THE
MUSEUMS &
GALLERIES
PASSPORT GUIDE 1990

EDITED BY SIMON TAIT

Produced by:
Spero Communications
Grampian House
Meridian Gate
Marsh Wall
Docklands
London E14 9XT

Editor: Simon Tait

Publishing Director: Connie Brighton

Production Manager: Lynda Thomas

Researcher: Martin Campfield

Publisher: Ian Spero

Cover & Passport
Illustration: Paul Bateman

Design: Spero Communications
Alan Cheung

Additional photography by John O'Grady
& Anita Corbin

Published by: Info Publishing Ltd.

Maps supplied by Oxford Cartographers.

The listings are entirely based on information supplied by the museums. The contents are believed correct at the time of printing. Nevertheless, neither the publisher nor The Times can accept responsibility for errors or omissions or changes in the details given.

ISBN 1 872765 00 9

Book cover printed by Brandprint, Middlesex.

Printed in Great Britain by William Clowes Limited, Beccles and London

CONTENTS

BUCKINGHAM PALACE

As Patron of Museums Year 1989 I have derived great pleasure in visiting museums and galleries across the country.

Museums fulfil a vital role in the culture of the nation, they provide a resource of education and learning, but above all they are exciting places that can enrich almost every aspect of our lives.

I am delighted that the publishers have decided to produce a second edition of this excellent guide. I would now urge you to take your Museums Passport in hand, and venture forth to explore as many of the museums and galleries listed within as possible.

Sarah,.

PREFACE

By **CHARLES WILSON** Editor of The Times

The Times is once again delighted to be supporting the Museums and Galleries Guide building on the success of last year.

In 1989, Museums Year, the custodians of our heritage proved how integral a part of our society they are. They organised special events, exhibitions and promotions with the visitor in mind, and demonstrated their unique value as places both of enlightenment and entertainment.

They got their reward. They aimed to increase the number of museum visits in one year by nearly 20 per cent, to a record 100 million. To some of us that seemed an ambition even a boom industry, such as museums, was unlikely to fulfil, but all indications are that they will make it.

Now they have a new decade to look forward to, and perhaps a feeling of new independence after their showing last year. There will be new challenges and new demands from a new public.

Museums are not just about the past, as they were at pains to prove to us in Museums Year. They are about the present, and also about the future. Just as The Times is a chronicle of our world, The Times Museums and Galleries Guide is a chronicle of the development of museums.

In the 1990s and the coming new millennium, let us look to our museums as a chronicle of our time, and as monitors of our perils - such as the threat to our environment - as well as of our triumphs.

CHARLES WILSON

Welcome to the second Times Passport Guide to Museums and Galleries. It's nice to be able to say that this new edition is here by public demand - you asked for it, both in letters to me and by buying more than 30,000 copies of the 1989 Guide.

But what you also wanted, you said, was a more comprehensive guide. Last year we restricted entry to those museums participating in the Passport scheme; this year we have opened the guide to all museums and galleries throughout the United Kingdom, and we have highlighted those museums offering Passport concessions.

This time you will find that the entry on each museum is fatter, including a little more of what I found during my museum visits over the past year. And because there has been such positive feedback, from both museum-goers and the museums themselves, I would like to involve you even more in the next guide. Help me with it by writing to me, at the address on page 10, about the museums you saw, liked or loathed. It's even possible that there is one you know of which isn't mentioned here and should be.

It was Sir Henry Cole, founder of the Victoria and Albert Museum and inspiration for both art and science education through public collections, who called museums " temples where all can worship in harmony", a ringing phrase. But he went on: "They teach good habits of order and cleanliness, and politeness .... Museums are antidotes to brutality and vice".

The image is one of a sort of Sunday School with scrubbed children sitting dutifully around glass cases filled with stuffed sparrows and lizards, while a large black-clad curator/teacher lectures in technical terms above the heads of his audience.

But the vision Cole had was quite different. He wanted museums to be places where people of all classes could go to improve their understanding of the arts and sciences; to be, in our terms, "user-friendly" educational resources.

Today, the relevance of his view is demonstrated by the fact that more Britons now go to museums than to football matches. Last year was Museums Year 1989, a great festival of achievement in showing museums as not only harmonious but sought after.

INTRODUCTION

The Museums Association's President, Dr. Patrick Boylan, set the agenda at the beginning of a year which was to be more than a celebration of the association's centenary, it was to be the museums' springboard into the higher public arena, focussed on by newspapers and the media.

The targets were to make the general public aware of the value and interest of the nation's museums and galleries, to get the same message across to decision-makers in government and business, and to give the country the biggest museum jamboree the world had ever seen. There was also an extra message: that museums are a good investment.

Hundreds of museums went to great lengths to prove that any image of a musty, cobweb-strewn barn, full of unwanted and unregarded bygones, bore no relation to museums of the 1980s. They seem to have got their message across because it is confidently predicted that returns will show Britain's museums had over 100 million visits in 1989.

What museums have done is to set the scene for the 1990s and the next millennium. Cole's picture is not so remote, even in his phraseology of the 1860s. Museums are proving to be places where one can go to get away from a brutal world, where one does not just have to look at objects hermetically sealed behind unbreakable glass panels, but can participate, make things work, have a "hands-on experience" in the words of the tourist agencies, who have also woken up to the potential of museums and galleries.

There are new types of museums growing too, such as science centres. The Science Museum itself, another direct offshoot of Cole's crusading work, opened an experiment called Test Bed five years ago to see how children would respond to physical experiments. Then they relaunched it in 1989 as 'Launch Pad', a permanent gallery. In 1989 they had to move it to another part of the museum where it could expand, so popular had it become.

But the experimental element does not have to be confined to science, as John Southern has proved at Liskeard in Cornwall with his enchanting Thorburn's Museum. He was a farmer who had a lifelong love of the work of the wildlife artist Archibald Thorburn. He turned his cowshed into an art gallery for his collection, and

then realised he had created a "mausoleum" for them.

Now the paintings are part of a growing display, which includes a reconstruction of Jermyn Street, where Thorburn sold much of his work, and of Thorburn's sitting room, studio and potting shed. It has smells to fit the pictures, and even a stream. Everywhere you go there are relevant stuffed birds and animals which you - and more importantly blind people, for blind people come here a lot - can touch.

Other art galleries around the country, and especially in Scotland, Wales and the North, have taken a similar path and are making more of their pictures.

Museum curators are worried that the theme park ethic is taking over, they fear that legitimate scholarship will take second place to entertainment, that historical and scientific facts will be "dressed up" to make them more acceptable to an untutored and otherwise uninterested public.

That is one of the reasons why the Museums and Galleries Commission, the museums' equivalent of the Arts Council, has instituted a registration system and insists that institutions which want official recognition as genuine museums, and the grants and sponsorship contacts which go with that, must satisfy certain basic criteria and the scrutiny of experts.

But what Museums Year has also shown is that the public knows a good museum when it sees one. There are too many good ones now for knowledgeable visitors to be fobbed off.

Instead museum enthusiasts have places like the Museum of the Moving Image, which provides entertainment which for many is more fun than going to the cinema (also, incidentally, less popular now than museum-going).

Museums are becoming more aware of the world around them, and both the Science Museum and the Natural History Museum in London have plans for major exhibitions and galleries addressing environmental problems.

Military museums are becoming aware that the public knows there is more to war than medals and torn flags, and are approaching the social side of military history. The Imperial War Museum is stuck

with a title which may be an anachronism; it is no longer just a war museum but a public institution for the study of conflict in the 20th century.

Five years ago the word "museum" was one which was desperately being cast off in favour of "heritage centre" or "local history visitor centre". Those who were saddled with the unenviable task of publicising these places despaired because they conjured up exactly the image that Henry Cole's phrases encourage.

Now the word conjures an entirely different image and is seen as a positive selling point. Not only that, they earn half a billion pounds a year for this country. Museums are the reason many foreign visitors cite for coming to Britain. Antidote to brutality they may be, harmonious temples, well, sometimes, but a positive force in a new age of leisure and learning they have proved themselves to be.

SIMON TAIT

Spero Communications
Grampian House
Meridian Gate
Marsh Wall, Docklands
London E14 9XT

REGIONS   The Guide is split into eleven regions. Museums in London are listed alphabetically by name. The towns with museums or galleries are pinpointed on the maps at the back, with **M** for museum or **G** for gallery.

LISTINGS   Each listing gives a name, address and telephone number. Opening times appear in most entries, but some were not available at the time of going to press so you are asked to "call for opening". Since most museums and galleries are closed on Christmas Day, Boxing Day, New Year's Day and Good Friday, only exceptions are noted. Wherever possible the text includes guidance as to special events and exhibitions in 1990. Up-to-date listings of events and exhibitions will appear every Saturday in the Times Saturday Review.

SYMBOLS   £ - where there is a charge for museum admission, though not when the charge is for temporary exhibitions only.

P - where there is parking available.

♿ - where there is full access for disabled visitors (NB this information is supplied by the museums themselves and the publishers cannot accept responsibility for its accuracy).

(EH) - denotes English Heritage ownership. There is a special coupon on Page 37, which entitles the bearer to special rates at these properties.

OPPS : - where there are opportunities to attend lectures, special events, openings, exhibitions, private views etc. Interested visitors should telephone or write to the museum for additional information.

B.H. - Bank Holidays.

Continuing the success of the scheme during Museum Year, we are again offering a Passport to Museums. This entitles its holders to special incentives at a number of museums and galleries, these include offers such as free or reduced price entry, a free guide or poster, discounts in museum shops or invitations to special previews. Concessions on shop purchases do not include books unless specifically stated.

For the first time this year younger museum-goers, between the ages of five and twelve, have their own Passport, and their own concessions.

Information of Passport concessions can be found along with the individual museum's entry in this Guide.

Both the Passport and the Junior Passport are available free upon application to The Times. Details appear throughout the year, in Simon Tait's Saturday Museum feature.

PASSPORT CONCESSIONS: - where museums are making special offers to holders of the MUSEUMS GUIDE PASSPORT. Visitors should check their Guides for concessions. Make sure you have your Passport with you when claiming Passport Concessions.

Junior Passport Concessions: - where, for the first time, visitors aged between 5 and 12 have their own set of concessions listed separately, and their own Passport.

Concessions on shop purchases do not include books unless specifically stated.

Review

By Simon Tait
Arts Correspondent, The Times

Museums Year 1989 was devised as a celebration of the achievement museums and galleries have made in modern times, not only to continue nourishing a public demand for their unique brand of education and entertainment, in the face of modern technological competition and fashion, but to keep experimenting, encouraging new ideas and putting them into practice.

In fact, they have created a new age for museums, and this needed special recognition.

Shell U.K. have a record of being concerned with communities - after all, Shell petrol stations are in the middle of each one. They agreed to join The Times, already sponsors of Museums Year, in a partnership to create The Museums Year Awards, which became one of the most generous museum sponsorships to date.

Ms Sarah Tombs

"Shell has a very long track record of support for the arts from the early days in the 1920s and 1930s, when our involvement was linked to the countryside" said Chris Bullock, Shell U.K.'s community affairs manager, when the company's involvement was announced in June. "In those days the company commissioned paintings, to be used in advertising."

For **THE MUSEUMS YEAR AWARD** a unique trophy was commissioned from the sculptor Sarah Tombs, whose design embodied the theme of collective inspiration, which she saw as the motivating force in museums' innovation.

It was to be the public who would choose the winners, nominating and then voting through the columns of The Times. There would be two main museum awards, and one for an individual.

The main prize would go to the museum or gallery which the public considered to be the most innovative and enterprising. It had to have done something which was influential within the museums world, whilst maintaining the essential values. The value of the award would be £20,000 sponsorship.

The second award would go to the best community museum, the one which had done more than any other to reach into the community it served, winning it £10,000 sponsorship.

The Museums Association, who devised Museums Year to celebrate their centenary, wanted a third recognition: for the museum professional of the year. The winner of that would be picked by the Museums Association Council.

Nomination forms appeared in The Times in August. From each of the two main categories, the 12 most often nominated were creamed off and set before a panel of judges, or assessors to be more accurate, since the ultimate judges were the museum-going public.

The panel was chaired by the President of the Royal Academy, Mr. Roger de Grey, and included Dr. Patrick Boylan, president of the Museums Association; Mr. Max Hebditch, director of the Museum of London; Mr John Letts, chairman of National Heritage,

organisers of the long-standing national Museum of the Year Awards; Mr Michael Hoy, managing editor of The Times; Mr. Chris Bullock, community affairs manager for Shell U.K.; Mr. Ian Spero, managing director of Spero Communications, organisers of the awards scheme and Mr Simon Tait, arts correspondent of The Times.

The judges visited all the most popular nominees to create a short list which the public could vote

Mr Roger de Grey

from. By the beginning of October there were two short lists of five museums.

"It was a staggeringly difficult task, because so many museums have striven so well and succeeded so spectacularly" said Mr. de Grey.

Shell U.K. wanted to ensure that the sponsorship awards would be used in an appropriate way, so the finalists were asked to specify what projects would benefit from the sponsorship money if they won. These were detailed in The Times, to help voters make their decision. The response from Times readers was enthusiastic, and over 8,000 votes were received.

The Times Shell Museums Year Awards were presented by HRH The Duchess of York, patron of Museums Year, on December 5th in the magnificent surroundings of the National Gallery's newly restored Barry Rooms.

Speaking at the ceremony, the Duchess said that the awards were a fitting climax to the year which she had participated in whole-heartedly, visiting over 30 museums and galleries. "I have never been more impressed, and I've loved every single second of it" she said, but urged museums to continue to strive on behalf of their collections and the growing museum-going public.

Mr David Francis and Ms Helen Mackintosh, Museum of the Moving Image.

HRH The Duchess of York receives a posy from Master George Bullock, watched by (L to R) The Hon. Jacob Rothschild, Dr Patrick Boylan, Mr Malcolm Raiser, Mr Charles Wilson and Mr Mark Taylor.

Mr Alan Borg, The Imperial War Museum; Mr & Mrs Roger de Grey.

Mr Stuart Smith and Michael Lowe, Ironbridge Gorge Museum.

HRH The Duchess of York presents the award to Mr Phillip Phillips.

Mr Graham King, News International, Ms Jane Clarke, Spero Communications, Mr John Stockley, The Times.

Dr Robert Anderson, Mr Nigel Pitman, Dr Patrick Greene and Professor Brian Morris.

Representatives of Shell U.K.: Ms Hazel Barbour, Mr & Mrs Richard Nye, Mr & Mrs Malcolm Raiser, Mr Peter Hunt, Mr & Mrs Chris Bullock.

THE TIMES SHELL MUSEUM PROFESSIONAL OF THE YEAR is PHILLIP PHILLIPS, the curator of palaeontology at Liverpool Museum.

He was responsible for creating the computer system for the museum's new Natural History Centre, which allows much greater public access to the collections and information about them.

Mr. Phillips, aged 40, is also well-known outside Liverpool as one of the country's leading experts in the application of computer processes to museum use, and his accolade, voted for by members of the Museums Association Council and therefore by his professional peers, also recognises his work outside his normal sphere of duties.

Runners up in the **COMMUNITY MUSEUM** section were:

THE HORNIMAN MUSEUM. Created in South East London 100 years ago by the daughter of Frederick Horniman, the tea tycoon, who was himself an inspired collector. The museum is now an intrinsic part of an enriching multi-cultural neighbourhood.

THE NATURAL HISTORY CENTRE, LIVERPOOL MUSEUM. A new facility designed to help the public make the best possible use of the museum's collections. The public are encouraged to bring in their own specimens and to become involved in field work.

THE HORNSEA MUSEUM OF VILLAGE LIFE. Based on the life and times of the North Humberside village of Hornsea. As well as having recreated room settings, it has a photographic room, with changing exhibitions taken from the ever-growing archive of local scenes.

THE GLYNN VIVIAN ART GALLERY. Built in Swansea 80 years ago by Richard Glynn Vivian, to house his collections of fine and decorative art. It has since developed into a community museum which specializes in appealing to youth, the disabled and the under-privileged. So popular are its exhibitions that it plans 24 in the next year.

The museums shortlisted for the main **INNOVATION AWARD** included:

THE IMPERIAL WAR MUSEUM in London, which has changed its profile from a celebrant of imperial victories, to a centre for the study of conflict in the 20th century. The museum recently completed the first phase of a £20 million conversion, including a realistic Blitz Experience.

THE ROYAL MUSEUM OF SCOTLAND, the centrepiece of the National Museums of Scotland. Its main exhibition during 1989 was Wealth of a Nation, which showed Scotland's natural, cultural, royal and even criminal history. It is also developing a unique computer information system.

THE FLORENCE NIGHTINGALE MUSEUM, at St. Thomas's Hospital, London, was brand new in 1989. The museum is an evocative recreation of Florence Nightingale's biographical story and the horror of the Crimea. It also provides research material on the history of modern nursing.

THE MUSEUM OF THE MOVING IMAGE, behind the National Film Theatre opened in 1988. In its first year it drew over half a million visitors, eager to learn about the development of film and television technology. The guides are actors playing appropriate parts, and there are optical toys and even a chance to read the television news.

THE TIMES SHELL COMMUNITY MUSEUM OF THE YEAR was **THE WEALD AND DOWNLAND MUSEUM** in Singleton, West Sussex. It is one of Britain's most successful open air museums.

THE WEALD AND DOWNLAND MUSEUM was launched in 1967 by enthusiasts, led by its founder, J.R. Armstrong, who wanted to rescue good examples of vernacular architecture, the humbler sort of buildings which

The staff of the Weald and Downland Open Air Museum, with the Community Museum Trophy.

tended not to be preserved in situ. Using a technique begun in Norway in the 1880s, historic buildings are moved to the museum to save them from destruction.

In 1971 the museum opened to the public, with four buildings from the surrounding area - a treadwheel, a cruck cottage, a market hall and an early granary. Now more than 30 buildings have been re-erected on the site, from a charcoal burner's camp to a water mill producing stone-ground flour. More are in store and still others are earmarked for rescue.

The nature of the rural community has completely changed in the course of the last 50 years, with the revolution in agricultural technology and crops. The museum's buildings tell the story of a series of communities from prehistoric time to the 19th century.

To give a perspective to the story, the museum organizes tours side-by-side with the local Goodwood Farm to give visitors, particularly children, the opportunity of comparing farming methods.

The £10,000 Shell sponsorship award which goes with the trophy, and was received by the museum's director, Mr. Christopher Zeuner, will be used to help visitors explore the construction of traditional buildings through three-dimensional computer images.

Ironbridge Gorge Museum Staff with the Museums Year Award

The winner of **THE TIMES SHELL MUSEUMS YEAR AWARD** for innovation is IRONBRIDGE GORGE MUSEUM, a complex of six museums which first opened in 1973.

The first museum was established beside the kiln, at Coalbrookdale in Shropshire, where Abraham Darby first smelted iron in 1709, and thus is generally accepted as having started the Industrial Revolution. Seventy years later his grandson built the world's first iron bridge there.

Added to the Museum of Iron now are the Jackfield Tile Museum, the Coalport Museum of pottery, and the Ironbridge itself. The newest addition is the Museum of the River, which examines the influence rivers have had on the industrial process, focusing on the River Severn at Ironbridge in particular.

The sixth museum is Blists Hill, a re-created Victorian village, now growing into a town, of transplanted 19th century buildings. You can buy bread in the bakery, and candles in the chandlers. You can get Victorian money from the bank, and spend it in the shops. There is a cobbler's, a doctor's surgery, a sweet shop, a locksmith's and a squatters' cottage. The museum also has the only works in the world producing wrought iron.

The complex has just announced a £20 million development programme for the rest of the century which will provide Blist's Hill with a school, a photographer's studio, a grocers, a post office, more houses and a park complete with bandstand and tea room.There will also be hotels, restaurants and car parks around the site perimeter.

The museum's winning sponsorship cheque of £20,000 will go towards providing new museum guides in period costume for Blist's Hill - a preacher, an organ-grinder and a policeman. The museum also wants to produce a range of foreign language literature.

A year ago we hoped that Museums Year 1989, the national celebration of a 100 years' services to the nation by the Museums Association and its more than 3,000 members, would be much the largest national festival of the arts and museums that the world has ever seen, and all of our hopes were fulfilled.

Never have museums been so much in the forefront of public and media concern and discussion, with widespread debates about museum and gallery standards, government funding and the civilised and much cherished British tradition of free admission to our national institutions.

There is no doubt that both sponsorship and the editorial support of The Times played an important part in the success of Museums Year, as did The Times Museums Year Guide. All the indications are that the Association's target of pushing UK museum and gallery admissions from an already remarkable 80 million in 1988 to at least 100 million in Museums Year 1989, has been achieved.

The Association very much welcomes this new and substantially expanded Guide and hopes that it will be an invaluable companion in the cars and pockets of many tens of thousands of UK supporters of our museums and galleries, both large and small, and of the many overseas visitors who support and enjoy the rich range and high quality of our museums and galleries.

DR. PATRICK J. BOYLAN
President, Museums Association

Get the m this g with free to the

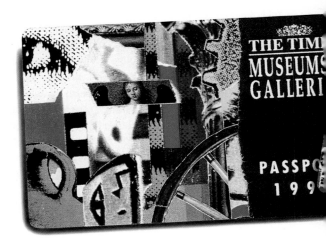

Free admission plus special offers.

The Times Museums' Passports are essential companions to this excellent Museums' Guide. They won't cost you a penny, but could save you a fortune.

Holders enjoy free or reduced entry to hundreds of museums and galleries, and exciting offers, like free posters and discounts in museum shops. *(Offer valid until March 30th 1991.)*

st out of
uide
passports
past.

Exclusive to readers of *The Times*.

For your free Passports to a fuller appreciation of our cultural heritage, simply fill in the special coupon, only in *The Times* on Saturdays. And use these invaluable little access cards to get more from our museums and galleries.

AGRICULTURAL

A R T

CHILDREN

INDUSTRIAL & TECHNICAL

MARITIME & WATERSIDE

MILITARY

OPEN AIR

TRANSPORT

An historic offer well worth repeating.

English Heritage, responsible for the protection of some of the most spectacular historic sites in England, has an offer simply too good to miss.

Pay to visit one of over 130 English Heritage sites listed as EH in this guide and a second person can join you, free of charge.*

From Cornwall to Kent, Northumberland to Hampshire, you'll discover our properties in almost every county.

Gaze across to France from the battlements of Dover Castle and you'll see why this magnificent fortress is called 'The Key Of England'. Or spend a day discovering the sumptuous elegance of Audley End House, and its Park.

Our sites and their tales are many and varied, covering some 5,500 years of fascinating history.

For further details of English Heritage, please turn this page.

* Your 'two for one' voucher offer does not include the following sites: The Iveagh Bequest: Kenwood, Marble Hill House, Ranger's House, Osborne House, Eynsford Castle, Lullingstone Roman Villa, Gainsborough Old Hall, Easby Abbey, Stokesay Castle, Bradford-on-Avon Tithe Barn, Mortimer's Cross Water Mill and Stonehenge.

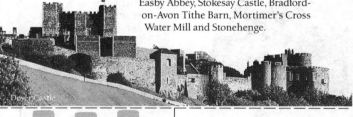

Dover Castle

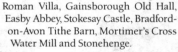

BUY ONE FULL ADULT ADMISSION AND ANOTHER PERSON ENTERS FREE

English ✠ Heritage

Conditions of offer
Voucher must be surrendered upon entry.
Not redeemable for cash and must not be used
in conjunction with any other offer.
Valid only at the properties indicated in this
advertisement. Not valid at special events.
Valid until 31 December 1990.

An historic offer well worth repeating.

Visit one of over 130 English Heritage sites listed, and a second person can join you, free of charge.

So make the most of what English Heritage has to offer, and explore your past with our present for the future.

For further details, please turn this page.

For further information of times of opening, please call:

(North) Tel: (091) 261 1585
(Midlands) Tel: (0902) 765105
(East Anglia) Tel: (0223) 455532
(South East) Tel: (0892) 548166
(South West) Tel: (0272) 734472

MEMBERSHIP

For just £12.50, you gain a year's membership, entitling you to FREE entry to every site across the country. You also get a free guidebook, map and quarterly copy of English Heritage Magazine filled with information about special activities and events at sites throughout the year.

For further membership information contact English Heritage, Membership Department, PO Box 1BB, London W1A 1BB.

Dover Castle

LONDON

With effect from 6th May 1990 the London 01 dialling code will be replaced by either 071, for inner London, or 081 for outer London.

Listed below are the first three digits of the existing London telephone numbers alongside their new codes.

Look up the first three digits of the current phone number, using this table.

This will show which of the two new codes applies to this area, eg 01-538 0101 will become 071-538 0101, and 01-657 0101 will become 081-657 0101.

1st 3 digits of no.	New code	1st 3 digits of no.	New code	1st 3 digits of no.	New code	1st 3 digits of no.	New code	1st 3 digits of no.	New code	1st 3 digits of no.	New code
200	081	253	071	304	081	360	081	422	081	474	071
202	081	254	071	305	081	361	081	423	081	475	081
203	081	255	071	308	081	363	081	424	081	476	071
204	081	256	071	309	081	364	081	426	081	478	081
205	081	257	071	310	081	365	081	427	081	480	071
206	081	258	071	311	081	366	081	428	081	481	071
207	081	259	071	312	081	367	081	429	081	482	071
208	081	260	071	313	081	368	081	430	071	483	071
209	081	261	071	314	081	370	071	431	071	484	071
210	071	262	071	316	081	371	071	432	071	485	071
214	071	262	071	317	081	372	071	433	071	486	071
215	071	264	071	318	081	373	071	434	071	487	071
217	071	265	071	319	081	374	071	435	071	488	071
218	071	266	071	320	071	375	071	436	071	489	071
219	071	267	071	321	071	376	071	437	071	490	071
220	071	268	071	322	071	377	071	438	071	491	071
221	071	269	071	323	071	378	071	439	071	492	071
222	071	270	071	324	071	379	071	440	081	493	071
223	071	271	071	325	071	380	071	441	081	494	071
224	071	272	071	326	071	381	071	442	081	495	071
225	071	273	071	327	071	382	071	443	081	496	071
226	071	274	071	328	071	383	071	444	081	497	071
227	071	275	071	329	071	384	071	445	081	498	071
228	071	276	071	330	081	385	071	446	081	499	071
229	071	277	071	332	081	386	071	447	081	500	081
230	071	278	071	335	081	387	071	448	081	501	081
231	071	279	071	336	081	388	071	449	081	502	081
232	071	280	071	337	081	389	071	450	081	503	081
233	071	281	071	339	081	390	081	451	081	504	081
234	071	282	071	340	081	391	081	452	081	505	081
235	071	283	071	341	081	392	081	453	081	506	081
236	071	284	071	342	081	393	081	455	081	507	081
237	071	286	071	343	081	394	081	456	081	508	081
238	071	287	071	345	081	397	081	458	081	509	081
239	071	288	071	346	081	398	081	459	081	511	071
240	071	289	071	347	081	399	081	460	081	512	071
241	071	290	081	348	081	400	071	461	081	514	081
242	071	291	081	349	081	401	071	462	081	515	071
243	071	293	081	350	071	402	071	463	081	517	081
244	071	294	081	351	071	403	071	464	081	518	081
245	071	295	081	352	071	404	071	466	081	519	081
246	071	297	081	353	071	405	071	467	081	520	081
247	071	298	081	354	071	406	071	468	081	521	081
248	071	299	081	355	071	407	071	469	081	523	081
249	071	300	081	356	071	408	071	470	081	524	081
250	071	301	081	357	071	409	071	471	081	526	081
251	071	302	081	358	071	420	081	472	081	527	081
252	071	303	081	359	071	421	081	473	071	529	081

1st 3 digits of no.	New code	1st 3 digits of no.	New code	1st 3 digits of no.	New code	1st 3 digits of no.	New code	1st 3 digits of no.	New code	1st 3 digits of no.	New code
530	081	597	081	671	081	745	081	834	071	920	071
531	081	598	081	672	081	746	081	835	071	921	071
532	081	599	081	673	081	747	081	836	071	922	071
533	081	600	071	674	081	748	081	837	071	923	071
534	081	601	071	675	081	749	081	839	071	924	071
536	081	602	071	676	081	750	081	840	081	925	071
537	071	603	071	677	081	751	081	841	081	927	071
538	071	604	071	678	081	752	081	842	081	928	071
539	081	605	071	679	081	754	081	843	081	929	071
540	081	606	071	680	081	755	081	844	081	930	071
541	081	607	071	681	081	756	081	845	081	931	071
542	081	608	071	682	081	758	081	846	081	932	071
543	081	609	071	683	081	759	081	847	081	933	071
544	081	618	071	684	081	760	081	848	081	934	071
545	081	620	071	685	081	761	081	850	081	935	071
546	081	621	071	686	081	763	081	851	081	936	071
547	081	622	071	687	081	764	081	852	081	937	071
549	081	623	071	688	081	766	081	853	081	938	071
550	081	624	071	689	081	767	081	854	081	940	081
551	081	625	071	690	081	768	081	855	081	941	081
552	081	626	071	691	081	769	081	856	081	942	081
553	081	627	071	692	081	770	081	857	081	943	081
554	081	628	071	693	081	771	081	858	081	944	081
555	081	629	071	694	081	773	081	859	081	946	081
556	081	630	071	695	081	776	081	861	081	947	081
558	081	631	071	697	081	777	081	863	081	948	081
559	081	632	071	698	081	778	081	864	081	949	081
560	081	633	071	699	081	780	081	866	081	950	081
561	081	634	071	700	071	783	081	868	081	951	081
562	081	635	071	701	071	785	081	869	081	952	081
563	081	636	071	702	071	786	081	870	081	953	081
564	081	637	071	703	071	788	081	871	081	954	081
566	081	638	071	704	071	789	081	874	081	958	081
567	081	639	071	706	071	790	071	875	081	959	081
568	081	640	081	707	071	791	071	876	081	960	081
569	081	641	081	708	071	792	071	877	081	961	081
570	081	642	081	709	071	793	071	878	081	963	081
571	081	643	081	720	071	794	071	879	081	964	081
572	081	644	081	721	071	796	071	881	081	965	081
573	081	645	081	722	071	798	071	882	081	968	081
574	081	646	081	723	071	799	071	883	081	969	081
575	081	647	081	724	071	800	081	884	081	974	081
576	081	648	081	725	071	801	081	885	081	976	071
577	081	650	081	726	071	802	081	886	081	977	071
578	081	651	081	727	071	803	081	888	081	978	071
579	081	653	081	728	071	804	081	889	081	979	081
580	071	654	081	729	071	805	081	890	081	980	081
581	071	655	081	730	071	806	081	891	081	981	081
582	071	656	081	731	071	807	081	892	081	983	081
583	071	657	081	732	071	808	081	893	081	984	081
584	071	658	081	733	071	809	081	894	081	985	081
585	071	659	081	734	071	820	071	897	081	986	081
586	071	660	081	735	071	821	071	898	081	987	071
587	071	661	081	736	071	822	071	900	081	988	081
588	071	663	081	737	071	823	071	902	081	989	081
589	071	664	081	738	071	824	071	903	081	991	081
590	081	665	081	739	071	826	071	904	081	992	081
591	081	666	081	740	081	828	071	905	081	993	081
592	081	667	081	741	081	829	071	906	081	994	081
593	081	668	081	742	081	831	071	907	081	995	081
594	081	669	081	743	081	832	071	908	081	997	081
595	081	670	081	744	081	833	071	909	081	998	081

EC3	All Hallows-by-the-Tower Crypt Museum

Byward St, London EC3. 071-481 2928. Open: Daily by appointment only. £ P &

This is a Saxon church whose crypt has been turned into a museum where the star object is a Roman pavement.

SE1	Bankside Gallery

48 Hopton St, London SE1 9JH. 071-928 7521. Open: During exhibitions Tue 10-8, Wed-Sat 10-5, Sun 1-5pm. £ &

This is the national centre for exhibiting watercolours and original prints and has a continuous and varied exhibition programme.

EC2	Barbican Art Gallery

Level 8, Barbican Centre, Silk Street, London EC2Y 8DS. 071-638 4141. Open: Mon-Sat 10-6.45, Sun 12-5.45. Closed: 9 Jul-9 Oct. £ &

A child of the 1980s within the Barbican Arts Centre, the gallery has become a major exhibition venue, with the 1990 programme concentrating on 19th and 20th century paintings, sculpture and photography, with other exhibitions featuring American, Canadian and Japanese art and culture.

PASSPORT CONCESSIONS: £1 off adult admission charge.

JNR. PASSPORT CONCESSIONS: Free schools information pack.

Reader reply service see page 453

W1 — Ben Uri Gallery

21 Dean Street
(4th floor), London
W1V 6NE.
071-437 2852.
Open: Mon-Thur 10-5.
Closed: Jewish Hols;
August. &

Dedicated to Jewish art, the gallery in the depths of Soho celebrates its 75th anniversary this year with an exhibition of the works of the founding artists taken from the permanent collection in May, contemporary Jewish artists in October and Solomon J Solomon in November, with a regular programme of exhibitions and events.

E2 — Bethnal Green Museum of Childhood

Cambridge Heath Road,
London E2 9PA.
081-980 3204.
Open: Mon-Thur/Sat
10-5.50, Sun 2.30-5.50.
P

Originally the prefabricated early buildings of the Victoria and Albert Museum, shifted to the East End in the 1870s to bring a bit of enlightenment. Now they contain one of the most thoughtful expositions on the history of childhood and childish things.

BEXLEY — Bexley Museum

Hall Place, Bourne
Road, Bexley, Kent
DA5 1PQ.
0322-526574.
Open: Mon-Sat 10-5
(Dusk in Winter), Sun
(Summer only) 2-6. P

This is the local history museum for one of London's largest boroughs, set in a Tudor and Jacobean house with permanent archaeological and natural displays and a temporary exhibition on social history. Between March and November an exhibition celebrates the borough's silver jubilee.

W1 — The British Council Collection

Visual Arts
Department,
11 Portland Place,
The British Council,
London W1N 4EJ.
071-389 3060. Open:
By appointment only.

This is a sort of peripatetic museum in that its homeless collections can be seen all over the world in exhibitions on British art or on loan to museums, galleries, community centres or the council's offices in more than 80 countries. With well over 5,000 works of art it is one of the most important national collections of 20th century British art. Special exhibitions in Venice, Japan and New York in 1990.

W1 — British Dental Association Museum

64 Wimpole Street,
London W1M 8AL.
071-935 0875.
Open: Mon-Fri 9-5.

The tooth of the matter, with the instruments, equipment, appliances of what Julia Marsh, the museums officer, describes as 'the art and science' of dental surgery.

WC1 — The British Library

Great Russell Street,
London WC1.
071-323 7593.
Open: Mon-Sat 10-5,
Sun 2.30-6.
&

As the vast new building rises by St. Pancras Station, you can still visit the Great Russell Street exhibition galleries where there is a full programme of changing themes. See gems on permanent view like two of the four copies of the Magna Carta and the Lindisfarne Gospels.

SW7 — British Library National Sound Archive

29 Exhibition Road,
London SW7 2AS.
071-589 6603.
Open: Mon-Fri 10-5
(Thur -9pm.)

This is the national repository for recordings of all kinds - music, speech, wildlife - all on cylinders, discs, audio and video tape. The long term exhibition, Revolutions in Sound, is a celebration of a century of the gramophone.

WC1 — The British Museum

Great Russell Street,
London WC1B 3DG.
071-636 1555.
Open: Mon-Sat 10-5,
Sun 2.30-6. Closed:
May B.H. &

The first national museum, founded by Act of Parliament in 1753, perhaps this is the world's greatest museum, tracing the works of man from prehistoric times to the present day. 1990's exhibition subjects include Celtic metalwork, fakes, Japanese art and Chinese art.

Woman looking in a mirror by Utamaro, 18th century.

BROMLEY — Bromley Museum

The Priory, Church
Hill, Orpington
BR6 OH4.
0689-31551.
Open: Mon-Sat 9-5.
(excl. Thur). P

The archaeology and social history of Bromley, plus the life of John Lubbock, the man who invented bank holidays. Special exhibition 27 March to 6 April to complement Bromley's first arts festival.

PASSPORT CONCESSIONS: Behind the scenes tours on application.

N17 — Bruce Castle Museum

Lordship Lane,
Tottenham,
London N17 8NV.
081-808 8772.
Open: Daily 1-5. P

Local history collections covering the London Borough of Haringey including a large photographic collection, fine postal history displays and the Museum of the Middlesex Regiment.

SE16 — Brunel Engine House

Railway Avenue,
Rotherhithe,
London SE16 4LF.
081-318 2489.
Open: 1st Sun of
every month 11-3. £

In here were the steam engines which drained the Thames Tunnel, the first underwater tunnel. It was built by Sir Mark Brunel and his son Isambard, and is what the main exhibition, Brunel's Tunnel and Where it Led, commemorates.

PASSPORT CONCESSIONS: 50% off adult admission charge; Special rate family entrance ticket- 50p for under 18's.

JNR. PASSPORT CONCESSIONS: Free Pencil.

SW1 — Cabinet War Rooms

Clive Steps, King
Charles Street,
London SW1A 2AQ.
071-930 6961.
Open: Daily 10-6.
Closed: 24 Dec.
£ &

Underneath the present Cabinet Office itself off Whitehall is the bunker headquarters from which Churchill ran the country and World War II during the Blitzkrieg on London, restored to the way it would have been a few minutes before a War Cabinet Meeting. Eerie to some, never less than intriguing, part of the Imperial War Museum family.

NW3 — Camden Arts Centre

Arkwright Road,
London NW3 6DG.
071-435 2643. Open:
Mon-Fri 10.30-5.30,
Sat/Sun 12-6.

Continuous exhibitions throughout the year in the galleries, with a complementary education programme, adult education classes and artists' shop.

SW3 — Carlyle's House

24 Cheyne Row,
London SW3 5HL.
071-352 7087.
Open: Wed-Sun 11-5.
Closed: Nov-Mar. £

Jane and Thomas Carlyle, the historian, lived here for 50 years and the house was bought by public subscription after Carlyle's death. It reverted to the National Trust in the 1930s and is kept as Carlyle had it.

W4 — Chiswick House

Burlington Lane,
Chiswick, London W4.
081-995 0508. Open:
Daily 10-6 Summer,
10-4 Winter. £ P (EH)

Lord Burlington designed this villa in about 1725, and William Kent decorated it and landscaped the gardens. Some of the original paintings remain and there is a new exhibition about the house and grounds.

NW4 — Church Farm House Museum

Greyhound Hill, Hendon, London NW4 4JR. 081-203 0130. Open: Mon-Sat 10-1/ 2-5.30 (Tues 10-1 only) Sun 2-5.30. P

This is a 17th century famhouse on what was then the rural hinterland of London. Its kitchen has been furnished to the style of 1820, its dining room to about 1850 and there are ten temporary exhibitions a year on local and social history and fine and decorative arts.

WC2 — Courtauld Institute Galleries

Somerset House, The Strand, London WC2R 0RN. 071-873 2777. Open: Mon-Sat 10-6, Sun 2-6. £ &

The event of the year will be when this fantastic collection opens in Somerset House's Fine Rooms, by the end of June if the contractors have finished. Worth going to London just to see this, with its matchless collection of Old Masters Impressionists and Post-Impressionists, now shifted from their fifth floor Woburn Place rooms.

PASSPORT CONCESSIONS: 50% off adult admission charge.

SW1 — Crafts Council

12 Waterloo Place, Lower Regent Street, London SW1Y 4AU. 071-930 4811. Open: Tue-Sat 10-5, Sun 2-5. &

The Crafts Council was established to promote the crafts in Britain, it offers support to crafts people in general and has a gallery, shop and free information service. The 1989 Wilding Report recommendation that the Crafts Council should be absorbed into the Arts Council has been strongly resisted and although, as we go to press, the distant future is unsure, there is a strong programme of temporary exhibitions throughout 1990.

Courtauld Institute Galleries

University of London
Will open at Somerset House, Strand, WC2
in early Summer 1990

Samuel Courtauld Collection of Impressionist paintings; Princes Gate Collection of Old Master paintings; Lee Collection; Gambier-Parry Collection; Witt & Spooner Collections of drawings.

SE19 — Crystal Palace Museum

Anerley Hill, London SE19 2BA.
081-676 0700.
Open: Sun 2-5 By arrangement at other times.

A new museum set in the old engineering school next to the remains of the Brunel water tower which served the lost exhibitions centre, it tells the sometimes joyous, sometimes tragic story of the Crystal Palace from 1850 to the present through photographs, with actual artefacts forming a new exhibition in mid-1990.

JNR. PASSPORT CONCESSIONS: Free Schools information pack - by application in advance only.

SE17 — Cuming Museum

155-157 Walworth Road, London SE17 1RS.
071-703 2850.
Open: Thur-Sat 10-5. Groups welcome all week by appointment.

This is Southwark's borough collection about its history from the Romans up, joined with the collections culled worldwide by the Cuming family. In the second half of 1990 there is a major temporary exhibition called Poverty and Pleasure, about Victorian life in Southwark.

PASSPORT CONCESSIONS: Reduction of 10% on shop purchases; Opportunity to attend Private View of 'Poverty & Pleasure' exhibition.

JNR. PASSPORT CONCESSIONS: Free 'Cuming Museum' sticker.

SE1 — Design Museum

Butlers Wharf, Shad Thames, London SE1 2YD.
071- 407 6261. Open Tue-Sun 11.30-6.30.
£ P ♿

Art, or at least design, in ordinary mass produced life, with constantly changing exhibitions.

PASSPORT CONCESSIONS: 50% off adult admission charge.

WC1 — The Dickens House Museum

48 Doughty Street, London WC1N 2LF.
071-405 2127. Open Mon-Sat 10-5. £

Charles Dickens lived here from 1837 to 1839 where he worked on the Pickwick Papers, Oliver Twist, Nicholas Nickleby and Barnaby Rudge. The rooms have been restored and contain his books, manuscripts and personal possessions.

PASSPORT CONCESSIONS: Free Guidebook.

SE22 — Dulwich Picture Gallery

College Road, London
SE22 9LE.
081-693 5254
Open: Mon-Sat 11-5,
Sun 2-5. £ P &

This is a collection of Old Masters in a gallery designed for them by Sir John Soane. It was Fine Art Museum of the Year in 1989 and it was commended in the European Museum of the Year competition in 1989. It is the oldest public art gallery in England, and until June 1990 there is an important exhibition on the care and conservation of paintings.

PASSPORT CONCESSIONS: Reduction of 10% on shop purchases; Inclusion on mailing list free for one year.

NW3 — Fenton House

Hampstead Grove,
London. 071-435 3471.
Open: Mar Sat/Sun 2-6,
Apr-Oct Sat-Wed 11-6.
Closed: Nov-Feb. £

The National Trust's 17th century house in a Hampstead walled garden which houses, among other things, the Benton Fletcher Collection of keyboard instruments still played regularly and on which there are concerts from May to September.

SE1 — Florence Nightingale Museum

2 Lambeth Palace Rd,
London SE1.
071-620 0374.
Open: Tue-Sun 10-4.
£ P &

This newcomer was a runner-up in the Times Shell Museums Year Awards within a year of its opening. It has not only a stark reconstruction of conditions at Florence Nightingale's Scutari hospital in the Crimea, but the details, through her words and those of her family and friends, of her long and fulfilled life.

PASSPORT CONCESSIONS: £1 off adult admission.

ENFIELD — Forty Hall Museum

Forty Hill, London
EN2 9HA.
081-363 8196.
Open: Apr-Sept Tue-
Sun 10-6. Oct-Mar
Tue-Sun 10-5. P &

This 17th century house contains collections of watercolours and drawings alongside local history displays.

NW3 — Freud Museum

20 Maresfield Gardens,
London NW3 5SX.
071- 435 2002.
Open: Wed-Sun 12-5.
£ &

This was Freud's home in the last two years of his life, a refugee from the Nazis. It is the psychoanalyst's complete working environment with his extraordinary collection of antiquities, his library and fine furniture including the famous couch. Special exhibitions and conferences in 1990 mark the 50th anniversary of his death.

PASSPORT CONCESSIONS: £1 off adult admission charge; Free Poster (while supply lasts); Free Museum Newsletter.

JNR. PASSPORT CONCESSIONS: Free Badge (while supply lasts).

E2 — Geffrye Museum

Kingsland Road,
London E2 8EA.
071-739 8368.
Open: Tue-Sat 10-5,
Sun 2-5. &

In the idyllic setting of an 18th century almshouse, this draws on the traditional trades of Hackney, personal memories, trade pattern books and photographs to look at home making and furnishings in ordinary dwellings from 1600 to 1940.

JNR. PASSPORT CONCESSIONS: Free Badge.

NW10 — Grange Museum of Community History

On the Neasden
Roundabout,
Neasden Lane,
London NW10 1QB.
081-908 7432.
Open: Tue-Thur 12-5,
Sat 10-12/1-5. P

This must be the only museum actually in the middle of a roundabout. As well as telling 200 years of the history of this bit of Neasden through photographs, objects and text, it has the largest collection of material from the 1924 British Empire Exhibition.

PASSPORT CONCESSIONS: Reduction of 10% on shop purchases.

JNR. PASSPORT CONCESSIONS: Free Badge; Free Pencil.

W1 — Guinness World of Records

The Trocadero Centre, Coventry Street, Piccadilly Circus, London W1V 7FD. 071-439 7331. Open: Daily 10am-10pm. £ &

Not really a museum, but nevertheless an absorbing anthology of record-breaking humans, animals, sportspeople, entertainers, structures and machines.

W3 — Gunnersbury Park Museum

Gunnersbury Park, London W3 8LQ. 081-992 1612. Open: Daily 1-4 Winter, 1-5 Summer. P &

Re-opening in the spring after rebuilding work with a new local history gallery and a special exhibition, From Plough to Platter.

PASSPORT CONCESSIONS: Free Guidebook.

JNR. PASSPORT CONCESSIONS: Free Pencil.

E8 — Hackney Museum

Central Hall, Mare Street, London E8 1HE. 081-986 6914. Open: Tue-Fri 10-12.30/ 1.30-5, Sat 1.30-5. Closed: B.H. &

The roots of the people - all the varieties of Hackney people - are here beside the Haitian store, the hospital doll, the piano player and the Matchbox toys. Breathtaking programme of exhibitions.

PASSPORT CONCESSIONS: Free Poster.

JNR. PASSPORT CONCESSIONS: Free Pen.

NW3 — Hampstead Museum

Burgh House, New End Square, London NW3 1LT. 071-431 0144 Open: Daily 12-5.

Hampstead's local history museum is set in a Queen Anne house and has special displays about Constable and his Hampstead connections, and about Helen Allingham, the watercolourist and book illustrator.

PASSPORT CONCESSIONS: Free Guidebook.

HARROW — Harrow Museum & Heritage Centre

Headstone Park, Pinner View, Harrow, Middlesex. 081-863 6407. Open: Wed-Fri 12.30-5, Sat/Sun & B.H. 10.30-5. P &

This is a 14th century manor house with a 16th century tithe barn.

EC3 — The Heralds' Museum at the Tower of London

HM Tower of London, London EC3N 4AB. 071-236 9857. Open: Mon-Sat 9.30-5.45, Sun 2-5.30. Closed: Oct-Mar. £

This is in the Tower of London and explains the point of heraldry and its development, with some of the best examples of crowns, crests, shields and banners. The main 1990 exhibition is about the Order of the Indian Empire and the Order of the Star of India.

PASSPORT CONCESSIONS: Free Poster.

Crest from the Carter Stall of HRH The Duke of Windsor (L) and HRH Prince Henry, Duke of Gloucester (R).

E1 — The Heritage Centre Spitalfields

19 Princelet St, London E1 6QH. 071-377 6901. Open: Mon-Wed 10-5.

Spitalfields is one of the most historical neighbourhoods of London, about to undergo another major change when the famous fruit and vegetable market moves. This museum, in a Huguenot weaver's house with a unique Victorian synagogue built over the back garden, examines the succession of immigrant cultures which have peopled the community, primarily Huguenot, Jewish and Bengali.

BRENTFORD — Heritage Motor Museum

Syon Park, Brentford, Middx TW8 8JF. 081-560 1378. Open: Daily Mar-Oct 10-5.30, Nov-Feb 10-4. £ P &

With over 90 vehicles, this is the world's largest collection of historic British cars, ranging from an 1895 Wolseley through veteran, vintage and classic grades of collectability, set in the beautiful Syon Park.

SE1 — HMS Belfast

Morgans Lane, Tooley Street, London SE1 2JH. 071-407 6434. Open: Daily Apr-Oct 10-5.30, Nov-Mar 10-4.30 £

Europe's largest surviving warship with personal recorded tours to help explore the seven decks. Special events such as a murder mystery weekend in March, Easter Egg Hunt April 15, the Telethon May 27-28. A new permanent exhibition on the Arctic convoys opening in July.

PASSPORT CONCESSIONS: £1 off adult admission charge.

JNR. PASSPORT CONCESSIONS: 50p off child admission.

W4   Hogarth's House

Hogarth Lane, Great West Road, London W4 2QN. 081-994 6757. Open: Winter Mon-Sat 11-4, Sun 2-4. After 1st Apr Mon-Sat 11-6, Sun 2-6. P

Once the home of the great 18th century artist on the river at Chiswick, it is now a gallery for his engravings and some reproductions of his paintings.

SE23   Horniman Museum and Gardens

100 London Road, Forest Hill, London SE23 3PQ. 081-699 2339. Open: Mon-Sat 10.30-6, Sun 2-6. &

Runner-up in the Times Shell Community Museum of the Year competition, this unflaggingly popular museum created from the collections of Frederick Horniman the tea man and ethnographer, it sets out to illustrate the world we live in through its cultures, arts, crafts, music and natural environment.

PASSPORT CONCESSIONS: Reduction of 5% on shop purchases.

JNR. PASSPORT CONCESSIONS: Free Badge.

SE1   Imperial War Museum

Lambeth Rd, London SE1 6HZ. 071-735 8922. Open: Daily 10-6. £ &

A runner-up in the Times Shell Museums Year Awards, the old IWM has emerged from a six month closure as a new IWM, with a transformation of galleries - three times as much space - and the famous Blitz Experience.

PASSPORT CONCESSIONS: £1 off adult admission.

JNR. PASSPORT CONCESSIONS: 50p off child admission.

WC2   Inns of Court & City Yeomanry Museum

10 Stone Buildings, Lincoln's Inn, London WC2A 3TG. 071-405 8112. Open: Mon-Fri 10-4 by appointment only.

Uniforms, medals, badges, weapons, equipment from 1798, with the unique set of drums dated 1803. Major refurbishment due this year, so ring to check before going.

N4   Islington Schools' Loan Collection

Ambler Primary School, Blackstock Road, London N4 2DR. 071-226 0674 Open: Mon-Thur Term time only.

This is an enterprising 'museum on wheels' idea: collections of natural history artefacts and items of British domestic and multi-cultural history which is loaned to schools in the borough of Islington.

SW1 — Jewel Tower At Westminster

Opp. Houses of
Parliament,
London SW1.
071-222 2219. Open:
Daily 10-6 Summer,
10-4 Winter (excl.
Mon). £ (EH)

This was built in about 1365 as part of the
Palace of Westminster by Edward III to house
the valuables from the King's wardrobe.

WC1 — The Jewish Museum

Woburn House,
Tavistock Sq,
London WC1H OEP.
071-388 4525. Open:
Apr-Sept Tue-Fri/Sun
10-4, Oct-Mar Tue-
Thur/Sun 10-4, Fri
10-12.45. Closed: B.H.
& Jewish Hols. ♿

Jewish life, particularly in Britain, covering the
religion, the history and the art.

PASSPORT CONCESSIONS: 10% off Shop
Purchases.

NW3 — Keats House

Keats Grove,
Hampstead, London
NW3 2RR. 071-435
2062. Open: Apr-Oct
Mon-Fri 2-6, Sat 10-
1/2-5, Sun & B.H. 2-5.
Nov-Mar Mon-Fri 1-5,
Sat 10-1/ 2-5, Sun 2-5.

Restored to the style of when John Keats lived
here between 1818 and 1820, with a lot of
Keatsiana, perhaps the most poignant being the
engagement ring he gave to Fanny Brawne.

NW3 — Kenwood, The Iveagh Bequest

Hampstead Lane,
London NW3 7JR.
081-348 1286. Open:
Daily 10-6 Summer,
10-4 Winter. P (EH)

Robert Adam's outstanding neo-classical
remodelling contains the Iveagh Bequest
printings including works by Rembrandt, Hals,
Gainsborough and Reynolds.

BRENTFORD — Kew Bridge Steam Museum

Green Dragon Lane,
Brentford, Middlesex
TW8 0EN.
081-568 4757
Open: Daily 11-5.
£ P

One of the newest and more successful of the
latest generation of industrial museums, this
one is in a Victorian waterworks by the Thames
and has a unique collection of huge steam-
powered beam engines, dating from 1820, with
a steam railway giving rides and a working forge.

PASSPORT CONCESSIONS: 50% off adult
admission charge.

KINGSTON UPON THAMES

Kingston upon Thames Museum & Heritage Centre

Wheatfield Way, Kingston upon Thames, Surrey KT1 2PS 081-546 5386. Open: Mon-Sat 10-5. P

The centrepiece of this local museum is the life and work of Eadweard Muybridge, the artist who used photography to record movement for figure sculptures and painters and by the way inspired potential movie makers and created works of art with his own photographs. There is also a display of the local Martinware pottery.

PASSPORT CONCESSIONS: Free Poster; Free Guidebook; OPP - send s.a.e. for details.

JNR. PASSPORT CONCESSIONS: Free Museum bag.

W14

Leighton House

12 Holland Park Road, London W14 8LZ. 071-602 3316. Open: Mon- Sat 11-5.

A high Victorian mansion designed and built for Lord Leighton, it has an outstanding collection of Pre-Raphaelite art, a unique display of Middle Eastern ceramics and temporary exhibitions.

PASSPORT CONCESSIONS: Reduction of 5% on shop purchases.

EC2

The Library & Collection of the Worshipful Company of Clockmakers

The Clock Room, Guildhall Library, Aldermanbury, London EC2P 2EJ. 071-606 3030 Open: Mon-Fri 9.30-5. &

The guild's collection founded in 1813 and on public display since 1873, now in the Guildhall's Clock Room, with mostly English 17th to 19th century watches, clocks and marine chronometers including Harrison's celebrated H5.

LONDON

W8 — Linley Sambourne House Museum

18 Stafford Terrace, London W8 7BM. 081-994 1019. Open: Wed 10-4, Sun 2-5. Closed: Nov-Feb. £

Sambourne was Punch's chief political cartoonist in the late 19th century and his home is a unique survival of a Victorian town house. The original decorations and furnishings have been preserved together with many of his own drawings and photographs..

SE15 — Livesey Museum

Old Kent Road, London SE15. 071-634 5604. Open: During exhibitions Mon-Sat please call for details. &

This is in Camberwell's former public library, the building being 100 years old. It was named after a noted local philanthropist and it examines Southwark's history through its changing exhibitions.

PASSPORT CONCESSIONS: 10% off shop purchases.

W2 — The London Toy & Model Museum

21 Craven Hill, London W2 3EN. 071-262 7905. Open: Tue-Sat 10-5.30, Sun/B.H. 11-5.30. £

Opened in 1982 and now under new ownership, the museum has more than 5,000 trains, boats, planes, dolls, animals and bears, all toys of course, with train rides in the garden .

PASSPORT CONCESSIONS: £1 off adult admission charge.

JNR. PASSPORT CONCESSIONS: Free Badge.

WC2

London Transport Museum

The Piazza, Covent Garden, London WC2E 7BB.
071-379 6344.
Open: Daily 10-6.
£ &

The development of London's transport systems and their impact on the growth of the capital, plus lots of interactive exhibits and temporary exhibitions. Until June there's an exhibition about transport maps, succeeded by one on Underground poster art, and in May there begins a centenary celebration of the first underground electric railway.

PASSPORT CONCESSIONS: 70p off adult admission charge.

JNR. PASSPORT CONCESSIONS: 30p off child admission charge.

N3

The London Museum of Jewish Life

The Sternberg Centre for Judaism, 80 East End Road, Finchley, London N3 2SY.
081-346 2288.
Open: Mon-Thur 10.30-5, Sun 10.30-4.30. Closed: Sun in August, Jewish Hols.

Jewish influence on London life has been profound since early in the Middle Ages and the permanent exhibition here traces their immigration and settlement with reconstructions of a tailor's workshop, a typical immigrant home and an East London bakery as well as temporary exhibitions, photographs and an oral history archive.

PASSPORT CONCESSIONS: 50% off adult admission charge to special exhibitions; OPPS.

JNR. PASSPORT CONCESSIONS: Free entry to Junior Passport holder to special exhibitions. Call for details of other benefits.

SW1

Mall Galleries

The Mall (Nr Admiralty Arch), London SW1.
071-930 6844. Open: Daily 10-5. £

The gallery of the Federation of British Artists which promotes contemporary artists through exhibitions and competitions and by finding sponsorship for young artists and encouraging commissions. There's a very busy exhibition programme throughout 1990.

TWICKENHAM — Marble Hill House

Richmond Road, Twickenham. 081-892 5115. Open: Daily 10-6 Summer, 10-4 Winter. P (EH)

An English Palladian villa of the 1720s with grounds flowing down to the Thames. The house contains important Georgian paintings and furniture including a unique set of architectural paintings by Panini.

N15 — Markfield Beam Engine and Museum

Markfield Road, South Tottenham, London N15 4RB. 076-387 331. Open: Call for details. £ P

This is an 1886 beam pumping engine in its original house and worked by steam on its open days, and there are several other steam engines, plus a graphic display on water supply and drainage.

PASSPORT CONCESSIONS: £1 off adult admission charge; Opportunity to attend advanced booked steam days.

JNR. PASSPORT CONCESSIONS: Free entry to Junior Passport holder accompanied by adult if under 12.

NW8 — MCC Museum

Lord's Cricket Ground, London NW8 8QN. 071-289 1611. Open: Mon-Sat 10.30-5, Sun 12-5. £

At Lord's, the shrine of cricket, this is thought to be the largest collection of cricketing memorabilia, and although the Ashes are spiritually in Australia for the time being, actually they are here.

PASSPORT CONCESSIONS: Free Poster.

JNR. PASSPORT CONCESSIONS: Free Literature.

W1 — Michael Faraday's Laboratory and Museum

The Royal Institution, 21 Albemarle St, London W1X 4BS. 071-409 2992. Open: Tue/Thur 1-4. £ &

Many of Faraday's most important discoveries were made in the laboratory in the Royal Institution. It has now been restored to its appearance when Faraday knew it in the 1840's, and there is now a museum adjoining which contains some of the key instruments he used.

EC1 — Museum & Library of the Order of St. John

St. John's Gate, St John's Lane, Clerkenwell, London EC1M 4DA. 071- 253 6644. Open: Mon-Fri 10-5 Sat 10-4. Closed: B.H. &

The medieval Knights Hospitallers from whom sprang the present day St. John Ambulance Brigade had their London headquarters here. Now it houses books, furniture, pictures, silver and objects with the history of the Order in England, Rhodes and Malta, where their distinctive cross insignia comes from. There is a separate archive and display on St. John Ambulance.

E14 — Museum in Docklands

Unit C14, Poplar Business Park, 10 Prestons Road, Poplar, London E14 9RL. 071-515 1162. Open: By appointment only. &

This is a museum in waiting - waiting for its permanent home in 1992 where it will be able to tell the story of the working port of London coherently. In the meantime there is a visitor centre in the Royal Victoria Dock where, by prior arrangement, you can see diving gear, coopers' and riggers' workshops and interactive displays on London trades such as printing. Museum on the move is the exhibition trailer for the collection, going out to schools, community events and roadshows.

E6 — Museum Nature Reserve and Interpretative Centre

Norman Road, East Ham, London E6 4HN. 081-470 4525. Open: Mon-Fri 9-5 or dusk if earlier, Sat/Sun 2-5. P &

In the depths of London's East End, this is in a nine acre churchyard around a 12th century church containing many species of birds, animals and plants which can be seen from marked trails, says the assistant curator - Colin Plant.

PASSPORT CONCESSIONS: Free Guidebook

JNR. PASSPORT CONCESSIONS: Free Badge or Free Pen or Free Pencil.

SE18 — Museum of Artillery in the Rotunda

Repository Road, Woolwich, London SE18. 081-316 5402. Open: Mon-Fri 12-5. Sat/Sun 1-5. Nov-Mar closes at 4pm daily. P

Beau Nash, the man who made Bath fashionable, designed a huge rotunda tent for the Prince Regent in 1814. It is a listed building now, and has a huge collection of artillery from the 14th century.

EC2 — Museum of London

150 London Wall, London EC2Y 5HN. 071-600 3699. Open: Tues-Sat 10-6, Sun 2-6. Closed: Mon except B.H. &

Two thousand years of London's history with displays which include a Roman kitchen, Newgate Gaol, the Lord Mayor's coach, an 18th century dolls' house and the spectacular Great Fire Experience. Temporary exhibitions in 1990-91 include one on London's gardens and another on the Blitz, 50 years on.

ST. JOHN'S GATE

Museum & Library of the Order of St. John

Formerly the southern entrance to the Priory of the Knights of St. John housing the most comprehensive collection of items relating to the Order of St. John outside Malta.

See listing for details

W1 — Museum of Mankind

(The Ethnography Department of the British Museum) Burlington Gardens, London W1X 2EX. 071-636 1555. Open: Mon-Sat 10-5, Sun 2.30-6. &

The British Museum's ethnography branch illustrating the lifestyles of non-Western societies and cultures, with special exhibitions in 1990 on Palestine, Arctic exploration and Bangladeshi rickshaws.

EC1 — Museum of Methodism and Wesley's House

49 City Road, London, EC1Y 1AU. 071-253 2262. Open: Museum Daily 9-5, House and Chapel Mon-Sat 10-4. £ P &

This ia a Georgian house and Methodist Chapel where John Wesley lived for the last 12 years of his life and where he died. It has his possessions and furniture, and there is a "Wesley Walkabout" each Sunday.

RICHMOND — Museum of Richmond

Old Town Hall, Whittaker Avenue, Richmond, Surrey TW9 1TP 081-332 1141. Open: Tue 11.30-5, Wed 11.30-8, Thur/Fri 11.30-6. £ &

This is a new museum, set up by a partnership between independent local enthusiasts who raised money and the local authority who provided the premises. It has superb models of the lost Richmond Palace and displays on local theatre and crafts.

PASSPORT CONCESSIONS: Free entry to Passport holder; Reduction on shop purchases.

JNR. PASSPORT CONCESSIONS: Free entry to Junior Passport holder. Free Badge.

SE1 — Museum of the Moving Image (MOMI)

Southbank Waterloo
London SE1 8XT
071-401 2636.
Open: Tues-Sat 10-8,
Sun (Oct-May) 10-6,
(June-Sept) 10-8 £ &

Runner-up in the Times Shell Museums Year Awards, this museum about the history of film and television and their forebears was already a multi-award winner before it was a year old. This year it sees its second birthday, and the popularity of its actor guides, 1,000 film and television clips and hands-on participation grows and grows.

PASSPORT CONCESSIONS: £1 off MOMI catalogue.

JNR. PASSPORT CONCESSIONS: Free Badge.

Hands on animation.

SE1 — Museum of the Royal Pharmaceutical Society of Great Britain

1 Lambeth High Street,
London SE1 7JN.
071-735 9141. Open:
By appointment only. &

The history of the science, profession and practice of pharmacy.

WC1 — Museum of Zoology and Comparative Anatomy

Medawar Building,
University College,
Gower Street, London
WC1E 6BT.
071-381 7050 Open:
By appointment only.

This is the teaching collection of the biology department of University College, London. It was started in 1828 and covers the whole range of the animal world, including many rare and extinct species.

BRENTFORD — The Musical Museum

368 High Street,
Brentford, Middlesex
TW8 0BD.
081-560 8108. Open:
Sat/Sun 2-5.30.
Closed: Nov-Mar. £

This is a museum of automatic instruments, the fore-runners of gramophones, mainly pianos and organs which reproduced sounds from music rolls made of perforated paper. It also tells you how it was done.

PASSPORT CONCESSIONS: Free Guidebook.

SW3 — National Army Museum

Royal Hospital Road, Chelsea, London SW3 4HT. 071-730 0717. Open: Mon-Sat 10-5.30, Sun 2-5.30. ♿

The museum has a new director and a new vibrancy, with a new permanent exhibition, The Road to Waterloo, opening in the summer, and temporary exhibitions on soldiers as collectors, the British Army at the time of Dunkirk, the 19th century Indian/Abyssinian paintings of Col. Cornelius Francis James, and the British Army postal services.

JNR. PASSPORT CONCESSIONS: Free Badge.

WC2 — The National Gallery

Trafalgar Square, London, WC2N 5DN. 071-839 3321. Open: Mon-Sat 10-6, Sun 2-6. ♿

One of the three most important collections of paintings in the world, with more than 2,000 pictures dating from the 13th to the 20th centuries.

SE10 — National Maritime Museum

Greewich, London SE10 9NF. 081-858 4422. Open: Mon-Sat 10-5, Sun 2-5. £ ♿

This is the nation's nautical memory, both for casual visitors and scholars, with over 2.5 million artefacts. It includes the Queen's House, designed by Inigo Jones and built in 1635, which re-opens on May 1, 1990 after a £5million refurbishment; and the Old Royal Observatory. The major exhibition in 1990 is about Captain Cook and opens on March 30.

WC2 — National Portrait Gallery

St. Martin's Place,
London WC2H 0HE.
071-930 1552.
Open: Mon-Fri 10-5,
Sat 10-6, Sun 2-6.
Closed: 24 Dec.

18th century galleries.

The most comprehensive family album in the world, founded in 1856 to record the appearances of famous Britons and now doing it with paintings, sculpture and photographs as well. How long before holograms? The newly sponsored BP Portrait Award in the summer is the NPG's salute to new talent, the young winners getting prestigious commissions. Continuous theme exhibitions through the year.

PASSPORT CONCESSIONS: 25% off souvenir guide.

ECI — National Postal Museum

King Edward Building,
King Edward St,
London, EC1A 1LP.
071-239 5420. Open:
Mon-Thur 9.30-4.30,
Fri 9.30-4.

An international philatelic collection from which are taken frequent exhibitions: in 1990 the inventor of postage, Rowland Hill, is the subject of a main gallery display until May and the Penny Black which launched his system.

SW7 — The Natural History Museum

Cromwell Road,
London SW7.
071-938 9123. Open:
Mon-Sat 10-6, Sun 1-6.
£ &

Formerly next door neighbours with The Geological Museum, now amalgamated, the NHM has a new image and new visitor services with new exhibitions to come in the course of 1990, and the Geological has plans for new attractions as well.

WC2 — Odontological Museum

Royal College of
Surgeons, 35-43
Lincolns Inn Fields,
London WC2A 3PN.
071-405 3474. Open:
Mon-Fri 10-5. Closed:
Aug.

This is part of the Royal College of Surgeons and has 10,000 specimens to aid the endeavours of students of teeth - animal and human.

HARROW — Old Speech Room Gallery

Harrow School, Harrow on the Hill, Middlesex HA1 3HP. 081-869 1205. Open: Term time daily (excl. Wed.

This is in Harrow School, one of our most famous public schools, and it has a varied but distinguished collection of Egyptian, Greek and Roman antiquities, English watercolours, modern British paintings, printed books, natural history and, of course, Harrowiana.

SE1 — The Operating Theatre Museum & Herb Garret

9A St Thomas' Street, Southwark, London SE1. 071-955 5000. Open: Mon/Wed /Fri 12:30-4. £

A unique survival, a 19th Century operating theatre which was in use before anaesthetics or antiseptics were discovered, with a collection of the medical and surgical instruments of the day on show.

TWICKENHAM — Orleans House Gallery

Riverside, Twickenham TW1 3DJ. 081-892 0221. Open: Tue-Sat 1-5.30. Sun 2-5.30. Oct-Mar closes 4.30. P &

The original Orleans House, where Louis Philippe, Duke of Orleans, lived in exile before becoming King of France was demolished in 1927, but the James Gibbs octagonal garden pavilion of about 1720 survives. Next to it is the art gallery which holds temporary exhibitions often featuring paintings from the Ionides Collection.

PASSPORT CONCESSIONS: 50% off 'The History of Orleans House' Guidebook.

JNR. PASSPORT CONCESSIONS: Free children's Passport Pack including questionnaire on The Octagon and Riverside Walk.

E15 — Passmore Edwards Museum

29 Romford Road, Stratford, London E15 4LZ. 081-519 4296. Open: Call for details.

After a major refurbishment the museum is due to re-open in the spring of 1990 with a new gallery devoted to the borough of Newham's natural history as well as its comprehensive local history and archaeology displays and changing exhibitions.

JNR. PASSPORT CONCESSIONS: Free Badge or Pen or Pencil.

WC1 — Percival David Foundation of Chinese Art

University of London, 53 Gordon Square, London WC1H 0PD. 071-387 3909. Open: Mon-Fri 10-5 Closed: B.H.

This is a University of London collection, with about 1,500 pieces of Chinese ceramics from the Song, Yuan, Ming and Qing dynasties, some of which were owned by Chinese emperors.

WC1   Petrie Museum of Egyptian Archaeology

University College London, Gower Street, London WC1E 6BT. 071-387 7050. Open: Mon-Fri 10-12/1.15-5. Closed: Week Xmas, Week Easter, One Month in Summer. Call for info.

Based on the collection of the great Victorian archaeologist Sir William Flinders Petrie and on his successors, the museum, part of the University College London, its central theme is the development of Egyptian domestic life, culture and technology from Palaeolithic to Roman times.

W5   Pitshanger Manor Museum

Mattock Lane, Ealing, London W5 5EQ. 081-567 1227. Open: Tue-Sat 10-5. ♿

First built by George Dance, rebuilt by his pupil, Sir John Soane, to try and encourage his sons to take up architecture (he failed), it is currently being restored, but there are temporary exhibitions from May to October and a collection of Martinware pottery.

PASSPORT CONCESSIONS: Free Poster; 30% off Martinware postcard pack; OPP - please apply for Newsletter.

The Breakfast Room.

W1   Pollock's Toy Museum

1 Scala Street, London W1. 071-636 3452. Open: Mon-Sat 10-5. £

Toys of every sort, from dolls made of all kinds of different materials and lead figures to board games and mechanical toys, all in a pair of 18th century houses. There are temporary exhibitions and demonstrations as well.

JNR. PASSPORT CONCESSIONS: Free entry to Junior Passport holder.

WC2   Public Record Office

Chancery Lane, London WC2. Open: Mon-Fri 9.30-5. Closed: fortnight beginning 1 Oct. ♿

This is the nation's official memory, one that can remember back to the Domesday Book, and it has a newly refurbished museum now in which its gems are recalled.

PASSPORT CONCESSIONS: 10% off shop purchases over £10.

SW1 — The Queen's Gallery

Buckingham Palace,
London SW1A 1AA.
071-930 4832. Open:
Mon-Sat 10.30-5, Sun
2-5. £ &

Part of Buckingham Palace on the site occupied by the private chapel before it was destroyed in the Blitz, the gallery is the showcase for the unparalleled Royal Collections of art with different themes for each year's displays. This year, from March 9, it is the collections in the Royal Library at Windsor Castle, treasures never before shown in public including jewellery, watercolours - many of them by members of the Royal Family - music written by the 11-year old Mozart, the shirt in which Charles 1 was executed, the clock Henry VIII gave to Anne Boleyn plus sovereign coins from Elizabeths I to II and original manuscripts by Byron, Dickens and Hardy.

E3 — Ragged School Museum

46-48 Copperfield
Road, Bow,
London E3 4RR.
081-980 6405.
Open: Please call for
details. P

This is a new museum, devoted to East End life and told through photographs, documents, memorabilia and room reconstructions, (including a Victorian classroom,) all set in the largest of Dr. Barnado's Ragged Schools in London.

SE10 — Rangers House

Chesterfield Walk,
London SE10.
O81-853 0035. Open:
Daily 10-6 Summer,
10-4 Winter. P (EH)

This red brick villa of about 1700, once the home of the 4th Earl of Chesterfield, contains a series of Jacobean paintings attributed to Larkin, and a collection of musical instruments.

W1 — Royal Academy of Arts

Burlington House,
Piccadilly, London
W1V 0DS.
071-439 7438.
Open: Daily 10-6.
£ &

It has very little by way of permanent collections so is this a museum? Whether it is or not, it's Britain's oldest fine arts society, run by our best artists as a school for, perhaps, the best of the future, but also the venue for outstanding exhibitions. In 1990 there are exhibitions on Royal Academicians from 1900 to 1950, Monet and the Impressionists.

PASSPORT CONCESSIONS: Passport holders will be eligible for the Concessionary Admission rate to each exhibition.

NW9 — Royal Air Force Museum

Grahame Park Way,
Hendon, London
NW9 5LL.
081-205 2266.
Open: Daily: 10-6.
£ P &

Britain's national museum of aviation tracing the story of flight through 60 historic aircraft, its wars, its personalities and its achievements. Special exhibitions this year reflect the 50th anniversary of the Battle of Britain.

PASSPORT CONCESSIONS: Two admissions for the price of one.

EC3 — The Royal Armouries

HM Tower of London,
London EC3N 4AB.
071-480 6358. Open:
Mar-Oct Mon-Fri
9.30-5, Sat 9.30-5.45
Sun 2-5.30, Nov-Feb
Mon-Sat 9.30-4.30.
£ &

The national museum of arms and armour, in the Tower of London, including the armours of Henry VIII, a unique collection of military and sporting firearms and the only surviving elephant armour.

Armour for Man and Horse.

SE18 — Royal Artillery Museum

Old Royal Military
Academy, Red Lion
Lane, Woolwich,
London SE18 4DN.
081-854 2242.
Open: Mon-Fri 12.30-
4, Sat/Sun 2-4.

The regimental story through pictures, models, uniforms and displays from its foundation in 1716.

RICHMOND — Royal Botanic Gardens

Kew, Richmond,
Surrey TW9 3AB.
081-940 1171. Open:
Daily 9.30-dusk.
£ P &

Or Kew Gardens as it's best known to us, founded by George III's mother in 1759, its job is to promote man's understanding and management of plant life, a sort of a botanical zoo, and in the spring of 1990 a new £4million Sir Joseph Banks building opens with a large

exhibition hall dedicated to focussing on the importance of plants to mankind. The Kew Gardens Gallery has exhibitions by botanical illustrators and craftsmen.

SW7   Royal College of Art Galleries

Kensington Gore, London SW7 2EU. 071-584 5020. Open: Mon-Fri 10am-6pm. Sat/Sun please call for details. ♿

This is the country's only post-graduate art school, and it now has its own art gallery, the Gulbenkian, where the degree shows in June and July give some idea of the styles of the future.

PASSPORT CONCESSIONS: 30 Free tickets to college fashion show mid-June, please call for details.

SW7   Royal College of Music Department of Portraits

Prince Consort Road, London SW7 2BS. 071-589 3643. Open: Mon-Fri by appointment only.

This has a comprehensive collection of musicians' portraits, as well as Britain's largest archive of concert programmes.

SW7   Royal College of Music Museum of Instruments

Prince Consort Road, London SW7 2BS. 071-589 3643. Open: Wed during term time 2-4.30. £

There are 500 instruments in the collection, dating from 1480 to 1980, and incorporating the Donaldson, Tagore, Hipkins and Ridley collections.

PASSPORT CONCESSIONS: 50% off adult admission; 20% off postcards; 10% off working drawings.

NW8 — Saatchi Collection

98A Boundary Road, London NW8 0RH. 071-624 8299. Open: Fri/Sat: 12-6. Closed: 2 weeks over Christmas and during the changeover of exhibitions twice a year.

The incomparable collection of modern art brought together by Charles Saatchi, half of the famous sibling advertising partnership, and his wife and opened in 1985. Now has special theme exhibitions: Leon Kossoff and Bill Woodrow until March 1990, further British Art from April on.

PASSPORT CONCESSIONS: Free Pamphlet.

SE1 — Schooner Kathleen & May

St Mary Overy Dock, Cathedral Street, Southwark, London SE1 9DE. 071-403 3965. Open: Daily 10-5. Closed: Weekends Nov-Feb. £

Built at Connah's Quay in 1900, this was the last wooden three-master topsail trading schooner, and as well as being its own exhibit it has a display about the coastal sailing trade.

PASSPORT CONCESSIONS: Free admission to child accompanying Passport holder.

JNR. PASSPORT CONCESSIONS: Free Badge; Free Pencil.

SW7 — Science Museum

Exhibition Rd, London SW7. 071-938 8000. Open: Mon-Sat 10-6, Sun 11-6. £ &

Properly, the National Museum of Science and Technology, it has begun a five year multi-million pound refurbishment programme and now has a new entrance, new shops, a new and absorbing Food and Nutrition Gallery - and a new admission charge.

W2 — The Serpentine Gallery

Kensington Gardens, London W2 3XA. 071-402 6075 Open: Mon- Fri May-Oct 11-6, Nov-Apr 11-dusk. &

Formerly a tea room in Hyde Park, the gallery is now one of the foremost for exhibitions of modern art, presenting younger artists' work, recognising the achievements of established British artists and reflecting international developments.

SE1 — Shakespeare Globe Museum

Bear Gardens, Bankside, London SE1. 071-928 6342. Open: Mon-Sat 10-5, Sun 1.30-5.30. £

This little museum is the core of the new museum which will go in the International Shakespeare Globe Centre which is being built. The collections have a new edge of interest since the campaign to save the 1587 Rose Theatre, found next door, and the more recent discovery of the Globe itself a few yards further away.

PASSPORT CONCESSIONS: 50% off adult admission

NW1 — The Sherlock Holmes Museum

221b Baker Street,
London NW1 6XE.
071-935 8866
Open: Daily 9-10. £

With some Sherlockian detective work, Mr John Aidiniantz and his associates actually found 221b Baker Street after two sets of renumbering the houses over the years, and not only did it have the correct number of stairs as mentioned in one of the stories, it was for sale. Due to open Spring 1990.

PASSPORT CONCESSIONS: Free Guidebook.

JNR. PASSPORT CONCESSIONS: Free Schools information pack.

SW1 — Tate Gallery

Millbank, London
SW1 4RG.
071-821 1313.
Open: Mon-Sat 10-5.50, Sun 2-5.50. &

These are the national collections of historic British art and of 20th century painting and sculpture, and there is now the extra attraction of the Turner collections in their own new gallery.

EC4 — Telecom Technology Showcase

135 Queen Victoria
Street, London
EC4V 4AT.
071-248 7444
Open: Mon-Fri 10-5.
Closed: B.H.

This is British Telecom's award-winning museum which uses working exhibits, models and video films to explain the development and future of telecommunications.

PASSPORT CONCESSIONS: Free Poster.

JNR. PASSPORT CONCESSIONS: Free decal Badge.

WC2 — Theatre Museum

1e Tavistock St,
London WC2 (main
entrance Russell St).
071-836 7891. Open:
Tue-Sun 11-7 £ &

The national collection of the history of the dramatic arts in the middle of London's theatreland.

WC1 — The Thomas Coram Foundation for Children

40 Brunswick Square,
London WC1N 1AZ.
071-278 2424. Open:
Please call for details. £

The old Foundling Hospital which now has art treasures including works by Hogarth, Gainsborough and Reynolds.

LONDON

SE1 — Tower Bridge Museum

Tower Bridge, London
SE1 2UP.
071-407 0922.
Open: Daily Apr-Oct
10-5.45, Nov-Mar 10-4.
£ ♿

The London tourism landmark which many tourists assume to be medieval is actually an astonishing tribute to Victorian engineering. Its heart, the original steam hydraulic machinery, can be seen, and a definitive exhibition on how and why the whole extraordinary thing came to be.

PASSPORT CONCESSIONS: 50p off adult admission.

JNR. PASSPORT CONCESSIONS: Free Schools information pack (phone or write in-not available on the day).

WC2 — Twinings Museum

216 Strand,
London WC2.
071-353 3511.
Open: Mon-Fri 9.30-
4.30. ♿

This museum - through the shop in 216 Strand - has the distinction of being on the premises of the oldest ratepayer in the city of Westminster. Twinings has been on the same site tendering tea and coffee since 1706, and the tiny museum reflects its refreshing history.

UPMINSTER — Upminster Tithe Barn Agricultural and Folk Museum

Hall Lane, Upminster,
Essex RM14 1AU.
04024-47535.
Open: 1st full weekend
of the month. Closed:
Nov-Mar. P ♿

This is a museum which has packed in everything but the kitchen sink - well, it's come close with plumbers' tools among the categories which also include agricultural material, Victoriana, an old schoolroom, coopering tools, bottles, dairy items and an old kitchen complete with ancient gadgets.

DAGENHAM — Valence House Museum

Becontree Avenue,
Dagenham, Essex
RM8 3HT.
081-592 4500. Open:
Mon-Fri 9-1.30/2-4.

Maps, archaeology, topographical paintings and portraits of the Fanshawes, the family which owned the 17th century house and its contents. Temporary exhibitions from May 21-July 13 on the spread of London into Essex.

E17 — Vestry House Museum

Vestry Road,
Walthamstow,
London E17 9NH.
081-509 1917. Open:
Mon-Fri 10-1/2-5.30,
Sat 10-1/2-5. P

An 18th century workhouse in old Walthamstow Village has become the town's memory, with a reconstructed police cell, a Victorian parlour, and the Bremner car, built locally in about 1894.

PASSPORT CONCESSIONS: Reduction of 10% on shop purchases.

JNR. PASSPORT CONCESSIONS: Free Badge.

SW7   Victoria & Albert Museum

Cromwell Road,
London SW7 2RL.
071-938 8500. Open:
Mon-Sat 10-5.50, Sun
2.30-5.50. ♿

The world's top museum of fine and applied art, undergoing major internal changes but with most of its popular delights available, and a series of temporary exhibitions.

SE21   Vintage Wireless Museum

23 Rosendale Road,
West Dulwich,
London SE21 8DS.
081-670 3667. Open:
By appontment only

In this private house is one of Europe's largest collections of wireless sets and a replica of a 1930s wireless shop.

W1   The Wallace Collection

Manchester Square,
London W1M 3BN.
071-935 0687.
Open: Mon-Sat 10-5,
Sun 2-5.

Whether its Rembrandts are real or, as a group of Dutch scholars are claiming, not, this is one of the world's finest private collections of fine and applied art in the world, given to the nation nearly 100 years ago by the widow of Sir Richard Wallace who had made the family home, Hertford House, and the family collections into a museum.

PASSPORT CONCESSIONS: Half price Guidebook.

SW15   Wandsworth Museum

5 Disraeli Road,
Putney, London
SW15 2DR.
071-871 7074. Open:
Mon-Sat 1-5. Closed:
Thur & B.H. ♿

A new museum of every day life from prehistory to today in the area now covered by the Borough of Wandsworth.

PASSPORT CONCESSIONS: Free Pencil.

WC2   Wellcome Museum of Human Anatomy

Royal College of
Surgeons of England,
35-43 Lincoln's Inn
Fields, London
WC2A 3PN.
071-405 3474 Open:
To medical
professionals and study
groups only.
Closed: Aug.

This is one of those specialist museums which are only available to specialists. Based in the Royal College of Surgeons, I reckon that if you find their own description appealing you're probably qualified to visit: Dissections demonstrating human anatomy; resin corrosion casts of blood vessels, tracheo-bronchial trees, biliary and renal tracts; transverse sections of human body; radiological and histological demonstrations.

W1 — Wellington Museum

149 Piccadilly, Apsley House, Hyde Park Corner, London W1. 071-499 5676. Open: Tue-Sun 11-4.50. £

This is Apsley House, the first Duke's London home, and known as Number One London in his day because it was the first major house coaches coming from the north saw within the bounds of the capital. It is now a museum showing Wellingtonia, but more importantly the private collections of painting and applied art of the old soldier.

SW1 — Westminster Abbey Chapterhouse and PYX Chamber

Westminster Abbey, London SW1. 071-222 5897. Open: Daily 10-6 Summer, 10-4 Winter. £ (EH)

The Chapter House was built by royal masons in about 1250 and contains two of the finest examples of medieval sculpture, a tiled floor and mural paintings; the 11th century Chamber has the Abbey Treasures.

SW1 — Westminster Abbey Museum

Westminster Abbey, London SW1P 3PA. 071-233 0019. Open: Daily 10.30-4. £ &

The fascinating collection of royal effigies of the likes of Henry VIII, Charles II and Queen Anne, plus some not-quite-royals are in this three-year-old museum set in the Abbey's 11th century vaulted undercroft, along with armour, medieval glass and replicas of coronation regalia.

E17 — William Morris Gallery

Lloyd Park, Forest Road, Walthamstow, London E17 4PP 081-527 3782. Open: Tue-Sat 10-1/2-5 and first Sun in every month: 10-12 /2-5. Closed: B.H. P &

A hundred years old when the great founder of the Arts and Crafts Movement brought his family to live in the Water House in 1848, it now houses the permanent collection celebrating William Morris's achievements as designer, craftsman, poet and socialist, in the town where he was born in 1834. Exhibition on Morris & Co tiles and ceramics from autumn 1990.

PASSPORT CONCESSIONS: Free Poster.

LION RAMPANT tile panel designed by William De Morgan.

SW19 — The Wimbledon Lawn Tennis Museum

The All England Club,
Church Road,
Wimbledon,
London SW19 5AE.
081-946 6131. Open:
Tue-Sat 11-5, Sun 2-5.
£ P &

The personalities, the fashions, the trophies, the equipment and the history of tennis, with a chance to see the Centre Court and regular special exhibitions.

PASSPORT CONCESSIONS: 50p off adult admission, 25p off OAP and Children's ticket.

SW19 — Wimbledon Society Museum of Local History

The Ridgway,
Wimbledon,
London SW19. Open:
Sat 2.30-5.

Archaeology, prints, watercolours, photographs, natural history, books, maps and manuscripts about Wimbledon, its Common and the less than common people who have lived there.

SE3 — Woodlands Art Gallery

90 Mycenae Road,
Blackheath, London
SE3 7SE.
081-858 4631. Open:
Mon-Fri 10-7.30, Sat
10-6, Sun 2-6 .
Closed: Wed. P

This Blackheath gallery organises 12 complete exhibitions a year in its four rooms, all of contemporary art but of various styles.

SW7 — Zamana Gallery

1 Cromwell Gardens,
London SW7 2SL.
071-584 6612. Open:
Tue- Sat 10-5.30, Sun
12-5.30. Closed: B.H.
£ &

This gallery, opposite the V&A, is dedicated to the arts, architecture and culture of non-Western societies, particularly Islamic ones, with special exhibitions all year.

PASSPORT CONCESSIONS: Free entry to Passport holders

The Wimbledon Lawn Tennis Museum

The Museum traces the development of Lawn Tennis from a polite pastime in Victorian England to the highly professional spectator sport seen at Wimbledon today. Displays feature costume, trophies, paintings, ephemera, memorabilia, equipment and much more.

**The All England Club,
Church Road, Wimbledon,
London SW19 5AE
Telephone: 081-946 6131**

SOUTH EAST

ASHFORD — Ashford Local History Room

Central Library,
Church Road,
Ashford, Kent. 0233-
20649. Open:
Mon/Tue 9.30-6,
Wed/Sat 9.30-5,
Thur/Fri 9.30-7. P

The historical geography of this ancient market town on the Stour, on the Roman road to Canterbury.

ASHFORD — Wye College Museum of Agriculture

Wye College, Wye,
Ashford, Kent TN25
5AH. 0233-812401.
Open: Wed: 2-5 May-
Sept & Sat 2-5 in Aug.
Closed: Oct-Apr.

This has an exhibition of vehicles, implements and tools from the days before the tractor took over from the horse as the main work-beast of the farm. It is housed in a 14th century barn and 19th century oast house.

BASILDON — National Motorboat Museum

Wat Tyler Country
Park, Wat Tyler Way,
Pitsea, Basildon,
Essex SS16 4UW.
0268-550077. Open:
Mon-Fri 10-4, Sat/Sun
11-5. P &

Boats for pleasure, for sport, for work and for war in this collection, with a conservation workshop and reference library.

BATTLE — Battle Abbey & Site of the Battle of Hastings

Battle High Street,
Battle, East Sussex.
04246-3792. Open:
Daily 10-6 Summer,
Tue-Sun 10-4 Winter.
£ P & (EH)

The site of the last successful invasion of England in 1066. William built the abbey around the spot where the English royal standard stood during the Battle of Hastings. There are still impressive remains, including the gate house.

BATTLE — Buckley's Museum of Shops

90 High Street, Battle,
Nr. Hastings, E.
Sussex. 04246-4269.
Open: Daily 10-5. £

There are over 30,000 objects, all about the business of going shopping between 1850 and 1950. Advertising and domestic memorabilia in a Victorian arcade and shop and room settings in Mrs Annette Buckley's delightful museum.

PASSPORT CONCESSIONS: Free Guidebook; 20% off admission charge.

JNR. PASSPORT CONCESSIONS: Free Badge; 20% off admission charge.

BEXHILL — Bexhill Museum of Costume and Social History

Bexhill Manor Gardens, Old Town, Bexhill. 0424-215361. Open: Apr-Oct Mon-Fri 10.30-5.30, Sat/Sun 2.30-5.30. Closed: Nov-Mar. £ P &

Original costumes dating from the early 18th century, and other memorabilia to go with them.

PASSPORT CONCESSIONS: Free entry to Passport holder.

JNR. PASSPORT CONCESSIONS: Free entry to Junior Passport holder.

BEXHILL-ON-SEA — Bexhill Museum

Egerton Road, Bexhill-on-Sea, East Sussex TN39 3HL. 0424-211769. Open: Tue-Fri 10-5, Sat/Sun 2-5. £ &

The star of this museum is not the usual run of the beach seaside creature. It's an iguanadon, a local one, and it sets off the displays on local history, geology and natural history in the sea-front museum. There are monthly changing temporary exhibitions.

PASSPORT CONCESSIONS: Free entry to Passport holder.

JNR. PASSPORT CONCESSIONS: Free entry to Junior Passport holder; Free Pencil.

BIRCHINGTON — Powell-Cotton Museum

Quex Park, Birchington, Kent CT7 0BH. 0843-42168. Open: Apr-Sept Wed/Thur/Sun 2.15-6. + Aug Fri 2.15-6. Winter Sun 2.15-6 only. P

The museum displays the extraordinary collections of Major Percy Powell-Cotton, one of the last great white hunters and a naturalist. His "trophies" are stuffed and set in dioramas of their habitats. Next door is the family home, and there is an outstanding collection of Chinese Imperial porcelain.

BRIGHTON — Booth Museum of Natural History

194 Dyke Road, Brighton, East Sussex BN1 5AA . 0273-552586. Open: Mon-Sat 10-5, Sun 2-5. Closed: Thur. &

Dating from 1874, this is a natural history museum typical of the popular Victorian type which still draws thousands of visitors today.This one has birds, butterflies, dinosaurs, fossils, minerals, whale and other skeletons. The service is broadened by nature conservation unit, a record centre, specimen loans and temporary exhibitions.

PASSPORT CONCESSIONS: Free Poster.

BRIGHTON — Brighton Museum and Art Gallery

Church Street, Brighton, East Sussex BN1 1UE. 0273-603005. Open: Tue-Sat: 10-5.45, Sun 2 -5.

This has an award-winning fashion gallery examining why we wear clothes as well as which clothes we wore. There is also furniture, paintings from Old Masters to modern, and archaeology, local history, ethnography, musical instruments and pottery.

PASSPORT CONCESSIONS: Free Poster.

BRIGHTON — Preston Manor

Preston Park, Brighton BN1 6SD. 0273-603005. Open: Tue-Sun 10-5. £ P

The country house of the Stanford family for 200 years, first built in 1251, rebuilt in 1738, remodelled in 1905. Fully furnished now in the mode of the gentry before World War One, including the servants' quarters.

PASSPORT CONCESSIONS: Free Poster.

JNR. PASSPORT CONCESSIONS: Free Poster.

BRIGHTON — The Royal Pavilion

Brighton BN1 1VE. 0273-603005. Open: Daily 10-5, Jun-Sept 10-6 . £ &

The crazy and beautiful seaside palace of George IV, now largely refurbished, with some furnishings on loan from the Queen.

PASSPORT CONCESSIONS: Free Poster; Special rate family entrance ticket.

JNR. PASSPORT CONCESSIONS: Free Pencil.

BROADSTAIRS — Crampton Tower Museum

Post Office, High Street, Broadstairs, Kent. 0843-64446. Open: Easter-Oct Mon/Tue/Thur/Fri 2.30-5, Sun only when followed by B.H. 2.30-5. Closed: Nov-Easter. £

Dedicated to Thomas Crampton, the Victorian engineer, architect and locomotive designer. The tower is a biographical museum, in a waterworks designed by Crampton. Also contains displays about Kent's tracked transport.

BROADSTAIRS — Dickens House Museum Broadstairs

Victoria Parade, Broadstairs, Kent. 0843-62853. Open: Apr-Oct Daily 2.30-5.30. Closed: Nov-Mar. £

Set in the house which was once the home of Miss Mary Strong, the model for Dickens's Betsy Trotwood, the museum commemorates the novelist's association with Broadstairs. The parlour is furnished according to the description in David Copperfield.

CANTERBURY — Canterbury Heritage Museum

Stour Street, Canterbury, Kent. 0227-452747. Open: Mon-Sat 10.30-5, Sun (June -Oct) 1.30-5. £ ♿

Opened by the Queen in 1987, in the medieval Hospital for Poor Priests, this museum features the city's treasures from Roman times to the Blitz. They include two Roman swords, the world's first passenger steam railway engine (Invicta), Rupert Bear and Joseph Conrad collections.

PASSPORT CONCESSIONS: 50% off adult admission charge; Special rate family entrance ticket.

JNR. PASSPORT CONCESSIONS: Free Badge; Free Museum bag.

CANTERBURY — Canterbury Pilgrim's Way

St Margaret's St. Canterbury, Kent. 0227-454888. Open: Daily 9.30-5.30. £ ♿

In a former church, the creators of the Jorvik Viking Centre have made a delightful interpretation of the journey from the Southwark tavern, and some of the tales the travellers told each other.

CANTERBURY — The Royal Museum & Art Gallery

High Street, Canterbury, Kent. 0227-452747. Open: Mon-Sat 10-.5

A new display of the Buffs Gallery, dedicated to the regiment famous for keeping steady, and the decorative arts gallery with a theme of Canterbury and Europe, are due to open in 1990. There is a gallery devoted to the animal painter Thomas Sidney Cooper, as well as a series of temporary art exhibitions.

CANTERBURY — St Augustine's Abbey

Canterbury, Kent. 0227-767345. Open: Daily 10-6 Summer, 10-4 Winter £ (EH)

Augustine founded the first Christian abbey on this site in 598. There are remains of the later Benedictine monastery, which includes a Norman church with a well-preserved crypt, and a site exhibition.

CANTERBURY — The Westgate Museum

St Peter's Street, Canterbury. 0227-452747. Open: Apr-Sept Mon-Sat 10-1/2-5, Oct-Mar Mon-Sat 2-4. £

Re-opening in April 1990 after structural repairs, this 14th century building is the last of the city's fortified gatehouses and has a display of arms and the history of defences, as well as panoramic views over the city.

PASSPORT CONCESSIONS: Free entry for under 18's.

JNR. PASSPORT CONCESSIONS: Free Badge; Free Museum bag.

CHATHAM — Fort Amherst

Dock Road, Chatham, Kent ME4 4UB. 0634-847747. Open: Sun all year 12-4.30. Mar-Oct Wed-Sun 12-4.30. Daily in School hols. £ P

Built in 1756 to guard the dockyard, it was allowed to deteriorate but is now being restored. It houses a growing display about the Napoleonic Wars.

PASSPORT CONCESSIONS: Free Poster.

CHATHAM — The Historic Dockyard Chatham

Chatham, Kent ME4 4TE. 0634-812551. Open: 25 Mar-28 Oct Wed-Sun 10-6. 31 Oct- 30 Mar Wed/Sat/Sun 10-4.30. £ P &

Four hundred years of dockland and maritime history in the former naval dockyard, Britain's largest collection of scheduled ancient monuments. New semi-permanent exhibition, Wooden Walls, on the building of the sailing warship, opens in 1990.

PASSPORT CONCESSIONS: Reduction of 10% on shop purchases; OPP.

JNR. PASSPORT CONCESSIONS: Free dockyard badges.

CHATHAM — Medway Heritage Centre Trust

St Mary's, Dock Road, Chatham, Kent ME4 4SH. 0634-407116. Open: Apr-Oct Wed-Sat 10-4 , Sun 2-5, Nov-Apr Wed & Sun only. £

The Medway through the centuries, its people, places, wildlife and crafts from Sheerness to Allington Lock.

CHELMSFORD — Chelmsford & Essex Museum - Essex Regiment Museum

Oaklands Park, Moulsh Street, Chelmsford, Essex. 0245-353066 Open: Mon-Sat 10-5, Sun 2-5. P

Local treasures from archaeology and coins to paintings and costume are to be found in this museum, which incorporates a history of the Essex Regiment in a purpose-built annexe museum.

COLCHESTER — Colchester Castle

Colchester, Essex CO1 1TJ. 0206-712939. Open: Apr-Sept Mon-Sat 10-5 , Sun 2.30-5, Oct-Mar Mon-Fri 10-5, Sat 10-4 . £

The largest medieval keep in Europe, built by William the Conqueror in about 1076. It now has a museum tracing the human occupation of Essex from the earliest evidence (at Clacton) to the Siege of Colchester in 1648.

PASSPORT CONCESSIONS: Free entry to Passport holder.

COLCHESTER — Hollytrees Museum

Colchester, Essex
CO1 1UG.
0206-712940. Open:
Apr-Sept Mon-Sat
10-5, Oct-Mar Mon-
Fri 10-5, Sat 10-4.

This early Georgian town house was built in 1718 and now has domestic displays relating to the 18th, 19th and 20th centuries, including toys and costumes.

JNR. PASSPORT CONCESSIONS: Free Pencil.

COLCHESTER — Mersea Museum

High Street, West
Mersea,
Colchester CO5.
0206-385191. Open:
May-Sept Daily 2-5.
Closed: Oct-May. £

This is a small museum telling the local story through postcards, photographs and paintings, with local marine items like a gun punt.

PASSPORT CONCESSIONS: Free entry to Passport holder; Reduction of 10% on shop purchases.

JNR. PASSPORT CONCESSIONS: Free entry to Junior Passport holder; Free Badge; Free Pencil.

COLCHESTER — The Minories Art Gallery

74 High Street,
Colchester, Essex
CO1 1UE.
0206-577067. Open:
Tue-Sat 10.30-5.30,
Sun 12-4.

This is an independent gallery which shows contemporary work by artists of regional, national and international reputation. There are historical shows connected with the perma-nent collection.

Italian Landscape by John Nash, 1915.

COLCHESTER — Natural History Museum

All Saints Church,
High Street,
Colchester, Essex
CO1 1DN.
0206- 712941. Open:
Apr-Sept Mon-Sat 10-
5, Oct-May Mon-Fri
10-5, Sat 10-4.

Housed in a church, the theme of this museum takes a slightly different twist from the usual approach to the subject, by looking at the impact of human society on the environment.

JNR. PASSPORT CONCESSIONS: Free Pencil.

COLCHESTER — Social History Museum

Holy Trinity Church,
Trinity Street,
Colchester, Essex
CO1 1JN.
0206-712942. Open:
Apr-Sept Mon-Sat 10-
5, Oct-Mar Mon-Fri
10-5, Sat 10 -4.

A 14th century church which is now dedicated to the country life and crafts of Essex.

JNR. PASSPORT CONCESSIONS: Free Pencil.

COLCHESTER — Tymperleys Clock Museum

Trinity Street, Colchester, Essex CO1 1JN. 0206-712943. Open: Apr-Sept Tue-Sat 10 -5, Oct Tue-Fri 10 -5, Sat & All B.H. 10 -4, Closed: Nov-Mar. £

This is a timber-framed house, dated about 1500 which houses the Mason Collection of Colchester clocks.

PASSPORT CONCESSIONS: Free entry to Passport holder.

DARTFORD — Dartford Borough Museum

Market Street, Dartford, Kent DA1 1EU. 0322-343555. Open: Mon/Tue/ Thur/Fri 12.30-5.30, Sat 9-1/2-5.

This local museum tells the human history of the area, with temporary exhibitions - 20 years of fashion from January 27 to April 14, Battle of Britain from May 1 to June 28, domestic Dartford from July 14 to October 13, transport from October 27 to January 19.

DEAL — Deal Archaeological Collection

Deal Library, Broad Street, Deal, Kent. 0304-374726. Open: Mon/ Tue/Thur 9.30-6, Wed 9.30-1, Fri 9.30-7, Sat 9.30-5. Closed: B.H. P

Local finds, including jewellery, weapons and pottery, from the Stone Age to the 16th century.

DEAL — Deal Castle

Victoria Road, Deal, Kent. 0304-372762. Open: Daily 10-6 Summer, Tue-Sun 10-4 Winter. £ P (EH)

This is the largest and most complete of the coastal forts built by Henry VIII, and it houses an exhibition on the king's Channel defences.

DEAL — Walmer Castle

Kingsdown Road, Walmer, nr Deal, Kent. 0304-364288. Open: Daily 10-6 Summer, Tue-Sun 10-4 Winter. Closed: Jan/Feb. P (EH)

Another of Henry VIII's forts, the next one on from Deal, and it is also the offical residence of the Warden of the Cinque Ports. The post is now held by the Queen Mother, but the first Duke of Wellington held it and died at Walmer, where his room has been left unchanged. He even left his boots.

DOVER — Crabble Corn Mill

Lower Road, River, Dover, Kent CT17 OUY. 0304-823292. Open: Wed-Mon 10-5. Closed: Oct-Easter. £ P

Winner of the 1989 Times/RIBA Community Enterprise Award, this is one of Europe's finest working mills. Restored from a ruin it offers a fascinating insight into the power of water at work.

PASSPORT CONCESSIONS: £1 off adult admission charge; reduction of 10% on shop purchases; OPP.

JNR. PASSPORT CONCESSIONS: Free Badge; Free Pencil.

DOVER — Dover Castle

Dover, Kent. 0304-201628. Open: Daily 10-6 Summer, 10-4 Winter. £ P ♿ (EH)

One of England's largest and most impregnable strongholds, its precincts contain a Roman lighthouse, a Saxon church, a Norman keep and an underground network of tunnels prepared for possible invasion, first by both Napoleon and then by Hitler.

DOWNE — Darwin Museum-Down House

Luxted Road, Downe (Orpington), Kent BR6 7JT. 0689-59119. Open: Wed-Sun 1-6. Closed: Feb. £ P ♿

The delightful house where the extraordinary Charles Darwin not only wrote his shattering book on the Origin of Species by Means of Natural Selection, but also brought up his family of extraordinarily gifted children. The garden he designed and walked and thought in is preserved.

PASSPORT CONCESSIONS: 50% off adult admission charge.

JNR. PASSPORT CONCESSIONS: Free entry to Junior Passport holder.

DYMCHURCH — Dymchurch Martello Tower

Dymchurch, Kent. 0303-873684. Open 10-6 Summer. Closed: Winter. £ (EH)

This is one of the 74 towers built along the coast between 1805 and 1812 to resist the threatened French invasion.

EASTBOURNE — Sussex Combined Services Museum

The Redoubt Fortress, Royal Parade, Eastbourne, East Sussex BN22 7AQ. 0323-410300. Open: Daily 9.30-5.30. Closed: Nov-Apr. £ &

All three of the armed services have histories in Sussex. This museum tells them, including those of the Royal Sussex regiments and the Queen's Royal Irish Hussars, each in their own little museums within this fortress which dates from the Napoleonic Wars. There is also an aquarium.

PASSPORT CONCESSIONS: Free entry to Passport holder.

JNR. PASSPORT CONCESSIONS: Free entry to Junior Passport holder.

EASTBOURNE — Towner Art Gallery and Local History Museum

High Street, Old Town, Eastbourne, East Sussex BN20 8BB. 0323-411688. Open: Mon-Sat 10-5, Sun 2-5. Closed: Mon Nov-Mar.

Mainly 19th and 20th century British art in the permanent collection, but all illustrating Eastbourne's development from prehistory to 1900, and a lively full programme of temporary exhibitions.

EASTBOURNE — Tower '73 The Wish Tower

King Edward's Parade, Eastbourne, East Sussex. 0323-410300. Open: Daily 9.30-5.30. Closed: Oct-Mar. £

This is a Martello Tower of 1804, a link in a chain of forts built to discourage Napoleon. They worked: he never came. Now it's a museum about coastal defences, especially of that period.

PASSPORT CONCESSIONS: Free entry to Passport holder.

JNR. PASSPORT CONCESSIONS: Free entry to Junior Passport holder.

EAST GRINSTEAD — East Grinstead Town Museum

East Court, College Lane, East Grinstead, Sussex RH19 3LT. 0342 322511. Open: Nov-Mar Wed/Sat 2-4, .Apr-Oct 2-5. P

Craft bygones and local pottery in the local history collections, with a new temporary exhibition every quarter.

PASSPORT CONCESSIONS: Free Guidebook.

JNR. PASSPORT CONCESSIONS: Free Badge or Free Pencil.

ERITH — Erith Museum

Erith Library, Walnut Tree Road, Erith. Kent 0322-526574. Open: Mon/Wed/Sat 2-5.

The Thames-side town from prehistory to modern industry, with displays about Maxim's flying machine, an Edwardian kitchen and a model of the Tudor warship Great Harry.

FALMER — The Barlow Gallery

University of Sussex, Falmer, Sussex. 0273-606755. Open: Tue/Thur 11.30-2.30. £ P

There are over 400 pieces of oriental ceramics, dating from the Ham period to the Qing period, in this museum in the University of Sussex.

FAVERSHAM — Chart Gunpowder Mills

Westbrook Walk, Faversham , Kent. 0795-534542. Open: Easter-31st Oct Sat/Sun 2-5. Closed: Nov-Easter.

Nelson's ships at Trafalgar, and Wellington's artillery at Waterloo, had powder made here. The oldest mills of their kind in the world.

FAVERSHAM — Fleur de Lis Heritage Centre

13 Preston Street, Faversham, Kent ME13 8NS. 0795-534542. Open: Mon-Wed/Fri/Sat 10-1/ 2-4.30. Closed: B.H. £

In a 15th century building owned by the Faversham Society, the heritage centre is an enthralling if sometimes intense description of this historic town's past. Part of the July Open House Scheme of the town, in which several Faversham historic houses are opened for holders of a special ticket, available at the centre.

PASSPORT CONCESSIONS: 50% off adult admission charge.

FAVERSHAM — Ospringe: Maison Dieu

Ospringe, Faversham, Kent. 0795-533751. Open: Daily 10-6 Summer. Closed: Winter. £ (EH)

This is an early 16th century timber-framed building which incorporates fragments of a 13th century hospital and pilgrims' shelter. There is a site museum telling its story.

FOLKESTONE — Folkestone Museum

Grace Hill, Folkestone, Kent CT20 1HD. 0303-850123. Open: Mon-Fri 9-5.30, Sat 9-5.

Founded by the Folkestone Natural History Society in 1868, the museum reflects the town's natural sciences and history in their collections, particularly Roman and Saxon finds. Now with a new display of Victorian Folkestone.

FOLKESTONE — Kent Battle of Britain Museum

Aerodrome Road, Hawkinge Airfield, Nr. Folkestone, Kent CT18 7AK. 0303-893140. Open: Daily Apr-Sept 10-5, Oct 11-4. Closed: Nov-Apr. £ P

It will be another half century before this museum has a more important year. It is housed in the original RAF buildings where the day-to-day developments of the battle in 1940 are itemised. The flight control tower has a comprehensive range of material. There will be special events at the crucial time, including a veterans' reunion.

JNR. PASSPORT CONCESSIONS: Free Pen.

GILLINGHAM — Royal Engineers Museum

Prince Arthur Road, Gillngham, Kent. 0634-844555. Open Tue-Fri 10-5, Sun 11.30-5. £ P &

This is a new museum giving an imaginative insight into the life and work of Britain's soldier engineers and their place in our military, social and imperial history from 1066 to 1945.

PASSPORT CONCESSIONS: 50% off adult admission.

JNR. PASSPORT CONCESSIONS: Free entry to Junior Passport holder.

A young 'sapper' officer defuzes an unexploded bomb.

GOUDHURST — Finchcocks Living Museum of Music

Finchcocks, Goudhurst, Kent TN17 1HH. 0580-211702. Open: Easter-Sept Wed-Sat 2-6. Closed: Nov-Mar. £

One of the most delightful ways to spend an afternoon is among Mr. Richard Burnett's matchless collection of historic keyboard instruments, all in good condition, on which he will give recitals whenever the Georgian house is open. In September there is the Finchcocks Festival of chamber music, and on October 12 to 14 the Finchcocks Fair.

PASSPORT CONCESSIONS: Free Poster; Reduction of 10% on shop purchases.

GRAVESEND — Gravesham Museum

High Street, Gravesend, Kent DA11 0BQ. 0474-323159. Open: Mon/Tue/Thur/Fri Sat 10 - 1/2-5. Closed: B.H. P

Once a key port on the Thames, Gravesend's story is a long and honourable one, as the museum shows.

GRAVESEND — Milton Chantry

Fort Gardens, Gravesend. 0474-321520. Open: Daily 10-6 Summer. Closed: Winter. £ (EH)

This is a 14th century building which once housed the chapel of the leper hospital and the chantry of the de Valence and Montechais families. It now has changing exhibitions of local arts and crafts.

GRAYS — Thurrock Local History Museum

Orsett Road, Grays, Essex RM17 5DX. 0375-383325. Open: Mon/Tue/Thur/Fri: 9-8, Wed/Sat: 9-5. Closed B.H. P &

A feature of these collections is the prehistoric, Romano-British and pagan Saxon archaeology. They also illustrate social, agricultural and industrial changes in Thurrock.

HARLOW — Harlow Museum

Passmores House, Third Avenue, Harlow, Essex CM18 6YL. 0279-446422. Open: Mon/Wed/Fri 10-6, Tue/Thur 10-9, Sat/Sun 10-12/1.30-5. P

Set in landscaped Essex grounds, this Tudor farmhouse is the centre for the area's archaeology, folk and farming history, geology and natural history.

HARLOW — Mark Hall Cycle Museum

Muskham Road, Off First Avenue, Harlow, Essex. 0279-39680. Open: Mon-Fri 10-1/2-5, Sat/Sun 10 -5. P &

Bikes from the 1818 hobby horse, which must have run rolling down a hill in a barrel of apples close for comfort, to the 1982 Plastic Itera in the Collins Collection here, along with the saddles, pumps, lamps and puncture outfits which go with them.

Harlow Museum

Mark Hall Cycle Museum & Gardens

Passmores House. Georgian Wing built 1727.

Courtyard with 52" penny-farthing.

HASTINGS — Hastings Museum & Art Gallery

Johns Place,
Cambridge Road,
Hastings, E. Sussex.
0424-721202. Open:
Mon-Sat 10-1/2-5.
Sun 3-5. P ♿

International ethnography collection, European
ceramics, North American Indians' work, Sussex
pottery, paintings and a regular, bewilderingly
busy programme of temporary exhibitions.

PASSPORT CONCESSIONS: Reduction of 5% on
shop purchases; OPP

HASTINGS — Old Town Hall Museum of Local History

High Street, Hastings,
East Sussex.
0424-721209. Open:
Mon-Sat: 10-1/2-5,
Oct-Easter Sun only
3-5.

Smuggling and shipwrecks are among the more
picaresque elements of the story of Hastings,
told here in the Georgian town hall.

PASSPORT CONCESSIONS: Free Hastings
Information Pack.

JNR. PASSPORT CONCESSIONS: Free Badge.

HEATHFIELD — Sussex Farm Museum Countryside Interpretation & Nature Trails

Horsham, Heathfield,
E. Sussex TN21 0JB.
Open: Easter-Oct
Daily 10-5. Closed:
Nov-Mar. £

How the surrounding fields and woods were
used for farming and for making iron and
bricks, with a working smithy.

PASSPORT CONCESSIONS: Free entry to Passport
holder; £1 off adult admission charge.

JNR. PASSPORT CONCESSIONS: Free entry to
Junior Passport holder.

HERNE BAY — Herne Bay Museum

Herne Bay Library,
High Street, Herne Bay,
Kent. 0227-374896.
Open: Mon/ Tue/Fri
9.30-7, Wed 9.30-1,
Thur/Sat 9.30-5. P

Housed in the old post office, the museum of
Herne - Saxon for corner - has treasures
including Pleistocene elephant jawbones, a
smuggler's 'creep' and dishes from a Roman
shipwreck.

HOVE — The British Engineerium

Off Nevill Road, Hove, East Sussex BN3 7QA. Open: Daily 10-5. £ P

Where places like the Science Museum send their old engines to be mended. You can watch the experts at work, with permanent residents including the restored 1876 beam engine in an original pumping station and hundreds of model engines.

PASSPORT CONCESSIONS: £1 off adult admission charge

JNR. PASSPORT CONCESSIONS: Free Badge.

HOVE — Hove Museum & Art Gallery

19 New Church Road, Hove, East Sussex BN3 4AB. 0273-779410. Open: Tue-Fri 10-5, Sat 10-4.30, Sun 2-5. &

Housed in a splendid Victorian villa, the collections embrace painting and applied art from the 17th century to the present. Comprehensive displays of porcelain and the South East Arts Collection of contemporary craft.

PASSPORT CONCESSIONS: Reduction of 10% on shop purchases; OPP.

JNR. PASSPORT CONCESSIONS: Free Museum bag.

HYTHE — Hythe Local History Room

Stade Street, Hythe, Kent CT21 6BG. Open: Mon 9.30-6, Tue-Thur 9.30-5, Fri 9.30-7, Sat 9.30-4. &

A founder Cinque Port, Hythe's growth, decline and resurgence is traced by the museum, with a new display about the Hythe School of Musketry.

LAMBERHURST — Mr. Heavers Noted Model Museum and Craft Village

Forstal Farm, Lamberhurst, Kent TN3 8AG. 0892-890711. Open: Daily 10-6 or dusk. £ P &

In the delightful Kentish town of Lamberhurst, the singular Mr. Alan Heaver has set up his model museum with a reconstructed village street 'housing crafts and silly things of interest', including a miniature fairground.

PASSPORT CONCESSIONS: Free Poster; Reduced entry for holder.

JNR. PASSPORT CONCESSIONS: Free Poster.

LEWES — Anne of Cleves House Museum

52 Southover High Street, Lewes, East Sussex BN7 1JA. 0273- 474610. Open: Mon-Sat 10-5.30, Sun 2-5.30. Closed: Nov-Mar & B.H. £

In one of England's loveliest old county towns, the museum tells of the area's social history, of the region's traditional ironwork and Lewes Priory's stonework. With furnished rooms and displays of toys and games.

PASSPORT CONCESSIONS: Free entry to Passport holder.

JNR. PASSPORT CONCESSIONS: Free entry to Junior Passport holder.

LEWES — Charleston Farmhouse

Nr. Firle, Lewes, East Sussex BN8 6LL. 032-183265. Open: Wed/Thurs/Sat/Sun 2-6. Closed: Nov-Mar. £ P

The nerve centre for the Bloomsbury Group of artists and writers, where Vanessa and Clive Bell, Duncan Grant and their circle worked and played. It is the only complete example of the domestic art of Bell and Grant anywhere in the world.

LEWES — Lewes Castle and Museum of Sussex Archaeology

Barbican House, 169 High Street, Lewes, East Sussex BN7 1YE. 0273-474379. Open: Mon-Sat 10-5.30, Sun 11-5.30. Closed: Sundays Nov-Mar. £

The progress of Sussex people from the Stone Age to the Middle Ages, with a Norman motte and bailey and 14th century barbican nearby. There is an exhibition on latest archaeological discoveries between Oct 20-Nov 17.

PASSPORT CONCESSIONS: Free entry to Passport holder.

JNR. PASSPORT CONCESSIONS: Free entry to Junior Passport holder.

LULLINGSTONE — Lullingstone Roman Villa

Lullingstone Lane, Eynsford, Kent. Open: Daily 10-6 Summer, 10-4 Winter except Mon. £ (EH)

You can see four distinct periods of this large country villa, which was occupied through much of the Roman occupation, thanks to a painstaking archaeological programme. There are splendid mosaics to be seen in the reception room.

LYDD — Lydd Town Old Fire Station

53 High Street, Lydd, Romney Marsh, Kent TN29 9AN. 0679- 20660. Open: B.H. weekends & Daily throughout school Summer vacations 2:30-5. Closed: Oct-Mar. P

There is an 1890 fire engine and a centenary exhibition in 1990, plus a horse bus of about 1900, a Victorian domestic scene and a Battle of Britain display.

MAIDSTONE — Boughton Monchelsea Place

Maidstone, Kent . 0622-743120. Open: Easter-Oct Wed/Sun/B.H. 2.15-6, Jul/Aug Sat 2.15-6. Closed: Oct-Easter. £ P

This is a battlemented Elizabethan house which contains important collections of furniture, pictures, tapestries and objets d'art, stretching from the Crimea to the Falklands Campaign, and including Florence Nightingale's carriage used at Scutari.

PASSPORT CONCESSIONS: 50% off adult admission charge.

MAIDSTONE — Lashenden Air Warfare Museum

Headcorn Aerodrome, Headcorn, Ashford, Kent TN27 9HX. 0622- 890226. Open: Sun & B.H. 10.30-6, other times by appointment only. Closed: End Oct - Easter. P &

An aviation museum with five complete aircraft, including the prototype of the piloted V1 flying bomb with uniforms and prisoners of war memorabilia. A major display on the Battle of Britain celebrates the 50th anniversary and the museum's own 21st birthday.

PASSPORT CONCESSIONS: 10% off shop purchases.

JNR. PASSPORT CONCESSIONS: Free Badge; Free Pencil.

MAIDSTONE — Maidstone Museum & Art Gallery

St. Faith's Street, Maidstone, Kent ME14 1LH. 0622- 54497. Open: Mon-Sat 10-5.30, Sun 2-5.

The Tudor Chillington Manor House was extended in the 19th century and now contains important collections of natural, local and social history, archaeology, fine and applied art, ethnography and the museum of the Queen's Own Royal West Kent Regiment.

PASSPORT CONCESSIONS: 10% off shop purchases.

MAIDSTONE — Museum of Kent Rural Life

Lock Lane, Cobtree Manor Park, Maidstone, Kent ME14 3AU. 0622- 763936. Open Mon-Fri 9-5, Sat 12-5, Sun 12-6. Closed: Oct-Feb. £ P &

Spread over 27 acres, this museum has an oast house, a dairy courtyard, hoppers' huts, livestock, hop gardens, a herb garden, a market garden, an apiary and some fields to make its point.

PASSPORT CONCESSIONS: Free entry to Passport holder; Free Guidebook.

JNR. PASSPORT CONCESSIONS: Free entry to Junior Passport holder.

MAIDSTONE — Tyrwhitt Drake Museum of Carriages

Mill Street, Maidstone, Kent ME14. 0622-54497. Open: Mon-Sat 10 -1/2-5, (Sun: 2-5 Apr-Sept only).

One of the country's finest collections of horsedrawn carriages is on show in the 14th century former stables of the Archbishop's Palace. With state, official and private carriages, some on loan from the Royal Family.

PASSPORT CONCESSIONS: 10% off shop purchases.

MARGATE — Margate Old Town Hall Local History Museum

Market Square, Margate, Kent. 0843-225511. Open: Tue-Sat 10-1 /2 -4. Closed: Oct-Apr. £

This is about Margate's social and local history over the last 200 years, with a Victorian police station and a court house on display.

MARGATE — Tudor House & Museum

King Street, Margate, Kent. 0843-225511. Open: Tue 10.30-1/2-4. Closed: Oct-Apr. £ .

This is a local authority museum which traces the human occupation of the Isle of Thanet from Neolithic to Tudor. There are also displays of tools used in the important local industries of brewing and ship building.

MEOPHAM GREEN — Meopham Windmill

Meopham Green, Kent. 0474-812110. Open: June-Sept Sun 2.30-4.30. Closed: Oct-May. P

This is an early 19th century mill which has almost been fully restored, and it is hoped that it will grind corn again when restoration is complete.

MILTON REGIS — The Court Hall Museum

High Street, Milton Regis, Sittingbourne, Kent. Open: Apr-Sept Sat 2-5. Closed: Oct-Mar. £

The strange and picturesque history of the five bastions of the French-facing coasts, which took a French collective name, the Cinque Ports. The exhibition focuses particularly on Winchelsea, and includes a model of the place as it looked in 1292.

PASSPORT CONCESSIONS: Free entry to Passport holder.

JNR. PASSPORT CONCESSIONS: Free entry to Junior Passport holder.

NEWHAVEN — Newhaven Fort

Fort Road, Newhaven, E. Sussex BN9 9DL. 0273-517622. Open: Easter-Oct 8th, Wed-Sun 10.30-6. Daily during School Summer Holidays, also open B.H. Closed: Oct 9-Easter. £ P

A cliff-top Victorian fort restored and containing military displays, particularly with World War II material.

PASSPORT CONCESSIONS: Free Guidebook.

JNR. PASSPORT CONCESSIONS: Free Badge.

NEWHAVEN — Newhaven Local and Maritime Museum

West Foreshore, Newhaven, East Sussex. Open: Easter-Oct Sat/Sun 2.30 -6 . Closed: Nov-Easter. £ P

In a prefab under the cliffs of the west foreshore, the local historical society has established its museum of local record.

PASSPORT CONCESSIONS: Free entry to Passport holder.

PETWORTH
Petworth House

Petworth, West Sussex GU28 0AE. 0798-42207. Open: Tue/Thur/Sat/Sun: 1-5. Closed: Tue after B.H. Mons. £ P ♿

The home of the Earls of Egremont, now run by the National Trust, it has an outstanding painting collection including works by Van Dyck, Lely, Claude, Reynolds and Turner, plus sculpture and wood carving by Grinling Gibbons.

PEVENSEY
Pevensey Castle

Pevensey, East Sussex. 0323-762604. Open: Daily 10-6 Summer, 10-4 Winter (excl. Mon). £ (EH)

This is a medieval castle which still has the remains of its keep, and within its walls is the 4th century Roman Fort Anderida.

RAMSGATE
Ramsgate Museum

Ramsgate Library, Guildford Lawn, Ramsgate, Kent. 0843-593532. Open: Mon-Wed 9.30-6, Thur/Sat 9.30-5, Fri 9.30-8. ♿

Much of the collection about the town was lost in a bombing raid in the last war, but it is being rebuilt to show Ramsgate's progress from a fishing harbour to a major holiday resort.

ROCHESTER
Guildhall Museum

High Street, Rochester, Kent ME1 1PY. 0634-848717. Open: Daily 10-5.30.

Local history, archaeology, arms and armour, dolls, toys, Victoriana, and models of sailing barges and flying boats.

ROCHESTER
Rochester Castle

Rochester, Kent. 0634-402276. Open: Daily 1-6 Summer, 10-4 Winter (excl Mon). £ (EH)

This is a large Norman castle partly founded on the Roman city wall, and it has a splendid keep built in about 1130.

ROCHESTER
Upnor Castle

High Street, Upper Rochester, Kent 0634-718742. Open: Daily 10-6 Summer. Closed: Winter. £ (EH)

This curious fort, with its angled bastion facing the river, was built by Queen Elizabeth's navy to protect her warships on the Medway.

ROLVENDEN

The C.M. Booth Collection of Historic Vehicles

Falstaff Antiques,
63-67 High Street,
Rolvenden, Kent
TN17 4LP
0580-241234. Open:
Mon-Sat 10-6. £

Mr. Booth's speciality is his collection of Morgan three-wheelers dating from 1913 to 1935, of which he usually has ten on display. There is the only known 1904 Humber Tri-car. Plus bikes, motorbikes and other automobilia.

PASSPORT CONCESSIONS: 50% off adult admission charge.

ROTTINGDEAN

The Grange Art Gallery & Museum

The Green,
Rottingdean, East
Sussex. 0273-301004.
Open: Tue/Fri:10-1/2-
5, Mon/Thur/Sat:
10-5, Sun: 2-5.

This was an 18th century vicarage which Lutyens remodelled in 1919. The ground floor is now an art gallery with temporary exhibitions featuring local artists. There is an exhibition of toys, a collection of books and pictures associated with Kipling, who lived in Rottingdean, and a historical display about the district.

PASSPORT CONCESSIONS: Free Poster

RYE

Rye Art Gallery / Easton Rooms

Ockman Lane, East
Street, Rye, East
Sussex TN31 7JY.
0797-223218. Open:
Mon-Sat 10.30-1/2-5,
Sun 2.30-5.

A new purpose-built gallery in the heart of the town, this has a programme of contemporary and historical exhibitions on such subjects as the one intriguingly entitled "Mendelssohn and the Blomfields Make Strange Bedfellows". Permanent collection of works by Burra, Nash and Piper.

PASSPORT CONCESSIONS: Free entry to Passport holder; Reduction of 10% on shop purchases.

Eric Gill, self portrait.

RYE — Ypres Tower Museum

Gungarden, Rye, Sussex. 0797-223254. Open: Mon-Sat 10.30-1/2.15-5.30, Sun 11.30-1/2.15-5.30. Closed: Nov-Mar. £

Historically an intrinsic activity on this part of the coast was smuggling, so it figures as part of the collections in this local museum, these include local history, country life, medieval pottery, Cinque Ports material, militaria, toys, dolls and shipping.

SANDWICH — Richborough Castle

Richborough, Sandwich, Kent. 0304-612013. Open: Daily 10-6 Summer, 10-4 Winter excl. Mon. £ P (EH)

This is where the Romans landed in 43AD, and the original defensive earthworks were replaced by massive stone walls which still survive. There is a site museum about the complex stronghold.

SANDWICH — White Windmill Folk Museum

Ash Road, Sandwich, Kent. 0304-612076. Open: Sun 2.30-5.30. Closed: Sept-Mar. £

A landmark for many miles before you get near Sandwich, it would seem a waste if somebody just lived in the 18th century mill and you couldn't go inside. Happily it's a museum all about itself, its wooden machinery and some of the work that went on in the rural community hereabouts a century or two ago.

SEAFORD — Seaford Museum of Local History

Martello Tower No. 74, Esplanade, Seaford, E. Sussex. 0323-898222. Open: Summer Wed/Sat 2.30-4.30, Sun 11-1/2.30-4.30. Winter Sun/B.H. only 11-1/2.30-4.30. £

Martello Towers are popular places for museums. This one is entirely volunteer-run, its theme being "How Seaforders Used to Live", with appropriate displays and photographs, along with a series of temporary exhibitions.

SEVENOAKS — Sevenoaks Museum

Buckhurst Lane, Sevenoaks, Kent. 0732-453118. Open: Mon-Fri 9.30-5.30, Thur -7, Sat 9-5. Closed: B.H. &

Re-established in 1986 with the district's geology, archaeology and local history as its theme.

SHEERNESS — Minster Gatehouse

Union Road, Minster-in-Sheppey, Sheerness, Kent ME12 2HW. 0795-872303. Open: Easter weekend, Sat/Sun from Spring B.H., mid Jul-mid Sept Daily (excl. Thur). £

Fossils, documents, photographs, tools, costumes and personal memorabilia, in three floors of the medieval abbey's gatehouse on the Thames Estuary.

PASSPORT CONCESSIONS: Free entry to Passport holder.

JNR. PASSPORT CONCESSIONS: Free entry to Junior Passport holder; Free Badge or Free Pencil.

SOUTHEND-ON-SEA — Central Museum

Victoria Avenue, Southend-on-Sea, Essex. 0702-330214. Open: Mon 1-5, Tues-Sat 10-5.

The human and natural history of South East Essex, with finds from a Saxon cemetery, toys from the early 19th century, aquaria and wildlife, in an Edwardian building.

SOUTHEND-ON-SEA — Prittlewell Priory

Victoria Avenue, Southend-On-Sea, Essex. 0702-342878 Open: Tues-Sat 10-5 P

The Clunial monastery of St. Mary Prittlewell, which was founded in about 1110, now has displays on the history of the priory, medieval religious history and local wildlife, and there is also a nationally important collection of radios and televisions based on EKCO, or E K Cole, the Southend based mamufacturers.

SOUTHEND-ON-SEA
Southchurch Hall

Southchurch Hall Close, Southend-on-Sea, Essex. 0702-467671. Open: Tues-Sat 10-5 &

This is a medieval timber-framed house in its own grounds, with an open central hall which has a buttery and a Tudor wing. In the 1920's it was restored and now has displays on life in the Middle Ages, and Victorian room settings.

STAPLEHURST
Brattle Farm Museum

Brattle Farm, Staplehurst, Kent. 0580-891222. Open: Apr-Oct Sun 9.30-6.30. By appointment at other times. £ P &

Vintage vehicles and hand tools, with a special section including hopping, blacksmithing, wheelwrighting, trapping and potting.

JNR. PASSPORT CONCESSIONS: Free Badge.

TENTERDEN
Dame Ellen Terry Museum

Smallhythe Place, Smallhythe, Nr. Tenterden, Kent. 05806-2334. Open: Mon-Wed/Sat/Sun 2-6. Closed: Nov-Mar. £ P

The home of the celebrated actress is now a museum of her theatrical mementoes and costumes collected during her long stage career.

TENTERDEN
South of England Museum of Agricultural Heritage

Tenterden Vineyard, Spots Farm, Small Hythe, Tenterden, Kent. 05806-3033. Open: Daily 10-6 Summer, 10-4 Winter. £ P (EH)

Not only are the traditional tools and implements restored and on display, along with old machinery, they are used to tend the farm the museum is part of.

TENTERDEN — Tenterden & District Museum

Station Road, Tenterden, Kent TN30 6HN. 05806-4310. Open: Daily 2-5. Closed: Nov-Feb. £

This is about life in a Victorian market town, about the hop-growing tradition, Wealden architecture, and light railways, the kind of things which people who want to know about Tenterden ought to be aware of, including the Cinque Ports. There is an exhibition throughout 1990 dedicated to the Battle of Britain, fought in the skies above the town.

PASSPORT CONCESSIONS: Free Guidebook.

TONBRIDGE — Whitbread Hop Farm

Beltring, Paddock Wood, Kent TW12 6PY. 0622-872068. Open: Apr 12-Nov 11 Daily 10 -5.30. £ P &

There are displays of hop farming, rural crafts, agricultural machinery and the ubiquitous Whitbread horses among this unique collection of Victorian oast houses.

TUNBRIDGE WELLS — Tunbridge Wells Museum & Art Gallery

Civic Centre, Mount Pleasant, Royal Tunbridge Wells, Kent TN1 1NS. 0892-26121. Open: Mon-Sat 9.30-5 . &

You can still take the waters at the wells by the Pantiles, and Tunbridge itself is steeped in colourful history, much of it told in this local museum with its art gallery and bewildering list of exhibitions.

PASSPORT CONCESSIONS: Free Postcard.

JNR. PASSPORT CONCESSIONS: Free Postcard.

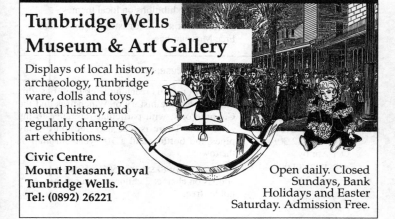

Reader reply service see page 453

UCKFIELD

The Bluebell Railway

Sheffield Park Station, Nr. Uckfield, East Sussex TN22 3QL. 082-572 2370. Open: Daily 9-5. £ P &

Ivor the Engine will never give way to Gavin the Intercity Sleeper in our children's books as long as there are museums like this keeping the steam heritage alive. With a collection of locomotives and coaches dating from 1872 to the 1960s, it steams between Sheffield Park and Horsted Keynes, as well as having a static display. It's 30 years old in 1990, and if you send a stamped addressed envelope they'll send you a timetable and brochure.

PASSPORT CONCESSIONS: Adult Passport holders receive reduced train fare ticket, valid only on timetable trains-not special or reserved trains.

JNR. PASSPORT CONCESSIONS: Junior Passport holders receive reduced train fare ticket valid only on timetable trains - not special or reserved trains.

WESTCLIFF-ON-SEA

Beecroft Art Gallery

Station Road, Westcliff-on-Sea, Essex SS0 7RA. 0702-347418. Open: Mon-Thur/Sat 9.30-5.30, Fri 9.30-5. Closed: B.H. P &

The permanent collection has works from the 16th to the 20th centuries, and includes 17th century Dutch paintings. There are also the local topography and a full list of exhibitions which include a sponsored open art exhibition with prizes.

WHITSTABLE

Whitstable Museum

The Foresters' Hall, Oxford Street, Whitstable, Kent. 0227-276998. Open: Mon/Tue/Thur/Fri/Sat 10.30-1/2-4.

A new museum, with its collections still growing, to tell of the sea-faring traditions of this town, famous for its oysters. There are temporary exhibitions on local themes.

JNR. PASSPORT CONCESSIONS: Free Badge; Free Museum bag,

WINCHELSEA

Court Hall Museum

High Street, Winchelsea, East Sussex. 0797-226365. Open: Apr-Oct Mon-Sat 10.30-12.30/ -5, Oct-Apr by appointment only. £ P

Thanks to records reaching back centuries, this museum has the history of Winchelsea and the Cinque Ports, with particular reference to the civic side. There is also a collection of clay pipes and bottles, and a 700-year-old map of the town.

PASSPORT CONCESSIONS: 50% off adult admission charge; 2 children accompanied by holder free.

SOUTH/
ISLE OF
WIGHT

ABINGDON — Abingdon Museum

County Hall, Market Place, Abingdon, Oxon. 0235-23703. Open: Tue-Sun 1-5 Summer, 1-4 Winter. £

The archaeology and social history of the area, housed in a splendid late 17th century building.

ABINGDON — Pendon Museum of Miniature Landscape and Transport

Long Wittenham, Abingdon OX14 4QD. 086730-7365. Open: Sat/Sun 2-5, B.H. Weekends Sat-Mon 11-5. £ P

There are model trains, farms, thatched cottages and the whole countryside recreating rural life in the 1930s.

PASSPORT CONCESSIONS: Two visitors in any category for price of one.

ALDERSHOT — Airborne Forces Museum

Browning Barracks, Aldershot GU11 2BU. 0252-24431. Open: Tue-Sun 10-4.30. P £ &

The largest collection of airborne weapons ever assembled, with a concise history of the airborne forces from 1940 to 1982. Their 50th anniversary is celebrated in a special exhibition during 1990.

PASSPORT CONCESSIONS: 50% off adult admission.

ALDERSHOT — Aldershot Military Museum

Evelyn Woods Road, Queens Avenue, Aldershot, Hants GU11 2LG. 0252-314598. Open: Mar-Oct Daily 10-5, Nov-Feb 10-4.30. Closed: 17-26 Dec. £ P &

Here is a look behind the scenes at 140 years of the domestic and military life of a soldier, in and around Aldershot. Discipline and the Hampshire air makes them long-lived. There is also a Canadian Gallery, Yeomanry and Volunteer uniforms.

PASSPORT CONCESSIONS: Adult card holders at party rates.

JNR. PASSPORT CONCESSIONS: Junior card holders at party rates.

ALDERSHOT — Army Physical Training Corps

Army School of Physical Training, Queens Avenue, Aldershot, Hants GU11 2LB. 0252-24431. Open: Mon-Fri 8.30-12.30/ 2-5 Sat/Sun by appointment. P &

The corps was founded in 1860; the museum tells its history and also has a technical and study area.

PASSPORT CONCESSIONS: Free Poster; Free Guidebook.

JNR. PASSPORT CONCESSIONS: Free Leaflet.

ALDERSHOT — QARANC Museum

Regimental Headquarters, QARANC, Royal Pavilion, Farnborough Road, Aldershot, Hants GU11 1PZ. 0252-349301. Open: Tue/Wed 9-12, 2-4.30, Thurs 9-12. Other times by arrangement. P

The QARANCS, for those who don't know, are the Queen Alexandra's Royal Army Nursing Corps, but their museum covers a broader spectrum than the corps.

ALDERSHOT — RAMC Historical Museum

Keogh Barracks, Ash Vale, Nr. Aldershot. 0252-24431. Open: Mon-Fri 8.30-4, Closed: B.H. P &

The Royal Army Medical Corps and the history of army medical services, including the Falklands campaign.

ALDERSHOT — Royal Corps of Transport Museum

Reg. HQ. Buller Barracks, Aldershot GU11 2BX. 0252-24431. Open: Mon-Fri 9 -12/2-4. Closed: B.H. P

Uniforms, badges, medals, dioramas and pictures dating from 1795, all about the corps and its predecessors.

PASSPORT CONCESSIONS: 10% off Museum guide.

JNR. PASSPORT CONCESSIONS: Free Badge.

ALTON — Curtis Museum & Allen Gallery

High St, Alton, Hants. 0420-82802. Open: Tue-Sat 10-5. &

There is a gallery here devoted to the work of the botanist William Curtis, but the museum also covers social and industrial history, with new displays designed to appeal to children.

PASSPORT CONCESSIONS: 10% off shop purchases.

JNR. PASSPORT CONCESSIONS: 10% off shop purchases.

ALTON — Jane Austen's House

Chawton, Alton, Hants GU34 1SD. 0420-83262. Open: Daily 11-4.30. Closed: Mon/Tues Nov-Mar, Jan-Feb Weekdays. £ P &

This is the 17th century cottage where Jane Austen lived for the last eight years of her life and where she wrote Mansfield Park, Emma, and Persuasion; here are memorabilia of Miss Austen and her family.

JNR. PASSPORT CONCESSIONS: Free Guidebook.

ANDOVER — Andover Museum

6 Church Close, Andover. 0264-66283. Open: Tue-Sat 10-5. P

This Georgian/Victorian town house has become a museum full of the area's geology, archaeology and natural history, with an art gallery attached. The exhibition until June is the History of Weyhill Fair, and in July the museum helps celebrate the Andover Arts Festival.

ANDOVER — Museum of the Iron Age

6 Church Close, Andover SP10 1DP. 0264-66283. Tue-Sat 10-5, Sun 2-5 . £ P

Twenty years of excavation at Danebury Ring, a hill fort, colour this comprehensive picture of life between 700BC and 50AD.

PASSPORT CONCESSIONS: Free entry to Passport holder; Free Poster; Free Guidebook; Special rate family entry ticket.

JNR. PASSPORT CONCESSIONS: Free entry to Junior Passport holder; Free schools information pack; Free Badge.

ARUNDEL — Amberley Chalk Pits Museum

Houghton Bridge, Amberley, Arundel, West Sussex BN18 9LT. 0798-831370. Open: 24 Mar-28 Oct Wed-Sun 10-5, 18 July-9 Sept Daily 10-5. Closed: Nov-Mar. £ P &

The Sussex working museum with teams of craftsmen, narrow gauge railway, vintage buses, stationary engines, village garage, ironmonger's shop and a whole series of events from spring to autumn.

PASSPORT CONCESSIONS: £1 off adult admission charge.

JNR. PASSPORT CONCESSIONS: 40p off admission charge.

ARUNDEL — Arundel Museum & Heritage Centre

61 High Street, Arundel, West Sussex BN18 9AJ. 0903-882268. Open: Tue-Sat 10.30-12.30/2-5, Sun 2-5. Closed: Nov-Easter. £

This tackles the story of this ancient town, its people, its industries, its historic events, from the Stone Age to the 20th century.

PASSPORT CONCESSIONS: 50% off adult admission charge; Free Guidebook; OPP.

JNR. PASSPORT CONCESSIONS: Free entry to Junior Passport holder.

ARUNDEL — Toy & Military Museum

23 High St, Arundel BN18 9AD. 0903-883101. Open: June-Aug Daily 11-5. Sat/Sun 11-5 Sumer, 2-5 Winter.

This is Sarah Henderson's collection of family toys, especially of toy soldiers, and there is a collection of Gossware in the museum, which is known as The Doll's House.

AYLESBURY — Buckinghamshire County Museum

Church Street, Aylesbury, Bucks HP20 2QP. 0296-88849. Open: Mon-Sat 10-1.30/2-5. &

In a group of 18th century buildings the county tells its story of geology, archaeology and rural life, and has temporary exhibitions throughout the year on subjects like photography, embroidery and medieval pottery.

AYLESBURY — Waddesdon Manor

Waddesdon, Aylesbury, Bucks HP18 0YH. 0296-651211. House Open: Apr-Oct Wed-Sun 1-5. Grounds & Aviary Wed-Sat 1-5, Sun 11.30-5. £ P &

A French chateau in the Buckinghamshire countryside, built in 1874 for Baron Ferdinand de Rothschild, with French decorations and English paintings, plus aviary. Bequeathed to the National Trust.

Jane Austens's House
Chawton, Alton, Hants Tel: 0420 83262

17th century house where Jane lived from 1809 to 1817 and wrote or revised her six great novels. Filled with mementoes of her and her family.

BALDOCK

Ashwell Village Museum

Swan Street, Ashwell, Baldock, Herts SG7 5NY. Open: Sun/B.H. 2:30-5. Parties by appointment. £

The history of an English village, from the Stone Age to the present, is displayed in a timber-framed building.

PASSPORT CONCESSIONS: Free entry to Passport Holders.

JNR. PASSPORT CONCESSIONS: Free entry to Junior Passport Holders.

BANBURY

Banbury Museum

8 Horsefair, Banbury, Oxon OX16 0AA. 0295-259855. Open: Apr-Sept Mon-Fri 10-5, Oct-Mar Tue-Sat 10-4.30.

Overlooking Banbury Cross, this museum's permanent displays tell of "Banburyshire" and the story of the area, with changing temporary exhibitions.

PASSPORT CONCESSIONS: OPP.

BANBURY

Bloxham Village Museum

Yew Tree House, Church Street, Bloxham, Banbury, Oxon OX15 4ET. 0295-720283. Open: Nov-Easter 2nd Sun each month 2.30-4.30 Easter-Oct all Sun/B.H. 2.30-5.30. £ P &

This lovely village near Banbury has its museum in the old courthouse, with an exhibition of old photographs from January to June, and one about the local school history from June to November.

BANBURY

Edgehill Battle Museum Trust

The Estate Yard, Farnborough Hall, Farnborough, Banbury, Oxon. 0926-332213. Open: Wed/Sat 2-6. Closed: Oct-Mar. £ P

It narrows the confusion of the Civil War by just commemorating the first battle, with a huge diorama of 3,000 model soldiers. Throughout the summer there are what are described as 'sporadic demonstrations' of activities such as pike drill. It sounds like guerrilla museology.

PASSPORT CONCESSIONS: 50% off adult admission charge.

JNR. PASSPORT CONCESSIONS: Free Badge.

BANBURY

The Granary Museum & Gift Shop

Butlin Farm, Claydon, Nr Banbury, Oxfordshire OX17 1EP. 0295-89258. Open: Mon-Sat 10-dusk, Sun 11-5. P

Gramophones, typewriters, tractor engines, a steamroller, all handleable, and all in four farm buildings.

PASSPORT CONCESSIONS: 5% reduction on shop purchases.

BASINGSTOKE — Willis Museum & Gallery

Old Town Hall, Market Place, Basingstoke RG21 1QD. 0256-465902. Open: Mon 9.30-5 (Gallery only), Tue-Fri 10-5, Sat 10-4.30.

The Basingstoke tale from 2500 BC - natural history, clocks and watches, embroidery, toys and changing exhibitions.

PASSPORT CONCESSIONS: Reduction of 10% on shop purchases

JNR. PASSPORT CONCESSIONS: Free Badge.

BEAULIEU — Beaulieu Abbey & Exhibition of Monastic Life (and Palace House)

John Montagu Building, Beaulieu, Hampshire SO42 7ZN. 0590-612345. Open: Daily Easter-Sept 10-6, Oct-Easter 10-5. £ P ⑂

In the 13th century abbey remains there is an exhibition of monastic life, showing how the Cistercian monks lived. Palace House, formerly the great gatehouse to the abbey, but the family home of the Montagu's since 1653, is also open to visitors.

PASSPORT CONCESSIONS: £1 off adult admission charge if accompanied by at least one other full-paying adult.

BEAULIEU — National Motor Museum

John Montagu Building, Beaulieu, Hampshire SO42 7ZN. 0590-612345. Open: Daily Easter-Sept 10-6, Oct-Easter 10-5. £ P ⑂

Lord Montagu's famous collection of more than 200 cars, commercial vehicles and motorcycles, which between them tell the story of motoring from 1895 to the present.

PASSPORT CONCESSIONS: £1 off adult admission charge if accompanied by at least one other full-paying adult.

BEDFORD — Bedford Museum

Castle Lane, Bedford MK40 3XD. 0234-53323. Open: Tue-Sat 11-5, Sun 2-5, B. H. Mon 2-5. P ⑂

There are displays of social and natural history here, including important local finds such as the Old Warden Iron Age Mirror, and there is a temporary exhibition programme and children's activities.

BEDFORD — Cecil Higgins Art Gallery & Museum

Castle Close, Bedford MK40 3NY. 0234-211222. Open: Tue-Fri 12.30-5, Sat 11-5, Sun 2-5. &

A decorative arts museum with European ceramics and glass, and regular exhibitions of the gallery's watercolour collection.

BIGGLESWADE — Shuttleworth Collection

Old Warden Aerodrome, Nr Biggleswade, Beds SG18 9ER. 076727-288. Open: Daily 10-5 Summer, 10-4 Winter. £ P &

The aircraft here date from a 1909 Bleriot to a 1941 Spitfire, and there is a collection of ancient road vehicles at this working aerodrome, where they boast that "time flies"

PASSPORT CONCESSIONS: £1 off adult admission (weekdays only); Free Poster; Free Guidebook.

JNR. PASSPORT CONCESSIONS: Free Guide.

BIGGLESWADE — The Swiss Garden

Biggleswade Road, Old Warden, Nr. Biggleswade, Beds. 0234-228330. Open: Wed-Sun 1-6. Closed: Nov-Mar. £

An early 19th century romantic landscaped garden with original buildings, ironwork, ponds, trees and shrubs, plus a popular lakeside picnic site.

PASSPORT CONCESSIONS: Free admission to adult Passport holders on weekdays.

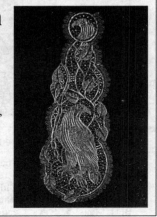

BISHOP'S STORTFORD

Rhodes Memorial Museum

South Road, Bishop's Stortford, Herts CM23 3JG. 0279-651746. Open: Tue-Sat 10-4. £ P

The house where Cecil Rhodes, founder of Rhodesia, was born in 1853, with memorabilia and photographs of Rhodes's career.

BISHOP'S WALTHAM

Bishop's Waltham Palace

Bishop's Waltham, Hampshire. 0489-892460. Open: Daily 10-6 Summer, 10-4 Winter (excl Mon). £ P (EH)

This is the fortified palace of the bishops of Winchester, founded in the 12th century. Here are ruined buildings of the 12th and 14th centuries, ranged about a courtyard within a moat. The ground floor of the Dower House is furnished as a 19th century farmhouse with an exhibition on the first floor.

BOURNEMOUTH

Russell Cotes Art Gallery & Museum

East Cliff, Bournemouth BH1 3AA. 0202-551009. Open: Mon-Sat 10-5.30. £

The collections in this Victorian house are rich in ceramics and oriental material, and the art gallery has good collections of Victorian and Edwardian paintings. In the autumn of 1990 a display area opens for a mixed arts collection and temporary exhibitions, and between August and January 1991 the museum will be celebrating Bournemouth's centenary.

PASSPORT CONCESSIONS: 50% off adult admission charge; Free Poster.

JNR. PASSPORT CONCESSIONS: Free entry to Junior Passport holder; Free Badge.

BOURNEMOUTH   Shelley Rooms

Russell Cotes Art Gallery & Museum, East Cliff, Bournemouth BH1 3AA. 0202-551009. Re-opening after refurbishment Sept 1990 call for details. £ P

This is the only museum in the world dedicated to Percy Byshe Shelley, with objects brought from the poet's home in Italy to his son's home to create the museum. But there are changes planned in 1990, so check before your visit.

PASSPORT CONCESSIONS: Free entry to Passport holder; Free Guidebook.

JNR. PASSPORT CONCESSIONS: Free entry to Junior Passport holder.

BOURNEMOUTH   The Terracotta Warriors

Bournemouth Exhibition Centre, Old Christchurch Lane, off Old Christchurch Road, Bournemouth, BH1 1NE. 0202-293544. Open: Daily 9.30-5.30. Closed: from Oct 1990. £

Not surprisingly, the 7,000 portrait sculptures of the entire army of a dead Chinese emperor found near his tomb have been described as the eighth wonder of the world. Here is an opportunity to wonder at just five of them.

BRADING, Isle of Wight   Nunwell House Home Guard & Military Museums

Nunwell House, Coach Lane, Brading, Isle of Wight. 0983-407240. Open: Sun-Thur 10-5. Closed: Oct-Jun. £ P

A family's uniforms and memorabilia of military service, plus a commemoration of the island's home guard of 1940-43.

PASSPORT CONCESSIONS: Reduction of 20% on shop purchases.

JNR. PASSPORT CONCESSIONS: Free Pencil

BREAMORE   Breamore Countryside Museum

Breamore, Nr Fordingbridge, Hampshire FP6 2DB. 0725-22468. Open: Apr Tue/Wed/Sun, May-Jul/Sept-Tue/Thur/Sat/Sun, August Daily. Closed: Oct-Mar. £ P &

A 19th century agricultural community recreated with a cottage shop, workshops and a fine collection of tractors and farm machinery, plus a steam rally May 12-13 and a craft fair the following weekend.

PASSPORT CONCESSIONS: £1 off adult admission charge.

JNR. PASSPORT CONCESSIONS: Free entry to Junior Passport holder.

BROCKENHURST — Buckler's Hard Maritime Museum & Historic Village

Buckler's Hard, Brockenhurst, Hampshire SO42 7ZN. 0590- 616203. Open: Daily 10-6 Summer, 10-4.30 Winter, July & Aug 10-9. £ P

An 18th century ship-building village, with cottages depicting life as it was and a maritime museum featuring the work of Master Builder Henry Adams, who, built some of Nelson's favourite ships. On the Montagu Estate which includes the National Motor Museum.

PASSPORT CONCESSIONS: Child party rate when accompanied by an adult.

BROMHAM — Bromham Mill and Art Gallery

Bromham, Beds. 0234-228330. Open: Tue-Fri 10.30-4.30, Sat/Sun/B.H. 11.30-6. Closed: Nov-Mar. £ P

A watermill with working machinery on show as part of a museum interpretation, but with the added attraction of an art gallery with special exhibitions in April, May, June, July and October.

PASSPORT CONCESSIONS: Free admission to adult Passport holders on weekdays.

BURFORD — Tolsey Museum

High Street, Burford, Oxford. 099-382 3236. Open: Mar 31-Oct 8 Daily 2.30-5.30. Closed: Oct 9-Mar. £

This has the social and industrial history of Burford, with royal charters from 1350, town maces, tools and the wares of the Burford trades of quarrying, bell-founding and leather-working.

BUSHEY — Bushey Museum Trust & Local Studies Centre

Church House, High Street, Bushey, Herts 081-950 5208.Open: Tue 7-10. £ P

Local history, with a special section on the Monro Circle of artists and the Herkomer Art School.

PASSPORT CONCESSIONS: Free entry to Passport holder.

CALSHOT — Calshot Castle

Calshot, Hampshire. 0703-892023. Open: Daily 10-6 Summer. Closed : Winter. £ (EH)

This was one of Henry VIII's links in his chain of fortified coastal defences, completed in 1540. There is an exhibition and a recreated World War One barrack room.

CAMBERLEY — Royal Army Ordnance Corps Museum

Blackdown Barracks, Deepcut, Camberley, Surrey. 0252-24431. Open: Mon-Fri 8.30-12.30/1.30-4.30. P &

Once through barracks security you find an intriguing story told through dioramas of the Corps' work in campaigns from the Indian Mutiny to World War II, with a history of the British service rifle to be a new attraction.

PASSPORT CONCESSIONS: OPP.

WWI Diorama showing ammunition supply in The Great War.

CAMBERLEY — Surrey Heath Museum

Knoll Road, Camberley, Surrey GU15 3HD. 0276-686252. Open: Tue-Sat 11-5. Closed: B.H. &

Displays on subjects as diverse as highwaymen and heathland crafts help this small museum tell the story of the Surrey Heath area. Includes the development of the military camp, Camberley - originally called Cambridge after the Duke of Cambridge, then Commander-in-Chief-but had to be changed after completely confusing the Post Office.

PASSPORT CONCESSIONS: OPP.

JNR. PASSPORT CONCESSIONS: Free set of 6 educational colour & cut out sheets.

CHALFONT ST GILES — Chiltern Open Air Museum

Newland Park, Gorelands Lane, Chalfont St Giles, Bucks HP8 4AD. 02407-71117. Open: Apr-Oct Wed-Sun 2-6. Closed: Nov-Mar. £ P

Where historic buildings of 16th to 19th centuries live again, saved from destruction and transplanted. Special events through the spring and summer, and in December a Victorian Christmas weekend.

PASSPORT CONCESSIONS: £1 off adult admission charge.

JNR. PASSPORT CONCESSIONS: Free Badge.

CHERTSEY — Chertsey Museum

33 Windsor Street, Chertsey, Surrey. 0932-565764. Open: Tue/Thur 2-5, Wed/Fri/Sat 10-1/2-5.

This is a local history museum in a Georgian house, with a good costume collection, archaeology, porcelain, glass and regular changing exhibitions.

CHICHESTER — Chichester District Museum

29 Little London, Chichester, West Sussex PO19 1AB. 0243-784683. Open: Tue-Sat 10-5.30.

This is in a Georgian corn store and has such items as a scale model of a Roman legionary and the city stocks, to tell the history of the district.

PASSPORT CONCESSIONS: Free Guidebook "Story of the District"; Free postcard of building exterior.

JNR. PASSPORT CONCESSIONS: Free Badge.

CHICHESTER — Fishbourne Roman Palace & Museum

Salthill Road, Fishbourne, Chichester, W. Sussex PO19 3QR. 0243-785859. Open: Winter Sun only 10-4, Daily Summer 10-6, Spring 10-5, Autumn 10-4. £ P &

These are the remains of a 1st century AD palace. There is a large collection of mosaic floors still in place, with others rescued from the area, Roman artefacts found in excavations and a replanted formal garden.

PASSPORT CONCESSIONS: £1 off adult admission charge.

JNR. PASSPORT CONCESSIONS: Free entry to Junior Passport holder.

CHICHESTER — Guildhall Museum

Priory Park, Priory Road, Chichester, West Sussex. 0243-784683. Open: Tue-Sat 1-5. Closed: Oct-May. &

This is in the medieval Greyfriars Church, which was once the city's Guildhall. It has a recently conserved 13th century wall painting, displays of Roman stonework and an 18th century bell from the Market Cross.

PASSPORT CONCESSIONS: Free Guidebook "Story of the District"; Free postcard of building exterior and park.

JNR. PASSPORT CONCESSIONS: Free Badge.

CHICHESTER — Mechanical Music & Doll Collection

Church Road, Portfield, Chichester, West Sussex. 0243-785421. Open: Apr 13th-Sept Daily 10-6, Oct-Apr Sat/Sun 10-5. £ P &

You can see and hear barrel organs, barrel pianos, polyphones, orchestrions, dance and fair organs, all fully restored to working order. There is also a collection of Victorian bisque dolls.

PASSPORT CONCESSIONS: Reduction of 20% on shop purchases.

JNR. PASSPORT CONCESSIONS: Reduction of 20% on shop purchases.

CHICHESTER — Pallant House

9 North Pallant, Chichester, West Sussex PO19 1TJ. 0243-774557. Open: Tue-Sat 10-5.30. £

This is a restored Queen Anne town house, with furnished rooms reflecting two centuries, a Georgian garden, a Victorian kitchen and a collection of modern British art. There are exhibitions and concerts scattered throughout the season.

PASSPORT CONCESSIONS: Free entry to Passport holder.

JNR. PASSPORT CONCESSIONS: Free entry to Junior Passport holders.

CHICHESTER — Red Cap Museum

RHQ RMP, Roussillon Barracks, Broyle Road, Chichester PO19 4BN. 0243-786311. Open: Tue-Fri: 10.30-12.30/ 2.30-4.30 + Sat/Sun 2.30-4.30 Apr-Sept. Closed: Jan.

The Red Caps are the Military Police and Chichester is their home. The museum was refurbished in 1984 and depicts the history of the MPs from Tudor times; in March 1990 a new medal room and a display about airborne MPs open.

PASSPORT CONCESSIONS: Free Poster.

CHICHESTER — Weald & Downland Open Air Museum

Singleton, Chichester, West Sussex PO18 0EU. 0243-63348. Open: Daily 11-5 Summer, Nov-Easter Wed/Sun only. £ P

Winner of the Times Shell Community Museum of the Year for Museums Year, this open air museum has more than 30 historical buildings from this part of England, rescued and reconstructed. They include a medieval farmstead, houses, barns, rural craft workshops, a village school and a working watermill.

PASSPORT CONCESSIONS: £1 off adult admission charge.

JNR.PASSPORT CONCESSIONS: Free Badge.

CHIPPENHAM — Fox Talbot Museum of Photography

Lacock near Chippenham Wilts. 0373-830474. Open: Mar-Oct Daily 11-5. £ P &

This is at Lacock Abbey, where the whole village is now owned by the National Trust. The Abbey now celebrates the inventor of photography in his own home.

PASSPORT CONCESSIONS: A third off admission charge; a third off special exhibition admission charge.

CHIPPENHAM — Yelde Hall Museum

Market Place, Chippenham, Wiltshire. 0249-651488. Open: Mon-Sat 10.30-12.30/2-4.30. Closed: Nov-Mid Mar + B.H.

The history of Chippenham is told through photographic displays in this late 15th-early 16th century house.

CHRISTCHURCH — The Red House Museum

Quay Road, Christchurch, Dorset. 0202-482860. Open: Tue-Sat 10-5, Sun 2-5. £ &

This was originally an 18th century parish workhouse, and is now a local and natural history museum, with a dress collection and a formal herb garden.

PASSPORT CONCESSIONS: Free entry for Passport holder; 5% off admission for family accompanying Passport holder, OPP.

JNR. PASSPORT CONCESSIONS: Free entry to Junior Passport holder; Free Pencil.

COGGES — Cogges Manor Farm Museum

Cogges near Witney, Oxfordshire OX8 6LA. 0993-772602. Open: Apr- 4 Nov Tue-Fri 10.30-5.30, Sat/Sun 12-5.30. Closed: 5 Nov-Mar. £ P &

This is largely a 17th century farm, but working as it was in the early 20th century, with a wide range of stock, as there would have been in Edwardian times.

PASSPORT CONCESSIONS: 50% off adult admission charge, and special family rate.

JNR. PASSPORT CONCESSIONS: 50% off adult admission charge.

COOKHAM VILLAGE
Stanley Spencer Gallery

King's Hall, High Street, Cookham Village, Berks. 06285-20890. Open: Easter-Oct Daily 10.30-5.30, Nov-Easter Sat/Sun 11-5. £ &

The paintings, drawings, letters, documents and memorabilia of Sir Stanley, in the village where he lived and worked; plus winter and summer exhibitions.

COWES, Isle of Wight
Library & Maritime Museum

Beckford Road, Cowes, Isle of Wight PO31 7SG. 0983-293341. Open: Mon-Fri 9.30-6, Sat 9.30-4.30.

There are 6,000 maritime books here, plus models, paintings, prints and photographs of the island's maritime history, a special exhibit about J Samuel White shipbuilders and the sailor and yacht designer Uffa Fox.

COWES, Isle of Wight
Osborne House

East Cowes, Isle of Wight. 0983-200022. Open: Daily 10-5 Summer. Closed: Winter. £ P &

Queen Victoria's favourite home, designed by Prince Albert and Thomas Cubitt and built at her own expense, where she died in 1901. Her private apartments have been restored and preserved.

DIDCOT
Didcot Railway Centre

Didcot, Oxfordshire OX11 7NJ. 0235-817200. Open: Tue-Sun 11-5 Summer, weekends only in Winter. £ P &

The golden age of the Great Western Railway recreated with steam locos, an original engine shed and a reconstructed typical country station

PASSPORT CONCESSIONS: £1 off adult admission.

JNR. PASSPORT CONCESSIONS: 50% discount on admission (not to Santa Steamings in Dec).

DORKING
Dorking & District Museum

62A West Street, Dorking, Surrey RH4 1BS. 0306-882589 Open: Wed/Thurs 2-5, Sat 10-5. £

The chalk of the Surrey Downs has yielded a very good fossil collection, and there is also local history and paintings by local artists.

EASTLEIGH — Eastleigh Museum

25 High Street,
Eastleigh, Hants
SO5 5LF.
0703-643026.
Open: Tue-Fri 10-5,
Sat 10-4. &

This tells of the history, life and culture of the
Hampshire town since the railway arrived in
about 1840.

PASSPORT CONCESSIONS: Reduction of 10% on
shop purchases; OPP.

JNR. PASSPORT CONCESSIONS: Free Pencil.

EGHAM — Egham Museum

Literary Institute, 51
High Street, Egham,
Surrey TW20 9EW.
Open: Thur 2-4.30,
Sat 10.30-12.30/2.30-
4.30.

Devoted to the archaeology and history of
Egham, Thorpe and Virginia Water, with
material about the Magna Carta which was
signed nearby at Runnymede.

ELSTOW — Elstow Moot Hall

Elstow Green, Elstow,
Nr Bedford.
0234-228330. Open:
Tue-Sat/B.H. 2-5,
Sun 2-5.30. Closed:
Nov-Mar. £ P

Ebenezer Hoard had the idea for a garden city.
How it was put into practice to create the
world's first garden city, Letchworth, is told
here, along with temporary exhibitions and, on
July 14, craft demonstrations.

PASSPORT CONCESSIONS: Free admission to
adult Passport holders on weekdays.

FAREHAM — Fort Nelson

Down End Road,
Fareham, Hants PO17
6AN. 0329-233734.
Open: Sat/Sun 12-
4.30, Other times by
appointment only.
Closed: Nov-Mar. £ P

A new branch of the Royal Armouries opened
in 1989 in a Victorian fort, with cannon firings
on certain Sundays through the summer.

FAREHAM — Porchester Castle

Porchester Castle,
Fareham, Porchester.
0705-378291. Open:
Daily 10-6 Summer,
10-4 in Winter (excl
Mon) £ P & (EH)

The Norman keep in this castle is almost intact.
There is an Augustinian priory church within
the walls, and the bastions of a large Roman
Fort. The permanent exhibition opening in 1990
covers 1,400 years of its history.

FARNHAM — Farnham Castle Keep

Farnham, Surrey.
0252-713393. Open:
Daily 10-6 Summer.
Closed: Winter.
£ P (EH)

A former residence of the bishops of Winchester, this was a motte and bailey castle enclosing a mound on which are the massive foundations of a Norman tower

FARNHAM — Farnham Museum

38 West Street,
Farnham,
Surrey GU9 7DX.
0252-715094. Open:
Tue-Sat 10-5. &

Costume, hops, brewing and William Cobbett are the main nodes of the subject matter in this local history museum, set in a Grade I listed building of 1718. Workshops, lectures and an exhibition on Farnham's theatre through the summer.

FARNHAM — Rural Life Centre

Old Kiln Museum,
Reeds Road, Tilford,
Farnham, Surrey
GU10 2DL.
025-125-2300. Open:
Wed-Sun 11-6. Closed:
Oct-Apr. £ P &

This is at the Old Kiln Agricultural Museum, and is one of the largest private collections of rustic village life, with a wheelwright's shop, a bakery, an arboretum and collections relating to forestry and agriculture.

PASSPORT CONCESSIONS: 50% off adult admission charge.

FARNHAM — Titchfield Abbey

24 Grove Avenue,
Porchester, Farnham.
0329-43016. Open:
Daily 10-6 Summer.
Closed: Winter. £ (EH)

This was a white Canons abbey founded in 1232, but after the Dissolution in 1537 it was converted into a mansion by the Earl of Southampton.

FORDINGBRIDGE — Rockbourne Roman Villa

Rockbourne, Nr.
Fordingbridge,
Hampshire.
0725-3541. Open:
Mon-Fri 2-6, Sat/Sun
10.30-6. Closed: Oct-
Early Apr. £

A site museum whose star pieces are the remarkable finds made in more than 30 years of digging, arranged thematically to tell the story of the villa.

PASSPORT CONCESSIONS: Free entry to passport holder; 10% off on shop purchases; 50% off for family accompanying Passport Holder; OPP.

JNR. PASSPORT CONCESSIONS: Free entry to Junior Passport holder; Free Pencil.

GODALMING — Godalming Museum

109a High Street, Godalming, Surrey GU7 1AQ. 0483-426510. Open: Tue-Sat 10-5.

This lively community museum, with its local studies library, nestles in a beautiful garden designed by Gertrude Jekyll.

GOSPORT — Fort Brockhurst

Gunners Way, Gosport, Hampshire. 0705-581059. Open: Daily 10-6 Summer, 10-4 Winter (excl Mon). £ P &

Five major forts were built in the mid-19th century to protect Portsmouth and its naval base, and this is one of them. It has an exhibition about the history of Portsmouth's defences.

GOSPORT — Gosport Museum

Walpole Road, Gosport, Hampshire PO12 1NS. 0705-588035. Open: Mon-Sat 9.30-5.30, May-Sept Sun 1-5 as well. &

The collections relate to the long and varied history of this naval/seaside town, with its interesting geology and fossils. The collections are being recast during 1990 on thematic lines. There is, however, a full programme of temporary exhibitions.

PASSPORT CONCESSIONS: Reduction of 10% on shop purchases OPP.

JNR. PASSPORT CONCESSIONS: Free Badge; Free Pencil.

GOSPORT — Royal Navy Submarine Museum

Haslar Jetty Road, Gosport, Hants PO12 2AS. 0705-510354. Open: Nov-Mar Daily 10-3.30, Spr-Oct Daily 10-4.30. £ P

History of the submarine service, with 'Holland' Navy's first submarine, restored. From Easter, a new video presentation and redesigned cinema, and reintroduction of the joint ticket with the Royal Marines Museum.

PASSPORT CONCESSIONS: One child free with every two full paying adults.

GUILDFORD — British Red Cross Museum & Archives

Barnett Hill, Wonersh, Guildford, Surrey, GU5 0RF. 0483-898595. Open: By appointment only. P

This is particularly about the British Red Cross between the 1860s and the 1980s, but also covers the whole Red Cross movement with uniforms, medals, equipment, photographs, memorabilia and archives.

PASSPORT CONCESSIONS: Half-price Poster.

GUILDFORD — The Watts Gallery

Down Lane, Compton,Nr. Guildford, Surrey GU3 1DQ. 0483-810235. Open: Mon/Tue/Fri/Sun 2-6, Wed/Sat 11-1/2-6. 1 Oct-31Mar Gallery closes at 4.30. &

This is a permanent display of the work of the Pre-Raphaelite George Frederick Watts, with paintings, drawings and sculptures by him, and photographs.

Lillie Langtry by F.F. Watts, 1879.

GUILDFORD — Women's Royal Army Corps

WRAC Centre, Queen Elizabeth Park, Guildford, Surrey GU2 6HQ. 0252-24431. Open: Mon-Fri 9-4, Sat by appoint. only. P &

The role of women soldiers in the British Army since 1917 in a small redesigned museum within the WRAC's training centre.

HARPENDEN — Harpenden Railway Museum

235 Luton Road, Harpenden, Herts AL5 3DE. 0582-713524. Open: May 5th-7th, Aug 24-27, 10.30-5.30. £ P

This is the collection of Sue and Geoff Woodward who have accumulated hundreds of artefacts. These include signal boxes, signs, lamps, tools, equipment, documents and 12 working signals, displayed in their home.

PASSPORT CONCESSIONS: Free entry to Passport Holder; Free Guidebook.

JNR. PASSPORT CONCESSIONS: Free entry to Junior Passport holder.

HASLEMERE — Haslemere Educational Museum

High Street, Haslemere, Surrey GU27 2LA. 0428-2112. Open: Apr-Oct Tue-Sat 10-5, Sun 2-5 Nov-Mar Tue-Sat 10-4. £

This is a delightful museum representing all the best tenets of the traditional sort, with comprehensive displays broadly tackling the history of the earth and of man.

PASSPORT CONCESSIONS: Free entry to Passport holders.

JNR. PASSPORT CONCESSIONS: Free entry to Junior Passport holders.

HATFIELD — Mill Green Museum & Mill

Mill Green, Hatfield, Herts AL9 5PD. 0707-271362. Open: Tue-Fri 10-5, Sat/Sun 2-5. P

This a restored water corn mill, which has craft demonstrations, temporary exhibitions and events through the year.

PASSPORT CONCESSIONS: 20p off any size bag of flour.

HAVANT — Havant Museum

56 East Street, Havant, Hants. 0705-451155. Open: Tue-Sat 10-5. P

The Vokes Collection of firearms is one of the star exhibits, filling three rooms, complementing the local material. A new gallery opens in 1990.

PASSPORT CONCESSIONS: Reduction of 10% on shop purchases; OPP.

JNR. PASSPORT CONCESSIONS: Free Pencil.

HERTFORD — Hertford Museum

18 Bull Plain, Hertford SG14 1DT. 0992-582686. Open: Tue-Sat 10-5. £

There are watercolours by the great Georgian - or anti-Georgian - cartoonist and caricaturist Thomas Rowlandson here, as well as changing exhibitions.

PASSPORT CONCESSIONS: 10% off shop purchases.

HIGH WYCOMBE — Wycombe Local History and Chair Museum

Castle Hill House, Priory Avenue, High Wycombe, Bucks HP13 6PX. 0494-23879. Open: Mon-Sat 10-1/2-5.

This is on a medieval site in a 17th century building with later additions, and is devoted to the area's social history, especially the design of the English country chair.

PASSPORT CONCESSIONS: Free Guidebook.

JNR. PASSPORT CONCESSIONS: Free School quiz.

HITCHIN
Hitchin Museum & Art Gallery

Paynes Park, Hitchin, Hertfordshire SG5 1EQ. 0462-434476. Open: Mon-Sat 10-5. Closed: B.H. P

This focuses on the history of the market town, and also has Hertfordshire's biggest costume collection and a very busy art and craft exhibition programme.

HODDESDON
Lowewood Museum

High Street, Hoddesdon, Herts EN11 8BH. 0992-445596. Open: Tue-Sat 10-1/2-4.

Re-opening after extensive repairs in March 1990, this museum tells of the natural history, archaeology and social history of the borough of Broxbourne.

PASSPORT CONCESSIONS: Free Gift.

JNR. PASSPORT CONCESSIONS: Free Gift.

HORSHAM
Horsham Museum

9 The Causeway, Horsham, West Sussex RH12 1HE. 0403-54959. Open: Tue-Sat 10-5. P

In a 16th century timber-framed building, the domestic and rural history of this Sussex centre are told. Complete with a barn and walled garden, and continuously changing exhibitions on sometimes apparently unrelated subjects, like 'Did Dinosaurs Get Toothache?".

KEYHAVEN
Hurst Castle

On Pebble Spit, South of Keyhaven, Hants. 05904-2344. Open: Daily 10-6 Summer, 10-4 weekends only Winter. £ (EH)

One of Henry VIII's coastal forts, added to extensively in the 19th and 20th centuries and with a site exhibition.

LETCHWORTH
The First Garden City Heritage Museum

296 Norton Way South, Letchworth Garden City, Herts SG6 1SU. 0462-683149. Open: Mon-Fri 2-4.30, Sat 10-1/2-4. ♿

A medieval timber-framed market hall restored to be a museum of 17th century furniture. With items relating to John Bunyan, along with a collection of his works and illustrations from The Pilgrim's Progress.

LETCHWORTH — Letchworth Museum & Art Gallery

Broadway, Letchworth, Herts SG6 3PF. 0462-685647. Open: Mon-Sat 9-5. P

There is a new natural history gallery, a rich archaeology collection and regular temporary exhibitions in the art gallery.

PASSPORT CONCESSIONS: Reduction of 10% on shop purchases.

JNR. PASSPORT CONCESSIONS: Free Museum bag.

LITTLEHAMPTON — Littlehampton Museum

12a River Road, Littlehampton, West Sussex BN17 5BN. 0903-715149. Open Tue-Sat 10.30-4.30.

A sea captain's house overlooking the harbour, with a fine collection of maritime paintings, archaeology, special history and photographs about the district. There are temporary exhibitions throughout the year.

PASSPORT CONCESSIONS: OPP.

LUTON — Luton Museum & Art Gallery

Wardown Park, Luton. 0582-36941. Open: Mon-Sat 10-5, Sun 1-5. P &

This has archaeology, local and natural history, lace, costume, toys and hat-making, plus the Beds and Herts Regimental Museum.

LUTON — Stockwood Craft Museum & Gardens

Stockwood Park, Farley Hill, Luton. 0582-38714. Open: 31 Mar-28 Oct Wed-Sat 10-5, Sun 10-6. Closed: 29 Oct-30

Bedfordshire rural craft and trades are displayed in and around an 18th century stable block , which has resident craftsmen.

MILTON COMMON Rycote Chapel

Rycote Park, Milton Common, Oxfordshire. 08447-346. Open: Daily 10-6 Summer, 10-4 Winter (excl. Mon). P &. (EH)

This private chapel was founded in 1449 and still has its medieval font and pews, and two 17th century roofed pews.

MILTON KEYNES Milton Keynes Museum of Industry & Rural Life

Stacey Hill Farm, Southern Way, Wolverton, Milton Keynes MK12 5EJ. 0908-316222. Open: Daily Wed-Sun 1.30-4.30. Closed: Nov-Apr. £ P &.

It's hard to think of Milton Keynes having a history, but it did and here's proof, in extensive collections of agricultural, industrial, domestic and rural pieces covering the last 200 years.

PASSPORT CONCESSIONS: Free entry to Passport holder; Special rate family entrance ticket.

JNR. PASSPORT CONCESSIONS: Free entry to Junior Passport holder. Children under 14 must be accompanied by an adult.

MINSTER LOVELL Minster Lovell Hall & Dovecot

Minster Lovell, Nr Witney, Oxon. 0993-775315. Open: Daily 10-6 Summer, 10-4 Winter. £ P (EH)

This is a 15th century manor house, with a great solar and kitchens. The medieval dovecot survives with its nesting boxes.

NEWBURY Newbury District Museum

The Wharf, Newbury, Berks RG14 5AS. 0635-30511. Open: Oct-Mar Mon-Sat 10-4, Apr-Sept Mon-Sat 10-6, Sun 2-6. P

Fossils to ballooning represents the range of collections in this local museum, in two pretty and historic buildings, a 17th century cloth mill and an 18th century granary.

JNR. PASSPORT CONCESSIONS: Free schools information pack; Free Pencil.

NEW MILTON Sammy Miller Museum

Gore Rd, New Milton, Hants BH25 6TF. 0425-619696. Open: Daily 10-4.30. £ P

One of the world's largest collections of classic bikes with over 200 on show and many record-breaking motorcycles.

PASSPORT CONCESSIONS: Free Poster.

NEWPORT, Isle of Wight
Carisbrooke Castle

Newport, Isle of Wight PO30 1X4. 0983-522107. Open: Daily 10-6 Summer, 10-4 Winter. £ P ♿ (EH)

Charles I was imprisoned in this medieval castle in the months before his trial and execution. The Governor's Lodge now houses the island's county museum.

NEWPORT, Isle of Wight
Newport Roman Villa

Cypress Road, Newport, Isle of Wight. 0983-529720. Open: Sun-Fri 10-4.30. Closed: Oct-Good Friday. £

This was discovered in 1926. It is a good example of a 2nd-3rd century AD winged corridor house, with an exceptionally well-preserved bath range.

PASSPORT CONCESSIONS: 50% off adult admission charge.

NEWPORT, Isle of Wight
Wireless Museum-Arreton Manor

Arreton Manor, Newport, Isle of Wight. 0983-67665. Open: Mon-Fri 10-6, Sun 12 - 6. Closed: Nov- Feb. £ P

This has a large range of radios from the crystal sets of the early 1920s, to the transistorised sets of today. In September there is the annual "Wireless Rally" for enthusiasts.

OXFORD
Ashmolean Museum

Beaumont Street, Oxford OX1 2PH. 0865-278000. Open: Tue-Sat 10-4, Sun 2-4. ♿

This is Britain's oldest public museum with international collections of fine and decorative arts; European paintings and sculpture, Egyptian, Greek and Roman antiquities, Oriental paintings, ceramics and metalware.

PASSPORT CONCESSIONS: Free Guidebook; Reduction of 10% on shop purchases over £1.

JNR. PASSPORT CONCESSIONS: Free Pencil.

OXFORD
Bate Collection of Historical Instruments

Faculty of Music, Oxford OX1 1DB. 0865-276139. Open: Mon-Fri 2-5. ♿

Britain's most comprehensive collection of woodwind, brass and percussion instruments, with over 1,000 on display, a bow-maker's shop and the oldest playable Javanese double gamelan in Britain.

PASSPORT CONCESSIONS: Free Guidebook; 5% reduction of shop purchases including guides.

JNR. PASSPORT CONCESSIONS: Free Badge.

OXFORD — British Telecom Museum

35 Speedwell Street, Oxford OX1 1RH. 0865-246601. Open: By appointment only.

There are over 100 telephones here, from Alexander Graham Bell's "Gallows" to modern instruments, as well as telegraph equipment to help illustrate the development of telecommunications. The museum is in the old telephone exchange, and calls can be made through early switchboards.

OXFORD — Chinese Arts Centre

50 High Street, Oxford OX1 4AS. 0865-242167. Open: Mon-Sat. 10-5, Sun 12-5 (only Apr-Oct.)

An unusual but engrossing find in the middle of Oxford: Chinese painting, both traditional and avant garde, antique and modern jewellery, ceramics, books, magazines, even cassettes.

OXFORD — Christ Church Picture Gallery

Christ Church, Oxford OX1 1DP. 0865-276172. Open: Easter-Sept Mon-Sat 10.30-1/2-5.30, Oct-Easter Closes at 4.30.

This is an important collection of mainly Italian Old Masters from the 14th to the 18th centuries, with works by Michelangelo, Leonardo, Tintoretto and Caracci, as well as non-Italians like Van Dyck and Frans Hals. There are also important temporary exhibitions through 1990 and 1991.

PASSPORT CONCESSIONS: 50% off adult admission.

OXFORD — Museum of the History of Science

Old Ashmolean Building, Broad Street, Oxford OX1 3AZ. 0865-277280. Open: Mon-Fri 10.30-1/2.30-4. Closed: B.H. & weeks at Easter & Christmas.

Scientific instruments, particularly old ones, are peculiarly fascinating, and the collection here is infinitely fascinating: astrolabes, sundials, microscopes, calculating instruments, navigating instruments and much more.

OXFORD — Museum of Modern Art

30 Pembroke Street, Oxford OX1 1BP. 0865-722733. Open: Tue-Sat 10-6/Sun 2-6. £ &

This is one of Europe's leading centres for the visual arts, celebrating its 25th anniversary in 1990. There are changing exhibitions of international 20th century art, design, architecture, photography, film, video and performance.

OXFORD

Museum of Oxford

St. Aldate's, Oxford
OX1 1BZ.
0865-815539. Open:
Tue-Sat 10-5.

In a city well served for museums, this is the only one which deals with its topography, history, social history and architecture, open displays of period interiors.

OXFORD

The Oxford Story

Broad Street, Oxford
OX1 3AJ.
0865-728822. Open:
Daily Apr-Oct 9.30-5.
Nov-Mar 10-4. £

The history of the university told in a tour of life-like sets, created by the Jorvik Viking Centre people.

PASSPORT CONCESSIONS: Free car sticker; 2 adults for the price of one.

JNR. PASSPORT CONCESSIONS: Free Badge for each child; 2 children for the price of one.

OXFORD

Pitt Rivers Museum

South Parks Road,
Oxford OX1 3PP.
0865-270927. Open:
Mon-Sat 1-4.30.

One of the world's greatest ethnographic collections, created by General Pitt Rivers who was a pioneer in the field and gathered thousands of treasures from all parts of the world and all periods of history.

PASSPORT CONCESSIONS: Reduction of 10% on shop purchases.

JNR. PASSPORT CONCESSIONS: Free Badge.

OXFORD

Pitt Rivers Museum Balfour Building

60 Banbury Road,
Oxford OX2.
0865-270927. Open:
Mon-Sat 1-4.30. &

This is the collection of hunter-gatherer societies from prehistoric times to the eskimos, plus musical instruments from all over the world.

PASSPORT CONCESSIONS: Reduction of 10% on shop purchases; 5% off tapes and records.

JNR. PASSPORT CONCESSIONS: Free Badge.

OXFORD
University Museum

Parks Road, Oxford, OX1 3PW. 0865-272950. Open Mon-Sat 12 -5.

The university's collections of insects, rocks, minerals and animals in a magnificent neo-gothic building.

PASSPORT CONCESSIONS: Reduction of 10% on shop purchases.

PORTSMOUTH
Fort Cumberland and Portsmouth Militaria Society

Broad St, Old Portsmouth. 0705-668981. Open: Mon 7.30pm-10pm, Sun 2-5. &

This has local history, ship, naval and Army memorabilia, and drill displays by men dressed in 1830s uniform.

PORTSMOUTH
Mary Rose Exhibition & Ship Hall

College Road, HM Naval Base, Portsmouth PO1 3LX. 0705-750521. Open: Daily 10-5.30. £ &

Henry VIII's flagship, raised in 1982 after 137 years on the seabed, is now on permanent display as a unique Tudor time capsule. Many of the treasures found on board are now in a permanent exhibition.

PASSPORT CONCESSIONS: Special family rate: 10% discount on all tickets - but not combined tickets.

JNR. PASSPORT CONCESSIONS: Free childrens book: either "Pirates" or "Shipwrecks".

PORTSMOUTH
Museum of the Dockyard Apprentice

Unicorn Trading Centre, Market Way, Portsmouth. 0705-822571. Open: Apr-Sept Mon-Fri 10-1/2-5. Closed: Oct-Mar. &

The test work of apprentices in the naval docks over a century and a half, including ship models and engines, covering every trade in the dockyard since the early 1800's.

PULBOROUGH
Bignor Roman Villa

Pulborough, West Sussex RH20 1PH. 07987-259. Open: Tue-Sun Mar-May 10-5, Daily Jun-Sept 10-6. Closed: Nov-Feb. £

First discovered in the 1820's, this has some of the finest Roman mosaics in the country.

PASSPORT CONCESSIONS: Free Guidebook.

JNR. PASSPORT CONCESSIONS: Free Mosaic colouring book.

READING — Cole Museum of Zoology

University of Reading, Whiteknights, Reading RG6 2AJ. 0734-875123. Open: Mon-Fri 9-5. P &

This is part of the University of Reading and was established in 1909 to display the "form and function" of the animal kingdom. It now has about 2,000 items many of them irreplaceable, and is renowned for its fine dissections.

READING — The Ure Museum of Greek Archaeology

The University of Reading, P O Box 218, Whiteknights, Reading RG6 2AA. 0734-875123. Open: Mon-Fri 9-5. Closed: 2 weeks Christmas, 1 week Easter, B. H. P &

This is the working museum within Reading University's classics department, Greek antiquities, mainly painted pottery, are a teaching aid. Ring to check opening before coming.

READING — Museum of English Rural Life

University of Reading, Whiteknights, Reading, Berks RG6 2AG. 0734-318663. Open: Tue-Sat 10-1/2-4.30. £ P

This national collection of farming, crafts and the countryside way of life over the last 150 years is also part of the University of Reading.

PASSPORT CONCESSIONS: 50% off adult admission charge. Free Guidebook.

JNR. PASSPORT CONCESSIONS: Free Pencil.

READING — REME Museum

Isaac Newton Rd, Arborfield, Reading RG2 9LN. 0734-760421. Open: Mon-Fri 9-12.30/2-4.30. Closed: B.H. P &

The Royal Electrical and Mechanical Engineers; the Army's repair men, the seldom-sung heroes whose speedy and perilous work in battle often ensured victory. Celebrated here in objects, pictures and dioramas.

JNR. PASSPORT CONCESSIONS: Join the dots handout.

REIGATE — Reigate Priory Museum

Reigate Priory Middle School, Bell Street, Reigate, Surrey RH2 7RL. 0737-245065. Open: Term time only Wed 2-4.30, 1st Sat in month 11-4. Closed: Aug. &

This is largely a children's museum in a school, but one which adults will enjoy. Set in an historic building.

PASSPORT CONCESSIONS: Free Poster; OPP.

JNR. PASSPORT CONCESSIONS: Free schools information pack; Free Pencil.

ROMSEY — Mountbatten Exhibition

Broadlands, Romsey, Hampshire, SO51 9ZD. 0794-516878. Open: 12 Apr-30 Sept Mon-Thur/Sat/Sun 10-4
£ P &

At Broadlands, the home of Earl Mountbatten of Burma, the lives of Lord and Lady Mountbatten are traced in a series of tableaux.

ROYSTON — Royston and District Museum

Lower King Street, Royston, Herts SG8 5AL. 0763-242587. Open: Wed/Thur/Sat 10-5, by appointment at other times.

This museum of local social history, about Royston and its acolyte villages, also has an impressive collection of 20th century ceramics and a temporary exhibitions programme.

PASSPORT CONCESSIONS: Free Booklet with every purchase above 50p, while stocks last.

JNR. PASSPORT CONCESSIONS: Free Booklet with every purchase above 50p, while stocks last.

ROYSTON — Wimpole Hall and Home Farm

Arrington, nr Royston. 0223-207257. Farm Open: 31 Mar-4 Nov Tue/Thur/Sat/Sun + B.H. 11-5. Hall Closed: Nov-Mar.
£ P &

In an 18th century house in a park which contains an exhibition on the historical development of the landscape, with a farm built as a model by Sir John Soane.

RYDE, Isle of Wight — The Isle of Wight Steam Railway Museum

The Railway Station, Havenstreet, Ryde, Isle of Wight PO33 4DS. 0983-882204. Open: Call for details. £ P &

Run by an independent trust from the main station at Havenstreet, the museum has archives, photographs and objects relating to the island's railways, and on certain days (ring to find out which) trains run on the preserved railway giving rides.

SALISBURY

The Museum of the Duke of Edinburgh's Royal Regiment

The Wardrobe, 58 The Close, Salisbury, SP1 2EX. 0722-336222 Open: Daily 10-4.30. Closed: Dec/Jan. £ P

In one of the most beautiful buildings in the Cathedral Close and set in heavenly pastoral surroundings, celebrates the regiment with its weapons, medals, uniforms and silver.

PASSPORT CONCESSIONS: Free Guidebook; Children free when accompanied by an adult.

JNR. PASSPORT CONCESSIONS: Free Badge.

SANDOWN, Isle of Wight

Brading Roman Villa

The Roman Villa, Brading, Sandown, Isle of Wight PO36 0EN. 0983-406223. Open: Daily 10-5.30. Closed: Oct-Mar. £

This is one of the most important villas of Roman Britain to be discovered and there are extensive remains on display, including unique mosaics, and an exhibition of excavation finds.

PASSPORT CONCESSIONS: 50% off adult admission

JNR. PASSPORT CONCESSIONS: Free Badge; Free Bookmark.

SANDOWN, Isle of Wight

Museum of Isle of Wight Geology

High Street, Sandown, PO36 8AF. 0983-404344. Open: Mon-Fri 9.30-5.30, Sat 9.30-4.30.

The island's rugged physiology and how it came about, in modern, well illuminated displays, with a special feature being the local dinosaur skeleton.

SELBORNE

Oates Memorial Museum & Gilbert White Museum

The Wakes, Selborne, Alton, Hants GU34 3JH. 042050-275. Open: Wed-Sun: 11-5.30. Closed: Nov-Mar. £

The Wakes was the home of the naturalist Gilbert White where he wrote his seminal work, The Natural History of Selborne, and is now partly a museum devoted to him and to his work, and to exploration of Africa and Antartica in memory of two members of the Oates family, one of them part of Captain Scott's ill-fated expedition.

SELBORNE
The Romany Folklore Museum and Workshop

Limes End Yard, High Street, Selborne, Nr Alton, Hampshire. 042050-486. Open: Daily 10.30-5.30. £

Museum of the gypsies, showing the migration from Northern India, language, dress, tents, living-vans and art. There's a small section on poaching and another on fortune-telling, while vans are repaired and even newly built in the yard.

PASSPORT CONCESSIONS: Free Guidebook; A lucky charm for Passport holders.

JNR. PASSPORT CONCESSIONS: A free lucky charm.

SHOREHAM-BY-SEA
Marlipins Museum

High Street, Shoreham-by-Sea, West Sussex. 0273-462994. Open: Tue-Sat 10.30-1/2-4.30, Sun 2-4.30. Closed: Oct-Apr.

The main exhibit of this museum is the building itself, basically Norman with a 14th century chequerwork facade. It contains local and maritime history displays

SILCHESTER
Calleva Museum

Sawyer's Lands, Silchester, Nr. Reading RG7-2NG. 0734-700362. Open: Daily daylight hours. P

This has a pictorial display of life on Roman Silchester. The entire circuit of the old town survives, and you can see the remains of the amphitheatre.

SLOUGH
Slough Museum

23 Bath Rd, Slough. 0753-26422. Open: Wed-Fri 12-4, Sat/Sun 2-5.

This is a small, lively, local museum about Slough's people, past and present.

PASSPORT CONCESSIONS: Comprehensive information pack.

JNR. PASSPORT CONCESSIONS: Free Pen.

SOUTHAMPTON
Maritime Museum

The Wool House, Town Quay, Southampton. 0703-224216. Open: Tue-Fri/ Sun 10-5, Sat 10-4. &

A medieval wool warehouse on the Town Quay has been turned into a museum with exhibitions and models detailing the development of the port over the past 150 years. Liners, and particularly the Titanic, are a special feature. There is an exhibition about the Blitz from September 1990.

PASSPORT CONCESSIONS: 5% off shop purchases; OPPS: Free museum news mailing & details.

JNR. PASSPORT CONCESSIONS: Free Badge.

SOUTHAMPTON Medieval Merchants House

58 French St, Southampton. 0703-221503. Open: Daily 10-6 Summer, 10-4 Winter (excl Mon). £ (EH)

This is a late 13th century house which has been restored and furnished, and the shop sells wine, beer, herbs and spices of the period.

SOUTHAMPTON Museum of Archaeology

God's House Tower, Winkle Street, Southampton. 0703-224216. Open: Tue-Fri 10-5, Sat 10-4, Sun 2-5.

God's Tower House, the home of this museum, was built in the 15th century as a fortress to defend the town. Now it features evidence of Southampton's Roman, Saxon and medieval past, with exhibitions focussing on trade and daily life.

PASSPORT CONCESSIONS: 5% off shop purchases; OPPS: Free Mailing of "Museum News" with details.

JNR. PASSPORT CONCESSIONS: Free Badge.

SOUTHAMPTON Netley Abbey

1 Abbey Hill, Netley, Southampton. 0703-453076. Open: Daily 10-6 Summer, weekends 10-4 Winter. £ P 🅰 (EH)

These are the extensive remains of a Cistercian Abbey, founded in 1239, with the church walls and cloister buildings still standing.

SOUTHAMPTON Southampton City Art Gallery

Civic Centre, Commercial Road, Southampton 0703-832769. Open: Tue-Fri 10-5, Sat 10-4, Sun 2-5. 🅰

In a 1930s building, it has one of the region's leading collections of contemporary art, plus good British and European Old Masters.

PASSPORT CONCESSIONS: Free Poster

SOUTHAMPTON Tudor House Museum

Bugle Street, Southampton 0703-224216. Open: Tue-Fri 10-5, Sat 10-4, Sun 2-5.

This Tudor House is furnished with its original 16th and 17th century furnishings, cooking equipment and family treasures.

PASSPORT CONCESSIONS: 5% off shop purchases; OPPS: Free mailing of "Museum News" with details.

SOUTHSEA

Royal Marines Museum

Royal Marines
Eastney, Southsea,
Hampshire PO4 9PX
0705-819385. Open:
Daily Easter-Sept 10-
5.30, Oct-Easter 10-
4.30. £ P

An award-winning museum re-telling the story
of the water-borne soldiers, with a film show
about their Falklands experiences, and a really
Arctic (refrigerated) display.

ST. ALBANS

Mosquito Aircraft Museum

Salisbury Hall,
London Colney, St.
Albans, Herts
0727-22051. Open:
Easter-Oct Sun 10.30-
5.30 and Thur Jul-Sept
2-5.30. £ P

Britain's oldest aircraft museum, with an open
day and flying display on July 14/15 and on
November 24, the 50th anniversary celebration
of the first flight of the DH Mosquito.

ST. ALBANS

Museum of St. Albans

Hatfield Road,
St. Albans,
Herts AL1 3RR.
0727-56679. Open:
Mon-Fri 10-5, Sat 10-
6, Sun 2-5.   P

The museum, refurbished during 1989-90 with
a series of innovative galleries, tells of historic
St. Albans and its developments since the
Romans left. New Salaman Galleries of trade
and craft tools opens in December 1990.

PASSPORT CONCESSIONS: Opps: Send SAE for
details.

JNR. PASSPORT CONCESSIONS: Free Badge.

ST. ALBANS

Roman Theatre of Verulamium

Blue House Hill, St.
Albans, Herts.
0727-35035. Open:
Daily 10-5, 10-4 in
Winter. £ P

A second century theatre used for religious
ceremonies connected with the nearby temple,
also plays and other events. Now a witness to a
past culture.

ST. ALBANS

St. Albans Organ Museum

326 Camp Road, St.
Albans, Herts AL1 5PB.
0727-69693. Open:
Sun 2-4.30, Mon-Sat
by appointment. £

Case organs, pianos, theatre organs, music
boxes, violano virtuosi in the permanent
working exhibition of mechanical musical
instruments, with concerts throughout the year.

ST. ALBANS — Verulamium Museum

St. Michael's, St. Albans, Herts. 0727-66100. Open: Mar-Oct Mon-Sat 10.30-5.30, Sun 2-5.30, Nov-Feb closes daily at 4. £ P

Set in a 100 acre park, this museum's exhibits relate to St. Albans in its Roman days when it was one of Britain's major cities, with mosaics, wall paintings, jewellery, coins and personal items.

PASSPORT CONCESSIONS: 50% off adult admission charge; Half price family ticket; Opps: Free membership of friends of St. Albans for 1990 - send SAE.

JNR. PASSPORT CONCESSIONS: Free entry to Junior Passport holder.

STEVENAGE — Stevenage Museum

St. George's Way, Stevenage, Hertfordshire SG1 1XX. 0438-354292. Open: Mon-Sat 10-5 + B.H. 艮

The story of Stevenage told through its natural and social history, archaeology and geology is told in the displays in this unusual museum in part of a modern church. There are also temporary exhibitions.

STEVINGTON — Stevington Windmill

Stevington, Beds. 0234-228330. Open: Daily 10-7 or dusk. P

Built in 1770, this post mill is the finest in the county and the last working windmill to have used cloth sails.

STEYNING — Steyning Museum

Saxon Cottage, Church Street, Steyning, West Sussex BN44 3YB. Open Tue/Wed/Sat 10.30-12.30/2.30-4.30. Sun 2.30-4.30.

This little local museum is moving in 1990 to a purpose-built home, but its erstwhile home, the 16th century timber-framed house called Saxon Cottage will continue its most prized exhibit.

STOCKBRIDGE — Museum of Army Flying

Middle Wallop, Stockbridge, Hants SO20 8DY. 0264-62121. Open: Daily 10-4:30. Closed: one week over Christmas. £ P 艮

Here is the story of Army flying from the balloons and giant kites of the 19th century through both world wars to the present day.

PASSPORT CONCESSIONS: 2 for the price of one.

JNR. PASSPORT CONCESSIONS: Free entry to Junior Passport holders; Free schools information pack.

SWINDON	Coate Agricultural Museum

Coate Water, Swindon SN3 6AA. 0793-493188. Open: Sun 2-5. Closed: Oct-Easter. P &

One of Thamesdown Borough Council's family of museums, this one showing temporary displays of larger agricultural items like waggons, carts and implements.

JNR. PASSPORT CONCESSIONS: Free Pencil or Poster.

SWINDON	Great Western Railway Museum

Faringdon Road, Swindon, Wilts SN1 5BJ. 0793-493189. Open: Mon-Sat 10-5, Sun 2-5. £

Locomotives, great numbers of evocative name plates, models, illustrations, posters tickets, from God's Wonderful Railway.

PASSPORT CONCESSIONS: 50% off adult admission charge; Free Poster

JNR. PASSPORT CONCESSIONS: Free entry to Junior Passport holder

SWINDON	Lydiard House

Lydiard Tregoze, Swindon Wilts SN5 9PA. 0793-770401. Open: Mon-Sat 10-1/2-5.30, Sun 2-5.30. P &

A Palladian mansion in parkland and with its state rooms restored with many of the contents of the original owners, the St John family.

PASSPORT CONCESSIONS: Free Poster

JNR. PASSPORT CONCESSIONS: Free Pencil.

SWINDON	Mobile Museum

c/o Museum & Art Gallery, Bath Road, Swindon SN1 4BA. 0793-493188. Open: By appointment only.

An old corporation bus transformed to become a travelling museum as part of the schools service, open to the public on certain days.

SWINDON	Railway Village Museum

34 Faringdon Road, Swindon SN1 5BJ. 0793-526161. Open: Mon-Sat 10-1/2-5, Sun 2-5. £

This is the foreman's house of the Great Western Railway Village, furnished as it was in the hey-dey of the GWR.

PASSPORT CONCESSIONS: 50% off adult admission charge.

JNR. PASSPORT CONCESSIONS: Free entry to Junior Passport holder.

SWINDON — Richard Jefferies Museum

Marlborough Road, Coate, Swindon SN3 6AA. 0793-52616. Open: Wed /Sat /Sun 2-5.

Another of Thamesdown's museums, this one dedicated to the writer with a reconstruction of his study and cheese room with many of his personal items and book collection.

PASSPORT CONCESSIONS: Free Poster.

JNR. PASSPORT CONCESSIONS: Free Pencil.

SWINDON — Swindon Museum & Art Gallery

Bath Road, Swindon, Wilts SN1 4BA. 0793-4931811. Open: Mon- Sat 10-6, Sun 2-5. P

Wiltshire's archaeology, natural history and geology, plus local memorabilia, coins, the Manners collections of pot lids and the Wiltshire Yeoman Room. 20th century British art in the gallery's permanent collection.

PASSPORT CONCESSIONS: Free Poster

JNR. PASSPORT CONCESSIONS: Free Pencil.

UFFINGTON — Tom Brown's School Museum

Broad Street, Uffington, Oxfordshire. 036782-675. Open: Easter-Oct Sat 2-5. Closed: Nov-Easter. £ P &

This is dedicated to the life and work of Thomas Hughes, author of Tom Brown's Schooldays, but it has much else that young Tom would have been fascinated by which is not in the book; the Uffington White Horse, Roman artefacts, a smithy and art gallery included.

VENTOR, Isle of Wight — Blackgang Sawmill - World of Timber & St Catherine's Quay Maritime World.

Blackgang, nr Ventor, Isle of Wight PO38 2HN. 0983-730330. Open: Daily 10-5. Closed: Dec-Mar. £ P

A world of timber with two exhibitions, one about the trade with working steam engines, and the other about the Royal National Lifeboat Institute and the celebrated local shipwrecks - including the skeleton of the whale found in 1986.

PASSPORT CONCESSIONS: Free Poster; Free Guidebook.

JNR. PASSPORT CONCESSIONS: Free Badge; Free Poster and Guide.

WALTHAM ABBEY — Epping Forest District Museum

39/41 Sun St, Waltham Abbey, Essex EN9 1EL. 0992-716882. Open: Fri-Mon 2-5 , Tue 12-5, Wed/Thur party bookings only.

The Tudor herb garden is a special feature of this local history museum, with the formal displays in two ancient buildings.

WANTAGE — Vale and Dowland Museum Centre

Church Street, Wantage, Oxon. 02357-66838. Open: Tue-Sat 10.30-4.30, Sun 2.30-5. &

The displays in this 17th century cloth merchants' house tells the history of the Vale of the White Horse, Wantage and local industries, added to by temporary exhibitions through 1990.

JNR. PASSPORT CONCESSIONS: Free Badge.

WATFORD — Watford Museum

194 High Street, Watford, Hertfordshire. 0923-32297. Open Mon-Sat 10-5, Sun - call for opening. &

Watford from prehistory to present, with a leaning to the local industries of printing and brewing. Special exhibitions throughout the year.

PASSPORT CONCESSIONS: Free Poster.

The West Front, Cassinbury by J.M.W Turner R.A.

WELWYN — Welwyn Roman Baths

Welwyn Bypass, Old Welwyn. 0707-271362. Open: Thurs-Sun, B.H. 2-5. £ P

Much of the 3rd century bath house survives, inspite of the motorway going overhead, and there are graphic displays to explain how it worked, including a model of how it must have looked.

PASSPORT CONCESSIONS: Free Guidebook.

JNR. PASSPORT CONCESSIONS: Free Badge.

WEYBRIDGE — Weybridge Museum

Church Street, Weybridge, Surrey KT13 8DE. 0932-843573. Open: Mon-Fri 2-5, Sat 10-1/2-5. Aug Mon-Sat 10-1/2-5.

The local exhibits here range in category from archaeology to social history, from natural history to costume.

WHITNEY — North Leigh Roman Villa

East End, Whitney, Oxon. 0993 881830. Open: Easter-Oct Daily 10-6. Closed: Winter. £ (EH)

The large villa on this site was first occupied in the 1st century AD, but it was altered and its present form dates from the 4th century. The remains include the living quarters with mosaics and baths.

WINCHESTER — The Royal Hampshire Regiment Museum

Serle's House, Southgate Street, Winchester, Hampshire SO23 9EG. 0962-63658. Open: Mon-Fri 10-12.30/2-4, Sat/Sun 12 -4. Closed: Sat/Sun Nov-Easter.

This is in Serle's House built about 1730 which has been used by the military for much of the last two centuries, and now tells the regiment's story since its formation in 1702.

PASSPORT CONCESSIONS: Tour of state rooms (by prior arrangement); Free Postcard.

JNR. PASSPORT CONCESSIONS: Free Badge.

WINCHESTER — Winchester Cathedral Library & Triforium Gallery

The Cathedral Office, 5 The Close, Winchester, Hampshire SO23 9LS. 0962-53137. Open: Easter-Oct Mon-Sat 10.30-1/2-4.30. Oct-Easter call for opening times. £

This is one of the most imaginative of the new generations of museums, set in the cathedral itself and with some of the finest sacred sculpture, woodwork and metalwork from eleven centuries, with the library housing, among other treasures, the great 12th century illuminated Winchester Bible.

PASSPORT CONCESSIONS: 50% off adult admission charge; Special rate family entrance ticket.

JNR. PASSPORT CONCESSIONS: Free entry to Junior Passport holder.

WINCHESTER — Winchester College Treasury

Winchester College, Winchester SO23 9NA. 0962-64242. Open: Sat/Sun 2-4. Or by appoint. Closed: Dec-Mar.

The memorabilia of this great public school include documents, manuscripts, silver antique scientific instruments, Greek ceramics and the Duberly Collection of Chinese pottery.

WINCHESTER — Wolvesey: Old Bishops Palace

College St, Winchester, Hants. 0962-54766. Open: Daily 10-6 Summer. Closed: Winter. £

These are the ruins of the medieval palace of the bishops of Winchester, built around a rectangular courtyard.

WOBURN — Woburn Abbey

Woburn, Bedfordshire MK43 0TP. 0525-290666. Open: Nov-Mar Sat/Sun 11-4, Apr-Oct Mon-Fri 11-5, Sat/Sun 11-5.30. £ P &

The seats of the Dukes of Bedford for over 400 years, the house, not largely 18th century and Palladian, set in a 3,000-acre deer park, has one of the finest private collections of furniture, paintings and silver in the country and a busy programme of special events from April - Oct.

PASSPORT CONCESSIONS: 50% off adult admission charge; Reduction of 10% on all purchases but *not* films, batteries etc.

WOKING — Gordon's School Museum

West End, Woking, Surrey GU24 9PT. 0276-858084. Open: by appointment only.

The personalia of General Gordon of Khartoum, including his revolver, writing desk, mandarin's costume and games table.

WOODSTOCK — Oxfordshire County Museum

Fletcher's House, Park Street, Woodstock OX7 1SN. 0993-811456. Open: Apr-Oct Mon-Fri 10-5, Sat 10-6, Sun 2-6, Nov-Mar Tue-Fri 10-4, Sat 10-5, Sun 2-5.   P

This has the archaeology and natural history of the county in a 17th century building surrounded by a peaceful garden, and there is a full exhibition programme for 1990.

PASSPORT CONCESSIONS: Free Booklet.

JNR. PASSPORT CONCESSIONS: Free Postcard.

WORTHING — Worthing Museum and Art Gallery

Chapel Road, Worthing, West Sussex BN11 1HD. 0903-39999. Open: Apr-Sept Mon-Sat 10-6, Oct-Mar 10-5. ♿

This award-winning museum has collections of costume, childhood items, ceramics and glass, local archaeology and history. There are temporary exhibitions throughout 1990.

PASSPORT CONCESSIONS: Reduction of 10% on shop purchases.

JNR. PASSPORT CONCESSIONS: Free Badge.

WROXALL, Isle of Wight — Appledurcombe House

Wroxall, Isle of Wight. 0983-852484. Open: Daily 10-6 Summer, 10-4 Winter (excl. Mon). £ P (EH)

This was a grand house, begun in 1701, which has now been re-roofed. It stands in a "Capability" Brown landscape.

YARMOUTH, Isle of Wight — Yarmouth Caste

Quay Street, Yarmouth, Isle of Wight. 0983-760678. Open: Daily 10-6 Summer. Closed: Winter. £ (EH)

This is the last of Henry VIII's coastal defence forts, completed in 1547. In the 17th century the coast was filled in and the castle reduced in size. It now has an exhibition about itself and a display of paintings.

SOUTH WEST/
CHANNEL
ISLANDS

ALDERNEY, Channel Islands

Alderney Society Museum

High St, Alderney, Channel Islands. 048-1823222. Open: Easter-Oct Mon-Sat 10-12, Sun 2-4. £

Materials from an Iron Age site, as well as items from the World War Two German occupation.

PASSPORT CONCESSIONS: Free entry to Passport holder.

JNR. PASSPORT CONCESSIONS: Free entry to Junior Passport holder.

APPLEDORE

North Devon Maritime Museum

Odun House, Odun Road, Appledore, North Devon. 0237-474852. Open: Mon-Fri 11-1/2-5.30, Sat/Sun 2-5.30. Closed: Nov-Easter. £ P

This 19th century ship-owner's home commands splendid views of the estuary, if you look past the collections of ship models, pictures and displays about local maritime history, ship building, smuggling, wreck and rescue.

PASSPORT CONCESSIONS: Free entry to under 18's.

JNR. PASSPORT CONCESSIONS: Free entry to Junior Passport holders; Free quiz sheet (entered for prize if completed).

BATH

The American Museum

Claverton Manor, Bath, Avon BA2 7BD. 0225-460503. Open: 31st Mar-28th Oct Tue-Sun 2-5. Closed: Nov-Mar. £ P ♿

Afternoon tea with cookies here, after seeing the period 17th to 19th century rooms, the galleries with silver, pewter, glass, textiles and folk art, the gardens and the American arboretum. Indian weekend June 16-17, Independence displays July 7-8, Civil War weekend September 15-16.

PASSPORT CONCESSIONS: £1 off adult admission charge; free into grounds; Half price guidebook; 10% reduction in Herb Shop, Country Store and Cafeteria.

BATH

Bath Industrial Heritage Centre

Camden Works, Julian Road, Bath. 0225-318348. Open: Feb-Nov Daily 2-5, Dec/Jan Mon-Fri 2-5. £

This is the Camden Works, once a real tennis court, now Jonathan Burdett Bowler's cluttered brass foundry and fizzy drinks factory, recreated.

BATH — Bath Postal Museum

8 Broad Street, Bath BA1 5LJ. 0225-460333. Open: Mon-Sat 11-5, Sun 2-5. Closed: Sun Nov-Mar. £ P &

This tackles the immense task of covering the history of written communications, from clay tablets to modern technology, including a model of an early post office. In May 1990 a special exhibition opens to commemorate 150 years since the invention of the Penny Black, the world's first postage stamp.

PASSPORT CONCESSIONS: 50% off adult admission charge.

JNR. PASSPORT CONCESSIONS: Free Badge.

BATH — Beckford Tower and Musem

Nr. Lansdown Cemetery, Lansdown, Bath BA1 9BH. 0225-312917. Open: Sat/Sun 2-5. Closed: Nov-Mar. £

The tower was built in 1825 by the collector William Beckford and now has a permanent exhibition devoted to Beckford and his life at Fonthill and Bath.

PASSPORT CONCESSIONS: Free entry to Passport holder.

JNR. PASSPORT CONCESSIONS: Free entry to Junior Passport holder.

BATH — Farleigh Hungerford Castle

Farleigh, Nr. Bath, Somerset. 0272-734472. Open: Daily 10-6 Summer, 10-4 Winter (excl. Mon). £ P (EH)

The chapel of this late 14th century castle, with its large 15th century outer court, contains the tomb of its builder, Sir Thomas Hungerford.

BATH — The Fashion Research Centre

4 Circus, Bath, Avon BA1 2EW. 0225-461111. Open: Mon-Sat 9.30-5.

The history of dress in an extension of the Museum of Costume, with study centre, and (by appointment) special study collections and an identification service.

BATH — Geology Museum

18 Queen Square, Bath. 0225-428144. Open: Mon-Fri 9.30-6, Sat 9.30-5. Closed: B. H. &

On display are examples of the minerals, rocks and fossils to be found in this geologically rich area.

BATH — The Herschel House & Museum

19 New King Street, Bath, Avon BA1 2BL. 0225-311342. Open: Daily 2-5. Closed: Nov-Mar Sat/Sun only. £

The Georgian first home of William Herschel, discoverer of Uranus, and his sister, who made his early telescopes for him out of cardboard. It has astronomical exhibits (not cardboard), musical instruments, a workshop, a kitchen and a little garden.

PASSPORT CONCESSIONS: Free Poster; Free Guidebook.

JNR. PASSPORT CONCESSIONS: Free Pencil.

BATH — The Holburne Museum & Crafts Study Centre

Great Pulteney Street, Bath, Avon BA2 4DB. 0225-466669. Open: Mon-Sat 11-5, Sun 2.30-6. Closed: mid Dec-mid Feb + Mons Nov-Mar. £ P &

Important paintings, including a number of Gainsboroughs, and silver are displayed in this beautiful school converted to a museum, which has now become an important crafts centre as well. There is a good collection of work by 20th century artist-craftsmen.

PASSPORT CONCESSIONS: 50p off adult admission charge and OAPs; 50p student.

JNR. PASSPORT CONCESSIONS: 50p off admissions to Junior Passport holder.

BATH — Museum of Bookbinding

Maners Street, Bath. 0225-466000. Open: Mon-Fri 9-1/2-5.30. £

This is an extension of George Baytun's business, where antiquarian books have been bound and sold for 50 years. The museum shows the history and art of bookbinding, with a reconstruction of the craft in the 19th century.

BATH — The Museum of English Naive Art

The Old School Room, The Paragon, Bath. 0225-446020. Open: Apr-Oct Mon-Sat 10.30-5.30, Sun 2-6. £

This is the first museum of English folk painting, the 18th and 19th century seen through often whimsical and always enchanting paintings by amateurs.

BATH — Roman Baths Museum

Pump Room, Stall Street, Bath, Avon. 0225-461111. Open: Daily Mar-Oct: 9-6, Jul/Aug: 9-7, Nov-Feb: Mon-Sat 9-5, Sun 10-5. £ &

This is a permanent exhibition about the site and the finds from the Roman temple and bathing complex, which was dedicated to the goddess Sulis Minerva. The hot spring, the point of the whole development, can also be seen.

BATH — 1 Royal Crescent

No. 1 Royal Crescent, Bath. 0225-428126. Open: Mar-Oct Tue-Sat 11-5, Sun 2-5, Nov/Dec Tue-Sat 11-3, Sun 1-3, B.H. & Good Friday. £

Built by John Wood the Younger, one of the architects of 18th century Bath whose masterpiece was this wonderful row, now with the lower two floors of No 1 restored by the Bath Preservation Trust.

BATH — The Royal Photographic Society

The Octagon, Milsom Street, Bath, BA1 1DN. 0225-462841. Open: Daily 9.30-5.30. £ &

There is a full series of changing exhibitions through the year here, some based on the massive archive collections held by the society and some on loan.

PASSPORT CONCESSIONS: 50% off adult admission charge.

BATH — Sally Lunn's Kitchen Museum

4 North Parade Passage, Bath. 0225-461634. Open: Mon-Sat 10-5. £

This was the home of a famous local 17th century cook whose kitchen has been restored. The museum also shows some of the Roman, Saxon and medieval finds from excavations there.

BATH — Victoria Art Gallery

Bridge Street, Bath BA2 4AT. 0225-461111. Open: Mon-Fri 10-6, Sat 10-5.

A permanent collection of 18th to 20th century British paintings, including Rowlandson's famous 'Comforts of Bath' drawings.

PASSPORT CONCESSIONS: OPPS-Invitation to Private View of your choice upon request.

BEAFORD — Beaford Centre Photographic Archive

Beaford, Winkleigh, Devon EX19 8LU. 08053-201. Open: Mon-Fri 10-4. P

Here is a wonderful and exquisitely detailed record of the changing life of North Devon, in a vast family album of 130,000 photographs covering 115 years, from 1848 to 1963, of transformation.

PASSPORT CONCESSIONS: Some archive prints at reduced rate.

BEAMINSTER — Parnham

Parnham House, Beaminster, Dorset DT8 3NA. 0308-862204. Open: Wed/Sun/B.H. 10-5. Closed: Nov-Mar. £ P &

The home of the modern furniture maker John Makepeace whose workshops are open to the public. The Tudor house, set in 14 acres, has changing exhibitions of work by living artists and craftsmen, and a museum of woodcraft - tools collected from around the world.

PASSPORT CONCESSIONS: Free entry to Passport holder

JNR. PASSPORT CONCESSIONS: Free entry to Junior Passport holder.

BERKELEY — The Jenner Museum

The Chantry, Church Lane, High Street, Berkeley, Glos GL13 9BH. 0453-810631. Open: Tue-Fri 12.30-5.30, Sun/B.H. Mons 1-5.30. Closed: Oct-Mar. £ P &

The home of the country doctor who turned his back on a glittering career in London to stay at home and discover vaccine, complete with the Temple of Vaccinia, the garden hut where he gave the poor free vaccinations against smallpox.

JNR. PASSPORT CONCESSIONS: 50% off adult admission charge.

BLANDFORD FORUM — Blandford Forum Museum Trust

Beres Yard, Market Place, Blandford Forum, Dorset DT11 7HU. 0258-451115. Open: Mon-Sat 10-4. Closed: Oct-Mar. £

The local history displays here have remains from prehistoric to medieval times, costumes and Victoriana, button-making, lace-making and brewing, militaria and the Blandford Fire of 1731. There are also regular exhibitions of the work of local artists and craftsmen.

BLANDFORD FORUM

Royal Signals Museum

Blandford Camp, Dorset DT11 8RH. 0258-452581. Open: Mon-Fri 10-5, Sat/Sun 10-4 (Jun-Sept). P

Army communications from the Crimean War (where they went badly wrong for the Light Brigade just before they charged) with vehicles, motorbikes, uniforms and equipment.

PASSPORT CONCESSIONS: Free Guidebook.

JNR. PASSPORT CONCESSIONS: A Royal Signals Museum gift pack.

BODMIN

Duke of Cornwall's Light Infantry Museum

The Keep, Bodmin, Cornwall PL31 1EG. 0208-72810. Open: Mon-Fri 8-5. £ P

The regiment's history from 1702 to 1959.

PASSPORT CONCESSIONS: Free entry to Passport holder

BRADFORD-ON-AVON

Bradford-on-Avon Tithe Barn

Bradford-on-Avon, Wilts. 0272-734472. Open: Phone for details. P (EH)

This 14th century barn is one of the best preserved examples of medieval rural architecture. It once belonged to Shaftesbury Abbey, a Benedictine nunnery, but now contains an exhibition about farming and country life in Victorian and Edwardian times.

BRIDPORT

Bridport Museum

South Street, Bridport, Dorset DT6 3NR. 0308-22116. Open: Mon-Sat 10-4.30. £

The galleries in this Tudor building include one on "rope, net and twine", essential ingredients in the working lives of the seafarers who have plied from this old town since at least Roman times.

BRIDPORT

The Chantry

128 South Street, Bridport, Dorset DT6 3NW. 0308-22116. Open: Sat 10-12. Closed: Oct-Mar.

This is a medieval priest's chantry with its columbarium, piscina, garederobe and cresset intact, and the remains of wall paintings.

BRISTOL

Ashton Court Visitor Centre

Long Ashton, Bristol BS18 9JW. 0272-639174. Open: Call for details. P &

This has a permanent exhibition called The Landscape Makers, showing how people have changed and re-arranged the original landscape of the area.

BRISTOL — Bristol Industrial Museum

Princes Wharf, City Docks, Bristol BS1 4RN. 0272-251470. Open: Mon-Wed/Sat/Sun 10-1/2-5. P &

Developing on the dockside, the growing museum relates the internationally important industrial and transport history of the Bristol area.

BRISTOL — City of Bristol Museum & Art Gallery

Queens Road, Bristol BS8 1RL. 0272-223571. Open: Daily 10-5. &

Wide-ranging collection of fine, applied and oriental art, archaeology, geology and natural history, with temporary exhibitions through 1990.

BRISTOL — The Exploratory

Bristol Old Station, Temple Meads, Bristol BS1 6QU. 0272-252008. Open: Daily 10-5. £ &

The hands-on science invented by Professor Richard Gregory, with its "plores" instead of experiments, which include gyroscopes, pendulums, pulleys, lights, colour mixing, illusions and mirrors. Now in a new, much larger, space in Temple Meads.

PASSPORT CONCESSIONS: Special rate family entrance ticket.

BRISTOL — The Georgian House

7 Great George Street, Bristol. 0272-211362. Open: Mon-Sat 10-1/2-5.

Built almost exactly 200 years ago, the house is furnished with all the elegance of the George III style, and is now maintained as a museum.

BRISTOL — Harveys Wine Museum

12 Denmark Street, Bristol BS1 5DQ. 0272-277661. Open: Fri 10-12 only. Tours Mon-Fri by appoint. Closed: B. H. £

This has fine displays of antique silver, bottles, cellar equipment and one of the best collections of 18th century English drinking glasses.

BRISTOL — Maritime Heritage Centre

Wapping Wharf, Gasferry Road, Bristol BS1 6TY. 0272-260680. Open: Daily Summer 10-6, Winter 10-5. £ P

The rather unlovely address is in a very historic part of the port, on the lip of the Channel. The museum has the Hillhouse Collection, which illustrates the history of ship-building in Bristol from medieval times, and is the ticketing point for one of the most famous ships to be built here, the SS Great Britain, the world's first transatlantic passenger liner.

BRISTOL — Monica Britton Exhibition Hall of Medical History

Frenchay Hospital, Frenchay BS16 1LE. 0272-701212. Open: Daily by appointment only. P

Many aspects of medical history are on display here, with special emphasis on local and regional development, aimed at both professional and non-specialist audiences.

BRISTOL — The Red Lodge

Park Row, Bristol BS1 5LJ. 0272-211360. Open: Mon-Sat 10-1/2-5.

The building dates from 1500 and has the only surviving suite of 16th century rooms in Bristol, with superb plasterwork, carved panelling and stone fireplaces. Elsewhere the house was altered in the 18th century.

BRISTOL — St. Nicholas Church Museum

St. Nicholas Street, Bristol. 0272-211365. Open: Mon-Sat 10-5.

This former church now shows some of the city's collection of topographical watercolours, church plate and furnishings, a brass-rubbing centre and archaeological finds relating to Bristol's earliest history.

BRIXHAM — Brixham

Bolton Cross, Brixham, Devon TQ5 8LZ. 08045-6267. Open: Mon-Sat 10-5.30. Closed: End Oct-Easter. £

This was purposely designed as a community museum to reflect the life and work of the oldest town in Torbay. In April 1990 a new extension opens, with a display on the Brixham industries of boatbuilding, fishing and the ancillary crafts. There will be more space for other new industrial displays, such as the ICI research works now here, and, in the summer, another new permanent exhibition on the history of education in the town. The National Coastguard Museum is incorporated here.

PASSPORT CONCESSIONS: 25% off adult admission charge; Special rate family entrance ticket.

BROKERSWOOD — The Woodland Heritage Museum

The Woodland Park, Brokerswood, Westbury, Wilts BA13 4EH. Open: Mon-Fri 9-4, Sat 2-6, (Winter to 4). £ P

Set in Woodland Park, this is an interpretation centre for broad-leaved woodlands, with flora, fauna, history and management.

BUDE — Bude Stratton Historical and Folk Exhibition

Lower Wharf, Bude, Cornwall. 0288-353576. Open: Daily 11-4, later in high season. Closed: Winter. £ P ☐

The history of this Cornish seaside town is told through photographs, memorabilia and models.

PASSPORT CONCESSIONS: 50% off adult admission charge.

BUDLEIGH SALTERTON — Fairlynch Museum and Art Centre

27 Fore Street, Budleigh Salterton, Devon EX9 6NP 03954-2666. Open: Easter-Oct Mon-Sat 2.30-5, Jul/Aug Mon-Sat 10.30-12.30/2.30-5, Sun 2.30-5. Closed: Mid Oct-Xmas, Mid Jan-Easter. £ ☐

Local history, archaeology and geology such as the Bunter Pebble Beds and radioactive formations, plus costume and lace. Exhibitions include Victorian childhood, from Easter to mid-October, and plants and gardens of the area from Easter to mid-September.

PASSPORT CONCESSIONS: Free entry to under 18s; Free admission to Friends of Fairlynch talks.

BUDLEIGH SALTERTON — Otterton Mill Centre and Working Museum

Otterton, Nr. Budleigh Salterton, Devon EX9 7HG. 0395-68521. Open: Daily 10.30-5.30. £ P

A working watermill museum, which produces three-quarters of a ton of flour a week, and has workshops, a co-operative crafts shop and summer exhibitions.

PASSPORT CONCESSIONS: 50% off adult admission charge; Free entry for under 18's; Invitation to private views (3-6 in 1990)

JNR. PASSPORT CONCESSIONS: Free entry to Junior Passport holder; Free Pencil.

CAMELFORD — North Cornwall Museum and Gallery

The Clease, Camelford, Cornwall. 0840-212954. Open: Mon-Sat 10.30-5. Closed: Oct-Mar. £

Award-winning private museum, in what was a coach builder's premises, which looks at local rural life between about 1890 and 1940. With a reconstructed moorland cottage built in 1900. Changing exhibitions in the gallery throughout the season.

PASSPORT CONCESSIONS: Free entry to Passport holder.

JNR. PASSPORT CONCESSIONS: Free entry to Junior Passport holder.

CHARD — Chard & District Museum

Godworthy House, High Street, Chard, Somerset TA20 1QL. 0460-65091. Open: Mon-Sat 10-4.30, Sun Jul/Aug 10.30-4.30. Closed: Oct-mid May.

John Stringfellow, a pioneer of powered flight, and James Gillingham, inventor of artificial limbs, are celebrated here, and there are reconstructed blacksmith's, carpenter's and wheelwright's workshops and a 1940s garage.

PASSPORT CONCESSIONS: Free Guidebook; 20% off entrance fees for special events during year.

JNR. PASSPORT CONCESSIONS: Free quiz booklet.

CHARD — Hill's Plumbing Museum

Victoria Works, Victoria Avenue, Chard, Somerset TA20 1HE. 0460-63567. Open: Mon-Fri 8-5 by arrangement. P

A museum about things that go bump in the night. 1,000 bits of ancient plumbing, and the tools that stopped the bumps, from ballcocks to blow-torches, collected on the commercial premises of D R Hill (Plumbers) Ltd.

CHEDDAR GORGE — Cheddar Showcaves Museum

Cheddar Gorge, Somerset BS27 3QF. 0934-742343. Open: Easter to end Sept Daily 10-5.30, Oct-Easter 10.30-4.30. £ P

This museum sets out to document 40,000 years of human history at Cheddar, with dioramas to recreate Mendip life through the ages and the oldest complete skeleton in Britain, found in Gough's Cave.

PASSPORT CONCESSIONS: One child admitted free with 2 paying adults. Offer applies to - tickets giving access to Showcaves, Fantasy Grotto, Museum, Jacob's Ladder.

CHELTENHAM — Cheltenham Art Gallery & Museum

Clarence Street, Cheltenham, Glos GL50 3JT. 0242-237431. Open: Mon-Sat 10-5.20. P &

There are special exhibitions throughout the year, but the permanent collections are especially strong in the Arts and Craft Movement There are Dutch 17th century and British 17th-20th century paintings, as well as the social history and archaeology of Cheltenham and the Cotswolds, in the galleries.

CHELTENHAM — Chedworth Roman Villa

Yanworth, Cheltenham GL34 3LJ. 0242-89256. Open: Mar-Oct Tue-Sun 10-5.30, Nov-Dec Wed-Sun 11-4 Mid-Dec-Feb by appoint. £ P &

In a part of the country rich in Roman remains, this is one of the largest Romano-British villas in the country, with two bath houses, fine mosaics from the fourth century and a new site museum with a shop.

CHELTENHAM — Gustav Holst Birthplace Museum

4 Clarence Road, Cheltenham, Glos. 0242-524846. Open: Tue-Fri 12-5.20, Sat 11-5.20. P

The composer of The Planets was born in this Regency house in 1874, and it has 19th century period furnishings, with a working Victorian kitchen and laundry.

CHELTENHAM — Hailes Abbey

Cheltenham, Glos. 0242-602398. Open: Daily 10-6 Summer, 10-4 Winter (excl. Mon). £ P & (EH)

Founded in 1246, the ruins of this Cistercian Abbey's monastic buildings and cloister remain, and there is a museum with a collection of architectural fragments and tiles.

CHELTENHAM — Pittville Pump Room Museum, Gallery of Fashion

Pittville Park, Cheltenham, Glos GL52 3JE. 0242-512740. Open: Tue-Sat 10.30-5, Sun Apr-Oct 10.30-5. £ P

The history of Cheltenham, the spa town made fashionable by George III, uses costumed figures in its historic setting of 1760 to 1960, including displays of jewellery and fashion accessories and changing temporary exhibitions.

CINDERFORD — Dean Heritage Museum

Camp Mill, Soudley, Cinderford, Glos GL14 7UG. 0594-22170. Open: Daily Apr-Oct 10-6, Nov-Mar 10-5. £ P &

This is a regional museum for the Forest of Dean, describing its geology, archaeology, industrial, social and natural history, with craft workshops and nature trails.

PASSPORT CONCESSIONS: Free Guidebook

JNR. PASSPORT CONCESSIONS: Free Badge.

CIRENCESTER — Corinium Museum

Park Street,
Cirencester,
Glos GL7 2BX.
0285-655611. Open:
Mon-Sat 10-5, Sun 2-
5. Closed: Mons Nov-
Mar. £ &

This is the regional museum for the Cotswolds,
with one of the finest collections of Roman
antiquities, taken from the original Roman
Cirencester, Corinium. There are reconstructions
from Romano-British life and a new gallery
devoted to Cotswold prehistory.

PASSPORT CONCESSIONS: 35% off standard
admission charge to Passport holders.

JNR. PASSPORT CONCESSIONS: Free Schools
information pack.

COMBE MARTIN — The Combe Martin Motorcycle Collection

Cross Street, Combe
Martin, North Devon
EX34 0DH.
0271-882346. Open:
Daily 10-6. Closed:
Oct-Apr. £ P &

Early and late British motorcycles set against a
backdrop of old petrol pumps, signs and garage
memorabilia.

PASSPORT CONCESSIONS: Free Guidebook;
Special rate family entrance ticket.

JNR. PASSPORT CONCESSIONS: Free entry to
Junior Passport holder.

CULLOMPTON — Coldharbour Mill Working Wool Museum

Uffculme,
Cullompton, Devon.
0884-40960. Open:
Daily 11-5. Closed:
Sat/Sun in Winter, 15
Dec-2 Jan. £

This old woollen mill still produces pure wool,
knitting yarn and weaving cloth on machines
from the turn of the century. Products made at
the mill can of course be bought in the mill
shop.

DARTMOUTH — Dartmouth Castle

Dartmouth, Devon.
08043-3588. Open:
Daily 10-6 Summer,
10-4 Winter (excl.
Mon). £ P (EH)

Begun in 1481, extended in the 16th century,
Dartmouth was one of the earliest castles built
for artillery. Now it has a 19th century coastal
defence battery, with fully equipped guns.

DARTMOUTH — Dartmouth Museum

The Butterwalk, Duke
Street, Dartmouth,
Devon TQ6 9PZ.
08043-2923. Open:
Apr-Oct Mon-Sat 11-
5. Nov-Mar Mon-Sat
1.15-4. £

Local history, maritime yarns, ship models,
pictures and artefacts of this ancient little town,
in the Merchants House which dates from 1640.

DEVIZES

Devizes Museum

41 Long Street,
Devizes,
Wilts SN10 1NS.
0380-77369. Open:
Mon-Sat 10-5. £

Run by the Wiltshire Archaeological and Natural History Society, this museum has jewellery, weapons, tools, metalwork and pottery from the county's buried past up to the Roman occupation; Roman, Saxon and medieval exhibits; and a new local history gallery which deals with Devizes since 1600. There are natural history displays and an art gallery as well, with temporary exhibitions all year.

DEVIZES

Kennet and Avon Canal Exhibition

Canal Centre, Couch
Lane, Devizes, Wilts
SN1Q 1EB.
0380-71279. Open:
Easter-Xmas Daily
10-5. Closed: Xmas-
Easter. £

The story of the creation of the waterway link between London and Bristol is told here, as is that of the canal's current restoration.

PASSPORT CONCESSIONS: 50% off adult admission charge; Free Leaflet; Children free if accompanied by an adult.

DEVIZES

Wiltshire Fire Defence Collection

Fire Brigade
Headquarters, Manor
House, Potterne,
Devizes SN10 5PP.
0380-3601. Open: By
appointment only. P

Two manual fire pumps, historic photographs, various fire buckets, extinguishers and types of breathing apparatus, together with a comprehensive collection of 18th to 20th century fire-fighting equipment.

DORCHESTER — The Dinosaur Museum

Icen Way, Dorchester, Dorset DT1 1EW. 0305-269880. Open: Daily 9.30-5.30. £

There are actual fossils here, skeletons, life-size reconstructions and audio-visual/interactive displays to bring the world of dinosaurs back to life.

DORCHESTER — Dorset County Museum

High West Street, Dorchester, Dorset DT1 1XA. 0305-262735. Open: Mon-Sat 10-5. £

Anything to do with Dorset, on, below or above the ground, from dinosaurs' footprints to Thomas Hardy's study, are here. A series of exhibitions and events throughout the year celebrate the 150th anniversary of Hardy's birth.

DORCHESTER — Dorset Military Museum

The Keep, Bridport Road, Dorchester, Dorset DT1 1RN. 0305-264066. Open: Mon-Sat 9-11/2-4 Oct-Jun Sat 10-1. £ P

Nazi relics, displayed on a desk 'liberated' from Hitler's chancellory, form a centrepiece for the regiment's military and social history displays.

DORCHESTER — Old Crown Court

58/60 High West Street, Dorchester, Dorset DT1 1UZ. 0308-22116. Open: Mon-Fri 9-4.

This is where the Tolpuddle Martyrs were tried in 1834. By arrangement with the curator of Bridport Museum, who has responsibility here, you can visit the cells beneath the court.

DORCHESTER — The Tutenkhamun Exhibition

High West Street, Dorchester, Dorset DT1 1UW. 0305-269571. Open: Daily 9.30-5.30. £ P &

This is the Egyptian boy king's tomb recreated to exactly as Howard Carter found it in the 1920s, complete with the odours.

EXETER — Devonshire Regiment Museum

Wyvern Barracks, Topsham Road, Exeter, Devon. 0392-218178. Open: Mon-Fri 9-12.30/2-4.30. Closed: B.H. P

The uniforms, weapons and other militaria which pinpoint the 300 year history of this regiment, helped along, for more recent times, by photographs.

EXETER — Exeter Maritime Museum

The Haven, Exeter
EX2 8DT.
0392-58075. Open:
Daily 10-5. Jul/Aug
10-6. £ P ᴋ̇ free for
disabled.

Unashamedly the world's finest display of working boats, in a hands-on museum which, says the director, Christine O'Neill, has 'stories of adventure, romance and bravery'. Events and exhibitions from May, including a Riverama on June 30.

EXETER — Fursdon House

Cadbury, Exeter,
Devon EX5 5JS.
0392-860860. Open:
Thur & BH 16 Apr-11
Oct. mid-Oct-mid-Apr
by appoint. only. £ P

Small family museum in the house still owned by the Fursdon family after over 750 years, with a costume collection which includes a rare 18th century court gown.

EXETER — Rougemont House Museum

Castle Street, Exeter.
0392-265858. Open:
Mon-Sat 10-5.30.

This is the quite recently (1988) recast museum for one of the finest and largest collections of costume and lace in the country.

A typical Period Room Setting at Rougemont House, Exeter.

EXETER — Royal Albert Memorial Museum

Queen Street, Exeter
EX4 3RX.
0392-265858. Open:
Tue-Sat 10-5.30.

A Victorian museum, this has local and natural history, Exeter silver, Devon pottery, glass and ethnography.

EXETER — St. Nicholas Priory

Mint Lane, Fore Street, Exeter. 0392-265858. Open: Tue-Sat 10-5. £

This is the former guest wing of a Benedictine priory and includes a Norman crypt, kitchen and guest hall where the prior entertained his visitors.

EXETER — Topsham Museum

Holman House, 25 The Strand, Topsham, Exeter. 0392-87 3244. Open: Feb-Nov Mon/Wed/Sat 2-5 & Sun Aug-Sept. £

The Holman family over 300 years is celebrated here, and in particular their maritime partnership with Topsham.

EXETER — Underground Passages

Off High Street, Exeter. 0392-265858. Open: Tue-Sat 2-5. £

Part of the Royal Albert's activities, there are guided tours of Britain's only ancient city passageways, with a new interpretation centre.

FALMOUTH — Falmouth Art Gallery

Municipal Buildings, The Moor, Falmouth, Cornwall TR11 2RT. 0326-313863. Open: Mon-Fri 10-4.30. Closed: Between exhibitions

This tells the story of Cornwall's maritime heritage, and of communications, ship-building, ports, yachts and wars, with instruments, tools, ship models, paintings and photographs.

PASSPORT CONCESSIONS: Free Guidebook; Free Postcards.

JNR.PASSPORT CONCESSIONS: Free Postcards.

FALMOUTH — Maritime Museum

Bell's Court & Custom Quay, Falmouth. 0326-250507. Open: Apr-Oct Daily 10-4. £ P

There are displays about shipbuilding, the sea trade and war wrecks in Cornwall in the museum, with a steam tug berthed alongside.

PASSPORT CONCESSIONS: 50% off adult admission; special family rate.

FALMOUTH — Pendennis Castle

Falmouth, Cornwall. 0326-316594. Open: Daily 10-6 Summer, 10-4 Winter (excl. Mon). £ P (EH)

This is one of the coastal forts Henry VIII built, and was surrounded later in the 16th century by fortifications. There is an exhibition and a gun deck display.

FALMOUTH — Steam Tug St. Denys

Custom House Quay, Falmouth. 0326-250507. Open: Daily 10-4. Closed: Nov-Mar. £

This old tug, built in 1929, laboured in and out of Falmouth Harbour for more than 50 years. Now it has retired and is open to the public, with museum displays on board.

PASSPORT CONCESSIONS: 50% off adult admission charge; Special rate family entrance ticket - 25% off.

FILKINS — Swinford Museum

Filkins, Nr Lechlade, Glos. 036-786376. Open: Apr-Sept First Sun of each month 2-5. Closed: Oct-Mar. P

Every day objects used in a small Cotswold village at the turn of the century. For 1990 there is a special exhibition of the tools used by a mason, a slater and a woodworker.

FROME — Frome Museum

1 North Parade, Frome, Somerset BA11 1AT. 0373-626641. Open: Wed-Sat 10-4. £

Moved to new premises in North parade three years ago, Frome Museum's collections represent the town's geology, archaeology and industry, which includes cloth, brewing, bell founding and printing. An old chemist's shop has been recreated.

GILLINGHAM — Gillingham Local History Museum

Church Walk, Gillingham, Dorset. Open: Wed 2.30-4.30 Sat 10.30-4.30. Closed: Oct-Mar. P

A pair of 18th century cottages have been converted to become a museum which uses themes to tell of the town's past and interests.

GLASTONBURY — Glastonbury Tribunal

The Tribunal, High Street, Glastonbury, Somerset. 0458-32949. Open: Daily 10-6 Summer, 10-4 Winter (excl. Mon). £ (EH)

This was the abbey courthouse of the late 15th century, refaced between 1493 and 1524 and later converted into a private house.

GLASTONBURY — Somerset Rural Life Museum

Abbey Farm, Chilkwell Street, Glastonbury, Somerset BA6 8DB. 0458-32903. Open: Easter-Oct Mon-Fri 10-5, Sat/Sun 2-6. Nov-Easter Mon-Fri 10-5, Sat/Sun 2-4. £ P &

Activities like cider-making tell the story of Somerset's social and domestic history in this museum, which includes the magisterial Abbey Barn of the 14th century.

PASSPORT CONCESSIONS: Free entry to Passport holder.

GLOUCESTER — Gloucester Blackfriars

Lady Bellgate Street, Gloucester. 0452-27688. Open: Daily 10-6 Summer. Closed: Winter. £ (EH)

A Dominican house founded in 1239, with the friary church and parts of the cloister buildings surviving.

GLOUCESTER — Museum of Advertising & Packaging

Albert Warehouse, Gloucester Docks, Gloucester GL1 2EH. 0452-302309. Open: Tue-Fri/Sun 10-6. £ P &

This is the Robert Opie Collection, about which the Daily Mirror said: "It was like standing on the three-legged stool and peering into the pantry of my childhood home in the thirties". This is nostalgia at its purest.

PASSPORT CONCESSIONS: 50% off adult admission charge; Special rate family entrance ticket .

JNR. PASSPORT CONCESSIONS: Free entry to Junior Passport holder.

GLOUCESTER — The National Waterways Museum

Llanthony Warehouse, Gloucester Docks, Gloucester GL1 2EH. 0452-307009. Open: Daily 10-6 Summer, 10-5 Winter. £ P ♿

Set in the refurbished and adapted Llanthony Warehouse, this new museum reveals the extraordinarily varied world of Britain's canals in a series of thematic displays.

JNR. PASSPORT CONCESSIONS: Free Badge.

GLOUCESTER — The Regiments of Gloucestershire Museum

Custom House, The Docks, Gloucester GL1 2HE. 0452-22682. Open: Tue-Sun 10.30-5. £ P ♿

A new museum, to be opened on June 24 in the old custom house of the burgeoning docks, tells of the Gloucestershire Regiment and the Royal Gloucestershire Hussars, all 300 years of them.

PASSPORT CONCESSIONS: 50% off adult admission charge.

GUERNSEY, Castell — Guernsey Folk Museum

Saumarez Park, Castell, Guernsey. 0481-55384. Open: Daily 16 Mar-19th Oct 10-5.30. Closed: 20 Oct-15 Mar. £ P

The didactic in this social history museum is in both English and Guernsey Norman French. It is in an 18th century set of farm buildings surrounding a courtyard in a park. Covering 150 years, there is a bedroom, kitchen, parlour - and dairy, and a plough room with a wooden Norman plough. There is also a working cider press.

GUERNSEY, St. Peter Port — Castle Cornet

St. Peter Port, Guernsey. 0481-26518. Open: Daily 10.30-5.30. £ ♿

This was originally a medieval castle, an ancient sentinel for the island, and it remained so for Elizabethan, Georgian and German (in World War II) occupants, who all made significant additions. It contains art galleries and military and maritime museums, abranch of Guernsey Museum.

PASSPORT CONCESSIONS: Free entry to Passport holder.

JNR. PASSPORT CONCESSIONS: Free entry to Junior Passport holder.

GUERNSEY, St Peter Port

Guernsey Museum & Art Gallery

Candie Gardens, St. Peter Port, Guernsey. 0481-26518. Open: Daily 10.30-5.30, Winter closes 4.30. £ P &

One of the most delightful museums in Britain, in a purpose-built 12-year-old building set in Candie Gardens and overlooking St. Peter Port. It won the Museum of the Year Award in 1979, and tells Guernsey's story through its displays, and frequent special exhibitions.

PASSPORT CONCESSIONS: Free entry to Passport holder.

JNR. PASSPORT CONCESSIONS: Free entry to Junior Passport holder.

GUERNSEY, St Peter Port

Hauteville House

Exile House of Victor Hugo, 38 Hauteville, St Peter Port, Guernsey. 0481-21511. Open: Mon-Fri 10-11.30/ 2-4.30. Closed: Oct-Mar. £

Victor Hugo's home during his 14 year exile from France.

GUERNSEY, St Peter's

Fort Grey Shipwreck Museum

Rocquaine Bay, St. Peter's, Guernsey. 0481-26518. Open: Daily 10.30-12.30/1.30-5.30. Closed: mid Oct-mid Apr. £ &

This is a Martello Tower which has been converted into a museum. Situated on an islet connected by a stone causeway in Rocquaine Bay, the museum features the shipwrecks which have been all too frequent victims of the island's vicious west coast. A branch of the Guernsey Museum.

PASSPORT CONCESSIONS: Free entry to Passport holder.

JNR. PASSPORT CONCESSIONS: Free entry to Junior Passport holder.

HARTLAND

Hartland Quay Museum

Hartland Quay, Hartland, Nr. Bideford, North Devon. 028883-353. Open: Easter week, Daily end May-end Sept 11-5. £ P

Near the site of the Elizabethan harbour, this museum's exhibitions includes material on the history of the quay, coastal trades and industries, shipwrecks, smuggling and the Hartland Point Lighthouse, as well as geology and natural history.

JNR. PASSPORT CONCESSIONS: Free entry to Junior Passport holder.

HELSTON

Flambards Triple Theme Park

Culdrose Manor,
Clodgy Lane, Helston,
Cornwall TR13 0AF.
0326-574549. Open:
Daily 10-5. Cosed:
Nov-Mar. £ P &

Although it's particularly topical this year, Britain in the Blitz is actually one of the permanent exhibitions here, augmented this year by the History of the RAF Fighter which opens in April. There is also a life-size replica Victorian village and the Cornwall Aeropark collection of aircraft.

PASSPORT CONCESSIONS: 50p off adult admission charge.

JNR. PASSPORT CONCESSIONS: Free schools information pack.

HELSTON

Poldark Mine & Heritage Complex

Wendron, Helston,
Cornwall.
0326-573173. Open:
Daily 10-6. Closed:
Nov-Mar. £ P

Cornish heritage based on an 18th century tin mine, with an 1850 beam engine and underground tours - you are warned to allow four hours for your visit.

PASSPORT CONCESSIONS: 10% Discount on presentation of card.

HENBURY

Blaise Castle House Museum

Henbury, Bristol
BS10 7QS.
0272-506789. Open:
Mon-Wed, Sat/Sun
10-1/2-5. &

Set in Humphrey Repton parkland, this is a museum of everyday life in a house dating from 1796, with domestic furniture, costume, toys and tools. Stratford Watermill opens in May, and in the high summer there are demonstrations of country skills and crafts.

HONITON — Allhallows Museum

High Street, Honiton, Devon EX14 8PE. 0404-44966. Open: Mon-Sat 10-5, Oct 10-4. Closed: Nov-Apr. £

The centrepiece here is the collection of Honiton lace, and there are demonstrations in the summer on how it is made. There are also examples of Honiton pottery and material on local history and industry.

PASSPORT CONCESSIONS: Free Poster

ILFRACOMBE — Ilfracombe Museum

Wilder Road, Ilfracombe, North Devon EX34 8AF. 0271-63541. Open: Daily 10-5.30, Mornings only Nov-Easter. £ P &

Over 20,000 items of Victoriana, natural history, maritime items, geological specimens and archaeology, paintings, costumes and a brass rubbing centre.

ILMINSTER — Perry's Cider Mills

Cider Mills, Dowlish Wake, Ilminster, Somerset. 0460-52681. Open: Mon-Fri 9-5.30, Sat 10-4.30, Sun 10-1. P

This has a small collection of farm tools, waggons, carts and cider jars, and a photographic display about village and farm life in about 1900.

JERSEY, Grouville — La Hougue Bie Museum

Near Five Oaks, Grouville, Jersey. 0534-53823. Open: Easter-Sept Daily 10-4, Oct-Easter Mon-Fri 10-4. £ P

A 40-foot high mound contains a 5,000 year old tomb, dominating the museum site, and an underground German communications bunker from World War Two can also be explored.

JERSEY, St. Helier — Jersey Museums Service

9 Pier Road, St. Helier, Jersey. 0534-30511. Open: Mon-Sat 10-5. Closed: 2 weeks in Jan. £

This was a granite-built private house of about 1815, and the museum took it over 97 years ago. Instead of being a museum as it was last year it has become a "museums service", but its collections illustrate the polychrome history of Jersey, with temporary exhibitions in 1990 centering on the occupation 50 years ago.

JERSEY, St. Oven

Jersey Battle of Flowers Museum

La Robeline, Mont Des Corvees, St. Oven, Jersey. 0534-82408. Open: Daily 10-5. Closed: Dec/Jan. £ P &

Over 200 animals including zebras, lions, flamingos, ostriches, llamas and pandas.

JERSEY, St. Peter's Village

Jersey Motor Museum

St. Peter's Village, Jersey. 0534-82966. Open: Daily 10-5. Closed: Nov-mid Mar. £ P

British and German military vehicles are included in these collections of veteran and vintage motors, aeroplane engines and the Jersey Steam Railway exhibition.

KINGSBRIDGE

Cookworthy Museum

The Old Grammar School, 108 Fore Street, Kingsbridge, Devon TQ7 1AW. 0548-3235. Open: Mon-Sat 10-5. Closed: Nov-Mar. £

This local museum has everything relevant to Kingsbridge from costumes (there's a new display of them) to carts, with a walk-in Victorian kitchen and pharmacy, a large farm gallery, toys and dolls' houses.

PASSPORT CONCESSIONS: Free entry to Passport holder on craft days July 13th, 27th, August 10th, 24th 'Big Day' August 22nd; Special rate family ticket; Free Museum pen.

JNR. PASSPORT CONCESSIONS: Free Pen.

LANGPORT

Muchelney Abbey

Muchelney, Langport, Somerset. 0458-250664. Open: Daily 10-6. Closed: Winter. £ (EH)

Founded more than 1,000 years ago, the Benedictine Abbey site has been excavated to reveal the plan of its later church, and there are well-preserved remains of the 15th century south cloister range and the abbot's lodging, which was later used as a farmhouse.

LAUNCESTON — Launceston Castle

Launceston, Cornwall. 0566-2365. Open: Daily 10-6 Summer, 10-4 Winter (excl. Mon). £ (EH)

This was founded by William the Conqueror's elder brother, Duke Robert of Normandy, but the remains are mostly 12th and 13th century. They include a walled bailey and a cylindrical keep on top of a mound, and there is a site exhibition.

LAUNCESTON — Potter's Museum of Curiosity

Jamaica Inn, Bolventor, Bodmin Moor, Launceston, Cornwall. 0566-86838. Open: Daily 10.30-Dusk. Closed: Nov-Mar. £ P

The life, times and work of the Victorian taxidermist John Potter are celebrated here, having been originally founded in Bramber, Sussex, in 1862, and it includes memorabilia and curiosities from all over the world.

LOOE — Lanreath Folk & Farm Museum

Churchtown, Lanreath, Looe, Cornwall PL13 2NX. 0503-20321. Open: Daily 10-6. Closed: Nov-Easter. £ P &

Objects ranging from a Bronze Age tomb to old telephones people this museum, in an old tithe barn in the centre of Lanreath Village.

PASSPORT CONCESSIONS: Free entry to Passport holder.

JNR. PASSPORT CONCESSIONS: Free schools information pack.

LOSTWITHIEL — Restormel Castle

Lostwithiel, Cornwall. 020887-2687. Open: Daily 10-6 Summer, 10-4 Winter (excl. Mon). £ P (EH)

This is a 12th century motte and bailey castle with examples of Norman ringwork.

LYME REGIS — Lyme Regis Museum

Lyme Regis, Dorset DT7 3QA. 02974-3370. Open: Mon-Sat 10.30-5, Sun 2.30-5. Closed: Nov-Easter. £

The area's varied geology is prominently featured, alongside the local history of Lyme Regis.

MALMESBURY — Athelstan Museum

Cross Hayes, Malmesbury, Wiltshire. 0666-822143. Open: Tue-Sat 10.30-12.30/ 1-3 Summer, Wed/Fri/ Sat 1-3 Winter. P

The fact that this free museum is named after the Saxon king buried here gives an idea of how far back the history of Malmesbury goes.It's recorded here where there are also regular lace-making demonstrations and travelling exhibitions.

MARLBOROUGH — Avebury Museum

Avebury, Nr. Marlborough, Wilts. 06723-250. Open: Daily 10-6 Summer, 10-4 Winter (excl. Mon). £ (EH)

Housing one of Britain's most important prehistoric archaeological collections, this museum was founded in the 1930s by Alexander Keiller, who excavated the immensely rich sites around Avebury and its famous Ring.

MINEHEAD — West Somerset Rural Life Museum

The Old School, Allerford, Minehead, Somerset TA24 8HN. 0643-862529. Open: Mon-Sat 10.30-12.30/2-4.30. Closed: Sun, Nov-Mar. £

Activities like cider-making set the scene for this museum about the social and domestic life of rural Somerset, which includes the 14th century Abbey Barn.

NEWQUAY — Dairyland and Countrylife Museum

Tresillian Barton, Summercourt, Newquay, Cornwall TR8 5AA. 0872-510246. Open: Daily Apr + Oct 12-5. Easter/May-Sept 10.30-5.30. Closed: Nov-Mar. £ P &

Award-winning interpretation of Cornish farming, then and now, with working exhibits.

PASSPORT CONCESSIONS: 50p off adult admission charge.

JNR. PASSPORT CONCESSIONS: Free Badge.

NEWTON ABBOT — The Devon Guild of Craftsmen

Riverside Mill, Bovey Tracey, Newton Abbot, Devon TQ13 9AF. 0626-832223. Open: Daily 10-5.30. £

Contemporary craftwork in a gallery with occasional demonstrations, and a showroom and a shop. Special exhibitions monthly.

PASSPORT CONCESSIONS: Free entry to Passport holder.

JNR. PASSPORT CONCESSIONS: Free entry to Junior Passport holder; Free Badge.

NORTHLEACH — Cotswold Countryside Collection

Northleach,
Gloucestershire
GL54 3JH.
0451-60715. Open:
Mon-Sat 10-5.30, Sun
2-5.30. Closed: Nov-
Mar. £ P &

In a former house of correction, the museum
has the Lloyd-Baker Collection of agricultural
history as its centrepiece. There is a social
history gallery, a new "below stairs" exhibition
of laundry, dairy and kitchen, and a restored
cell block and courtroom.

**PASSPORT
CONCESSIONS:**
35% off standard
admission charge
to Passport holder.
**JNR. PASSPORT
CONCESSIONS:**
Free Schools
information pack.

*Prisoner Thomas
Trustrance behind bars in
the reconstructed display
in the cells at the former
Northleach House of
Correction.*

OKEHAMPTON — Finch Foundry Trust

Sticklepath,
Okehampton, Devon
EX20 2NW. 0837-
840286. Open:
Easter-Oct 10-5. £ P

Formerly a foundry for clay and copper mining
tools, this has become a museum for them.
PASSPORT CONCESSIONS: 50% off adult
admission charge; Free Poster; Free
Guidebook.

OKEHAMPTON — Okehampton Castle

Castle Lodge,
Okehampton, Devon.
Open: Daily 10-6
Summer, 10-4 Winter
(excl. Mon). £ P (EH)

This was founded in the 11th century and there
is a Norman keep and motte, with a 14th
century hall, chapel lodgings and gatehouse.

PAIGNTON — Kirkham House

Kirkham St, Off Cecil
Rd, Paignton, Devon.
0803-522775. Open:
Daily 10-6 Summer.
Closed: Winter. £ (EH)

This 15th century stone house, originally the
home of a merchant, burgher or diocesan
official, now has an exhibition of modern
furniture.

PENZANCE — Chysauster Ancient Village

Penzance, Cornwall.
0736-61889. Open:
Daily 10-6 Summer,
10-4 Winter (excl.
Mon). £ P (EH)

This Roman-Cornish village was built between
the third and fourth centuries AD, probably on
an Iron Age site, and there are a number of
stone houses with rooms arranged around an
open court.

PENZANCE — Gevor Tin Mining Museum

Pendeen, Penzance, Cornwall. 0736-788662. Open: Apr-Oct Daily 10.30-5. Closed: Nov-Mar. £ P &

The Trevithick collection is included in this Cornish tin mining museum, and so is an undeground tour.

PENZANCE — Newlyn Orion Galleries

Newlyn Art Gallery, Penzance, Cornwall TR18 5PZ. 0736-63715. Open: Mon-Fri 10-5. £

This is Cornwall's main visual arts centre for contemporary work, with a continuous exhibition programme, touring exhibitions and a branch now at Trelissick near Truro.

PENZANCE — Penzance and District Museum and Art Gallery

Penlee House, Penlee Park, Morrab Road, Penzance, Cornwall. 0736-63625. Open: Mon-Fri 10.30-4.30, Sat 10.30-12.30. £ P

The rain it raineth every day, Norman Garstin.

The archaeology, natural, social and industrial history of West Cornwall, with a permanent exhibition of the painters of the Newlyn School. There is a special exhibition about these artists in December and January, and in August an exhibition about tourism in the region.

PASSPORT CONCESSIONS: Free entry to Passport holder.

JNR. PASSPORT CONCESSIONS: Free Badge.

PLYMOUTH — The Elizabethan House Museum

New Street, Plymouth. 0752-264878. Open: Easter-Sept Tue-Sat 10-1/2-5.30, Sun 2-5. Oct-Easter Tue-Sat 10-4.30. £

This is a Tudor house dating from 1590, with authentic 16th century furniture, situated in the city's historic Barbican area.

PLYMOUTH — The Merchant's House Museum

St. Andrews Street, Plymouth. 0752-264878. Open: Tue-Sat 10-1/2-5.30, Sun from Easter until 30 Sept 2-5, B.H. 10-5.

The city's social history is told in this 16th century merchant's house, each room taking a theme from the rhyme "Tinker, Tailor, Soldier, Sailor, Apothecary, Thief".

PLYMOUTH — Plymouth City Museum and Art Gallery

Drake Circus, Plymouth PL4 8AJ. 0752-264878. Open: Tue-Sat 10-5.30, Sun 2-5. £ &

The municipal collections include contemporary art, Old Masters, topographical paintings, porcelain, Egyptology, natural history, minerals, an aquarium and a beehive.

PLYMOUTH — Saltram

Plympton, Plymouth, Devon PL7 3UH. 0752-336546. Open: House Mon-Thur 12.30-6, Garden & Art Gallery 11-5. Closed: Nov-Mar. £

This Georgian mansion has its original contents, including fine period furniture, china, and pictures including many Reynolds portratits. There are two important rooms by Robert Adam, and an art gallery in the chapel.

PASSPORT CONCESSIONS: £1 off adult admission charge; 50p off child admission charge; Free Guide leaflet; Free Parking.

PORTLAND — Portland Castle

Castle Town, Portland. 0305-820539. Open: Daily 10-6 Summer. Closed: Winter. £ P (EH)

This Henry VIII fort saw action. Having been extended in the 17th century it changed hands several times during the Civil War and was eventually taken by Parliamentary forces in 1646. The tale is told in an exhibition.

PORTLAND — Portland Museum

Wakeham, Portland. 0305-772444. Open: Daily 10-4.30. £

Avice's home from Thomas Hardy's *Well Beloved* is one of the pair of thatched cottages which have been turned into this local history museum.

PASSPORT CONCESSIONS: 50% off adult admission charge; Free entry for under 18's.

JNR. PASSPORT CONCESSIONS: Free entry to Passport holder.

REDRUTH — Camborne School of Mines Geological Museum & Art Gallery

Pool, Redruth,
Cornwall TR15 3SE.
0209-714866. Open:
Mon-Fri 9-5. P

Minerals may have been the source of Cornwall's wealth once, but this museum looks beyond, to display rocks and minerals from all over the world, including fluorescent and radio-active ones, gems and ore. A recent addition is an exhibition of local art.

PASSPORT CONCESSIONS: Free Poster; 5% off on shop purchases.

JNR. PASSPORT CONCESSIONS: Free schools information pack.

REDRUTH — Museum of Cornish Methodism

Carharrack Methodist
Church, Carharrack,
Redruth, Cornwall.
Open: Jul-Aug Tue-
Thur 2-4.

Wesleyana, chapel crockery and artefacts connected with Wesley's visits, and the development of Cornish Methodism.

PASSPORT CONCESSIONS: Free Guidebook.

SALISBURY — Duke of Edinburgh's Royal Regiment Museum

The Wardrobe, 58 The
Close, Salisbury
SP1 2EX.
0722-336222. Open:
Feb-Nov Mon-Fri 10-
4.30, Apr-Oct Sun 10-
4.30, Jul/Aug Daily
10-4.30. £ P

In one of the most magnificent houses in the Cathedral Close, this is about the regiment which was formed in 1959 from a combination of the Berkshire and Wiltshire Regiments. The museum is now houseed in its present 13th century home (which was used by the 14th century bishops as a wardrobe) to become one of the finest military museums.

PASSPORT CONCESSIONS: 50% off adult admission.

SALISBURY — Old Sarum

Salisbury, Wiltshire.
0722-335398. Open:
Daily 10-6 Summer,
10-4 Winter (excl.
Mon). £ P (EH)

First an Iron Age hill fort, Old Sarum became a Roman settlement, then a Saxon burgh, then a Norman town complete with motte and bailey castle. It was the site of the first Salisbury Cathedral and bishop's palace, which was begun in 1078 and finally abandoned 150 years later when the new town was built.

SALISBURY — Old Wardour Castle

Tisbury, Nr. Salisbury,
Wilts. 0747-870487.
Open: Daily 10-6
Summer, Sat/Sun 10-4
Winter . £ P (EH)

Built about 600 years ago around a central courtyard, this hexagonal castle was altered in the Renaissance style in the 16th century and badly damaged in the Civil War 100 years later, but preserved in the 18th century.

SALISBURY — Salisbury & South Wiltshire Museum

The King's House, 65 The Close, Salisbury, Wilts SP1 2EN. 0722-332151. Open: Mon-Sat 10-5, Sun (Jul & Aug only) 2-5. £ &

This enterprising museum has spent the last nine years opening new galleries, the last in the series being the costume gallery. There are also the Pitt Rivers archaeological collection, Dr. Neighbour's Surgery, the Giant and Hob Nob and a great deal more which have recently won The Museum Heritage Award.

PASSPORT CONCESSIONS: Free entry.

JNR. PASSPORT CONCESSIONS: Free entry to Junior Passport holder.

SALISBURY — Stonehenge

Nr. Amesbury, Salisbury, Wilts. 0980-623108. Open: Daily 10-6 Summer, 10-4 Winter. £ P (EH)

English Heritage have taken custody of Britain's most famous prehistoric monument, dating from between 3100 and 1100 BC. It consists of a series of concentric stone circles surrounded by a ditch and approached by an avenue. Why, no-one knows, but there is a new "time tunnel" devoted to world history which might give some clues.

SALTASH — National Maritime Museum at Cotehele Quay

Cotehele Quay, St. Dominick, Saltash, Cornwall. Open: Mon-Fri 11-6. Closed: Nov-Mar.

This is a branch of the national museum at Greenwich and is jointly owned with the National Trust. In a room in one of the quay warehouses it tells the story of river traffic on the Tamar.

SANDHURST — Nature in Art

The International Centre for Wildlife Art, Wallsworth Hall, Sandhurst, Glos GL2 9PA. 0452-731422. Open: 10-5 Tue-Sun + BH. £ P &

The world's first museum of wildlife art, with changing exhibitions throughout the year, complementing the permanent collections.

PASSPORT CONCESSIONS: 20% off adult adm. charge; 5% off shop purchases; Discount on membership of museum.

JNR. PASSPORT CONCESSIONS: Free Pencil, Pen and mini paintbox.

SHAFTESBURY — Shaftesbury Local History Museum

Gold Hill, Shaftesbury, Dorset. 0747-52157. Open: Mon-Sat 11-5, Sun 2.30-5. Closed: Oct-Easter. £

A 1744 fire engine sets the scene for the display of the Shaftesbury Historical Society's collections of photographs, clothes, tools, toys, school books, coins, letters, posters and bottles.

SHEPTON MALLET — The East Somerset Railway (The Strawberry Line)

The Station, Cranmore, Shepton Mallet, Somerset. 074-988417. Open: May-Sept Daily 10-5.30, Apr/Oct closes at 4. Closed: Jan/Feb. £ P &

The East Somerset is a standard gauge railway with eight locomotives, a signal box, an art gallery and, of course, a museum.

PASSPORT CONCESSIONS: Party rates for holders on steam days - please call to check steam days.

SHERBORNE — Sandford Orcas Manor House

The Manor House, Sandford Orcas, Sherborne, Dorset. 096-322206. Open: Mon 10-6, Sun 2-6. Closed: Oct-Apr. £ P

This is a Tudor manor house with a gatehouse, spiral stairways, 17th century panelling, medieval stained glass, Queen Anne furniture, and terraced gardens.

SHERBORNE — Sherborne Museum Association

Abbey Gate House, Sherborne, Dorset DT9 3BP. 093581-2252. Open: Tue-Sat 10.30-12.30/2.30-4.30, Sun 2.30-4.30. Closed: Christmas-Easter. £

There is a model of a 12th century castle, colour reproductions from the Sherborne Missal of 1400, the Sherborne Dolls House of 1870 and much more about the life, history and neighbourhood from Roman times, with a silk mill as a special exhibit.

PASSPORT CONCESSIONS: Free entry to Passport holder.

JNR. PASSPORT CONCESSIONS: Free entry to Junior Passport holder.

SHERBORNE — Sherborne Old Castle

Sherborne, Dorset. 093581-2730. Open: Daily 10-6 Summer, 10-4 Winter excl. Mon. £ P ♿ (EH)

This castle was owned by Sir Walter Raleigh, but was built by an early 12th century Bishop of Salisbury. The main buildings and curtain wall with towers and gates date from then.

SIDMOUTH — Sidmouth Museum

Hope Cottage, Church Street, Sidmouth, Devon EX10 8LY. 0395-516139. Open: Mon-Sat 10-12.30/2-4.30, Sun 2-4.30. Closed: Nov-Easter. £

This has the costumes, lace, prints, Victoriana and newspapers which speak of Sidmouth's life from the early 19th century onwards.

PASSPORT CONCESSIONS: Free entry to Passport holder.

JNR. PASSPORT CONCESSIONS: Free entry to Junior Passport holder.

SIDMOUTH — The Vintage Toy and Train Museum

First Floor, Field's, Market Place, Sidmouth, Devon EX10 8LU. 0395-515124. Open: Mon-Sat 10-5. Closed: Nov-Mar. £ P

A celebration of Frank Hornby's great Meccano company, with Hornby Dublo trains, Dinky toys, and the lamented Meccano sets themselves. Special exhibition this year of a toy gun emplacement of 1940 showing an AA gun firing at a German aeroplane.

PASSPORT CONCESSIONS: 50% off adult admission charge.

JNR. PASSPORT CONCESSIONS: Free Museum bag.

SOUTH MOLTON — South Molton Museum

The Town Hall, South Molton, North Devon EX36 3AB. 07695-2951. Open: Tue/Thur/Fri 10.30-1/2-4, Wed/Sat 10.30-12.30. Closed: Dec-Feb.

This small museum concentrating on local history and lifestyle is an award winner for its displays, which include a Newsham fire engine of 1736 and an 1886 horse-drawn Merryweather fire engine.

ST. AUSTELL — Charlestown Shipwreck and Heritage Museum

Charlestown, St. Austell, Cornwall. 0726-67955. Open: Daily 10-4. Closed Nov-Feb. £ P &

The largest collection of shipwreck flotsam and jetsam in the country, and a portrait of the heritage of this beautiful fishing village.

ST. AUSTELL — Wheal Martyn Museum

Carthew, St. Austell, Cornwall. 0726-850362. Open: Easter-Oct Daily 10-6. £ P &

This open air museum is about the china clay industry in Cornwall and the resulting environment.

ST. IVES — Barbara Hepworth Museum & Sculpture Garden

Barnoon Hill, St. Ives, Cornwall TR26 1AD. 0736-796226. Open: Mon-Sat 10-5.30. £

In the home of the headmistress of the St. Ives School of Artists where she lived from 1949 to 1975 is a permanent exhibition of her paintings and sculptures, with carving studios also on view.

ST. IVES — Penwith Galleries

Back Rd West, Saint Ives, Cornwall. 0736-795579. Open: Tue-Sat 10-1/2.30-5. £

Continuous exhibitions of paintings, sculpture and pottery.

ST. IVES — Wayside Museum

Zennor, Nr. St. Ives, Cornwall TR26 3DA. 0736-796945. Open: Daily 10-6.30. Closed: Nov-Mar. £ P

The theme of this extraordinary museum - a collector's paradise - is life in Zennor from 3000 BC to the 1930s when Colonel Freddie Hirst first began putting it together. Looks like he hasn't missed a single second.

PASSPORT CONCESSIONS: Free Guidebook.

JNR. PASSPORT CONCESSIONS: Free Pencil.

ST. MARY'S, Isles of Scilly

Isles of Scilly Museum

Church Street, St Mary's, Isles of Scilly. 0720-22638. Open: Mon-Sat 10-12/1.30-4.30, Nov-Mar Wed only 2-4. £

The special exhibits in this museum about Scillonian archaeology, history and natural history, are a full-rigged gig and a late 19th century local kitchen.

ST. MAWES

St. Mawes Castle

St. Mawes, Cornwall. 0326-270526. Open: Daily 10-6 Summer, 10-4 Winter (excl. Mon). £ P (EH)

Yet another of Henry VIII's forts which English Heritage have in their care, this one in a clover-leaf shape made by a central tower surrounded by three semi-circular bastions.

STREET

The Shoe Museum

40 High Street, Street, Somerset BA16 OYA. 0458-43131. Open: Easter-Oct Mon-Fri 10-4.45, Sat 10-4.30. Closed: Nov-Mar. &

Footwear from Roman times to the present with 19th century photographs of shoes being made. Set in the oldest part of the C & J Clark factory.

STROUD

Stroud District Museum

Lansdown, Stroud, Glos GL5 1BB. 0453-763394. Open: Mon-Sat 10.30-1/2-5. &

There is a life-size model of a dinosaur which is the star of this local history museum, and less imposing, yet to some more interesting, is the 1865 lawn mower.

PASSPORT CONCESSIONS: Free copy of 19c poster; 10% off souvenirs and most published items; OPPS.- invitation to join members at meetings and on field visits.

STURMINSTER NEWTON

Fiddleford Manor

Fiddleford, Nr. Sturminster Newton, Devon. 0258-72597. Open: Daily 10-6 Summer. Closed: Winter. £ P (EH)

This is part of a 14th century house altered 200 years later, comprising a hall and solar block with elaborate roofs.

SWANAGE

Coach House Museum

St George's Close, Langton Matravers, Swanage, Dorset. Open: Mon-Sat 10-12/ 2-4. Closed: Nov-Mar. or by appoint. £ (EH)

This is not a museum of coaches, as you might expect, but of the purbeck stone industry. It has a life-size underground quarry model, a capstan, tools, a quarry forge and specimens of masons' work.

JNR. PASSPORT CONCESSIONS: Free Pencil.

TAUNTON

Somerset County Museum

Taunton Castle, Taunton, Somerset TA1 4AA. 0823-255504. Open: Mon-Sat 10-5. £ P

Around the great hall of Taunton Castle, where Judge Jeffreys held his Bloody Assize in 1685, are displays of antiquities, including the Low Ham Mosaic and finds from the Somerset Levels - ceramics, industrial history, geology, costume, dolls, coins, medals and the Somerset Military Museum.

PASSPORT CONCESSIONS: Free entry to Passport holder; OPPS.

JNR. PASSPORT CONCESSIONS: Free entry to Junior Passport holder.

TAUNTON

Somerset Military Museum

Taunton, Somerset TA1 4AA. 0823-255504. Open: Mon-Sat 10-5. £

Three hundred years of the Somerset Light Infantry, West and North Somerset Yeomanry, Somerset Militia and the Rifle Volunteer Corps.

TAVISTOCK

Morwellham Quay

Morwellham, Tavistock, Devon. 0822-832766. Open: Daily 10-5.30 Summer, 10-4.30 Winter, allow 2 hours for visit. £ P

This is an open air museum on the site of a once busy river port on the Tamar, recalling the 19th century use of some of the buildings. there is a cooper's, a chandler's and a Victorian cottage among them, showing the life of this tin mining community.

TEIGNMOUTH — Teignmouth Museum

29 French Street, Teignmouth, Devon TQ14 8ST. 0626-773818. Open: Mon-Fri 10-12.30/2-4.30, + Thur eve 7-9, Sun 2-4.30. Closed: Oct-Apr. £

The town and its maritime history, plus the Atmospheric Railway Experiment, and displays about what life was like in an early seaside resort.

PASSPORT CONCESSIONS: Free entry to Passport holders.

TEWKESBURY — The John Moore Countryside Museum

41 Church Street, Tewkesbury, Glos GL20 5SN. 0684-297174. Open: Tue-Sat 10-1/2-5. Closed: Nov-Easter. £

A commemoration of Gloucestershire life in the name of Tewkesbury naturalist and author John Moore. Tools and domestic rural bygones from the Holland-Martin collection. The museum is ten years old this year.

PASSPORT CONCESSIONS: 50% off adult admission charge; Special rate family entrance ticket.

JNR. PASSPORT CONCESSIONS: Free entry to Junior Passport holder.

TEWKESBURY — The Little Museum

45 Church Street, Tewkesbury, Glos. Open: Tue-Sat 10-5. Closed: Nov-Easter.

Dedicated to John Moore (1907-67) and set in one of a row of 15th century cottages, furnished to the period.

TEWKESBURY — Tewkesbury Town Museum

64 Barton Street, Tewkesbury, Glos GL20 5PX. 0684-295027. Open: Mon-Fri 10-1/2-5. Closed: Nov-Mar. £

This local history museum is in a 16th century half-timbered house. The Battle of Tewkesbury, in which the House of York defeated the House of Lancaster in the Wars of the Roses, is the subject of a diorama. The Walker fairground collection is also here.

PASSPORT CONCESSIONS: Party rate £1 for up to 20 persons.

TINTAGEL — Tintagel Castle

Tintagel, Cornwall. 0840-770328. Open: Daily 10-6 Summer, 10-4 Winter (excl. Mon). £ P (EH)

One of the most romantic ruins in the West. The fact that it has had nothing to do with King Arthur, as legend and the local gift shops have it, does not detract from its eerie charm. It was founded in the 1100s by Reginald, Earl of Cornwall, on a Dark Ages site, and is now split in two by the insistent sea. A bigger exhibition about the castle opens in the summer of 1990.

TIVERTON — Bickleigh Castle Museum

Bickleigh, Tiverton, Devon EX16 8RP. 08845-363. Open: Sun-Fri 2-5. Closed: Oct-Easter. £ P

Bickleigh Castle has an exhaustive collection of World War II spy and escape gadgets, contrasted with 19th century toys, including ridable rocking horses and model ships.

PASSPORT CONCESSIONS: Free Guidebook; Special rate family entrance ticket.

JNR. PASSPORT CONCESSIONS: Free Schools information pack.

TIVERTON — Tiverton Castle

Tiverton, Devon EX16 6RP. 0884-253200. Open: Sun-Thur 2.30-5.30. Closed: Oct-Easter. £

Built by Henry I in 1106, it has a medieval gatehouse, tower and ruins, with a Civil War armoury, a notable clock collection and the New World Tapestry on display.

PASSPORT CONCESSIONS: £1 off adult admission charge.

JNR. PASSPORT CONCESSIONS: Free entry to Junior Passport holder.

TIVERTON — Tiverton Museum

St. Andrew Street, Tiverton, Devon EX16 6PH. 0884-256295. Open: Mon-Sat 10.30-4.30. Closed: Dec 22-Jan 30. P &

This place records the town, and the section of Devon which surrounds it, from the 1st century AD. There's a GWR tank locomotive, a Heathcoat lace machine, farm waggons and a Roman fort display.

TORPOINT — Mount Edgcumbe House

Cremyll, Torpoint, Cornwall PL10 1HZ. 0752-822236. Open: Wed-Sun 11-5.30. Closed: Nov-Easter. £ P &

Built in 1550, the house was all but destroyed by World War Two incendiary bombs and has now been rebuilt to its 16th century appearance.

PASSPORT CONCESSIONS: £1 off adult admission charge; 50p off OAP admission charge.

JNR. PASSPORT CONCESSIONS: Free Badge; Free Pencil.

Mount Edgcumbe, Cornwall

TORQUAY — Torre Abbey

The King's Drive, Torquay TQ2 5JX. 0803-293593. Open: Apr-Oct Daily 10-5. £

Converted after the dissolution in the 16th century, this 12th century monastery is now art galleries with furnished period rooms.

PASSPORT CONCESSIONS: Free entry to holders.

TORQUAY — Torquay Museum

529 Babbacombe Road, Torquay TQ1 1HG. 0803-293975. Open: Mon-Fri 9-5, + Sat Easter-Sept 2-5 Sun Mid-Jul-mid-Sept 12-4. £

Important archaeological finds from Kent's Cavern and other South Devon sites are here, as well as a natural history gallery and items from Devon folk life, Victoriana, local pottery and more.

TORRINGTON — Torrington Museum

The Town Hall, Torrington, Devon EX38 8HN. 0805-24324. Open: Mon-Fri 10.15-12.45/2.15-4.45, Sat 10.15-12.45. Closed: Oct-Apr

The Coronation Robes of the late Earl and Countess Orford of Rosemoor are among the items in this local history museum.

PASSPORT CONCESSIONS: Free Guidebook.

TOTNES — Berry Pomeroy Castle

Totnes, Devon. 0272-734472. Open: Daily 10-6 Summer. Closed: Winter. £ P (EH)

This is a late medieval fortified house which the Duke of Somerset, sometime Lord Protector to Edward VI, remodelled and extended in the manner of a French chateau, but it was still unfinished when he was executed in 1552. English Heritage are opening it this season, 1990, for the first time.

TOTNES — British Photographic Museum

Totnes, Devon. 0803-863664. Open: Easter-Sept Sun-Thur 11-5. £ P &

There are vintage cameras here, along with a Victorian studio, an Edwardian darkroom, and replica shops and cafe.

PASSPORT CONCESSIONS: 10% off purchases of collectors' cameras; Free glass of wine with meal.

JNR. PASSPORT CONCESSIONS: Free Badge

TOTNES — Devonshire Collection of Period Costume

Bogan House, 43 High Steet, Totnes, Devon TQ9 5RY. 0803-862423. Open: Mon-Fri 11-5, Sun 2-5. Closed: Oct-May. £

This is a private collection of costumes dating from 1750. The summer exhibition for 1990 will focus on holidays between 1920 and 1939.

TOTNES — Totnes Castle

Totnes, Devon. 0803-864406. Open: Daily 10-6 Summer, 10-4 Winter (excl. Mon). £ (EH)

The curtain wall of this Norman motte and bailey castle was built in the early 13th century and reconstructed in the 14th century.

TOTNES — Totnes Motor Museum

Steamer Quay, Totnes, Devon. 0803-862777. Open: Daily 10-5.30. Closed: Nov-Easter. £

Eighty years of motoring are recorded here, from a child's pedal car to exotic racers. All are in working order, and some can even be seen at major race meetings around Europe.

PASSPORT CONCESSIONS: 20% off adult admission charge.

TOTNES — Totnes Museum

70 Fore St, Totnes, Devon. 0803-863821. Open: Easter-Oct Mon-Fri 10.30-1/2-5. £

A rich merchant built this house for himself in 1575, and it now houses rich and varied exhibitions about local life.

PASSPORT CONCESSIONS: 50% off adult admission charge.

JNR. PASSPORT CONCESSIONS: Free for Junior Passport holder.

TROWBRIDGE — Trowbridge Museum

The Shires, Trowbridge, Wiltshire. 0225-751339. Opening Spring 1990.

This local museum, with its paintings, household objects and toys, is due to re-open in its new premises in the spring of 1990.

TRURO
County Museum & Art Gallery

River Street, Truro, Cornwall TR1 2SJ. 0872-72205. Open: Mon-Sat 9-5. £ &

As well as the toys, costumes and bits and pieces of Cornwall's social past, the museum has an important collection of minerals, the county's life blood in the past, archaeology and art, both fine and decorative, from Europe and the East. Two new galleries and new facilities, including a coffee shop, toilets and full disabled access, open in July 1990.

PASSPORT CONCESSIONS: 50% off adult admission charge.

JNR. PASSPORT CONCESSIONS: Free Badge.

WAREHAM
The Tank Museum

Bovington Camp, Wareham, Dorset BH20 6JG. 0929-462721. Open: Daily 10-5. Closed: 10 days at Christmas. £ P &

The largest, most comprehensive museum collection of armoured fighting vehicles in the world, with over 240 on show.

PASSPORT CONCESSIONS: Free Poster and Postcard; Special rate family entrance ticket

JNR. PASSPORT CONCESSIONS: Free Charlie Challenger games.

WATCHET
Cleeve Abbey

Washford, Watchet, Somerset. 0984-40377. Open: Daily 10-6 Summer, 10-4 Winter (excl. Mon). £ P & (EH)

Many of the buildings of this late 12th century Cistercian Abbey survive, including the frater with its fine timber roof, although little remains of the abbey church. There is an exhibition about its past.

WELLS
Wells Museum

8 Cathedral Green, Wells, Somerset BA5 2UE. 0749-73477. Open: Easter-Oct Mon-Sat 10-5.30, Sun 11-5.30, Nov-Easter Wed-Sun 11-4. £

There is a Somerset kitchen, a miniature antique shop, an icthyosaur and needlework samplers, along with the local archaeology, geology and social history in this museum on the cathedral green.

PASSPORT CONCESSIONS: 50% off adult admission charge.

JNR. PASSPORT CONCESSIONS: Free entry to Junior Passport holder.

WESTON-SUPER-MARE

Woodspring Museum

Burlington Street, Weston-Super-Mare, Avon BS23 1PR. 0934-621028. Open: Mon-Sat 10-5. P

Set in the old Gaslight Company's workshops, this has displays in local industries, not least of which is the seaside. Plus the Peggy Nisbet collection of costume dolls and a changing programme of exhibitions with Museum Week May 28-June 2.

WEYMOUTH

Diving Museum & Shipwreck Museum

Custom House Quay, Weymouth. 0305-772444. Open: Daily 10-6, Jun-Aug 10-9. £ P &

This has interactive displays, a children's submarine and live diving demonstrations.

WEYMOUTH

The New Timewalk Museum Weymouth

Brewers Quay, Weymouth. 0305-772444. Open: Daily 10-dusk from late May B.H. £

Opening in the spring of 1990, this is a local museum with a difference. Set in the old Brewery Buildings, historical cameos of the town's past have been constructed so you stroll back to the Black Death, the Spanish Armada, a Georgian ballroom, a smugglers' den and a Victorian brewery.

PASSPORT CONCESSIONS: 25% off adult admission charge; Free entry for under 18's.

JNR. PASSPORT CONCESSIONS: Free entry to Junior Passport holder; Free Museum bag.

WEYMOUTH

Nothe Fort

Nothe Gardens, Weymouth. 0305-772444. Open: June-Sept Daily 11-dusk, Winter Sun pm only. £ P

This Victorian coastal fort offers an insight into late Victorian military life, and spectacular views of the harbour.

JNR. PASSPORT CONCESSIONS: Free entry to Junior Passport holder if accompanied by adult.

WEYMOUTH

Tudor House Museum

No. 3 Trinity Street, Weymouth. 0305-772444. Open: Jun-Sept Tue-Thur 11-4.15. Closed: Oct-May. £

In this late 15th century house, now in Tudor livery, there are displays and reconstructions of social and domestic life, with a Tudor knot garden outside.

WILTON

Wilton Windmill

Wilton, Nr. Marlborough, Wiltshire. 0672-870427. Open: Sun/B.H. 2-5. Closed: Oct-Easter. £ P

Wiltshire's only working windmill, restored in 1976 but built in 1821 to replace five watermills made powerless by the building of the Kennet and Avon Canal.

WIMBORNE MINSTER

Priest's House Museum

23 High Street, Wimborme Minster, Dorset BH21 1HR. 0202-882533. Open: Daily 10.30-4.30. Closed: Oct-Xmas/ Jan-Easter. £ P &

A local museum set in a Tudor house with a walled garden.

PASSPORT CONCESSIONS: 50% off adult admission charge.

WINCHCOMBE

Winchcombe Railway Museum and Gardens

23 Gloucester Street, Winchcombe, Gloucestershire GL54 5LX. Open: Daily 1.30-6. Closed: Weekends Nov-Mar. £ &

Working exhibits from the days of steam, in a hands-on railway museum set in half an acre of the Victorian Cotswold gardens.

PASSPORT CONCESSIONS: Free Guidebook; Two adult admissions for the price of one.

JNR. PASSPORT CONCESSIONS: Free entry to Passport holder; Free Schools information pack.

YELVERTON — Buckland Abbey

Yelverton, Devon
PL20 6EY.
0822-853607. Open:
Apr-Sept Daily 10.30-
5.30, Oct 10.30-5,
Nov-Mar Wed/Sat/Sun
2-5.   £ P &

Sir Francis Drake's home, formerly a 13th
century Cistercian monastery, with lots of
sailor's relics. The Drake Legend Gallery is
due to open during the Summer.

YELVERTON — Yelverton Paperweight Centre

4 Buckland Terrace,
Leg o' Mutton,
Yelverton, Devon
PL20 6AD.
0822-854250. Open:
Mon-Sat 10-5, Nov-
Easter Wed 1-5, Sat
10-5.   P

Illuminated display of the Broughton
Collection, with hundreds of antique and
modern glass paperweights.

PASSPORT CONCESSIONS: 5% off Paperweight
sale.

YEOVIL — Brympton Country Life Museum

Brympton d'Evercy,
Yeovil, Somerset.
Open: Mon-
Wed/Sat/Sun 2-6.
Closed: Oct-Apr. £

Country life in Somerset has much to do
with cider, either the producing of it or the
consuming of it, and with many exhibits
rescued from a smallholding it tells the story of
in-cider trading, from apples to barrels.

PASSPORT CONCESSIONS: Free entry to Passport
holder.

JNR. PASSPORT CONCESSIONS: Free entry to
Junior Passport holder.

YEOVIL — Museum of South Somerset

Hendford, Yeovil,
Somerset BA20 1UN.
0935-24774. Open:
Mon-Sat 12-5.

A new social history gallery about life in South
Somerset over the last few hundred years opens
in the spring of 1990, complementing displays
of archaeology, firearms and costume.

YEOVILTON — The Fleet Air Arm Museum

Royal Naval Air
Station, Yeovilton,
Somerset BA22 8HT.
0935-840565. Open:
Daily 10-5.30 £ P &

One of the world's major aviation museums,
with over 50 historic aircraft-including
Concorde, part of the Science Museum's
collection. The exhibitions and displays
concentrate on the history of naval aviation
since it began in 1908, and there is a new
annual exhibiton each year; for 1990 it is The
Jump Jet Story.

WEST
MIDLANDS

BAGINTON — Lunt Roman Fort

Coventry Rd, Baginton, Warks. 0203-832433. Open: 26 May-Sept Tue/Wed/Fri-Sun 12-6, all week on B.H. Closed: Oct-Easter. £ P &

One of the finest displays on the Roman army in Britain is laid out in the granary of this excavated and partly reconstructed first century turf and timber fort, with the headquarters building being reconstructed.

BARLASTON — Wedgwood Visitor Centre

Barlaston, Nr Stoke-on-Trent, Staffs ST12 9ES. 0782-204218. Open: Mon-Fri 9-5, Sat 10-4 Easter-Oct Sun 10-4. Closed: Xmas week. £ P &

At the Barlaston works, where you can see Josiah Wedgwood's first wares from 1759 and potters and decorators at work on today's products.

PASSPORT CONCESSIONS: 50% off adult admission charge; Free Guidebook; Free entry to under 18's.

JNR PASSPORT CONCESSIONS: Free entry to Junior Passport holder.

BEWDLEY — Bewdley Museum

Load St, Bewdley, Worcs DY12 2AE. 0299-403573. Open: Mar-Nov Daily. Closed: Dec-Feb. £

This working brass foundry has not only a waterwheel, hydraulic rams and a Victorian reciprocating saw, but demonstrations of rope-making and claypipe-making.

BIRMINGHAM — Aston Hall

Aston, Birmingham B6 6JD. 021327-0062. Open: Daily 2-5. Closed: 4 Nov - 24 Mar. P

The Holte family built this house between 1618-1635 and lived in it until 1917, and it is one of the last great Jacobean houses with over 20 rooms open, furnished with pieces from the 17th to 19th centuries, and with outstanding original plasterwork and panelling.

BIRMINGHAM — Birmingham Museum & Art Gallery

Chamberlain Square, Birmingham B3 3DH. 021235-2834. Open: Mon-Sat 9.30-5, Sun 2-5. &

One of the great municipal museums with one of our finest art collections, especially of the Pre-Raphaelites. There is an extensive programme of temporary exhibitions.

BIRMINGHAM   Birmingham Nature Centre

Peshore Road, Birmingham. 021 4727775. Open: Apr-Sept Daily 10-5, Oct-Mar Sat/Sun only. P &

This museum brings natural history to life by combining a zoo, a nature trail and a museum on a six acre site, and there are events through the year, too.

BIRMINGHAM   Birmingham Railway Museum

670 Warwick Road, Tyseley, Birmingham BII 2HL. 021-707 4696. Open: Daily May-Sept 10-5, Oct-Apr Mon-Fri/Sun 10-5. £ P &

This is a working museum where locomotives are not only restored but seen to be restored - and ridden, with steam passenger rides every Sunday from Easter. On April 1 1990 there's the grand opening of the Tyseley Extension Railway and Tyseley Warwick Road Station.

BIRMINGHAM   Blakesley Hall

Blakesley Road, Yardley, Birmingham. 021-783 2193. Open: Daily 2-5. Closed: 5 Nov-23 Mar.

Richard Smallbroke, a prosperous Birmingham merchant, built this timber-framed farmhouse in Elizabethan times, all furnished according to an inventory of 1684, and you can see the original bedchamber wall paintings.

BIRMINGHAM   Lapworth Museum of Earth Sciences

School of Earth Sciences, University of Birmingham, Birmingham B15 2TT. 021-4146147. Open: Mon-Fri 9-5. P

This is part of Birmingham University, and the main displays are about stratigraphically arranged fossils and minerals. Many other aspects of earth sciences are also illustrated.

The Lunt Fort

Coventry Road, Baginton, Warwickshire
Telephone: 0203-832381/832433

This unique site is open June to September (inclusive), daily, 12 noon to 6pm. Closed Monday and Friday.

The museum shop has a good selection of postcards and books relating to the Roman Army generally.

Free car and coach park and picnic area.

Guided tours available for groups who book in advance.

BIRMINGHAM — Museum of Science & Industry

Newhall Street, Birmingham B3 1RZ. 021-236 1022. Open: Mon-Sat 9.30-5, Sun 2-5. ♿

The world's oldest working steam engine is here, along with locomotives, trams, cars, motorbikes, World War Two fighter planes, computer displays and a new Light on Science Gallery.

BIRMINGHAM — The Patrick Collection

180 Lifford Lane, Kings Norton, Birmingham B30 3NT. 021-459 9111. Open Easter - 28 Oct Sat/ Sun/B.H./School Hols 10-5.30, Other days 2-5.30. Winter - Call for opening. £ P ♿

Mr Patrick, the garage owner who has personally put together this collection, calls it Autoworld and it has 80 classic cars on display from the early 1900s to the supercars of the 1990s, set in Victorian papermills.

BIRMINGHAM — Sarehole Mill

Cole Bank Road, Hall Green, Birmingham. 021-7776612. Open: Daily 2-5. Closed: Nov-mid Mar.

This is the last working cornmill within the city boundary, still used commercially until 70 years ago. The Georgian buildings have rural life displays, and there's an 1850s engine house, a blade-grinding workshop and a bakehouse.

BIRMINGHAM — Selly Manor Museum and Minworth Greaves Exhibition Hall

Maple Rd & Sycamore Rd, Bournville, Birmingham. 021-472 0199. Open: Tue-Fri 10-5. Closed: mid Dec-mid Jan.

This is a half-timbered house of the 14th to 16th centuries which is a museum of furniture and household utensils now, and Minworth Greaves, a 14th century 'cruck' house, is now an exhibition hall now with displays changing through the year.

BIRMINGHAM — Weoley Castle

Alwold Road, Birmingham. 021-4274270. Open: Mon-Fri 2-5. Closed: Oct-Mar.

Within the ruins of this medieval moated castle is a small museum with the objects excavated in the 1930s and 1950s.

BREWOOD — Boscobel House and the Royal Oak

Brewood, Nr. Wolverhampton, Staffs. 0902-850244. Open: Daily 10-6 Summer, 10-4 Winter (Tue-Sun). Closed: Jan. £ P (EH)

Charles II hid in the branches of an oak tree in the grounds of this hunting lodge after the Battle of Worcester in 1651. The lodge, built at the start of that century, has now been fully refurbished, and has exhibitions.

BRIDGNORTH — Bridgnorth Museum

Northgate High St, Bridgnorth, Salop. 0746-762100. Open: Apr-Sept Sat 2-4, B.H. mid-July/Aug Mon-Wed 2-4.

Built in the town's walls, there are local objects from the Bronze Age to the Civil War in this museum, including the pistol hidden in the governor's house.

BRIDGNORTH — Dudmaston

Dudmaston, Quatt, Bridgnorth, Shropshire. 0746-780866. Open: Apr-Sept Wed/Sun 2.30-6. Closed: Oct-Mar. £ P &

Seventeenth century with fine furniture and Dutch paintings which belonged to Francis Darby of Coalbrookdale, modern pictures, botanical art, family and natural history.

PASSPORT CONCESSIONS: Special family rate.

BRIDGNORTH — Midland Motor Museum

Stourbridge Road, Bridgnorth, Shropshire WV15 6DT. 0746-761761. Open: Daily 10-5. £ P &

This has over 100 sports and racing cars and motorbikes from the 1920s onwards, along with other "motorabilia".

PASSPORT CONCESSIONS: £1 off adult admission charge.

JNR. PASSPORT CONCESSIONS: Free entry to Junior Passport holder.

BRIDGNORTH — The Northgate Museum

Northgate High Street, Bridgnorth, Shropshire. Open: Apr-Sept Sat, B.H. 2-4, Mid Jul-Aug Mon-Wed 2-4. Closed: Oct-Feb.

This is run by the Bridgnorth and District Historical Society and covers local history from Bronze Age tools to Civil War weapons to discoveries from the most recent archaeological excavations. A set of unique firemarks, the latest acquisition, are on show.

BROMSGROVE — Avoncroft Museum of Buildings

Stoke Heath,
Bromsgrove, Worcs
B60 4JR.
0527-31886. Open:
Daily 11.30-5.30.
Closed: Dec/Jan.
£ P &

This open air museum has a working windmill,
a 15th century timber-framed house, an 18th
century ice house, an earth closet, a cidermill
and a 19th century toll house, with the 14th
century Guesten Hall Roof as the newest exhibit.

PASSPORT CONCESSIONS: £1 off adult
admission charge.

JNR. PASSPORT CONCESSIONS: Free entry to
Junior passport holder (if accompanied by a
paying adult).

BROMSGROVE — Bromsgrove Museum

2 Birmingham Rd,
Bromsgrove B61 0DD.
0527-77934. Open:
Daily 10-12.30/1.30-5,
Sun 2-5. £ P &

The special feature here is the Victorian/
Edwardian street of different shops and there is
also a room devoted to local history, all put
together by Dennis Norton who has been
collecting for more than 40 years.

BURTON UPON TRENT — Heritage Brewery Museum

Anglesey Road,
Burton Upon Trent,
Staffs DE14 3PF.
0283-69226. Open:
Easter-Sept Mon-Sat
10-4, Oct-Easter Tue-
Sat 10-2. £ P &

The first working brewery museum in England
in a group of listed Victorian buildings with the
original steam engine and one of the world's
largest collections of bottled beer.

PASSPORT CONCESSIONS: £1 off adult
admission charge.

JNR. PASSPORT CONCESSIONS: Free entry to
Junior Passport holder.

BUXTON — Buxton Micrarium

The Crescent, Buxton,
Derbyshire SK17 6BQ.
0298-78662. Open:
Daily 10-5. Closed:
Nov-Apr. £

The world's first micrarium - easy-to-use
projection microscopes which reveal the beauty
and intricacy of the natural world.

PASSPORT CONCESSIONS: 50p off adult
admission charge.

JNR. PASSPORT CONCESSIONS: Free schools
information pack.

BUXTON — Buxton Museum and Art Gallery

Terrace Road, Buxton,
Derbyshire SK12
6DU. 0298-24658.
Open: Tue-Fri 9.30-
5.30, Sat 9.30-5.

The Peak District's extraordinary physique is
the theme of the Wonders of the Peak galleries
here with geology, archaeology and historical
specimens plus photographs and other archive
material. There's a busy diary of art exhibitions
too.

JNR. PASSPORT CONCESSIONS: Free Badge.

CASTLE DONINGTON

The Donington International Collection

Donington Park, Derby DE7 2RP. 0332-810048. Open: Daily 10-5. £

This is the world's largest collection of single seater racing cars. It is also the world's only speedway museum, and has the Speedway Hall of Fame.

CHEDDLETON

Cheddleton Flint Mill

Cheddleton, Nr. Leek, Staffs. 0782- 502907. Open: Daily 10-5. P

You can see one of the two water wheels working flint grinding pans daily, with the Robey steam engine working on request and the flint grinding process simulated.

PASSPORT CONCESSIONS: Reduction on shop purchases; Free Poster; Conducted tours available.

JNR. PASSPORT CONCESSIONS: Free schools information pack.

CHEDDLETON

Cheddleton Railway Centre

Cheddleton Station, Station Road, Cheddleton, Nr Leek, Staffs ST13 7EE. 0782-503458. Open: Easter-Sept Sun + B.H. Mon 11-5.30, Oct-Mar Sun 11-4.30. £ P

This is at the Victorian Cheddleton Station in the beautiful Churnet Valley in Staffordshire. There is a locomotive display hall with mainline engines, a working signal box and steam rides in the summer.

PASSPORT CONCESSIONS: Free guided tour on steam days.

CHESTERFIELD — Bolsover Castle

Castle Street, Bolsover, Nr. Chesterfield. 0246-823349. Open: Daily 10-6 Summer, 10-4 Winter (excl. Mon). £ (EH)

This was a 17th century house built for the Cavendish family by Robert and John Smythson. Its keep is decorated with paintings and carved fireplaces, and it has one of the earliest indoor riding schools on which there are displays, as well as on the keep itself.

CHESTERFIELD — The Revolution House

High Street, Old Whittington, Chesterfield, Derbyshire. 0246- 453554. Open: 13 Apr-26 Oct Daily 10-4, 27 Oct-12 Apr Sat/Sun 10-4. P

This is a 17th century former alehouse which takes its name from the 1688 "Glorious Revolution", and as well as its revolutionary presentation there is an exhibition of Derbyshire customs and traditions until the end of October 1990.

CHURCH STRETTON — Acton Scott Working Farm Museum

Wenlock Lodge, Acton Scott, Nr. Church Stretton, Shrops SY6 6QN. 06946-306. Open: Mon-Sat 10-5, Sun 10-6. Closed: Nov-Mar. £ P &

Great shire horses still labour here in the way they did 100 years ago, and butter is made regularly in the dairy in the traditional manner.

PASSPORT CONCESSIONS: Free entry to Passport holder.

JNR. PASSPORT CONCESSIONS: Free entry to Junior Passport holder.

COVENTRY — The Coventry Toy Museum

Whitefriars Gate, Much Park St, Coventry, Warwickshire CV1 2LT. 0203-227560. Open: Daily 2-6. £ P

In a 14th Centry monastery gatehouse, 200 years of toys of every description.

PASSPORT CONCESSIONS: 50% off adult admission charge.

COVENTRY — Herbert Art Gallery & Museum

Jordan Well, Coventry CV1 5RW. 0203-832381. Open: Mon-Sat 10-5.30, Sun 2-5.

The collections include Graham Sutherland's studies for the Coventry Cathedral's tapestry, plus live animal display with natural and social history exhibits. Poignant exhibition on the Blitz in November.

PASSPORT CONCESSIONS: Free Poster; 10% off shop purchases.

JNR. PASSPORT CONCESSIONS: Free Pencil.

COVENTRY — Museum of British Road Transport

St. Agnes Lane, Hales Street, Coventry CV1 1PN. 0203-832425. Open: Daily 10-5, Nov-Easter Fri-Sun. £ &

150 cars, 200 bikes, 80 motorbikes representing Coventry's unique contribution to road transport, with an A/V show about the world land speed record.

COVENTRY — Whitefriars Museum

Whitefriars Street, London Road, Coventry. 0203-832433. Open: Thur-Sat 10-5.

These are the remains of a 14th century Carmelite monastery, the best example left in Britain, and the museum shows a collection of artefacts found there, and includes sculpture from medieval to the 19th century. Temporary exhibitions all year.

PASSPORT CONCESSIONS: Free Poster; 10% off shop purchases.

CRAVEN ARMS — Clun Local History Museum

Clun Town Hall, Clun, Craven Arms, Shropshire. 05884-576. Open: Tue/Sat 2-5, B.H. Weekends Sat & Mon 10-1.

Over 2000 flint artefacts, tools and weapons made of the local picrite, plus some roman and medieval pieces, with domestic and agricultural items from the 18th and 19th centuries.

CRAVEN ARMS — Stokesay Castle

Craven Arms, Shropshire. 0588-672544. Open: Mar/Oct 10-4.30 (Wed-Mon), Apr-Sept 10-5.30, Nov Sat/Sun 10-dusk. Closed: Dec-Feb. £ P (EH).

This was a large fortified manor house, built in the late 13th century and with a 17th century gatehouse, but well preserved and little altered. The great hall is in superb condition, and there is a fine timber fire-surround in the solar.

DAVENTRY — Daventry Museum

Market Square, Daventry, Northants NN11 4BH. 0327-300277. Open: Apr-Sept Mon-Sat 10-5, Oct-Mar Tue-Sat 10-3.30. P

Natural and social history displays, with an exhaustive series of temporary art exhibitions and demonstrations throughout the year, and a medieval settlement from 17 Nov-15 Dec.

PASSPORT CONCESSIONS: OPPS.

JNR. PASSPORT CONCESSIONS: Free Museum bag.

DROITWICH — Droitwich Heritage Centre

St. Richard's House, Victoria Square, Droitwich Spa, Worcestershire WR9 8RF. 0905-774312. Open: Mon-Fri 10-5, Sat 10-4. P &

It took Droitwich 2,000 years to move from becoming a salt town of the Iron Age to a luxury spa, and this museum tells what happened. Temporary exhibitions in 1990 vary from the famous Body in the Bog excavation to the 21st anniversary of the Apollo moon mission.

PASSPORT CONCESSIONS: Free Poster.

JNR. PASSPORT CONCESSIONS: Free Badge.

DROITWICH — Hanbury Hall

Hanbury Hall, Hanbury, Nr. Droitwich, Worcs WR9 7EA. 0527-84214. Open: Apr/Oct Daily 2-5, May-Sept Wed-Fri 2-6. Closed: Nov-Mar. £ P &

Wren style house of 1701 with Thornhill painted ceilings and staircase. Furnished in keeping, and has the Watney porcelain collection. National Trust-owned, with events throughout the summer season.

PASSPORT CONCESSIONS: 50% off adult admission charge.

DUDLEY — The Black Country Museum

Tipton Road, Dudley, West Midlands DY1 4SO. 021-557 9643. Open: Daily 10-5. £ P &

This is an open air museum where a village has been created from buildings rescued and brought together here to show some of the facts of Black Country life in its most successful decades when, paradoxically, existence for the ordinary working man and his family was never harsher.

PASSPORT CONCESSIONS: £1 off admission charge.

JNR. PASSPORT CONCESSIONS: Free Badge.

DUDLEY

Dudley Museum & Art Gallery

St. James's Road, Dudley. 0384-456000. Open: Mon-Sat 10-5.

This has a definitive collection of fossils from the local limestone and coal measures, the Brooke Robinson collection of 18th and 19th century European paintings, ceramics, furniture and temporary exhibitions all year.

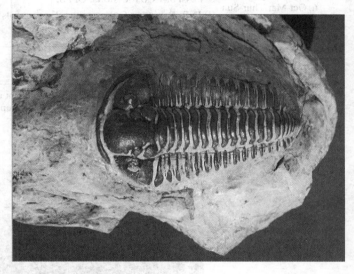

ECCLESHALL

Mill Meece Pumping Station Preservation Trust

Cotes Heath, Nr. Eccleshall, Staffs. 0270-873683. Open: Sat/Sun 11-5. £ P

This is a 1914 water pumping station restored to working order, with steaming weekends once a month from May to September.

PASSPORT CONCESSIONS: Free Guidebook.

JNR. PASSPORT CONCESSIONS: Free Badge; Free Pencil.

ELVASTON

Elvaston Castle Working Estate Museum

Borrowash Lane, Elvaston, Derbys. 0332-57134. Open: Apr-Oct Wed-Sun. £

This attempts to recreate life on the Elvaston Estate as it was in 1910, with original craft workshops showing how the estate depended on self-sufficiency.

HALESOWEN

Halesowen Abbey

Halesowen, nr Birmingham. Open: 2 Jun-1 Sept Sat/Sun/ B.H. 10-6. Closed: Winter. £ (EH)

The abbey was founded by King John in the year of Magna Carta, 1215. It is one of English Heritage's latest sites, and parts of the church can be seen as well as the monks' infirmary

HEDNESFORD — Valley Heritage Centre

Valley Road, Hednesford, Staffs WS12 5QX. 05438-77666. Open: Apr-Sept Wed-Sun 11-6, Oct-Mar Thur-Sun 11-4. P &

This is a former mining site in the Hednesford Hills with a blacksmith woodturner, glass engraver and furniture restorer as well as an events arena.

PASSPORT CONCESSIONS: OPPS.

JNR. PASSPORT CONCESSIONS: Free schools information pack.

HEREFORD — The Broomy Hill Engines at Herefordshire Waterworks Museum

Broomy Hill Pumping Station, Hereford HR4 OLF. 0432-273635. Open: Call for details. £ P &

A mid-Victorian waterworks pumping plant and its artefacts on the River Wye, with steam up on fixed spring and Summer weekends.

PASSPORT CONCESSIONS: 50% off adult admission charge; OPPS.

HEREFORD — Churchill Gardens Museum and Hatton Gallery

Venns Lane, Aylestone Hill, Hereford. 0432-268121. Open: Tue-Sun afternoons in Summer, Tue-Sat Winter. £

Furniture, costume and paintings from the 18th and 19th centuries, plus a Victorian nursery, parlor and butler's pantry. The Hatton Gallery is dedicated to Brian Hatton, the local artist killed in the First World War.

PASSPORT CONCESSIONS: 50% off adult admission charge.

HEREFORD — Hereford Cathedral

St John St, Hereford. 0432-56250. Open: Library Summer 10-12.30/2-4; Winter 11-11.30/3-3.30; Treasury Summer 10.30-12.30/2-4, Winter 10.45-11.15/2.45-3.15 .£

The cathedral has the world's largest chained library, treasures displayed in the crypt and, when its new mounting is made, the Mappa Mundi back home and on show.

HEREFORD — Hereford Cider Museum Trust

Pomona Place, Whitecross Road, Hereford. 0432-354207. Open: Easter-Oct Daily 10.30-5.30, Nov-Mar Mon-Sat 1-5. £ P

The museum in this working cider brandy distillery has a massive 17th century French beam press, an old farm cider house, 1920s hydraulic presses, original champagne cider cellars and an off-licence.

PASSPORT CONCESSIONS: Party rates to Passport holder.

JNR. PASSPORT CONCESSIONS: Free entry to Junior Passport holder.

HEREFORD — Hereford City Museum and Art Gallery

Broad St, Hereford HR4 9AU. 0432-268121. Open: Tue-Sat 10-5 Summer, 10-4 Winter. &

Archaeology, natural and local history, plus 19th century watercolours and local artists' work.

HEREFORD — The Old House

Hightown, Hereford. 0432-268121. Open: Mon morning only, Tue-Sat 10-5.30 Summer, 10-1 Winter. £

Jacobean house of 1621, originally part of Butcher's Row furnished on three floors to the period, with a kitchen, hall and bedrooms.

PASSPORT CONCESSIONS: 50% off adult admission charge.

HEREFORD — Piano Museum

Royal National College for the Blind, College Rd, Hereford HR1 1EB. 0432-265725. Open: Term time Mon-Fri 9-5, or by appointment. P &

The early and modern keyboard instruments used in the tuning department of the Royal National College for the Blind and for recitals include a clavichord, harpsichord, square pianos and grand pianos.

PASSPORT CONCESSIONS: OPPS. Behind the scenes tour.

HEREFORD — St. John and Coningsby Medieval Museum

Widemarsh St, Hereford. 0432-272837. Open: Easter-Sept Tue-Thur/Sat/Sun 2-5, or by arrangement. Closed: Oct-Easter. £ P

This was a hospice and chapel of the Knights of St. John, and it has tableaux illustrating the life of the pensioners who lived there, descriptions of the Crusades and material about a local girl, Nell Gwynn.

PASSPORT CONCESSIONS: Free entry to Passport holder.

JNR. PASSPORT CONCESSIONS: Free entry to Junior Passport holder.

ILKESTON — Erewash Museum

High Street, Off East Street, Ilkeston, Derby. 0602-440440. Open: Thur/Fri 10-12/1-4, + Apr-Oct Sat 10-12/1-4. Or by appt.

This local museum is housed in a Georgian and Victorian lace manufacturer's house.

KENILWORTH — Kenilworth Castle

Kenilworth, Warwickshire. 0926-52078. Open: Daily 10-6 Summer, 10-4 Winter (excl. Mon). £ P (EH)

This was the home Robert Dudley, Earl of Leicester, where Queen Elizabeth visited him and where Sir Walter Scott set the dramatic event surrounding the death of Leicester's wife, Amy Robsart, in his novel. It is one of the finest castles in Britain with remains dating from the 12th to the 16th centuries, a keep and great hall behind the gatehouse, and a good exhibition about the castle's past.

KIDDERMINSTER — Hereford & Worcester County Museum

Hartlebury Castle, Hartlebury, Nr. Kidderminster, Worcestershire DY11 7XZ. 0299-250416. Open: Mon-Fri 2-5, Sun 2-6. Closed: Dec-Feb. £ P

This is in part of Hartlebury Castle, "the fayre maner place"' where the county museum follows the lives of former Hereford and Worcester people, and has a collection of toys, costume, domestic life, room settings and horse-drawn vehicles.

PASSPORT CONCESSIONS: Free entry to Passport holder; Free Guidebook; Special rate family entrance ticket; Free entry to under 18's.

JNR. PASSPORT CONCESSIONS: Free entry to Junior Passport holder; Free Badge; Free Museum bag.

KINGSWINFORD — Broadfield House Glass Museum

Barnett Lane,
Kingswinford
DY6 9QA.
0384- 273011. Open:
Tue-Fri 2-5, Sat 10-
1/2-5, Sun 2-5.   P

This is the only museum to specialise in 19th and 20th century glass, and its collections are getting an international reputation; cameos, rock crystal, engraving, etching and a wide range of coloured glass plus glassmaking studios are all included.

PASSPORT CONCESSIONS: Reduction of 10% on shop purchases.

LEAMINGTON SPA — Leamington Spa Art Gallery & Museum

Avenue Road, Royal
Leamington Spa,
Warwickshire
CV31 3PP. 0926-
426559. Open: Mon-
Sat 10-1/2-5, Thur 6-
8. Re-opening 4 July
1990. &

There are permanent collections of Dutch and Flemish Old Masters, 19th and 20th century British artists and local artists represented, with a new local history gallery due to open, but not until July 1990.

PASSPORT CONCESSIONS: OPPS.

LEEK — The Brindley Mill & James Brindley Museum

Mill Street, Leek,
Staffs. 0538-381446.
Open: Easter-
Jun/Sept/Oct Sat 2-5,
Jul/Aug Sat-Wed 2-5.
Closed: Nov-Easter. £

The great 18th century canal builder and engineer James Brindley designed the water-powered cornmill, which is truly operational, and the museum is a centre for information about his life and work.

LEOMINSTER — Mortimers Cross

Leominster,
Herefordshire. Open:
1 Apr-30 Sept
Thur/Sun/B.H. 2-6.
Closed: Winter. £
(EH)

This mill was built in the 18th century and was still in use in the 1940s. The outer housing is sandstone, and the mechanism, which could be worked by one man, is on three floors and still in working order.

LICHFIELD — Wall Roman Site

Watling Street,
Letocetum, Nr.
Lichfield, Staffs.
0543-480768. Open:
Daily 10-6 Summer,
10-4 Winter (excl.
Mon). £ P & (EH)

This was a roadside settlement beside Watling Street and there are the remains of the public baths and lodging house and a museum of finds.

LICHFIELD — Lichfield Heritage Exhibition & Treasury

St. Mary's Centre, Market Square, Lichfield. 6543-256611. Open: Mon-Sat 10-5, Sun 10.30-5. £ &

In St. Mary's Church, in part of which worship still takes place, the exhibition traces Lichfield's 2,000 year history and the treasure is the civic silver.

LICHFIELD — Samuel Johnson Birthplace Museum

Breadmarket Street, Lichfield, Staffs WS13 6LG. 0543-256611. Open: Daily 10-5. £

Recreated rooms with paintings, furniture, books and personal items about the life and work of the lexicographer and wit.

PASSPORT CONCESSIONS: 50% off adult admission charge

LICHFIELD — The Staffordshire Regiment Museum

Whittington Barracks, Lichfield, Staffs WS14 9PY. 0543-433333. Open: Mon-Fri 9-4.30, Sat/Sun by appointment only. Closed: 2 weeks over Xmas. P

The regiment is the result of the 1959 amalgamation of the North and South Staffs Regiments, descended from the old numbered foot regiments, the first being raised here in 1705. So there are uniforms, relics, medals and memories going back 300 years, with a giant diorama (it has over 1,000 figures) of a battle in the Zulu War, a 1915 army biscuit and the prayer book which stopped an enemy bullet.

LONGTON — Gladstone Pottery Museum

Uttoxeter Road, Longton, Stoke-on-Trent. 0782-319232. Open: Mon-Sat 10-5, Sun 2-5. Closed: Mons Nov-Feb. £ P &

This is in a unique Victorian 'potbank' which has bottle ovens, a cobbled yard and a steam engine, with demonstrations of traditional skills in the original workshops.

PASSPORT CONCESSIONS: Free Guidebook.

LUDLOW — Dinham House Exhibition & Craft.

Dinham House, Ludlow, Salop SY8 1EH. 0584-874240. Open: Daily 10-5. £ P

The 18th century town house is now a museum with historical displays, fossils, period furnishing, permanent and changing exhibitions of arts and craftsmen at work.

PASSPORT CONCESSIONS: 50% off adult admission charge.

LUDLOW — Ludlow Museum

The Butter Cross, Broad Street, Ludlow, Shropshire. 0584-873857. Open: Mon-Sat 10.30-1/2-5, Sun Jun-Aug 10.30-1/2-5. Closed: Oct-Mar. £

This museum is more than 150 years old and is devoted to the history of Ludlow with geology, natural history and two Victorian room displays.

LUTTERWORTH — Percy Pilcher Flying Machine Exhibition

Stanford Hall, Lutterworth, Leicestershire LE17 6DH. 0788- 860250. Open: Sat/Sun 2.30-6, Thur (July & Aug only) 2.30-6, 12-6, B.H. & Tue following 12-6. Closed: Oct-Easter. £ P &

Stanford is mentioned in Domesday, but this house was built in the 1690s. It's still occupied by the Cave family after more than 550 years and contains antique furniture, good pictures and family costumes. In the grounds is the flying machine display named after Lt. Percy Pilcher RN who flew The Hawk, built in 1898, here and was killed at Stanford in 1899 in a flying accident. There is a full-size replica of The Hawk.

Whilst airborne during his 1st flight.

LUTTERWORTH — Stanford Hall Motorcycle Museum

Stanford Hall, Lutterworth, Leicestershire 0788-860250. Open: Sat/Sun 2.30-6, Thur Jul/Aug 2.30-6, B.H. & following Tue 12 - 6. Closed: Oct-Easter. £ P &

Also in the grounds of the Cave family seat, this collection includes historic and unique motorcycles, like George Brough's Brough Superior, all in running order, with some bikes, three cycle-cars and Henry Laird's yellow Morgan three-wheeler.

MALVERN — Malvern Museum

The Abbey Gateway, Abbey Road, Malvern, Worcs WR14 3ES. 0684-567811. Open: Easter-Oct Daily 10.30-5, (excl Wed in Term time). Closed: Nov-Mar. £

This museum, in a medieval gatehouse, tells of the famous hills, the water cure their springs are supposed to provide, the growth of the Victorian town and its life during the two world wars and since.

PASSPORT CONCESSIONS: Free entry to Passport holder.

JNR. PASSPORT CONCESSIONS: Free entry to Junior Passport holder.

MILFORD — Shugborough Park Farm

Shugborough, Millford, Nr. Stafford ST17 0XB. 0889-881388. Open: Daily 11-5 Summer, Mon-Fri 11-4 Winter. Closed: Jan-Mar (Booked parties only). £ P ♿

This is about working life on a Georgian Estate Farm, with demonstrations of the buildings, of working with the livestock, the equipment and the skills of 150 years of Staffordshire farming.

PASSPORT CONCESSIONS: Admission at party rate for holders.

MILFORD — Staffordshire County Museum

Shugborough, Milford, Nr. Stafford ST17 0XB. 0889-881388. Open: Daily 11-5 Summer, 11-4 Winter. Closed: Jan-Mar (Booked parties only) £ P ♿

This is in the servants quarters of Shugborough Hall, with rooms recreated to show the daily life of working people in the late 19th and early 20th centuries.

PASSPORT CONCESSIONS: Admission at party rate for holders.

MORETON MORRELL — Warwickshire Museum of Rural Life

Warwickshire College of Agriculture, Moreton Hall, Moreton Morrell, Warks. 0926-651367. Open: By appt. P

Part of the Warwickshire College of Agriculture, this is a display of farming implements, cared for by the county museum in Warwick.

Priceless artefacts,

from The Times.

The Times Museums' Passports are invaluable, yet cost nothing. Exclusive to readers of *The Times*, they are essential companions to this excellent Guide.

Free or reduced entry to hundreds of museums and galleries, plus special offers like free posters and discounts in museum shops, are just a few of the privileges you will enjoy.

For your free Passports to the past, simply fill in the special coupon, only in *The Times* on Saturdays.

MUCH WENLOCK Wenlock Priory

Much Wenlock, Shropshire. 0952-727466. Open: Daily 10-6 Summer, 10-4 Winter (excl. Mon). £ P (EH)

This was a large Cluniac priory, and there is an early 13th century church and Norman chapter house.

NEWCASTLE UNDER LYME Borough Museum & Art Gallery

Brampton Park, Newcastle Under Lyme, Staffs ST5 0QP. 0782- 619705. Open: Mon-Sat 9.30-1/2-6, Sun 2-5.30. P

A natural history garden and an aviary have been added to the collections of ceramics, militaria, clocks, textiles and a Victorian street scene in this museum. There are temporary exhibitions of contemporary art and sculpture, there will also be celebrations of the borough's charter awarded 400 years ago.

NEWPORT Lilleshall Abbey

Newport, Shropshire. 0952-604431. Open: 10-6 Daily in Summer. Closed: Winter. £ P &. (EH)

Augustinian canons built this evocative abbey in the 12th & 13th centuries. There are cloister buildings surviving, and a church with an aisleless nave.

NUNEATON — Nuneaton Museum & Art Gallery

Riversley Park, Nuneaton, Warwickshire CV11 5TU. 0203-376473. Call for info.

This museum collects geology, archaeology, ethnography, social history, fine and decorative arts, and particularly the personalia of the novelist George Eliot. But it is closed for major development and refurbishment work until autumn 1990.

RIPLEY — Midland Railway Centre

Butterley Station, Ripley, Derbyshire DE5 3TL. 0773-570140. Open July-Sept Mon-Fri 11.30-4.15, Apr-Oct Sat/Sun 11.30-4.15. £ P &

Building is due to be completed and the museum fully open this year giving more space to see the display of locomotives and rolling stock.

PASSPORT CONCESSIONS: 50% off adult admission charge.

ROSS ON WYE — Goodrich Castle

Goodrich, Ross on Wye, Herefordshire. 0600-890538. Open: Daily 10-6 in Summer, Tue-Sun 10-4 in Winter. £ (EH)

This castle, with a 12th century keep and additions from the 13th and 14th century was built into the red sandstone from which it watches over the River Wye.

RUGELEY — Puppet Theatre Museum

Edinburgh House, Bagot Street, Abbots Bromley, Rugeley, Staffs WS15 3DA. Open: Sun 2-6. £

This is the only museum in the country entirely devoted to puppets and puppet theatre, with at least 250 figures representing all types of puppets dating from 1850 and always on display.

SHIFNAL — Aerospace Museum

Cosford, Shifnal, Shrops TE11 8UP. 090722-4872. Open: Daily Mar-Oct 10-5, Nov-Feb 10-4. £ P

More than 60 British, American, German and Japanese designed aircraft in their hangars, plus the British Airways Exhibition Hall for temporary displays - Battle of Britain photographs February to May - and collection of historic airliners.

PASSPORT CONCESSIONS: Reduction of 10% on shop purchases.

JNR. PASSPORT CONCESSIONS: Free Badge.

SHREWSBURY — Haughmond Abbey

Upton Magna, Offington, Shrewsbury. 074377-661. Open: Daily 10-6 Summer, 10-4 Winter excl. Mon. £ (EH)

The church of this Augustinian Abbey, built in about 1135, was demolished in the Dissolution in 1539, but the abbot's lodge, the great hall and the kitchens which were turned into a mansion have survived. The exhibition about the place includes some splendid medieval sculpture.

SHREWSBURY — Rowley's House Museum

Barker St, Shrewsbury. 0952-61196. Open: Mon-Sat 10-5, Sun (Easter-Sept) 12-5. £ &

The town's main museum, with archaeology, geology and costume displays, is now housed in a 17th century timber-framed building.

PASSPORT CONCESSIONS: Free entry to holders; Free Poster.

SHREWSBURY — The Shropshire Regimental Museum

The Castle, Shrewsbury, Shropshire SY1 2AT. 0743-58516. Open: Mon-Sat 10-5, Sun (Easter-Oct) 10-5. £

Among the prizes here are an American flag captured when the White House was burned, a lock of Napoleon's hair and the baton of Grand Admiral Doenitz, the last fuhrer, but it is the museum of the King's Shropshire Light Infantry, the Shropshire Yeomanry Cavalry and the Shropshire Royal Horse Artillery, all housed in Shrewsbury Castle, 900 years old and last fought from in the Civil War.

PASSPORT CONCESSIONS: Free entry to Passport holder; Free Poster; Free Guidebook.

JNR. PASSPORT CONCESSIONS: Free entry to Junior Passport holder.

SIDBURY — Commandery Civil War Centre

Sidbury, Worcester WR1 2HU. 0905-355071. Open: Mon-Sat 10.30-5, Sun 2-5. £

Formerly a medieval hospital, the building was the home of the Wylde Family, hosts to Charles II who held a council of war here before the Battle of Worcester. Now you can join in. Civil War Festival July 9-13.

PASSPORT CONCESSIONS: 50% off adult admission charge.

SMETHWICK — Avery Historical Museum

Foundry Lane, Smethwick, Warley 021-5581112. Open: Mon-Fri 9-4 by appt. only. P

Weighed in the balance and not found wanting in scales, balances, weights, trade catalogues, records, even art and literature illustrating the history of weighing - but only open by appointment.

STAFFORD — Ancient High House

Greengate Street, Stafford, Staffs. 0785-40204. Open: Mon-Fri 9-5, Sat 10-3. £

John Dorrington, an Elizabethan wool merchant, built the house in 1595 and it has just been restored to its Tudor splendour. Now it houses a permanent collection of furniture, paintings, costume and pottery in period room settings, and there are changing exhibitions too.

PASSPORT CONCESSIONS: 50% off adult admission charge; Free Guidebook; Special rate family entrance ticket; OPPS.

JNR. PASSPORT CONCESSIONS: Free Badge; Info on Junior heritage Club.

STAFFORD — Regimental Museum of 16th/5th The Queen's Royal Lancers and the Staffordshire Yeomanry.

Kitchener House, Lammascote Rd, Stafford. 0785-45840. Open: Mon-Fri 9.30-1/2-4.30. P ♿

Medals, uniforms, pictures, models, weapons, photographs.

STOKE-ON-TRENT — Chatterley Whitfield Mining Museum

Tunstall, Stoke-on-Trent, Staffs ST6 8UN. 0782-813337. Open: Daily 10-4 incl. B.H. £ P

Now housing the national mining collection allocated by British Coal in 1989, ex-miners guide visitors who can ride the cage underground and travel on the subterranean locomotive. Exhibitions, related and unrelated to mining, through the year.

PASSPORT CONCESSIONS: Free Poster; Special rate family entrance ticket; Study facilities and guided tours can be arranged if pre-booked; Video films available at living history plays.

STOKE-ON-TRENT

City Museum & Art Gallery

Bethesda Street, Hanley, Stoke-on-Trent. 0782-202173. Open: Mon-Sat 10.30-5, Sun 2-5. &

This award winner covers fine and decorative art, natural history, archaeology, social history and has a ceramics collection of international standing.

JNR. PASSPORT CONCESSIONS: Free Pencil.

STOKE-ON-TRENT

Etruria Industrial Museum

Lower Beford Street, Etruria, Stoke-on-Trent. 0782-287557. Open: Wed-Sun 10-4. P

The latest manifestation of Jesse Shirley's Etruscan Bone and Flint Mill, the last steam-powered potters' mill in Britain, is as part of a museum, at Etruria Lock, with canalside buildings, which will open officially in the Summer of 1990.

JNR. PASSPORT CONCESSIONS: Free Pencil.

STOKE-ON-TRENT

Ford Green Hall

Ford Green Road, Smallthorne, Stoke-on-Trent. 0782-534771. Open: Daily 1-5.

A collection of furniture and household items in period settings are to be found inside the half-timbered Tudor farmhouse with its 18th century brick wings.

JNR. PASSPORT CONCESSIONS: Free Pen.

STOKE-ON-TRENT

Spode

Church Street, Stoke-on-Trent ST4 1BX. 0782-744011. Open: Mon-Thur 9-5, Fri 9-4, Sat 9-1. £ P

The Spode factory was founded in 1770, and the museum which is now in it has examples of the earliest pottery, the later bone china and the figures popular in the late 19th and early 20th century.

STRATFORD-UPON-AVON

Stratford-Upon-Avon Motor Museum

1 Shakespeare St. 0789-69413. Open: Easter-Sept Daily 9.30-6, Oct-Easter 10-4. £ &

Elegant Rolls Royces, exotic Bugattis, exciting Lagondas and excessive Bentleys are here, in an exuberant 1920s setting.

STRATFORD-UPON-AVON

Royal Shakespeare Company Collection

RSC Theatre, Waterside, Stratford-Upon-Avon, Warwickshire CV37 6BB. 0789-296655. Open: Mon-Sat 9.15-8, Sun 12-5 (Nov-Mar 11-4). £ P &

Permanent exhibition on the changing of staging from the Middle Ages to now, with a theatre exhibition of costumes, props, photographs and paintings from the RSC collection.

PASSPORT CONCESSIONS: Free entry to Passport holder

JNR. PASSPORT CONCESSIONS: Free entry to Junior Passport holder.

SUDBURY

Museum of Childhood & Sudbury Hall

Sudbury, Derbyshire DE6 5HT. 028-378305. Open: Apr-Oct Wed-Sun 1-5.30, B.H. Closed: Nov-Mar. £ P &

This not only studies childhood through the ages but compares the lifestyles of rich and poor children. There is also a collection of 20th century studio ceramics to see.

PASSPORT CONCESSIONS: Free entry to Passport holder.

JNR. PASSPORT CONCESSIONS: Free entry to Junior Passport holder.

TELFORD

Buildwas Abbey

Iron Bridge, Telford, Shrops. 095245-3274. Open: Daily 10-6 Summer, 10-4 Winter excl. Mon. £ P & (EH)

This was founded by the Cistercians in 1135, and the church is almost complete except for its roof.

TELFORD — Ironbridge Gorge Museum

Ironbridge, Telford, Shropshire TF8 7AW. 0952-453522. Open: Daily 10-6 Summer, 10-5 Winter. Only a few sites close Nov-Jan.   P ♿

A series of museums at the point where the Industrial Revolution started, the latest being the Museum of the River. New elements for 1990 are the Victorian estate office, and school at Blists Hill and the development of the Jackfield Tile Museum. Times Shell Museums Year Award winner 1989.

PASSPORT CONCESSIONS: Reduction of 5% on shop purchases.

JNR. PASSPORT CONCESSIONS: 50p off the price of a normal child passport.

WALSALL — Walsall Leather Centre Museum

Wisemore, Walsall WS2 8EQ. 0922-721153. Open: Tue-Sat 10-5, Sun 12-5, Nov-Mar closes at 4.   P ♿

A unique working museum in the centre of Britain's leather goods trade, with new gallery, made in Walsall, opening in the spring. Regular demonstrations.

WARWICK — St. Johns House

St. Johns, Warwick CV34 4NF. 0926-412132. Open: Tue-Sat 10-12.30/1.30-5.30, Sun (May-Sept) 2.30-5.   P

This is a Jacobean mansion house containing costume and social history displays and period rooms. A branch of Warwick Museum, it has interesting long-term temporary exhibitions planned for 1990, including one on women's life in World War Two, another on weights, measures and packaging, another is a multi-cultural look at games, and there is to be a selection from the Warwickshire Museum collections.

PASSPORT CONCESSIONS: Reduction of 10% on shop purchase valued at £1 or more.

JNR. PASSPORT CONCESSIONS: Reduction of 10% on shop purchases valued at £1 or more.

WARWICK — Warwick Doll Museum

Oken's House, Castle Street, Warwick CV34 4BP. 0926-495546. Open: Mon-Sat 10-5, Sun 2-5. Closed: Oct-Easter. £

This is the permanent exhibition of the Joy Robinson Collection run by Warwickshire Museum, which includes wood, bisque and wax dolls from 1800 onwards, and there are games, toys and automata on display as well.

PASSPORT CONCESSIONS: Adult admission charge reduced to 50p children to 30p. Reduction of 10% on shop purchases valued at £1 or more.

JNR. PASSPORT CONCESSIONS: Reduction of 10% on shop purchases valued at £1 or more.

WARWICK — Warwickshire Museum

Market Hall, Market Place, Warwick CV34 4SA. 0926-412500. Open: Mon-Sat 10-5.30, Sun (May-Sept) 2.30-5. ⅙

The county museum is in the county town's 17th century market hall and has displays of archaeology, geology and natural history, and includes the giant plesiosaur fossil and the medieval Sheldon Tapestry Map. There is also a busy schedule of temporary exhibitions.

PASSPORT CONCESSIONS: Reduction of 10% on shop purchases when £1 or more is spent.

JNR. PASSPORT CONCESSIONS: 10% off shop purchases valued at £1 or more.

WARWICK — The Warwickshire Yeomanry Regimental Museum

The Court House Vaults, Jury Street, Warwick CV34 4EW. 0926- 492212. Open: Easter-Sept Fri/Sat/Sun 10-1/2-4.

A small regimental museum covering the last 200 years with medals, uniforms, weapons and photographers

WOLVERHAMPTON — Bantock House Museum

Bantock Park, Wolverhampton WV3 9LQ. 0902-312132. Open: Mon-Fri 10-7, Sat 10-5, Sun 2-5. P ⅙

There is a new display of japanned ware in this 18th century farmhouse museum, which also has displays of other decorative arts and of local history.

WOLVERHAMPTON — Bilston Art Gallery and Museum

Mount Pleasant,
Bilston,
Wolverhampton.
0902-312032. Open:
Daily 10-5.30. &

The area's applied art industries are celebrated here, through 18th century enamels, japanning and ironstone ware.

WOLVERHAMPTON — Wolverhampton Art Gallery and Museum

Lichfield St,
Wolverhampton.
0902-312032. Open:
Mon-Sat/B.H. 10-6.
£ &

There is a collection of paintings here ranging from Gainsborough to Duncan Grant, and some oriental applied art.

WORCESTER — Worcester City Museum & Art Gallery

Foregate Street,
Worcester WR1 1DT.
0905-25371. Open:
Mon-Fri (excl.Thur)
9.30-6, Sat 9.30-5

The museum traces Worcester's history since Roman times, and has a reconstructed Victorian chemist's shop. The art gallery has a new watercolour gallery opening in May 1990, and there is a programme of regularly changing exhibitions.

JNR PASSPORT CONCESSIONS: Free balloon to under-5's.

WORCESTER — Tudor House Museum

Friar Street,
Worcester.
0905-20904. Open:
Daily 10.30-5.
Closed: Thur & Sun.

Worcester social history is told in open displays and period room settings here, with dolls and toys, an Edwardian bathroom and a Victorian kitchen. The principal theme for most of 1990, though, will be "Worcester At War", celebrating the 50th anniversary of the Battle of Britain.

PASSPORT CONCESSIONS: Reduction of 10% on shop purchases.

JNR. PASSPORT CONCESSIONS: Free Toy.

WROXETER — Wroxeter Roman City

Wroxeter, Nr.
Shrewsbury,
Shropshire. 074375-
330. Open: Daily 10-
6 Summer, 10-4
Winter excl. Mon. £ P
& (EH)

This was the Roman city of Virconium, and archaeologists have excavated its civic centre uncovering the 2nd century AD municipal baths. There is a museum about the place and the earlier legionary fortress.

EAST
MIDLANDS/
EAST ENGLIA

ALFORD

Alford Manor House Folk Museum

West Street, Alford, Lincolnshire. 05212-6385. Open: Mon-Fri 10.30-1/2-4. Closed: Nov-Apr. £ P

Craftsmen's tools, domestic knick-knacks, clothes, a schoolroom, local archaeology and Captain John Smith in a 16th century thatched manor house.

ASHBY DE LA ZOUCH

Ashby De La Zouch

South Street, Ashby De La Zouch. 0530-413343. Open: Daily 10-6 Summer, Tue-Sun 10-4 Winter. £ P (EH)

Edward IV's chamberlain, Lord Hastings, who was executed by Richard III, built the castle around an earlier manor house.

BLICKLING

Blickling Hall

Blickling, Norwich NR11 6NF. 0263-733084. Open: Apr-Oct. Tue/Wed/Fri -Sun 1-5 Closed: Nov -Mar, B.H. Mons. £

State rooms, tapestries, and fine furniture in this 17th century red brick house, with gardens and parkland outside, owned by the National Trust.

BOSTON

Boston Guildhall Museum

South Street, Boston, Lincolnshire PE21 6HT. 0205-65954. Open: Mon-Sat 10-5, Sun Apr-Sept only 1.30-5. £

Built in 1450 as the hall of St. Mary's Guild and later the town hall, it is now the borough museum, with the cells and courtroom where the Pilgrim Fathers were imprisoned and tried in 1607. There is a programme of temporary exhibitions.

BOSTON

Sibsey Trader Windmill

Sibsey, Boston, Lincs.
0205-750036. Open:
Daily 10-6 Summer.
Closed: Winter. £ P
(EH)

This was built in about 1877 with a brick-built tower and six sails. Its machinery is still intact. There is an exhibition about the work it did, and still does on its occasional milling days.

BURGH LE MARSH

Lincolnshire Railway Museum

Station Yard, Burgh
Le Marsh, Nr
Skegness, Lincolnshire
PE24 5EZ. 075485-
347. Open: Mar/Nov
Sun 2-4.30, Apr/Jun-
Aug Sun-Fri 11-5,
May/ Sept Sun-Thur
11-5, Oct Sun-Wed +
School hols 11-5, Dec
Suns 2-4 excl
Christmas. £ P &

Large and small exhibits, operational equipment and models, with a scenic $10^1/_4$ inch gauge passenger railway.

PASSPORT CONCESSIONS: 50p off adult admission.

JNR PASSPORT CONCESSIONS: Free Badge.

BURY ST. EDMUNDS

The Clock Museum

8 Angel Hill, Bury St.
Edmunds, Suffolk
IP33 1UZ.
0284-757063. Open:
Mon-Sat 10-5,
Sun 2-5.

Within this elegant Queen Anne house is one of the finest collections of time measuring instruments in the country, with early German and English clocks, watches, sundials and turret clocks.

PASSPORT CONCESSIONS: OPPS.

JNR. PASSPORT CONCESSIONS: Free attendance at talks and events; see local press for details.

BURY ST. EDMUNDS

Ilkworth House & Garden

The Rotunda,
Horringer.
0284-48270. Open:
Mar/Apr/Oct Sat/Sun.
House: May-Sept
Tue/Wed/Fri-Sun
1.30-5.30. £ P &

This is a spectacular house with an eliptical rotunda and curved wings, in which there are important collections of painting and silver. Outside are formal gardens, woodland and park walks.

PASSPORT CONCESSIONS: One child free for each paying adult.

BURY ST. EDMUNDS

Moyse's Hall Museum

Cornhill, Bury St. Edmunds, Suffolk. 0284-757063. Open: Mon-Sat 10-5, Sun 2-5.

Relics of the notorious and gruesome 19th century "Red Barn Murder" are to be found here in the oldest secular building in East Anglia, along with the largest Bronze Age hoard in Europe.

PASSPORT CONCESSIONS: OPPS.

JNR. PASSPORT CONCESSIONS: Free attendance at talks and other events - See local press for details.

CADEBY

Cadeby Steam & Brass Rubbing Centre

The Old Rectory, Cadeby, Nuneaton. 0455-290462. Open: 2nd Sat of every month, or by appt. P

Pixie, a Bagnall 0-4-0 loco, rides a narrow gauge steam railway, a large GWR model railway operates on a 1935 timetable and there are over 70 facsimiles in the brass rubbing centre.

CAMBRIDGE

Cambridge & County Folk Museum

2/3 Castle Street, Cambridge. 0223-355159. Open: Mon-Sat 10.30-5, Sun 2-5. £

Established in the mid-1930s, the museum has household and trade artefacts with folklore items, all of which are arranged to illustrate the lives of the Cambridgeshire folk from the 17th century onwards.

PASSPORT CONCESSIONS: Free Guidebook.

JNR. PASSPORT CONCESSIONS: Free Pencil.

CAMBRIDGE

Cambridge Museum of Technology

Riverside, Cambridge CB5 8HN. 0223-68650. Open: 1st Sun of every month 2-5 & steam weekends. £

This is in a Victorian pumping station with original gas, steam and electric powered pumps, plus other examples of local industry, like letterpress printing.

PASSPORT CONCESSIONS: 50% off adult admission charge.

JNR. PASSPORT CONCESSIONS: Free Badge.

CAMBRIDGE Fitzwilliam Museum

Trumpington Street, Cambridge CB2 1RB. 0223-332900. Open: Tue-Sat 10-5, Sun 2.15-5. Closed: 10 days over Xmas and May Day B.H. ♿

With collections of international importance, this is the art museum of the university with European paintings, antiquities, ceramics, sculpture, manuscripts and miniatures, all in the permanent displays, and a dizzying array of temporary exhibitions.

PASSPORT CONCESSIONS: Reduction of £1 off "Treasures of the Fitzwilliam"; 50% off guided tour charge.

CAMBRIDGE Sedgwick Museum of Geology

Department of Earth Sciences, University of Cambridge, Downing Street, Cambridge CB2 3EQ. 0223-333437. Mon-Sat 10-1. Closed: Xmas & Easter.

Part of the university's department of earth sciences, with spectacular specimens at close quarters such as dinosaurs, sea dragons and fish. New permanent galleries, including one about the world's largest spider, due to open in 1990.

CAMBRIDGE Univeristy Museum of Zoology

Downing Street, Cambridge CB2 3EJ. 0223-336650. Open: Mon-Fri 2.15-4.45. Closed: 1 week at Christmas & Easter.

Marine life, exotic birds, insects, mammal skeletons and fossils on spectacular display in this university teaching collection.

CAMBRIDGE Whipple Museum of the History of Science

Free School Lane, Cambridge CB2 3RH. 0223-334540. Open: Mon-Fri 2-4.

Scientific instruments from the Renaissance to now, with a regular programme of special exhibitions.

COLMWORTH — Bushmead Priory

Colmworth, Bedfordshire. 023062-614. Open: Sat/Sun 10-6. Closed: 1 Oct-Maundy Thur. £ (EH).

Deep in the Bedfordshire countryside, this medieval refectory of an Augustinian priory has a rare timber frame roof, wall paintings and stained glass, as well as an exhibition about itself.

CORBY — Kirby Hall

Deene, Corby, Northants. 0536-203230. Open: Daily 10-6 Summer, Tue-Sun 10-4 Winter. £ P (EH)

This is a stone-built Tudor mansion, begun in 1570 and with 17th century alterations. It is currently being restored by English Heritage.

COTTESMORE — Rutland Railway Museum

Cottesmore Iron Ore Siding, Ashwell Rd, Cottesmore, nr Oakham, Leicestershire. 0780-63092. Open: Sat/Sun by appointment only. £ P

There is the biggest collection of preserved freight wagons in Britain at this museum, as well as industrial locomotives. Check for steam-up days.

PASSPORT CONCESSIONS: Free entry for under-18's accompanied by adult.

CROMER — Cromer Museum

East Cottages, Tucker Street, Cromer, Norfolk NR27 9HB. 0263-513543. Open: Mon-Sat 10-5, Sun 2-5. £

The curator, Mr. Warren, says this is about "the character and history of the area", so the sea has a significant influence on what you can see - fishing, lifeboats, even a fisherman's cottage - but there is also geology, natural history and archaeology.

PASSPORT CONCESSIONS: Adult entry at student rate.

DERBY — Derby Industrial Museum

The Silk Mill, off Full Street, Derby. 0332-255308. Open: Mon 11-5, Tue-Sat 10-5, Sun + B.H. 2-5. £ P &

Chiefly about the development of railway engineering in Derby, the museum also has the Rolls Royce aero engines the town is famous for.

PASSPORT CONCESSIONS: Free entry to Special Exhibitions.

DERBY · Derby Museum and Art Gallery

The Strand, Derby DE1 1BS. 0332-255586. Open: Mon 11-5 Tue-Sat 10-5 Sun 2-5.

The paintings of Joseph Wright have pride of place in this local museum, but there is also archaeology, social history, militaria, Derby porcelain and a temporary exhibitions programme.

Key Gavioli Fairground Organ (1897).

DERBY · Pickford's House Museum

41 Friargate, Derby DE1 1DA. 0332-255363. Open: Mon 11-5, Tue-Sat 10-5, Sun & B.H. 2-5. £ &

This Georgian townhouse has a working kitchen of the period among its historical room settings, plus costume displays. The Georgian garden opens in the spring and summer. There is also a full temporary exhibition programme for the whole year.

PASSPORT CONCESSIONS: Free entry to Passport holder.

DEREHAM · Bishop Bonner's Cottages Museum

St Withburgs Lane, Dereham NR19 1ED. 0362-693107. Open: May-Sept Tue-Sat 2.30-5. P

The displays of local history are set in cottages dating from 1502.

PASSPORT CONCESSIONS: Free Pamphlet.

DISS · Bressingham Steam Museum

Bressingham, Diss, Norfolk IP22 2AB. 037988-382. Open: Daily 14th Apr-14 Oct 10-5.30. Call for details about steam days.

There are hundreds of steam driven things in this live museum, with 50 road, rail, traction and stationary engines, including the Royal Scot and the Oliver Cromwell, Victorian fairground gallopers and the Dell Garden next door. There is a busy summer and autumn of rallies and events.

PASSPORT CONCESSIONS: Free Guidebook.

DUXFORD
Imperial War Museum

Duxford Airfield, Duxford, Cambridgeshire CB2 4QR. 0223- 833963. Open: Daily 10-4 Oct-Mar, 10-6 Mar-Oct. £ P &

The air wing of the London IWM in a former Battle of Britain fighter station. Now it has the finest collection of civil and military aircraft in Britain, with a recreated ops room and other special exhibitions.

EAST RETFORD
The Bassetlaw Museum

Amcott House, 40 Grove Street, East Retford, Notts DN22 6JU. 0777-706741. Open: Mon-Sat 10-5. &

Amcott House is an 18th century town house, and now it is the chink in the curtain on the district's past with displays of archaeology, civic, local and agricultural history, as well as fine and applied art.

ELY
The Stained Glass Museum

The Cathedral, Ely, Cambs. 0223-60148. Open: Mon-Sat 10.30-4. Sun 12-3. Closed: Nov-Feb. £ P

In the triforium of Ely Cathedral, the national collection of stained glass windows, highlighting the Gothic Revival, Pre-Raphaelite and Arts & Crafts work. Exhibition of the prize-winning entries in the annual competition for young stained glass designers from June to October.

PASSPORT CONCESSIONS: 50% off adult admission charge

JNR. PASSPORT CONCESSIONS: Free entry to Passport holder.

FELIXSTOWE — Landguard Fort

Felixstowe, Suffolk.
Open: 27th May-30th
Sept. Wed,Thur/Sun
2.45-4. Closed: Oct-
May 26. £ (EH)

This 18th century fort was built on the site of an earlier one, and added to in the 19th and 20th centuries. The exhibition inside explains more.

FRAMLINGHAM — Framlingham Castle

Framlingham, Suffolk.
0728-723330. Open:
Daily 10-6 Summer,
Tue-Sun 10-4 Winter.
£ (EH)

The local museum is within the massive walls and towers of this castle, built about 1200, and the site of the great hall is now occupied by an 18th century poor house.

FRAMLINGHAM — 390th Bomb Group Memorial Air Museum

The Control Tower,
Parham Airfield, Nr.
Framlingham, Suffolk.
0359-51209. Open:
Sun/B.H. Mon 1-6.
Closed: Nov-Mar.
P &

Volunteer-run museum with bits of World War II aircraft, uniforms, documents, photographs and other memorabilia in an old control tower.

GAINSBOROUGH — Gainsborough Old Hall

Parnell Street,
Gainsborough DN21
2NB. 0427-612669.
Open Mon-Sat 10-5,
Sun 2-5. £

The great hall, kitchens, tower and wings of this medieval manor house are unchanged since 1480, and have connections with Richard III and the Mayflower pilgrims. Fairs and medieval and Tudor events during the year.

JNR. PASSPORT CONCESSIONS: Free Schools information pack.

GLANDFORD — Shell Museum

Shell Museum,
Glandford, Holt,
Norfolk NR25 7JR.
0263-740081. Open:
Mar-Oct Mon-Thur
10-12.30/2-4.30,
Fri/Sat 2-4.30, Nov-
Feb Mon-Thur 10-
12.30. £ P

A museum of shells, from all over the world, plus fossils and minerals.

GRANTHAM — Grantham Museum

St. Peter's Hill, Grantham, Lincs NG31 6PY. 0476-68783. Open: Apr-Sept Mon-Sat 10-5, Sun 2-5. Oct-Mar Mon-Sat 10-12.30/1.30-5. £

The history of the town plus displays on Sir Isaac Newton and Margaret Thatcher, and temporary exhibitions.

PASSPORT CONCESSIONS: Free entry to Passport holder.

JNR. PASSPORT CONCESSIONS: Free entry to Junior Passport holder.

GREAT YARMOUTH — Berney Arms Windmill

Great Yarmouth, Norfolk. 0493-700605. Open: Daily 10-6 Summer. Closed: Winter. £ (EH)

Seven storeys high, its mighty sails still in working order, this windmill is a landmark for miles around and is one of the best and largest marsh mills in Norfolk.

GREAT YARMOUTH — Elizabethan House Museum

4 South Quay, Great Yarmouth, Norfolk NR30 2QH. 0493-855746. Open: Mon-Fri 10-5.30, Sun Jun-Sept 10-5.30. £

This house is a bit of a fraud, but a very acceptable one because behind the Georgian facade is a Tudor merchant's home, with its panelled rooms and displays of silver, glass, ceramics, toys and domestic equipment.

PASSPORT CONCESSIONS: Adult entry at student prices.

GREAT YARMOUTH — Maritime Museum for East Anglia

25 Marine Parade, Great Yarmouth, Norfolk NR30 2EN. 0493-842267. Open: Sun-Fri 10-5.30. (Out of Season closed 1-2 & Sun.) £

Number 26 Marine Parade was a shipwrecked sailors' home, and is now the home of Norfolk's maritime heritage, with everything from life-saving and shipbuilding, to Nelson.

PASSPORT CONCESSIONS: Adult entry at student prices.

GREAT YARMOUTH

Nelson's Monument

South Beach Parade, Great Yarmouth, Norfolk. 0493-855746. Open: Jul/Aug & Trafalgar day, Mon-Fri/Sun 2-6. Closed: Sept-June. £ P

For all his connections with Merton, Portsmouth and Chatham, Horatio Nelson was actually born in a Norfolk rectory, and this monument, built 14 years after his death at Trafalgar, was erected to honour him. There are 217 steps to the viewing platform.

PASSPORT CONCESSIONS: Adult entry at student prices.

GREAT YARMOUTH

Old Merchants Houses

South Quay, Great Yarmouth, Norfolk. 0493-857900. Open: Daily 10-6 Summer. Closed: Winter. £ (EH)

These are typical of the 17th century, one in particular having splendid plaster ceilings and containing large displays of local architectural and domestic fittings.

GREAT YARMOUTH

Tolhouse Museum

Tolhouse Street, Great Yarmouth, Norfolk. 0493-858900. Open: Mon-Fri/Sun 10-5.30 Summer season only.

This is a former courthouse and jail with prison cells in the dungeons, and less harrowing displays about the history of Great Yarmouth.

GRESSENHALL

Norfolk Rural Life Museum

Beech House, Gressenhall, Nr. Dereham, Norfolk NR20 4DR. 0362-860563. Open: Easter-Oct Tue-Sat 10-5, Sun 2-5.30. Closed: Nov-Easter. £ P &

As well as farming exhibits and craft workshops, there is an Edwardian cottage and garden, and a 1920s working farm with rare breeds of sheep, cattle, poultry and pigs.

HUNTINGDON — Cromwell Museum

Grammar School Walk, Huntingdon, Cambs. 0480-425830. Open: Apr-Oct Tue-Fri 11-1/2-5, Sat/Sun 11-1/2-4, Nov-Mar Tue-Fri 2-5, Sat 11-1/2-4, Sun 2-4 .

This was a medieval hospital and became a school relatively late in life, a school where Cromwell was a pupil. He was born in Huntingdon in 1611, and the collection has family portraits, his personal belongings and documents.

HUNTINGDON — Norris Museum

The Broadway, St. Ives, Huntingdon, Cambs PE17 4BX. 0480-65101. Open: Tue-Fri 10-1/2-4, May-Sept Sat 10-12/2-5, Sun 2-5. ♿

Can you, have 'former' counties, or do they only cease to exist for the bureaucrats? This museum celebrates Huntingdonshire, now administratively just part of Cambridgeshire, but here are archaeology, fossils, geology and a whole research library about Hunts and its history, to prove it's far from 'former'.

PASSPORT CONCESSIONS: Free Poster.

IPSWICH — Christchurch Mansion

Christchurch Park, Soane Street, Ipswich. 0473-213761. Open: Mon-Sat 10-5, Sun 2.30-4.30. (Closes Dusk in Winter).

This is a Tudor house with collections of furniture, paintings and ceramics, and works by Constable, Gainsborough and other Suffolk artists.

IPSWICH — Ipswich Museums & Galleries

High Street, Ipswich IP1 3QH. 0473-213761. Open: Mon-Sat 10-5. Closed: B.H.

This is a Victorian museum building, with its displays extremely up-to-date. They include natural history, geology and archaeology, and there is a new Roman Suffolk display plus ethnography, and a temporary exhibitions gallery.

KETTERING — Alfred East Gallery

Sheep Street, Kettering, Northants. 0536-410333. Open: Mon-Sat 9.30-5.

This has a permanent collection of the works of Sir Alfred East RA (1849-1918) given to his home town, and also the works of T.C. Gotch, there are temporary exhibitions throughout the year.

KETTERING — Manor House Museum

Sheep Street, Kettering, Northants. 0536-410333. Open: Mon-Sat 9.30-5.   P &

Here are glimpses of Kettering's past through collections of social and industrial history, archaeology and geology.

KING'S LYNN — Castle Acre Priory

Stocks Green, Castle Acre, King's Lynn. 0760-755394. Open: Daily 10-6 Summer. Closed: Winter. £ (EH)

The 12th century church of the Cluniac priory has an elaborate west front. The monastic buildings, including the prior's lodge and chapel and a 15th century gatehouse, have also survived.

KING'S LYNN — Castle Rising Castle

Castle Acre, King's Lynn, Norfolk. 0842-810656. Open: Daily 10-6 Summer, 10-4 Winter (excl.Mon). £ (EH)

The bridge and gatehouse survive still to serve the 12th century keep.

KING'S LYNN — The Lynn Museum

Old Market Street, King's Lynn, Norfolk PE30 1NL. 0553-775001. Open: Mon-Sat 10-5. Closed: B.H. £ &

This is about West Norfolk, its farm tools, model ships and fairground machinery. There are new galleries on the area's natural history and geology.

PASSPORT CONCESSIONS: Adult entry at student prices.

KING'S LYNN — Museum of Social History

27 King Street, King's Lynn, Norfolk PE30 1HA. 0553-775004. Open: Tue-Sat 10-5. £

Childhood is becoming a curiously popular theme for museums, and this one has picked it as a main topic, with a dolls' house made by a former Mayor of Lynn the centrepiece. There is also the Taylor collection of glass and a brass-rubbing centre.

PASSPORT CONCESSIONS: Adult entry at student rate.

KING'S LYNN — Oxburgh Hall

Oxborough, King's Lynn. 036621-258. Open: 29 Mar-Oct Sat-Wed 12-5, Oct Sat/Sun. Closed: Nov-Mar. £ P &

The National Trust now owns this moated house, built in 1492, now with a Tudor gatehouse. The period rooms stretch from medieval to Victorian, and there is a garden, a French parterre and woodland walks.

KIRBY MUXLOE — Kirby Muxloe Castle

Oakcroft Avenue, Kirby Muxloe. 0533-386886. Open: Daily 10-6 Summer, 10-4 Winter (excl. Mon). £ P (EH)

William, Lord Hastings, was executed by Richard III three years after he began this moated, brick-built quadrangular castle, so it was never able to live up to its promise of being a magnate's residence of grandeur.

LAVENHAM — Lavenham Guildhall

Market Place, Lavenham, Suffolk CO10 9QZ. 0787-247646. Open: 31 Mar-5 Nov Daily 11-1/2-5.30. Closed: 6 Nov-30 Mar. P

This building is one of the magnificent badges of Lavenham's medieval wealth, when it was the centre of Norfolk's wool trade, though the Guildhall actually dates from about 1529. Since then it has been the town hall, a jail, a workhouse, an almshouse, a wool store, a restaurant and a nursery school. It has an exhibition about the cloth industry with models and an original loom.

LEICESTER — Belgrave Hall

Church Road, Leicester. 0533-666590. Open: Mon-Fri 10-5.30, Sun 2-5.30. P

There are period rooms from the late 17th to the mid 19th centuries in this Queen Anne house, coaches in the stable block and botanic gardens with over 6,500 species of plants.

PASSPORT CONCESSIONS: 10% off shop purchases.

LEICESTER — The Guildhall

Guildhall Lane, Leicester. 0533-532569. Open: Mon-Sat 10-5.30, Sun 2-5.30. P ♿

The town hall from the late 15th century until 1876, and then a police station, this was the hall of Corpus Christi Guild from its building in the 14th century until the 16th century.

PASSPORT CONCESSIONS: 10% off shop purchases.

LEICESTER — Jewry Wall Museum and Site.

St. Nicholas Circle, Leicester. 0533-544766. Open: Mon-Sat 10-5.30, Sun 2-5.30. P ♿

This is the county's archaeological museum, including the Bronze Age Welby Hoard and Romano-British mosaics, in a modern building which overlooks the Roman baths site and the massive 2nd century Roman Jewry Wall. There is to be a major refurbishment of galleries and displays in the summer, and an archaeology open day on September 1.

PASSPORT CONCESSIONS: 10% off shop purchases.

LEICESTER — John Doran Gas Museum

British Gas East Midlands, Leicester Service Centre, Aylestone Road, Leicester LE2 7QH. 0533-535506. Open: Tue-Fri 12.30-4.30. P

The history of the gas industry in a wide range of exhibits.

JNR. PASSPORT CONCESSIONS: Free Schools information pack.

LEICESTER — Leicestershire Museum & Art Gallery

New Walk, Leicester LE1 6TD 0533-554100. Open: Mon-Sat 10-5.30, Sun 2-5.30. ♿

There is English art from the 16th century onwards, plus some Old Masters and 19th and 20th century French paintings; important ethnic collections, particularly Gujerati, and natural history and geology galleries.

PASSPORT CONCESSIONS: 10% off shop purchases.

LEICESTER — Leicestershire Record Office

57 New Walk, Leicester. 0533-544566. Open: Mon-Thur 9.15-5, Fri 9.15-4.45, most Sats 9.15-12.15. Closed: B.H. weekends + annual stocktaking weeks, phone to check.   P

Some of the most appealing fragments of our history are behind the unassuming doors of county record offices, and this is one of the largest CRO's. An extensive collection of private and public, urban and rural archives relating to the county.

PASSPORT CONCESSIONS: 10% off shop purchases.

LEICESTER — Museum of Costume

Wygston's House, Applegate, St. Nicholas Circle, Leicester. 0533-554100. Open: Mon-Sat 10-5.30, Sun 2-5.30.

Leicester's varied collection of costume and textiles dating from the 18th to the 20th century, with reconstructed 1920s draper's and shoe shops, housed in an important late medieval building.

PASSPORT CONCESSIONS: 10% off shop purchases.

LEICESTER — Museum of the Royal Leicestershire Regiment

The Magazine, Oxford Street, Leicester. 0533-555889. Open: Mon-Sat 10-5.30, Sun 2-5.30.

The regimental museum of what was once the 17th Foot is housed in the early 15th century Newarke Gateway.

PASSPORT CONCESSIONS: 10% off shop purchases.

LEICESTER — Museum of Technology

Abbey Pumping Station, Corporation Road, Leicester. 0533-661330. Open: Mon-Sat 10-5.30, Sun 2-5.30. P &

In the 1891 Abbey Pumping Station which used to be part of the city's sewer and drainage system, there are the original four giant beam engines, plus other engines, a transport collection, knitting gallery and 84 ton Steam Navvy.

PASSPORT CONCESSIONS: 10% off shop purchases.

LEICESTER — Newarke Houses Museum

The Newarke, Leicester LE2 7BY. 0533-554100. Open: Mon-Sat 10-5.30, Sun 2-5.30.

One of the county-run museums, this one is dedicated to Leicestershire's social history, with room reconstructions and splendid furniture, the later pieces by Gimson, and a display dedicated to Daniel Lambert, the world's heaviest man.

PASSPORT CONCESSIONS: Reduction of 10% on shop purchases.

Leicestershire
Museums
Arts and
Records
Service

With fourteen museums, Leicestershire offers an exciting day out for the family, school or party visit. We have period gardens, historic buildings and displays covering a wide range of interests. You can see local history, dinosaurs, decorative arts, biology, archaeology, technology, military history, costume displays and art galleries across the city and county.

Disabled access details, parking information and telephone numbers are included in this guide.

a Leicestershire County Council service

LEISTON — The Long Shop Museum

Main Street, Leiston, Suffolk IP16 4ES. 0728-832189. Open: Daily 10-5. Closed: Nov-Mar. £

Based in the 200-year-old Richard Garrett engineering works, the award-winning collection takes in steam engines, agriculture, social history of the area and the US Air Force occupation of Leiston Airfield.

PASSPORT CONCESSIONS: 50% off adult admission charge; Free Guidebook.

LINBY — Newstead Abbey

Linby, Nottinghamshire NG15 8GE. 0623-793557. Open: Daily 11.30-6. Closed: Oct-Good Friday. £ P

'Dangerous to know' as Lord Byron, was described; so might his home be to those of a nervous disposition aware of Byron's poems about its ghostly legends. It is a medieval priory converted in Tudor times for domestic use, and could be the setting to a hundred Victorian Gothic novels.

LINCOLN — Bishops Palace

Minster Yard, Lincoln. Open: Daily 10- 6 Summer. Closed: Winter. £ (EH)

Two halls and a 15th century gatehouse are included in the remains of this medieval palace of the bishops of Lincoln.

LINCOLN — City & County Museum

Broadgate, Lincoln LN2 1HQ. 0522-530401. Open: Mon-Sat 10-5.30, Sun 2.30-5. £

The riches of Lincoln's archaeological and natural heritage in an inspiring medieval building, now with one of the four copies of Magna Carta, loaned by Lincoln Cathedral.

PASSPORT CONCESSIONS: Free entry to Passport holder.

JNR. PASSPORT CONCESSIONS: Free entry to Junior Passport holder.

LINCOLN — Museum of Lincolnshire Life

Burton Road, Lincoln. 0522-528448. Open: May-Sept Daily 10-5.30, Oct-Apr Mon-Sat 10-5.30, Sun 2-5.30. £ P &

This is the county council's heritage showcase which examines every aspect of the county of 'yellow-bellies' from period shops to dialect, and with temporary exhibitions and events all year.

LINCOLN — Usher Gallery

Lindum Road, Lincoln LN2 1NN. 0522-27980. Open: Mon-Sat 10-5.30, Sun 2.30-5. £ P &

The county's main repository for fine and decorative arts - especially watches, coins and objets d'art - now with its famous new acquisition, the £2 million Gainsborough portrait of Sir Joseph Banks, on display. A busy temporary exhibition schedule as well.

PASSPORT CONCESSIONS: Free entry to Passport holder.

JNR. PASSPORT CONCESSIONS: Free entry to Passport holder.

LOUGHBOROUGH — The Bellfoundry Museum

Freehold Street, Loughborough, Leicester LE11 1AR. 0509-233414. Open: Tue-Sat 9.30-12.30/1.30-4.30. £

The exhibits here show the evolution of the bellfounder's craft and the techniques of moulding, casting, tuning and fitting up bells.

PASSPORT CONCESSIONS: 20% off each admission.

JNR. PASSPORT CONCESSIONS: 20% off each admission.

LOWESTOFT — East Anglia Transport Museum

Chapel Road, Carlton, Colville, Nr. Lowestoft, Suffolk. 0502-569399. Open: Aug Mon-Fri 2, June-Sept Sat 11, May-Sept Sun 11. Closed: Oct-Apr. £ P &

Working trams, trolleybuses, a narrow gauge railway and other period vehicles all in a reconstructed 1930s street scene. There is a London event on July 14/15, with visiting buses, taxis and so on from the capital.

JNR. PASSPORT CONCESSIONS: One free child entry per party.

LOWESTOFT — Lowestoft Maritime Museum

Whaplao Rd, Lowestoft, Suffolk. 0502-61963. Open: May-Sept Daily 10-5. £ P &

This is a small museum at Ness Point, the most easterly point in Britain.

PASSPORT CONCESSIONS: 50% off adult admission charge; Free Guidebook.

LYDDINGTON — Lyddington Bede House

Blue Coat Lane, Uppingham, Lyddington. 057282-2438. Open: Daily 10-6 Summer. Closed: Winter. £ (EH)

This is the only surviving part of a manor house belonging to the bishops of Lincoln which, was converted into an almshouse in 1602. The first floor has an elaborate 16th century timber ceiling.

MANSFIELD — Mansfield Museum & Art Gallery

Leeming Street, Mansfield, Nottinghamshire NG18 1NG. 0623-663088. Open: Mon-Sat 10-5. &

An exhaustive programme of exhibitions, mostly about local artists, augments a permanent collection of social and natural history displays, watercolours of Mansfield by A.S. Buxton, porcelain and lustreware.

PASSPORT CONCESSIONS: Free Poster.

JNR. PASSPORT CONCESSIONS: Free Poster.

MARKET BOSWORTH — Bosworth Battlefield Visitor Centre & Country Park

Sutton Cheeney near Market Bosworth, Leics. 0455-290429. Open: Mon-Sat 2-5.30 & July/Aug Sun/B.H. Mons 1-6. £ P &

The site that saw the end of Richard III and the Middle Ages, it has an award-winning interpretation with models, film, theatre and illustrated battle trails.

PASSPORT CONCESSIONS: One child free for each paying adult.

MARKET HARBOROUGH — Harborough Museum

Council Offices, Adam & Eve St, Market Harborough, Leics. 0858-32468. Open: Mon-Sat 10-4.30, Sun 2-5. P &

This shows how the medieval town was designed and how it worked as a market, social and hunting centre. There are displays from the Symington Collection of Corsetry. There are four-monthly temporary exhibitions on different aspects of Market Harborough.

PASSPORT CONCESSIONS: 10% off shop purchases.

MARKET HARBOROUGH — Hunsbury Hill Ironstone Railway Museum

Camp Hill, Northampton, 9 High Street, Hallaton, Market Harborough, Leics LE16 8UD. 085889-216. Open: Sun 11-5 or by appt. £ P

This is the museum of the ironstone extraction industry, with tools and the locomotives which carried the ironstone, dating back to 1883, with the railway open from Easter.

PASSPORT CONCESSIONS: 50% off adult admission charge.

JNR. PASSPORT CONCESSIONS: Free entry to Junior Passport holder.

Archaeology, Egyptology, Hieroglyphics…

…all Greek to you?

Read Simon Tait every Saturday.

Not content with editing this excellent Guide, Simon Tait also finds time to produce his own column, every Saturday in *The Times*. His expert guidance and advice will help you get the most out of our museums and galleries.

He'll keep you up to date with exactly what's going on and where. And tell you about any extra concessions or free gifts Museum Passport holders are entitled to.

If you haven't already taken advantage of *The Times* Museums' Passport offer, simply fill in the coupon in *The Times* on Saturdays, for your free Passports to the past.

THE  TIMES

MATLOCK — Caudwell's Mill

Rowsley, Matlock, Derbyshire DE4 2EB. 0629-734374. Open: Daily 10-6 Summer, Sat/Sun 10-4.30 Winter. £ P ♿

Five working craftsmen are in residence, with changing exhibitions of their work. There are also permanent exhibitions of milling, water power and the Caudwell family.

PASSPORT CONCESSIONS: 50% off adult admission charge; Free Guidebook; Free entry to changing exhibition and new video films.

JNR. PASSPORT CONCESSIONS: Free Badge.

MATLOCK — Derbyshire Museum Service

John Turner House, The Parkway, Darley Dale, Matlock, Derbyshire DE4 2FW. 0629-733226. Open: Mon-Fri 2-5. P ♿

This is the brainbox for the county's official memory sorting, with research facilities coming soon and a discovery room, maps, microfiches, photographs, slides all to be available, along with temporary exhibitions already under way.

MATLOCK — National Tramway Museum

Crich, Nr. Matlock, Derbyshire DE4 5DP. 0773-852565. Open: Sat-Thur 10-5.30, 20th July-Aug Fri also. Closed: Nov-Mar. £ P ♿

The museum is a mile long, with an international collection of 40 electric, horse-drawn and steam vintage trams, some of which shuttle along the scenic track.

PASSPORT CONCESSIONS: Special rate family entrance.

MATLOCK BATH — Peak District Mining Museum

The Pavilion, Matlock Bath, Derbyshire. 0629-583834. Open: Daily 11-4. £ P ♿

The terrifying magic of the underearth is a source of fascination being made more and more available by museums. Here is one which offers a maze of shafts, and tunnels, working models. Trevithick's giant water pressure engine, 2,000 years of lead mining and a permanent exhibition about Millclose

PASSPORT CONCESSIONS: 50% off adult admission charge; Special family entrance ticket; Free certificate to anyone who climbs the shafts and tunnels.

JNR. PASSPORT CONCESSIONS: Free entry to Junior Passport holder; Free certificate to anyone who climbs the shafts and tunnels.

MELTON MOWBRAY

Melton Carnegie Museum

Thorpe End, Melton Mowbray, Leics. 0664-69946. Open: Mon-Sat 10-5, Sun 2-5 Summer, Mon-Fri 10-4.30, Sat 10-4 Winter.

If you thought pork pies and the Royal Army Veterinary Corps were the only claims to fame of Melton, allow Janet Legget, the curator of this growing museum, to put you right. What, for instance, about the two-headed calf? And the sporting life, which in this county means fox hunting, is the subject of the new extension expected to open in November.

PASSPORT CONCESSIONS: Admission to events organised by Friends of Melton Carnegie Museum; 10% off museums items only.

NEWARK

Millgate Folk Museum

48 Millgate, Newark, Notts NG24 4TS. 0636-79403. Open: Mon-Fri 10-5, Sat/Sun 1-5. Closed: Weekends Nov-Mar. &

This is a former Trent mill and warehouse, which has been turned into a museum of everyday things in reconstructed rooms and shops covering the hundred years from about 1850.

PASSPORT CONCESSIONS: Free Poster; Half price Guidebook.

JNR. PASSPORT CONCESSIONS: Free Badge; Children's Guidebook half price.

NEWARK — Newark Air Museum

The Airfield, Winthorpe, Newark, Notts NG24 2NY. 0636-707170. Open: Mon-Fri 10-5, Sat 11-5, Sun 10-6. Nov-Mar Sat/Sun only. £ P ♿

There are over 40 aircraft, plus aero engines and aviation relics, on display in one of the largest privately managed aviation museums in the country. A new engine display and aircraft display hall opens at Easter 1990.

PASSPORT CONCESSIONS: Party admission rates for passport holders.

JNR. PASSPORT CONCESSIONS: Party admission rates for passport holders.

NEWARK — Newark Museum

Appletangate, Newark, Notts. 0636-702358. Open: Mon-Sat (excl. Thur.) 10-1/2-5, Sun 2-5.

Housed in a former grammar school, this museum has the local history and archaeology of Newark and the surrounding area.

NEWARK — Vina Cooke Museum of Dolls and Bygone Childhood

The Old Rectory, Cromwell, Newark, Notts NG23 6JE. 0636-821364. Open: Daily 10-12/2-6. £ P

Vina Cooke's private collection of dolls, toys, prams, dolls houses, trains, baby-wear and portrait dolls are on display in a 17th century rectory.

PASSPORT CONCESSIONS: For each paying adult, one adult or two children free.

JNR. PASSPORT CONCESSIONS: Free entry to Passport holder.

NEWMARKET — National Horseracing Museum

99 High Street, Newmarket, Suffolk CB8 8JL. 0638-667333. Open: Tue-Sat 10-5, Sun 2-5. Closed: Dec-Apr. £ P ♿

The story of racing is told in five galleries through paintings, bronzes, trophies, memorabilia of famous horses, jockeys and personalities. There are videos of famous races, and equine tours can be arranged.

PASSPORT CONCESSIONS: 50% off adult admission charge; Free Poster.

JNR. PASSPORT CONCESSIONS: Free Badge.

NORTHAMPTON   Althorp House

Althorp, Northampton NN7 4HG.
0604-769368. Open: Daily 1-5, Jul/Aug Daily 11-6. £ P

Home of the Earl of Spencer, famous for its picture collection which includes works by Rubens, Van Dyke, Lely and Wootten. Its porcelain and furniture collection has recently been restored.

PASSPORT CONCESSIONS: £1 off adult admission charge.

NORTHAMPTON   Central Museum & Art Gallery

Guildhall Road, Northampton NN1 1DP 0604-39415. Open: Mon-Sat 10-5, Thur - 8. ♿

Northampton being historically the centre of the shoe-making industry, it is no surprise that the town's museum should have a strong collection of boots and shoes, but this is the largest in the world. The museum also covers the history of Northampton from the Stone Age, and has decorative and fine arts on show.

PASSPORT CONCESSIONS: Free Guidebook.

JNR. PASSPORT CONCESSIONS: Free Badge.

NORTHAMPTON   Leathercraft Museum

Bridge Street, Northampton.
0604-34881. Open: Mon-Sat 10-5.

Leatherwork from Ancient Egypt, Roman Britain, the early Middle Ages, gloves, Spanish leather, saddlery and the work of leathersellers are all part of this large collection.

PASSPORT CONCESSIONS: Free Guidebook.

JNR. PASSPORT CONCESSIONS: Free Badge.

NORWICH   Bridewell Museum

Bridewell Alley, Norwich, Norfolk NR2 1AQ.
0603-667228. Open: Mon-Sat 10-5. £

Norwich's trades and industries over the last two centuries are the display theme. They may seem history to us but would look like science fiction to the original owner of this house - he was a medieval merchant.

NORWICH   Felbrigg Hall

Felbrigg, Norwich NR11 8PR. 026375-444. Open: Apr-Oct Daily 1.30-5.30. Closed: Nov-Mar. £ P ♿

The National Trust's 17th century house, with its original 18th century furniture and pictures intact, and an outstanding library, all complemented outside by the walled garden, dovecote, lake and woodland.

NORWICH — The John Jarrold Printing Museum

Jarrold Printing, Whitefriars, Norwich, NR3 1SH. 0603-660211. Open: Tue evenings 7.30-9.30 & July-Sept Tue 10-12.30/2-4. £

A working museum with letterpress, lithographic and binding equipment going back nearly 200 years and still in use, as the continuous demonstrations testify.

PASSPORT CONCESSIONS: Free entry to Passport holder; Free Poster.

JNR. PASSPORT CONCESSIONS: Opportunity to print something for themselves.

NORWICH — Norwich Castle Museum

Castle Meadow, Norwich, Norfolk NR1 3JU. 0603-222222. Open: Mon-Sat 10-5, Sun 2-5. £ &

Norfolk's regional museum, in the 12th century castle, covering the county's archaeology, art, ceramics, natural and local history and glass, with a special exhibition of the world's greatest teapot collection.

PASSPORT CONCESSIONS: Adult entry at student rate.

NORWICH — Sainsbury Centre for Visual Arts

University of East Anglia, Norwich NR4 7TJ. 0603-592470. Open: Tue-Sun 12-5. £ P &

Norman Foster's building, with an extension under way (there is to be an exhibition about it here in the Summer of 1990), contains collections combining modern Western art with the arts of Africa, Oceania and North and South America, and boasts works by Picasso, Modigliani, Degas, Moore, Giacommetti, Bacon and John Davies.

PASSPORT CONCESSIONS: Free entry to Passport holder.

JNR. PASSPORT CONCESSIONS: Free entry to Junior Passport holder.

Mother & Child, Henry Moore.

NORWICH — St. Peter Hungate Church Museum & Brass Rubbing Centre

Princes Street,
Norwich, Norfolk
NR3 1AE.
0603-667231. Open:
Mon-Sat 10-5. &

The displays in this 15th century church, with its notable hammer beam roof and stained glass, assay the service art has paid to Christianity and the history of the church in Norfolk, in exhibits ranging in date from the 9th to the 20th centuries.

NORWICH — Strangers' Hall Museum

Charing Cross,
Norwich, Norfolk
NR2 4AL.
0603-667229. Open:
Mon-Sat 10-5. £

Once the home of well-to-do medieval burghers of Norwich, and still a private home until quite recently, the house reflects the progress of city life with the rooms furnished in various period styles from the 16th century on. There is also an intriguing toy collection and an archive of city shop signs.

PASSPORT CONCESSIONS: Adult entry at student rate.

NORWICH — Strumpshaw Old Hall Steam Museum

Strumpshaw,
Norwich, Norfolk
NR13 4HR.
0603-714535. Open:
Sun-Fri 2-5. Closed:
Nov-Apr. £

This private museum has a working beam engine as well as traction, ploughing and other steam engines, and a railway running every open day.

NOTTINGHAM — Brewhouse Yard Museum

Castle Boulevard,
Nottingham NG6
1FB. 0602-483504.
Open: Daily 10-5.

Nottingham daily life from 1600 to 1900 in five 17th century cottages with period rooms, shops, caves, gardens. Talks, displays and demonstrations all year.

NOTTINGHAM — Castle Museum

The Castle,
Nottingham NG1
6EL. 0602-483504.
Open: Daily 10-5.45
Summer, 10-4.45
Winter. £ &

The 17th century fortress guards the city's collection of silver, glass, ceramics and fine art, and has a gallery about the history of Nottingham, as well as a varied temporary exhibition programme.

PASSPORT CONCESSIONS: Free Poster.

NOTTINGHAM — D. H. Lawrence Birthplace Museum

8A Victoria Street, Eastwood, Nottingham NG16 3AW. 0773-763312. Open: Daily Apr-Oct 10-5, Nov-Mar 10-4. £

This is the miner's cottage in Eastwood, where Lawrence was born in 1885, furnished as it would have looked then.

NOTTINGHAM — Framework Knitter's Museum

Chapel Street, Ruddington, Nottingham NG11 6HE. 0602-846914. Open: Tue-Fri 10-4, & Sun 2-4 Jul-Aug. Closed: Nov-Mar. £

An award-winning independent working museum, housed in a restored early 19th century framework knitters' cottages and workshops.

PASSPORT CONCESSIONS: 50% off adult admission charge.

JNR. PASSPORT CONCESSIONS: Free Badge.

NOTTINGHAM — Green's Mill and Centre

Belvoir Hill, Sneinton, Nottingham NG2 4LF. 0602-503635. Open: Wed-Sun 10-5 + B.H. P &

The restored windmill home of George Green, mathematical genius, with interactive exhibits demonstrating his work.

NOTTINGHAM — The Natural History Museum

Wollaton Hall, Nottingham NG8 2AE. 0602-281333. Open: Apr-Sept Mon-Sat 10-7, Sun 2-5, Oct/Mar Mon-Sat 10-5.30, Sun 1.30-4.30, Nov-Feb Mon-Sat 10-4.30, Sun 1.30-4.30. £ P &

Displays on fish and British birds, plus exotic wildlife from Africa, America and Australasia, a room entirely devoted to British mammals, and insect and geology exhibits, all set in a fascinating Elizabethan mansion.

NOTTINGHAM — Nottingham Industrial Museum

Courtyard Buildings, Wollaton Park, Nottingham NG8 2AE. 0602-284602. Open: Oct-Mar Thur-Sat 10-4.30, Sun 1-4.30, Apr-Sept Mon-Sat 10-6, Sun 2-6. £ P &

This is in buildings on the old Wollaton Estate, and is devoted to the engineering which ran such Nottingham industries as pharmaceuticals and tobacco.

NOTTINGHAM — University of Nottingham Art Gallery

University of Nottingham, University Park, Nottingham NG7 2RD. 0602-484848. Open: Term time only Mon-Fri 10-7, Sat 11-5. P &

Temporary exhibitions of old masters and contemporary paintings - due to move to a new arts centre in the autumn.

OAKHAM — Oakham Castle

Market Place, Oakham, Leics. 0572-723654. Open: Apr-Oct Tue-Sat + B.H. Mon 10-1/2-4.30, Sun 2-5.30; Nov-Mar Tue-Sat 10-1/2-4. &

This 12th century castle has a unique collection of horseshoes in its great hall, each one given by a visiting peer.

PASSPORT CONCESSIONS: 10% off shop purchases.

OAKHAM — Rutland County Museum

Catmos Street, Oakham, Leics. 0572-723654. Open: Tue-Sat/B.H. Mon 10-1/2-5, + Sun 2-5 (Apr-Oct). P &

Largely an agriculture museum dedicated to the rural life of the old county, with farming equipment, implements and waggons. There are also local crafts, archaeology and a special gallery devoted to the Volunteer Soldier, all in an 18th century cavalry riding school.

PASSPORT CONCESSIONS: 10% off shop purchases.

OLNEY — Cowper & Newton Museum

Orchard Side, Marketplace, Olney, North Bucks. 0234-711516. Open: Easter-Oct Tue-Sat 10-12/2-5; Nov-Easter Tue-Sat 2-4 Closed: 8 Dec - 8 Jan. £

The home of the poet and hymn writer William Cowper where he entertained friends such as John Newton the author of the hymn "Amazing Grace". There is a costume gallery, a lace exhibition and gardens.

PASSPORT CONCESSIONS: 50% off adult admission charge.

JNR. PASSPORT CONCESSIONS: Free Badge.

PETERBOROUGH — Longthorpe Tower

Thorpe Road, Longthorpe, Peterborough. 0733-268482. Open: Daily 10-6 Summer, Tue-Sun 10-4 Winter. £ (EH)

The wall paintings of biblical and domestic scenes in this 14th century tower of a manor house form the most complete set of the period in England.

PETERBOROUGH — Peterborough City Museum and Art Gallery

Priestgate, Peterborough PE1 1LF. 0733-43329. Open: Mon-Sat 10-5.

A busy local treasury of an historic town's arts, crafts, geology, wildlife, archaeology and militaria, with relentless programme of high standard temporary exhibitions.

PETERBOROUGH — Railworld (Museum of World Railways)

Oundle Road, Peterborough PE2 9NR. 0733-44240 Not yet open to the public. P

Trains past and present, the people who run them and the places where they run them, but not due to open until 1991 so check before coming.

PETERBOROUGH — Sacrewell Farm and Country Centre

Sacrewell, Thornhaugh, Peterborough PE8 6HJ. Open: 0780-782222. Always open. £ P &

A working farm dating from at least Domesday, which has preserved its history from flint tools to a working water mill.

PASSPORT CONCESSIONS: Free entry to Passport holder; Special family entrance rate - 50% discount.

JNR. PASSPORT CONCESSIONS: Free entry to Passport holder; Free Pencil.

PINCHBECK

The Pinchbeck Engine & Museum of Land Drainage

West Marsh Road, Pinchbeck Marsh, Spalding, Lincs. 0775-725468. Open: Daily Oct-Mar by appointment only. P

The original pump house sports a simple 'A' frame beam engine erected in 1833. It was superceded in 1952 to become the last of its type working in the fens.

RUSHTON

Rushton Triangular Lodge

Rushton, Northants. 0536-710761. Open: Daily 10-6 Summer. Closed: Winter. £ (EH)

This is a unique piece of personal architecture, designed to represent the Holy Trinity and built between 1593 and 1597 by Sir Thomas Gresham, after being jailed for his religious beliefs.

SAFFRON WALDEN

Audley End House & Park

Saffron Walden, Essex. 0799-22399. Open: Tue-Sun 1-6 Summer. Closed: Winter. £ P (EH)

The plaster ceilings and reception rooms in this originally Jacobean house are by Robert Adam, and there was further remodelling in the 19th century. The house is shown with its original furniture and pictures, with the park landscaped by Capability Brown and garden buildings designed by Adam.

SAFFRON WALDEN

Saffron Walden Museum

Museum Street, Saffron Walden, Essex CB10 1JL. 0799-22494. Open: Mon-Sat 11-5, Sun 2.30-5 Summer, Mon-Sat 11-4 Winter. £ P ♿

This local museum in a beautiful medieval market town bursts out of its municipal boundaries with some of its collections, and now has a new Ancient Egyptian room. There are also ethnographic and ceramic collections, and 12th century castle ruins in the grounds.

PASSPORT CONCESSIONS: Free entry for under 18's; Special Offer Saffron Crocus Corms = £1.00 post paid.

SKEGNESS — Church Farm Museum

Church Road South, Skegness. 0754-66658. Open: Daily 10.30-5.30. Closed: Nov-Easter. £

This is another of the county service's 'Life in Lincs' museums, on the farm this time, with Lincoln Longwool sheep, a period farmhouse, agricultural tools and machinery and a thatched, timber frame cottage and garden.

PASSPORT CONCESSIONS: Free entry to Passport holder.

JNR. PASSPORT CONCESSIONS: Free entry to Junior Passport holder.

SOUTHWOLD — Southwold Museum

Batholomew Green, Southwold, Suffolk IP18. Open: Daily 2.30-4.30. Closed: Oct-Spring B.H. excl. Easter.

A characteristic feature of this local museum is that there is always a fresh display of wild flowers, plucked from the neighbourhood to augment the local and natural history displays, and the temporary exhibitions.

SPALDING — Ayscoughfee Hall Museum

Churchgate, Spalding, Lincs PE11 2RA. Open: Mon-Thur/Sat 10-5, Fri 10-4.30, Sun 11-5. Closed: Sat/Sun Nov-Feb. P &

Restored medieval manor house with agriculture, horticulture, drainage and wildfowling displays, plus a panelled 18th century library.

PASSPORT CONCESSIONS: Free information Pack.

JNR. PASSPORT CONCESSIONS: Free Badge.

Ayscoughfee Hall Museum

Churchgate, Spalding,
PE11 2RA (0775) 725468

Ayscoughfee Hall Spalding houses South Holland District Council's recently established museum service. Displays cover land drainage agriculture and horticulture as well as local history. Visitors can also see the panelled library and cased birds on loan from the Spalding Gentlemen's Society.

STAMFORD — Burghley House

Stamford,
Lincolnshire PE9
3JY. 0780-52451.
Open: Daily 11-5.
Closed: Early Oct-
Easter.   £ P

Built by Elizabeth I's Chancellor, Lord
Burghley, the scion of the Cecils and still their
home. It was stayed at by the Queen herself,
and was one of the grandest houses of the age.
All 18 state rooms are on view.

STAMFORD — Stamford Museum

Broad Street,
Stamford PE9 1PJ.
0780-66317. Open:
Oct-Mar Mon-Sat 10-
12.30/1.30-5. Apr-
Sept Mon-Sat 10-5,
Sun 2-5. £

The history and archaeology of one of Britain's
most historic towns, including special displays
on 52-stone Daniel Lambert and P. T. Barnum's
prize exhibit, 'General' Tom Thumb. Temporary
exhibitions throughout the year.

PASSPORT CONCESSIONS: Free entry to Passport
holder.

JNR. PASSPORT CONCESSIONS: Free entry to
Junior Passport holder.

STAMFORD — Stamford Steam Brewery Museum

All Saints St,
Stamford, Lincs TE9
2PA. 0780-52186.
Open: Tue-Sun 10-4.
Closed: Oct-Apr. £

A Victorian steam brewery, complete with
coppers, barrels and steam engine.

PASSPORT CONCESSIONS: Free Guidebook.

STOWMARKET — Museum of East Anglian Life

Stowmarket, Suffolk
IP14 1DL. 0449-
612229. Open: Mon-
Sat 11-5, Sun 12-5,
(Jun-Aug 12-6). Closed:
Nov-Apr. £ &

This is an open air museum of agriculture, rural
domestic life, crafts and industry, with events
and demonstrations through the summer.

PASSPORT CONCESSIONS: £1 off adult
admission charge.

JNR. PASSPORT CONCESSIONS:
Child 'school' rate of admission,
90p per child.

SUDBURY — Ancient House Museum

High Street, Clare, Sudbury, Suffolk. 0787-277865. Open: Easter-Sept Wed-Sat 2.30-4.30, Sun 11-12.30/2.30-4.30. Closed: Oct-Easter. £

Clare's town history, agricultural implements and artefacts, and room of costume from the late 19th and early 20th centuries.

SUDBURY — Nether Hall

Nether Hall, Cavendish, Sudbury, Suffolk CO10 8BX. 0787-280221. Open: Daily 11-4. £ P

This listed period manor house has a collection of rural artefacts and an arboretum.

PASSPORT CONCESSIONS: Free Poster; Free Guidebook; Free entry for under 18's; Free tasting of own wine.

JNR. PASSPORT CONCESSIONS: Free Schools Info Pack.

SUDBURY — The Sue Ryder Foundation Museum

Sue Ryder Foundation Headquarters, Cavendish, Sudbury, Suffolk. 0787-280252. Open: Daily 10.30-5.30, Sun 10-11/12-5.30. £ P &

The small museum tells the remarkable story of how this foundation was established, what it does and its hopes for the future.

SWAFFHAM — Cockley Cley Iceni Village and Museums

Estate Office, Cockley Cley Hall, Swaffham, Norfolk PE37 8AG. 0760-721339. Open: Daily in the afternoon-please call for details. Closed: Nov-Mar. £ P &

Reconstructed village from Boudicca's day, plus a medieval cottage and forge housing an East Anglian museum, a 7th century church, a farm implements museum and a nature trail.

PASSPORT CONCESSIONS: Free Guidebook; Discount admission charge.

JNR. PASSPORT CONCESSIONS: Free Badge.

TATTERSHALL — The Guardhouse Museum

The National Trust, Tattershall Castle, Tattershall, Lincoln. 0526-42543. Open: Apr-Oct Daily 10.30-6, Nov-Mar 12-4.30. £ P

In the National Trust's Tattershall Castle, the museum is mostly centred on the fascinating bits and pieces Lord Curzon found when he was restoring the castle in 1912-1914, plus a model of the castle as it looked 300 years ago.

THETFORD — Ancient House Museum

White Hart Street, Thetford, Norfolk. 0842-752599. Open: Mon-Sat 10-5, Sun 2-5 Summer, Mon-Sat 10-5 Winter. £

As ancient as the 1400s, the house belonged to a wealthy merchant who could afford to build them to last, and now tells of the Thetford and Breckland life.

PASSPORT CONCESSIONS: Adult entry at student rate.

THETFORD — Grime's Graves

Lynford, Thetford, Norfolk. 0842-810656. Open: Daily 10-6 Summer, 10-4 Winter (excl. Mon). £ (EH)

A lugubrious name for an extensive set of Neolithic flint mines, ranging from shallow pits to deep shafts with radiating galleries, all unique to this country.

THETFORD — Thetford Priory

Thetford, Norfolk. 0842-766127. Daily 10-6 Summer. Closed: Winter. £ (EH)

This was a Cluniac priory founded in 1103, and the cloisters remain along with a 14th century gatehouse.

TILBURY

Tilbury Fort

No 2 Office Block, The Fort, Tilbury, Essex. 0375-858489. Open: Daily 10-6 Summer, Tue-Sun 10-4 Winter. £ P (EH)

One of Henry VIII's many coastal forts, this one was remodelled and extended during the reign of Charles II and is an outstanding example of 17th century fortification.

TOWCESTER

The Canal Museum

Stoke Bruerne, Towcester, Northants NN12 7SE. 0604-862229. Open: Daily 10-6, Oct-Easter Tue-Sun 10-4. £ P

Beside the Grand Union Canal, in a restored cornmill, this museum covers the 200 year history and traditions of our canal system.

WALSINGHAM

Shirehall Museum

Shirehall, Common Place, Walsingham, Norfolk, NR22 6BP 0328-820510. Open: Easter-Sept Mon-Fri 10-1/2-5, Sun 2-5; Oct Sat/Sun only. Closed: Nov-Easter. £ P

This museum is in what was originally a medieval building, but now its centrepeice is a Georgian court room, preserved with its original fittings and the prisoners' cells. There is also a display on the history of pilgrimages to the shrine of Our Lady of Walsingham and other local history material.

PASSPORT CONCESSIONS: Adult admission at student prices.

WATERBEACH

Denny Abbey

Ely Road, Chittering, Waterbeach, Cambs. 0223-86489. Open: Daily 10-6 Summer, Tue-Sun 10-4 Winter. £ P (EH)

There was a series of "tenants" of this abbey after its 12th century foundation by the Benedictine order, including the Knights Templar and Franciscan nuns. The remains of the original church, and the 14th century dining hall.

WELLINGBOROUGH — Irchester Narrow Gauge Railway Museum

Irchester Country Park, Wellingborough, Northants. 0234-750469. Open: Sun 10-5. P &

A trust, dedicated to displaying and operating narrow gauge locomotives and rolling stock which were commonly used in the East Midlands, runs this museum, and so far there are four steam and five diesel locomotives, and 30 wagons.

PASSPORT CONCESSIONS: Free Guidebook; 10% off shop purchases.

JNR. PASSPORT CONCESSIONS: Free Badge; Free Pencil; Free Toy.

WIDDINGTON — Priors Hall Barn

Widdington, Essex. 0799-41047. Open: Daily 10-6 Summer. Closed: Winter. £ P (EH)

This is one of the finest surviving medieval barns in this part of England.

WISBECH — Wisbech and Fenland Museum

Museum Square, Wisbech, Cambs PE13 1ES. 0945-583817. Open: Oct-Mar Tue-Sat 10-4, Apr-Sept 10-5.

This purpose-built museum was opened in 1847 and contains a variety of collections including ceramics, ethnography, local history, geology, items relating to Thomas Clarkson's anti-slavery campaign, and a library of material about the draining of the Fens.

WISBECH — Peckover House & Garden

North Brink, Wisbech, Cambs. 0945-583463. Open: House - Sat/Sun/B.H. 2-5.30; Garden - Sat-Wed 2-5.30. £

The National Trust own this early 18th century town house, with plaster and rococo decoration plus a collection of Cornwallis family portraits and a Victorian garden.

PASSPORT CONCESSIONS: One child free for each paying adult.

WOLLASTON — Wollaston Museum

102 High St, Wollaston, Northamptonshire NN9 7PQ. Open: Sun 2.30-4.30. Closed: Oct-Easter.

Village life from 3000 BC to the 1940's (AD), including lace-making, rushwork and boot-making.

WOODBRIDGE — Easton Farm Park

Easton, Wickham Market, Woodbridge, Suffolk IP13 0EQ. 0728-746475. Open: Daily 10.30-6. Closed: Nov-Easter. £ P &

Farm animals including rare breeds and Suffolk Punch horses, a dairy centre with milking every afternoon, and vintage machinery.

PASSPORT CONCESSIONS: £1 off adult admission charge.

JNR. PASSPORT CONCESSIONS: Free schools information pack; Free badge.

WOODBRIDGE — Orford Castle

Orford, Woodbridge, Suffolk. 03944-50472. Open: Daily 10-6 Summer, 10-4 Winter (excl. Mon). £ (EH)

This was a royal castle built in 1165 to 1172 by Henry II, and its magnificent keep survives to tower almost intact 90 feet high.

WOODBRIDGE — Saxstead Green Post Mill

The Mill House, Saxstead Green, Woodbridge, Suffolk. 0728-82789. Open: Mon-Sat 10-6. Closed: Winter. £ (EH)

This is a four-sailed corn mill, with a 19th century wooden superstructure mounted on a brick round-house, and still in working order.

WOODBRIDGE — Woodbridge Museum

5A Market Hill, Woodbridge, Suffolk. 0394-380502. Open: Thur-Sat 11-4, Sun 2.30-4.30. Closed: Nov-Easter (Good Friday). £

Run entirely by volunteers, this local history museum has exhibitions about the Sutton Hoo finds, local personalities and the town in Napoleonic times as long-term exhibitions in 1990.

Passport Concessions: 50% off adult admission charge; Free Poster; OPPS.

WOOTTON — Royal Pioneer Corps Museum

Royal Pioneer Corps Headquarters, Simpson Barracks, Wootton, Northampton NN4 0HX. 0604-762742. Open: Mon-Fri 9-4. P

Set inside Simpson barracks (so arrange your visit in advance to be sure of getting in), here is the historical display about a much under rated corps and its wartime contribution.

NORTH WEST/
ISLE OF MAN

ACCRINGTON — Haworth Art Gallery

Haworth Park, Manchester Road, Accrington, Lancs . 0254-33782. Open: Sat-Thur 2-5. P

This house belonged to a cotton manufacturer who gave it to the town in the 1920's to be made into an art gallery. It now has European paintings, English watercolours, and the largest collection of Tiffany glass in Europe.

ALTRINCHAM — Dunham Massey Hall

Altrincham, Cheshire . 061-9411025. Open: Daily 1-4.30, Sun/B.H. 12-4.30, Garden 12-5.30, Sun/B.H. 1-5.30. £ P &

Home of the Earls of Stamford until it came to the National Trust in 1976, the 18th century mansion has more than 30 furnished rooms open, including kitchen, laundry, stables, and a working Tudor mill powered by the moat.

AMBLESIDE — Rydal Mount

Ambleside, Cumbria. 09663-3002. Open: Mar-Oct Daily 9.30-5, Nov-Mar Tue-Sun 10-4. £ P &

This was William Wordsworth's last home and contains family portraits, furniture and personal possessions still owned by the family. Wordsworth designed the garden himself.

ASHTON UNDER LYNE — The Museum of the Manchesters

Town Hall, Market Place, Ashton Under Lyne, Manchester. 061-344 3078. Open: Mon-Sat 10-4.

The Manchester Regiment recruited here and this unusual museum is one of military social history, looking past the medals and the battle honours, to the turmoil that was wreaked at home by military life.

ASHTON UNDER LYNE — Portland Basin Industrial Heritage Centre

Heritage Centre, 1 Portland Place, Portland Street South, Ashton Under Lyne, Manchester. 061-308 3374. Open: Tue-Sat 10-5, Sun 1-5. P &

Two hundred years of Tameside's industrial and social history are displayed in a former canal warehouse, with a waterwheel on the wharf.

BARROW-IN-FURNESS

Furness Abbey

Barrow-in-Furness, Cumbria. 0229-23420. Open: Daily 10-6 Summer,Tue-Sun 10-4 Winter. £ P &. (EH)

King Stephen founded this abbey in 1123. First it belonged to the Order of Savigny and then to the Cistercians, and it has a museum and exhibition.

BEBINGTON

Lady Lever Art Gallery

Port Sunlight Village, Bebington, Wirral L62 5EQ. 051-645 3623. Open: Mon-Sat 10-5, Sun 2-5. P &.

A treasury of the rich collections of Lord Leverhulme which he dedicated to his wife, with Reynolds, Constable and Turner all represented, plus pottery and porcelain. Lectures throughout the year.

JNR. PASSPORT CONCESSIONS: Free schools information pack on request.

BEESTON

Beeston Castle

Beeston, Taporley, Cheshire. 0829-260464. Open: Daily 10-6 Summer, 10-4 Winter (excl. Mon). £ (EH)

There are spectacular views of the Cheshire countryside from the walls of this castle, built about 1220 and there is an exhibition about the castle's history.

BIRKENHEAD

Birkenhead Priory & St. Mary's Church Tower

Priory Street, Birkenhead L41 5JH. 051-666 1249. Open: Mon-Sat 9.30-12.30/1-4, Sun 1-4. &.

A Benedictine monastery was founded here in the 12th century and the priory survives as Merseyside's oldest building. Displays in the undercroft trace the development of the buildings. The church was demolished in 1978 leaving the tower, and in a second phase on the site this is being refurbished by the Williamson Art Gallery and Museum, and opens during 1990 as a visitor centre with a history of Birkenhead and panoramic views.

BIRKENHEAD

Williamson Art Gallery and Museum

Slatey Road, Birkenhead, Wirral L43 4UE. 051-652 4177. Open: Mon-Sat 10-5 (Thur -9pm) Sun 2-5. P &.

In its 14 galleries the museum has displays of British watercolours, ceramic collections featuring Liverpool porcelain and Della Robbia pottery, local history (focussing on Cammell Laird shipbuilding) the history of the Wirral and the Mersey Ferry. The Baxter Collection of vintage motor vehicles is also here, and at Easter 1990 two new museums open as outstations at Shore Road Pump Station and Woodside Ferry Terminus.

BLACKBURN — Blackburn Museum & Art Gallery

Museum Street,
Blackburn, Lancs BB1
7AJ. 0254-667130.
Open: Tue-Sat 10-5.

There are strong collections of manuscripts and books in this local museum as well as paintings, watercolours, ceramics, Japanese prints and icons, and galleries devoted to social and local history.

PASSPORT CONCESSIONS: Free Poster.

JNR. PASSPORT CONCESSIONS: Free Badge.

BLACKBURN — Lewis Textile Museum

Exchange Street,
Blackburn, Lancs.
0254-667130. Open:
Tue-Sat 10-5.

tLancashire not only provided much of the world's textiles in the 19th century, it provided the men in the 18th century who invented the machinery to make it. This museum shows the early machines they created and demonstrations

of them can be arranged for visiting parties.

PASSPORT CONCESSIONS: OPPS. - to see working machines, appoint. needed.

JNR. PASSPORT CONCESSIONS: Free Badge.

BLACKBURN — Witton Country Park Visitor Centre

Preston Old Road,
Blackburn, Lancs.
0254-55423. Open:
Mon-Sat 1-5,
Sun/B.H. 11-5. P &

The centre is in the restored coach houses of the Witton Estate and has displays of carts, carriages and tools as well as temporary exhibitions which in 1990 include "King Cotton" and "The Romans in the North West".

BLACKPOOL — Grundy Art Gallery

Queen Street,
Blackpool, Lancashire.
0253-23977. Open:
Mon-Sat 10-5.

There is a permanent collection of 20th century British art, including work by Augustus John, Eric Ravilious and Paul Nash.

BOLTON — Bolton Museum & Art Gallery

Le Mans Crescent, Bolton, Lancs. 0204-22311. Open: Mon/Tue/Thur/ Fri 9.30-5.30, Sat 10-5. Closed: B.H. &

This museum boasts that it is the only one in the North West where you can see everything from Egyptian mummies, through English watercolours to live reptiles.

BOLTON — Bolton Steam Museum

The Engine House, Atlas No 3 Mill, Chorley Old Road, Bolton BL1 4JR. 02572-65003. Open: Sun 11-4. £

Steam engines which ran the Lancashire textile industry for nearly 100 years are preserved in an original engine house, with seven engines working on steam days - one each in April, May, August, October and December.

PASSPORT CONCESSIONS: 50% off adult admission charge.

JNR. PASSPORT CONCESSIONS: Free entry to Junior Passport holder.

BOLTON — Halli'th Wood

Green Way, off Crompton Way, Bolton, Lancs. 0204-51159. Open: Mon-Sat 11-5, Sun 2-5. Closed: Oct-Mar. £

This late medieval merchant's house which dates from 1485 was later the home of Samuel Crompton, the inventor of the Spinning Mule, and there is material about him and local history. It is furnished in Stuart and Georgian style.

PASSPORT CONCESSIONS: 50% off admission charge.

BOLTON — Local History Museum

All Saints Street, Bolton, Lancs. 0204-22311. Open: Mon-Sat (excl Thur) 10-12/1-5. Closed: B.H. &

This is in Bolton's first town hall, built in 1826 and covers social and industrial history with exhibits such as a horse-drawn fire engine, Civil War armour and a basket weavers' workshop.

BOLTON — Smithills Hall Museum

Off Smithills Dean Road, Bolton, Lancs. 0204-41265. Open: Mon-Sat 11-5, Sun 2-5. Closed: Oct-Mar. £

Dating from the 14th century, this is one of Lancashire's oldest manor houses. It has Tudor oak pannelling, 17th century furniture and a nature trail in the grounds.

PASSPORT CONCESSIONS: 50% off admission charge.

BOWNESS

Windermere Steamboat Museum

Rayrigg Road, Bowness-on-Windermere, Cumbria LA23 1BN. 09662-5565. Open: East-Oct Daily 10-5. £ P &

This has lake boats powered by steam, petrol and sail, but with some classic steamers in the collection.

BRAMPTON

Lanercost Priory

Brampton, Cumbria. 06977-3030. Open: Daily 10-6 Summer. Closed: Winter. £ (EH)

The church nave of this Augustinian priory of 1166 is still in use, contrasting with the ruined chancel, transepts and priory buildings.

BROMLEY CROSS

Turton Tower

Chapeltown Road, Bromley Cross, Nr Bolton, Lancs BL7 0HG. 0204-852203. Open: Mon-Fri 10-12/1-5, Sat/Sun 1-5. Closed: Dec-Jan. £ P

The tower dates from the early 15th century and now houses a fine collection of Tudor and Jacobean furniture, Civil War armour and weapons .

PASSPORT CONCESSIONS: 50% off adult admission; Free Poster; Free Guidebook; 50% off Family rate.

JNR. PASSPORT CONCESSIONS: Free Badge; Free Pencil; Free T. Shirt.

BUNBURY

Bunbury Watermill

Mill Lane, off Bowes Gate Lane, Bunbury,Tarporley, Ches. 061-480 6271. Open: Easter-Sept Sat/Sun 2-5. Or by appoint. Closed: Oct-Easter. £ P

The local water authority acquired this, along with a sewage works, and they restored it to working order, thanks to the help of a retired miller, Tom Parker.

PASSPORT CONCESSIONS: Free Guidebook; 20% off flour purchases and bookmarks.

BURNLEY

Towneley Hall Art Gallery & Museums

Burnley, Lancashire BB11 3RQ. 0282-24213. Open: Mon-Fri 10-5, Sun 12-5. P

A 14th century country house with a 12th century furnished chapel, long gallery, kitchen and early entrance hall and Regency drawing room. Natural history and archaeology, plus important paintings from the 18th and 19th centuries, and a natural history centre just opened with an aquarium.

BURNLEY — Weaver's Triangle Visitor Centre

The Wharfmaster's House, 85 Manchester Road, Burnley, Lancs BB11 1JZ. 0282-52403. Open: Tue/Wed/Sat/Sun 2-4. Closed: Oct-Mar.

Set in a Victorian industrial estate astride the Liverpool - Leeds Canal, the museum (for that's what it is despite its title) is about the triangle's life and work and that of the Burnley cotton industry.

PASSPORT CONCESSIONS: Free tea and biscuits in the Victorian parlour.

JNR. PASSPORT CONCESSIONS: Free Badge.

BURY — Lancashire Fusiliers' Regimental Museum

Wellington Barracks, Bolton Road, Bury. 061-764 2208. Open: Tue/ Wed/ Fri-Sun 9.30-12.15/12.45-4.30. Closed: B.H. £ P &

The regiment, which goes back 300 years, numbers General James Wolfe among its alumni, buried Napoleon in St. Helena, and has won four VCs, all elements of the story told here.

JNR. PASSPORT CONCESSIONS: Free admission to Junior Passport holder.

CARK-IN-CARTMEL — Craft and Countryside Exhibition

Holker Hall, Cark-in-Cartmel, nr Grange-over-Sands, Cumbria. 0539-58328. Open: Easter-Oct Sun-Fri 10.30-6. £ P &

This is at Cark-in-Carmel, and the crafts include bobbin-making, fishing and slate-working.

CARLISLE — The Border Regiment and King's Own Royal Regiment Museum

Queen Mary's Tower, The Castle, Carlisle. 0228-32774. Open: Daily 13 Apr-30 Sept. 9.30-6, Oct-14 Apr 9.30-4. £

Cumbria's county regiment and its 300 year history, from red coats to combat kit.

PASSPORT CONCESSIONS: Free Guidebook

JNR. PASSPORT CONCESSIONS: Free Badge.

CARLISLE — Carlisle Castle

Carlisle, Cumbria. 0228-31777. Open: Daily 10-6 Summer, Tue-Sun 10-4 Winter. £ (EH)

Mary Queen of Scots was imprisoned in this 12th century castle. It now has an exhibition about the city in about 1745, the Museum of the King's Own Regiment, a furnished suite of medieval rooms in the outer gatehouse and a living history centre.

CARLISLE — Carlisle Guildhall Museum

Greenmarket.
0228-34781. Open:
Mon-Sat 9-5.

This is a 15th century timber-framed house which now has exhibitions about the history of the medieval guild, open again after a major rebuild of its galleries.

CARNFORTH — Steamtown Railway Museum

Warton Road,
Carnforth, Lancashire.
Open: Daily 9-5
Summer, 10-5 Winter.
£ P &

On a huge site, there is a large collection of locos and coaches, plus workshops, a signal box, a turntable, offices and a coaling plant.

CASTLETON — Peveril Castle

Market Place,
Castleton, Nr. Sheffield.
0433-20613. Open:
Daily 10-6 Summer,
10-4 Winter excl. Mon.
£   (EH)

This evocative Norman keep with its herringbone brickwork, built by a companion of William the Conqueror's and visited by both English and Scottish kings, stands dramatically on a spur above the town and has splendid views of the Peak District.

CASTLETON — Treak Cliff Cavern

Castleton, Derbyshire
S30 2WP.
0433-20571. Open:
Daily 9.30-6 Summer,
9.30-4 Winter. £ P

If this is a museum, its objects must be the oldest in any collection, and perhaps it's more of a geological zoo. It's a quarter of a mile downwards to see the remarkable and beautiful blue john mine, still working, as well as stalactites and flowstone formations.

PASSPORT CONCESSIONS: Free entry to Passport holder; 10% off shop purchases over £1.

CASTLETOWN, Isle of Man — Castletown Grammar School

Castletown, Isle of
Man. 0624-75522.
Open: Easter-Sept
Tue-Sat 10-1/2-5, Sun
2-5.   P &

This was the old island capital's first church, built about 1200, and later the grammar school.

CASTLETOWN, Isle of Man — Castle Rushen

Castletown, Isle of Man. 0624-75522. Open: Easter-Sept Daily 10-5. Winter by appoint. £

This is a preserved medieval castle built on the site of a Viking stronghold in the old capital of the island, developed between the 13th and 16th centuries by successive kings and Lords of Man.

PASSPORT CONCESSIONS: Free entry to Passport holder.

JNR. PASSPORT CONCESSIONS: Free entry to Junior Passport holder.

CASTLETOWN, Isle of Man — Nautical Museum

Bridge Street, Castletown, Isle of Man. 0624-75522. Open: Easter-Sept Mon-Sat 10-1/2-5, Sun 2-5. £.

The centrepiece of this museum is the 18th century armed yacht Peggy in her boathouse, augmented by other nautical exhibits and photographs of Manx vessels.

PASSPORT CONCESSIONS: Free entry to Passport holder.

JNR. PASSPORT CONCESSIONS: Free entry to Junior Passport holder.

CHESTER — Cheshire Military Museum

The Castle, Chester CH1 2DN. 0244-327617. Open: Daily 9-5. Closed: 2 weeks over Xmas. £

This represents the four regiments historically connected with the county with uniforms, head-dress, medals, weapons and silver.

CHESTER — Chester Toy Museum

13 Lower Bridge St, Chester. 0244-316251. Open: Mon-Fri 11-5, Sat/Sun 10-5. £

This is the permanent home of the largest collection of Matchbox toys in the world, some of them never released by the makers, Lesney, and there are 7,000 items in all.

PASSPORT CONCESSIONS: 50% off adult admission; Special famiy rate.

CHESTER — St. Mary's Centre

St. Mary's Hill, Chester CH1 2DW. 0244-603320. Open: 2-4.30 or by appoint. Closed: B.H. & Aug.

The redundant St. Mary-on-the-Hill, a 15th century church at the top of Britain's steepest hill, has become a museum of itself, the objects being its chantry chapel, its tombs, its wall paintings, its memorials and its medieval corbels and gargoyles.

CLITHEROE — Clitheroe Castle Museum

Castle Hill, Clitheroe BB7 1BA. 0200-24635. Open: Easter-Oct Daily 1.30-5. Closed: Nov-Mar.

There are archaeology, geology, social and local history relating to Clitheroe in this museum which hopes to have its new economic geology gallery ready to open in 1990.

COCKERMOUTH — Wythop Mill

Embleton, Cockermouth, Cumbria CA13 9YP. 059 681-394. Open: Mon-Thur/Sun 11-5. Closed: Nov-Mar. £

In one of the Lakeland's loveliest hamlets, this mill has an exhibition of vintage woodworking machinery powered by an overshot water wheel, and there's also a display of traditional hand tools.

PASSPORT CONCESSIONS: 50% off adult admission charge.

COLNE — British in India Museum

Sun Street, Colne, Lancs BB8 0TT. 0282-63129. Open: Wed-Sat 10-4 + May-Sept 1st Sun in month 2-5. Closed: B.H. £ P

Through photographs, coins and model railways, this museum presents the days of the Raj and the sahibs who ran it.

PASSPORT CONCESSIONS: 50% off adult admission charge; Free copy "Short History of the Indian Army".

JNR. PASSPORT CONCESSIONS: Free copy of "Short History of the Indian Army".

COLNE — Heritage Centre

Old Grammer School, Church St, Colne, Lancs. 0282-695366. Tel for opening times. £ P

The former grammar school, built in 1812, has been restored and now has small displays about Colne in World War Two, and the textile industry.

PASSPORT CONCESSIONS: Free entry to Passport holder.

CONISTON — Brantwook

Cumbria LA21 8AD. 05394-41396. Open: mid Mar-mid Nov Daily 11-5.30, mid Nov-mid Mar Tue-Sun 11-4. £ P &

This was the home of the artist, critic, social and education reformer John Ruskin, now with his studio restored and a great collection of his drawings and watercolours.

PASSPORT CONCESSIONS: £1 off adult admission charge; Free to under-18's.

CREGNEISH, Isle of Man

Cregneish Village Folk Museum

Cregneish, nr Port St Mary, Isle of Man. 0624-75522. Open: May-Sept Mon-Sat 10-1/2-5, Sun 2-5. £ P

This has thatched cottages, which include a crofter-fisherman's home, a weaver's shed with a hand loom, a turner's shop with treadle lather, a farmstead and a smithy, and there are craft demonstrations.

PASSPORT CONCESSIONS: Free entry to Passport holder.

JNR. PASSPORT CONCESSIONS: Free entry to Junior Passport holder.

CROSBY, Isle of Man

Manx Motor Museum

Glen Vine, Crosby, Isle of Man. 0624-851236. Open: Mon-Sat 10-5, Sun 11-5. Closed: mid Sept-mid May. £.

There are about 30 vehicles here, illustrating the development of motoring between 1902 and 1977.

DOUGLAS, Isle of Man

Manx Museum

Crellins Hill, Douglas, Isle of Man. 0624-75522. Open: Mon-Sat 10-5. P ♿

The island's national museum has a new extension, opened by the Queen in 1989, and covers all aspects of man's past and nature, using such objects as a reconstructed farmhouse and dairy to help.

ECCLES

Eccles Parish Church

Church Rd, Eccles, Lancs. 061-7891034. Open: Tue/Thur-Sat 10-4. P ♿

The church which is also a museum has an important collection which includes the Celtic Cross and Waterloo medals.

PASSPORT CONCESSIONS: Free Poster; Free Guidebook.

ELLESMERE PORT

The Boat Museum

Dockyard Rd, Ellesmere Port, S. Wirral. 051-3555017. Open: Apr-Oct Daily 10-5, Nov-May Sat-Thur 11-4. £ P ♿

Working museum set in a restored dock complex on the Shropshire Union Canal with workers' cottages and forge, and special events.

PASSPORT CONCESSIONS: Free Guidebook; Special rate family entrance ticket.

JNR. PASSPORT CONCESSIONS: Free Badge.

FINSTHWAITE — Stott Park Bobbin Mill

Finsthwaite, Nr Ulverston, Cumbria. 0448-31087. Open: Daily 10-6 Summer. Closed: Winter. £ (EH)

This mill has been restored as a working industrial monument, and is now much as it was when it was built in 1835, with the steam turbine engine still there.

FLEETWOOD — Fleetwood Museum

Dock Street, Fleetwood. 03917-6621. Open: Sun/Mon/Thur/Sat 2-5, Tue/Fri 10-12.30/2-5. Closed: Nov-Mar.

Local history here means fishing, deep sea and inshore, so that is what the town's museum is about.

GLOSSOP — Dinting Railway Centre

Dinting Lane, Glossop, Derbys. 04574-5596. Open: Daily 10-5. £ P &

This is the home of the preserved steam locomotives Bahamas and Scots Guardsman, which give brake van rides on summer Sundays and Bank Holidays.

GRASMERE — Dove Cottage & The Wordsworth Museum

Grasmere, Cumbria. 09665-544. Open: Daily 9.30-5.30. Closed: mid Jan-mid Feb. £ P

Manuscripts, portraits and memorabilia of Wordsworth, his family and his distinguished literary and artistic circle.

GREEN HEAD — Roman Army Museum

Carvoran, Green Head, Carlisle, Cumbria. 06972-485. Open: Mar-Oct Daily 10-6.30, Nov-Feb Sat/Sun 10-4. Closed: Dec/Jan. £ P &

At the western end of the Hadrian's Wall, where there was a garrison, the museum has exhibitions about the life and work of the Roman soldier, with a large model of the fort which once stood here.

HELMSHORE — Helmshore Textile Museums

Holcombe Road, Helmshore, Lancs. 0706-226459. Open: Easter-Oct Mon-Fri 2-5, Sat 2-5, Sun 11-5, Jul-Sept Mon-Fri 12-5, Nov-Easter 2-5. £ P &

This is a water-powered mill built in 1789 with a large, rim-geared waterwheel, fulling stacks and machinery for finishing. There is a collection of early textile machines, a Hargeaves spinning jenny and several pieces from Arkwright's mill at Cromford.

KENDAL — Abbot Hall Art Gallery

Kirkland, Kendal, Cumbria LA9 5AL. 0539-722464. Open: Mon-Sat 10.30-5, Sun 2-5 Summer, Mon-Fri 10.30-5, Sat/Sun 2-5 Winter. £ P &

A Georgian house with furniture by the famous Gillows of Lancaster cabinet makers, and paintings by George Romney, locally born, and John Ruskin, plus temporary exhibitions.

PASSPORT CONCESSIONS: 50% off adult admission charge; Free Guidebook; Special rate family entrance ticket; 10% off shop purchases; Complimentary copy of 'Two Interesting Walks between Abbot Hall and Kendal Museum'.

JNR. PASSPORT CONCESSIONS: Free Pencil; Free questionnaire; Two children for price of one.

KENDAL — Kendal Museum of Natural History & Archaeology

Station Road, Kendal, Cumbria. 0539-721374. Open: Mon-Sat 10.30-5, Sun 2-5. £ P &

One of Britain's earliest museums, dating back to 1796, with the story of the Kendal inhabitants from the Stone Age to its development as a medieval wool town, plus natural history and wildlife galleries.

PASSPORT CONCESSIONS: 50% off adult admission charge; Special rate family entrance ticket; 10% off shop purchases; Complimentary copy of 'Two Interesting Walks'.

JNR. PASSPORT CONCESSIONS: Free Pencil; Free Questionnaire; Two children for the price of one.

From a Kendal Window.

KENDAL — Museum of Lakeland Life & Industry

Kirkland, Kendal, Cumbria LA9 5AL. 0539-722464. Open: Mon-Sat 10.30-5, Sun 2-5. £ P.

Reconstructed workshops full of hand-worn tools and intimate farmhouse rooms catch the flavour of traditional everyday life in the Lake District.

PASSPORT CONCESSIONS: 50% off adult admission charge; Free Guidebook; Special rate family entrance ticket; 10% off shop purchases; Complimentary copy of 'Two Interesting Walks'.

JNR. PASSPORT CONCESSIONS: Free Pencil; Free Questionnaire; Two children for the price of one.

KESWICK — Keswick Museum and Art Gallery

Fitz Park, Keswick, Cumbria. 0596-73263. Open: Mon-Sat 10-12.30/2-5. Closed: Nov-Mar. £

The museum was built to celebrate Queen Victoria's diamond jubilee, and to provide the people of Keswick with 'rest and relaxation', the art gallery coming in 1905. Its displays are of the art and objects of the Lake District, plus Joseph Fintoff's relief model of the area made between 1817 and 1834.

PASSPORT CONCESSIONS: Free entry to Passport holder; Free entry to under-18's.

KIRKBY STEPHEN — Brough Castle

High Street, Brough, Kirkby Stephen, Cumbria. Open: Daily 10-6 Summer, Tue-Sun 10-4 Winter. £ (EH)

Lesley Anne Clifford, Countess of Pembroke, restored this 12th century castle in the 17th century. It was built on the site of a Roman fort.

KNUTSFORD — Tatton Park

Knutsford, Cheshire WA16 6QN. 0565-54822. Open: Call for details. £ P &

This former Tenants' Hall houses the Egerton family museum, with the fourth lord's hunting trophies, and porcelain, glass, silver, paintings, horsedrawn vehicles and Gill furniture. There are special events almost constantly through the year.

PASSPORT CONCESSIONS: 20% off admission charge to Mansion and Garden.

LANCASTER — Cottage Museum

15 Castle Hill, Lancaster. Open: Daily 2-5. Closed: Nov-Easter. £ P

Part of a house dating from at least 1739 which was divided in two in the 1820s, the right-hand half is a private house while the left-hand has been returned to its 1825 state and furnished as an artisan's cottage.

PASSPORT CONCESSIONS: Free entry to Passport holder.

JNR. PASSPORT CONCESSIONS: Free entry to Junior Passport holder.

LANCASTER — Judges Lodgings

Church Street, Lancaster. 0524-32808. Open: Good Fri-30 Jun/Oct Daily 2-5. Jul-Sept Mon-Fri 10-1/2-5, Sat/Sun 2-5. Closed: Nov-Good Fri. £

This town house was bought by the Lancashire Justices in the 1820's, and evidence of the place's forensic past can be seen in the judges' bedroom and in the rest of the house. The second floor is being furnished as a private house, and there are plans for a gallery devoted to Gillow furniture and a billiard room with the world's largest billiard table - made by Gillow - in it. There is also a museum of childhood here.

LANCASTER — King's Own Regimental Museum

Market Square, Lancaster LA1 1HT. 0524-64637. Open: Mon-Sat 10-5.

This is part of Lancaster City Museum. The council acquired the collections of the King's Own Royal Regiment in 1929, and with them a splendid array of medals, early uniforms, books, photographs and medals now dating from 1680 to 1959.

LANCASTER — Lancaster City Museum

Market Square, Lancaster LA1 1HT. 0524-64637. Open: Mon-Sat 10-5.

Formed in 1923 but able to trace its origins back to 1835, the museum's collections trace the past of the city, whose catchment includes Morcambe and Heysham.

PASSPORT CONCESSIONS: Free Guidebook.

LANCASTER — Lancaster Maritime Museum

St. Georges Quay, Lancaster, Lancs LA1 1RB. 0524-64637. Open: Easter-Oct Daily 11-5, Nov-Easter 2-5. £ P

Housed in the former 18th century Custom House and opened in 1985, the museum tells the history of the port of Lancaster, with a reconstruction of a collector of customs' office of about 1800.

PASSPORT CONCESSIONS: Free entry to Passport holder.

JNR. PASSPORT CONCESSIONS: Free entry to Junior Passport holder.

LAXEY, Isle of Man

Laxey Wheel

Laxey, Isle of Man. 0624-75522. Open: Easter-Sept Daily 10-5. £ P.

Built in 1854 and called Lady Isabella after the wife of the then Lieutenant Governor, the Great Wheel at Laxey is the largest of its kind in the world.

PASSPORT CONCESSIONS: Free entry to Passport holder.

JNR. PASSPORT CONCESSIONS: Free entry to Junior Passport holder.

LEYLAND

The British Commercial Vehicle Museum

King Street, Leyland, Lancs. 0772-451011. Open: Apr-Sept Tue-Sun 10-5, Oct-Mar Sat/Sun only. £

This is the largest commercial vehicle exhibition in Europe, with over 40 exhibits dating from 1896 to the present day, with buses, fire engines, trucks and steam wagons.

LEYLAND

South Ribble Museum and Exhibition Centre

The Old Grammar School, Church Road, Leyland, Lancs. 0772-422041. Open: Tue/Fri 10-4, Thur 1-4, Sat 10-1. P

The borough's collections of local history and archaeology are housed in a Tudor grammar school, and there are monthly exhibitions of the work of local artists.

PASSPORT CONCESSIONS: Free Poster; Free Leaflet.

JNR. PASSPORT CONCESSIONS: Free Poster; Free Leaflet.

LIVERPOOL — Liverpool Museum

William Brown Street, Liverpool L3 8EN. 051-207 0001. Open: Mon-Sat 10-5, Sun 2-5. P &

A museum of long-standing quality with one of Britain's finest collections brought from around the world - and beyond it. There are also the award-winning Natural History Centre and Planetarium. Temporary exhibitions on Bulgarian art, Viking silver, and the work of members of the Association of Weavers, Spinners and Dyers.

LIVERPOOL — Merseyside Maritime Museum

Albert Dock, Liverpool L3 4AA. 051-207 0001. Open: Daily 10.30-5.30. Maritime Park closed in winter months. £ P &

The first to put its faith in the attractions of Albert Dock, which now draws over a million people a year, the museum is dedicated to the history of the port of Liverpool, its ships and its people, with special exhibitions this year on Falkland Islands shipwrecks and the 150th anniversary of the founding of the Cunard Line.

PASSPORT CONCESSIONS: Special family rate ticket.

JNR. PASSPORT CONCESSIONS: Free schools information pack.

LIVERPOOL — Museum of Labour History

Islington, Liverpool L3 8EE. 051-207 0001. Open: Daily 10-5.

Working life on Merseyside from 1840 to now, covering housing, employment, leisure, education and trade unionism, with reconstructions of a street, a scullery and an Edwardian classroom.

JNR. PASSPORT CONCESSIONS: Free schools information pack.

LIVERPOOL — Sudley Art Gallery

Mossley Hill Road, Liverpool L18 8BX. 051-207 0001. Open: Mon-Sat 10-5, Sun 2-5. P

A blend of Victorian family home and art gallery, with important 19th century paintings and furniture.

LIVERPOOL — Tate Gallery

Albert Dock, Liverpool L3 4BB. 051-709 3223. Open: Tue-Sun 11-7 Summer, Tue-Fri 11-5, Sat/Sun 11-6 Winter. P &

This is the new northern presence of the famous modern art gallery, with a permanent collection and an internationally important programme of temporary exhibitions.

PASSPORT CONCESSIONS: Free entrance to special exhibition for holder, families at single rate.

LIVERPOOL — University of Liverpool Art Gallery

3 Abercromby Square, Liverpool L69 3BX. 051-7942347. Open: Mon/Tue/Thur 12 -2, Wed 12-4. Closed: Aug.

The university's collections include sculpture, paintings (notably Audubon, Turner and Freud), watercolours, drawings, prints, furniture, ceramics, silver, glass, all from the late 17th century to the present and displayed in a Neo-Classical house.

LIVERPOOL — Walker Art Gallery

William Brown Street, Liverpool L3 8EL. 051-207 0001. Open: Mon-Sat 10-5, Sun 2-5.

Now with a majestic new gallery to show its magnificent collection of 19th century sculpture, there are also paintings and the gallery covers the 14th to 20th centuries - particularly British 19th century painting.

JNR. PASSPORT CONCESSIONS: Free schools information pack.

MACCLESFIELD — Paradise Mill Museum

Park Lane, Macclesfield. 0625-618228. Open: Tue-Sun 1-5. £ &

There are 26 Jacquard hand looms here, preserved, restored and in working order in a 19th century silk mill. There are tours guided by former silk workers, with demonstrations of the hand-weaving process.

PASSPORT CONCESSIONS: 50% off admission charge; 10% off shop purchases.

MACCLESFIELD — The Silk Museum

The Heritage Centre, Roe Street, Macclesfield. 0625-613210. Open: Tue-Sat 11-5, Sun 1-5. £ &

This award-winning museum traces the history of the silk industry from its origins with costumes, models and period settings.

PASSPORT CONCESSIONS: 50% off admission charge; 10% off shop purchases.

MACCLESFIELD — West Park Museum

Prestbury Road, Macclesfield. 0625-24067. Open: Tue-Sun 2-5.

This is a small Victorian gallery set in a public park, with a fine Egyptian collection, 19th and 20th century paintings and a varied programme of temporary exhibitions.

PASSPORT CONCESSIONS: 10% off shop purchases.

MANCHESTER — Gallery of English Costume

Platt Hall, Rusholme,
Manchester M14 5LL.
061-224 5217. Open:
Mon/Wed-Sat 10-6,
Sun 2-6 (Nov-Feb
closes at 4).   P &

Part of the Manchester City Art Gallery's
family, this one in Platt Hall in Rusholme, the
museum in a Georgian country house has what
probably amounts to the most important
costume collection outside London, with dress
and accessories from 1600 to the 1980s..
Because of textile conservation requirements
the costumes are rotated in thematic
exhibitions.

1956 Paton Dress.

MANCHESTER — Heaton Hall

Heaton Park,
Prestwich, Manchester
M25 5SW. 061-773
1231. Open:
Mon/Wed-Sat 10-1/2-
5.45, Sun 2-5.45.
Closed: Oct- Mar.

This is a late 18th century house designed by
James Wyatt for Sir Thomas Egerton, and the
restored period rooms are furnished with
paintings, furniture and ceramics. There is a
changing programme of exhibitions and events.
This is a branch of Manchester City Art
Gallery.

MANCHESTER — Holden Gallery

Grosvenor Building,
Manchester Poly,
Cavendish St, All
Saints, Manchester.
061-288 6171. Open:
Mon-Fri 9-4.30.
Closed: Jul-Sept.

Part of Manchester Polytechnic, the Holden has
its own craftwork collection on display and a
changing programme of temporary exhibitions.

PASSPORT CONCESSIONS: Free Poster.

MANCHESTER — Manchester City Art Gallery

Mosley Street &
Princess Street,
Manchester M2 3JL.
061-236 5244. Open:
Mon-Sat 10-5.45, Sun
2-5.45.

This municipal gallery has the work of Gainsborough, Stubbs, Turner, the Pre-Raphaelites, Victorian and Edwardian paintings, silver, pottery, porcelain, furniture and major temporary exhibitions.

PASSPORT CONCESSIONS: OPPS.

JNR. PASSPORT CONCESSIONS: Free Badge.

MANCHESTER — Manchester Jewish Museum

190 Cheetham Hill
Rd, Manchester M8
8LW. 061-834 9879.
Open: Mon-Thur 10-
4, Sun 10-5. Closed:
Jewish Hols. £ &

Housed in a Victorian synagogue, this tells the story of Manchester's Jewish community over the last 200 years, with exhibitions and demonstrations.

PASSPORT CONCESSIONS: 50% off adult admission charge.

JNR. PASSPORT CONCESSIONS: Free Badge.

MANCHESTER — Museum of Science and Industry

Liverpool Road,
Castlefield,
Manchester M3 4JP.
061-832 2244. Open:
Daily 10-5. £ P &

Set in the historic Castlefields railway station and its buildings, this is Europe's largest industrial museum, with the launch of the Planet Project - complete restoration of Stephenson's 1830s locomotive - in June.

PASSPORT CONCESSIONS: £1 off adult admission charge.

JNR. PASSPORT CONCESSIONS: Free entry to Junior Passport holder.

MANCHESTER — Museum of Transport

Boyle Street,
Cheetham,
Manchester M8 8UL.
061-205 2122. Open:
Wed-Sun 10-5. £ &

Mainly buses, coaches and commercial vehicles which plied around Manchester, the oldest being the 1890 horse bus and the newest the 1975 coach.

PASSPORT CONCESSIONS: 50% off adult admission charge; Special rate family entrance ticket.

JNR. PASSPORT CONCESSIONS: 50% off admission charge (must be accompanied).

MANCHESTER — Whitworth Art Gallery

University of Manchester, Oxford Road, Manchester M15 6ER. 061-273 4865. Open: Mon-Sat 10-5, (Thur -9pm). P &

This is part of the university and has outstanding collections of British watercolours, historic and modern prints, textiles, wallpapers, contemporary art and sculpture, and has major temporary exhibitions through 1990.

Gilbert and George.

MANCHESTER — Wythenshawe Hall

Wythenshawe Park, Northenden, Manchester. 061-998 2331. Open: Daily (excl. Tue) 10-1/2-5.45. Closed: Oct-Mar.

Once the home of the Tatton family, the 1540 hall has paintings and furniture from the 17th century on, and there is a programme of exhibitions and events.

MARYPORT — Maryport Maritime Museum and Steamboats

1 Senhouse Street, Maryport, Cumbria. 0900-813738. Open: Mon-Sat 10-5, Sun 2-5 Summer, Mon/Tue/Thur-Sat 10-12/2-4 Winter. £ P

Objects, pictures, models and paintings about Maryport's maritime past, with the Flying Buzzard, a preserved steam tug, open to visitors.

MARYPORT — The Senhouse Roman Museum

Camp Hill, Maryport, Cumbria. 0900-65611. Call for opening times. £ P &

Due to open in April 1990, this is the museum of Alauna, the command headquarters for the coastal defences of Hadrian's Wall's western end, and has the Netherhall Collection of inscriptions, sculptures and artefacts from the Roman-British site.

PASSPORT CONCESSIONS: A Free Poster of this major new museum.

NANTWICH — Nantwich Museum

Pillory Street, Nantwich, Cheshire. 0270-627104. Open: Mon/Tue/Thur-Sat 10.30-4.30.

This local museum has just opened a new exhibition about Cheshire cheese.

NELSON — Pendale Heritage Centre

Park Hill, Barrowford, Nelson, Lancs BB9 6JQ. 0282-695366. Open: Phone for details. £ P ♿

This 17th century farmhouse, with its restored 18th century walled garden is now devoted to the story of the beautiful Pendle district and the famous witches - there are even witch tours organised.

PASSPORT CONCESSIONS: 50% off adult admission charge.

JNR. PASSPORT CONCESSIONS: Free entry to Junior Passport holder.

NORTHWICH — The Salt Museum

162 London Road, Northwich, Cheshire CW9 8AB. 0606-41331. Open: Tue-Sun 2-5. £ P

Salt has been made in Cheshire since Roman times, and this museum, in the old Northwich Workhouse, tells how and why.

PASSPORT CONCESSIONS: Free Guidebook.

JNR. PASSPORT CONCESSIONS: Free Badge.

NORTHWICH — Stretton Mill

162 London Road, Northwich, Cheshire CW9 8AB. 0606-41331. Open: Tue-Sun 2-6. Closed: Nov-Feb. £ P

This little working watermill gently dominates the beautiful countryside ten miles out of Chester and there are regular tours and demonstrations.

JNR. PASSPORT CONCESSIONS: Free Badge.

OLDHAM — Oldham Art Gallery

Union Street, Oldham OL1 1DN. 061-678 4653. Open: Mon/Wed-Fri 10-5, Tue 10-1, Sat 10-4. P ♿

Seven exhibition spaces showing the best of contemporary art and photography, with thematic exhibitions drawn from the gallery's collection of 19th and 20th century paintings. Temporary exhibitions changing all year.

OLDHAM — Oldham Local Interest Museum

Greaves Street, Oldham OL1 1DN. 061-678 4657. Open: Mon/Wed-Fri 10-5, Tue 10-1, Sat 10-4. P

Dedicated at the moment to its major exhibition Going Up Town, which records the history and development of Oldham's town centre and a life-size street scene of about 1920.

From the Ice Age to the Space Age, find out what's happening, in The Times every Saturday.

For all the latest news on exhibitions and special events, from still life at the Tate, to the Museum of the Moving Image, read *The Times* on Saturdays. Simon Tait's weekly column will tell you what's on and where.

And it keeps Museum Passport holders informed of any additional concessions or free gifts they're entitled to.

If you haven't already taken advantage of *The Times* Museums' Passport offer, simply fill in the coupon in *The Times* on Saturdays, for your free Passports to the past.

THE TIMES

OLDHAM

Saddleworth Museum

High St, Upper Mill, Oldham OL3 6HS. 0457-874093. Open: Mon-Sat 10-5, Sun 12-5 Summer, Daily 1-4 (Wed 10-4) Winter. £ P

There is a textile room and a mill room in this local history museum in the middle of textile country, with a weaver's cottage recreated Victorian rooms, a transport gallery and an art gallery.

PEEL, Isle of Man

Odin's Raven

Peel, Isle of Man. 0624-75522. Open: Easter-Oct Mon-Fri/Sun 11-4. Closed: Nov-Easter. £ P &

In 1979 a thousand years of the Tynwald, the island's Parliament, was commemorated by a 50 foot Viking longship which sailed here from Norway. This museum houses a replica of it.

PASSPORT CONCESSIONS: Free entry to Passport holder.

JNR. PASSPORT CONCESSIONS: Free entry to Junior Passport holder.

PEEL, Isle of Man

Peel Castle

Peel, Isle of Man. 0624-75522. Open: Easter-Sept Daily 10-5. Closed: Oct-Easter. £

This is on St. Patrick's Isle. The medieval curtain wall encloses the castle and ecclesiastical buildings which include the ruins of the Cathedral of St. German serving the diocese of Sodor and Man - the island plus the Western Isles of Scotland.

PENRITH

Brougham Castle

Penrith, Cumbria. 0768-62188. Open: Daily 10-6 Summer, Tue-Sun 10-4 Winter. £   (EH)

The keep dates from the 13th century and later buildings surround a paved courtyard. The castle was restored by Lady Anne Clifford in the 17th century, and it now has an exhibition on Roman tombstones from the cemetary of the nearby Roman fort.

PENRITH

Penrith Museum

Robinson's School, Middlegate, Penrith, Cumbria CA11 7PT. 0768-64671. Open: Mon-Sat 10-5 + Sun (Apr-Sept) 1-6.

The building is now the Eden District's local history museum, but when it was built, in 1670, it was a girls' charity school, the museum re-opens in March 1990 after refurbishment and extension.

PENRITH — Wetheriggs Pottery

Clifton Dykes,
Penrith, Cumbria.
0768-62946. Open:
Daily 10-6. £ P &

This is a unique working Victorian pottery with a 19th century steam engine and machinery, a large beehive kiln and a museum of industrial relics. Events throughout the summer.

PASSPORT CONCESSIONS: Free entry to Passport holder; Free Poster; 10% off shop purchases.

JNR. PASSPORT CONCESSIONS: Free entry to Junior Passport holder; Free Badge; Free Pencil.

PRESTON — Harris Museum & Art Gallery

Market Square,
Preston PR1 2PP.
0772-58248. Open:
Mon-Sat 10-5. &

A magnificent Greek Revival cultural palace splendidly restored, this museum has fine and decorative art displays, costume and watercolour galleries and a permanent exhibition about the history of Preston. It is developing a renown for its temporary exhibitions of contemporary art and social history.

PASSPORT CONCESSIONS: Free Poster.

JNR. PASSPORT CONCESSIONS: Free Pencil.

PRESTON — Lancashire County and Regimental Museum

Stanley Street, Preston
PR1 4YP. 0772-
264075. Open: Mon-
Wed, Fri/Sat 10-5. P
&

Lancashire from its origins to the present day, as well as its martial contribution to the nation - the Queen's Lancashire regiment, the Duke of Lancaster's Own Yeomanry and the 14/20th King's Hussars, each in its own gallery. The main 1990 exhibition commemorates 150 years of the Lancashire Constabulary.

PRESCOT — Prescot Museum

34 Church Street,
Prescot L34 3LA.
051-430 7787. Open:
Tue-Sat 10-5, Sun 2-5.
P

This is a clock and watch museum in an 18th century town house in the middle of the town which was South Lancashire's centre for the trade. There is a reconstruction of a traditional Lancashire watchmaker's workshop.

RAMSEY, Isle of Man

Grove Rural Life Museum

Andreas Road, Ramsey, Isle of Man. 0624-75522. Open: Mon-Fri 10-5, Sun 2-5. £ P.

This is a Victorian house furnished in style with toys, costumes and a garden.

RAWTENSTALL

Rossendale Museum

Whitaker Park, Rawtenstall, Rossendale, Lancs BB4 6RE. 0706-217777. Open: Mon-Fri 1-5, Sat 10-12/1-5, Sun (Apr-Oct) 1-5, (Nov-Mar) 1-4.   P

This was a Victorian mill owner's mansion which now houses collections of fine and decorative art, natural and local history and a reconstructed late 19th century drawing room.

RIBCHESTER

Ribchester Museum of Childhood

Church Street, Ribchester, Lancs PR3 3YE. 0254-878520. Open: Tue-Sun 10.30-5. £

A persistent winner of awards, this atmospheric museum has more than 50 dolls houses and over 250,000 objects on display, with a traditional toyshop. Temporary exhibitions all year.

PASSPORT CONCESSIONS: Free Museum Postcard & Pencil; Free Museum Guide; 5% off shop purchases.

JNR. PASSPORT CONCESSIONS: Free Pencil & Museum Guide; Free Colour-in Poster.

ROCHDALE

Rochdale Art Gallery

Esplanade, Rochdale, Lancs OL16 1AQ. 0706-342154. Open: Mon-Fri 10-5, Sat 10-4.

This has been described as the major centre in the north for politically and socially committed work. Whatever the reasons for making it, the art, contemporary and historical, is lively and worth seeing, as is the imaginative temporary exhibition programme which includes such subjects as Gracie Fields, music hall and local myths.

RUNCORN — Norton Priory Museum & Gardens

Tudor Road, Runcorn WA7 1SX. 0928-569895. Open: Mar-Oct Mon-Fri 12-5, Sat/Sun 12-6; Nov-Feb Daily 12-4.   £ P ♿

The priory site was excavated in the 1970s and the interpretative museum is one of the most comprehensive displays about monastic life in Britain, with a 12th century undercroft and 30 acres of woodland gardens.

PASSPORT CONCESSIONS: Two for the price of one.

JNR. PASSPORT CONCESSIONS: Two for the price of one.

ST. HELENS — Pilkington Glass Museum

Prescot Rd, St. Helens. 0744-692 499. Open: Daily 10-5. Closed: Xmas-New Year. P ♿

At the famous factory, the 4,000 year old story of glass-making is told, from imperial goblets to periscopes.

ST. HELENS — St. Helens Museum & Art Gallery

College Street, St. Helens, Merseyside WA10 1TW. 0744-24061 Open: Mon-Fri 10-5, Sat 10-4. ♿

Work and home life in St. Helens in the early years of this century, with a working class bedroom and a middle class parlour, plus fine art displays and temporary exhibitions.

SALFORD — Ordsall Hall Museum

Taylorson Street, Salford M5 3EX. 061-872 0251. Open: Mon-Fri 10-12.30/1.30-5, Sun 2-5.   P

This building with its Tudor timber-framed great hall and period rooms, tells the everyday story of Salford through social history and archaeology displays.

PASSPORT CONCESSIONS: Free Guidebook.

SALFORD — Salford Mining Museum

Buile Hill Park, Eccles Old Road, Salford M6 8GL. 061-736 1832. Open: Mon-Fri 10-12.30/1.30-5, Sun 2-5. P

In the Georgian-style mansion of 1825, built by Sir Charles Barry, is an exhibition tracing the history of coal mining, with full-scale displays an archive and a mining library.

PASSPORT CONCESSIONS: Free entry to Passport holder.

JNR. PASSPORT CONCESSIONS: Free entry to Junior Passport holder.

SALFORD — Salford Museum & Art Gallery

Peel Park, Crescent, Salford M5 4WU. 061-736 2649. Open: Mon-Fri 10-4.45, Sun 2-5. P.

This museum has the most comprehensive collection of the works of local boy L S Lowry, with a recreation of a street of the time in which he was flourishing, Lark Hill Place.

PASSPORT CONCESSIONS: Free Guidebook to Lark Hill Place.

SALFORD — Viewpoint Photography Gallery

Vulcan House, The Crescent M5 4NY. 061-737 1040. Open: Tue-Fri 10-5, Sun 2-5. £ &

This has a changing programme of temporary exhibitions and a technical library.

PASSPORT CONCESSIONS: Free Poster.

SETTLE — Museum of North Craven Life

Chapel Street, Settle, North Yorks. 07292-2854. Open: Easter-Sept Sat/Sun 2-5, Jul/Aug Tue-Sun 2-5. Closed: Nov- Easter. £

How the landscape has influenced all changing aspects of life in North Craven with, all year, a special exhibition on a 100 years of tourism.

PASSPORT CONCESSIONS: 50% off adult admission charge; Free entry for under 18's.

SOUTHPORT — The Atkinson Art Gallery

Lord Street, Southport, Merseyside PR8 1DM. 0704-33133. Open: Mon/Wed-Fri 10-5, Thur 10-1, Sat 10-1.

English watercolours from the 18th and 19th centuries, Victorian paintings and work by painters from this century associated with the New English Art Club are all part of the permanent collections in this gallery which has a rolling temporary exhibition programme through the year.

SOUTHPORT — Botanic Gardens Museum

Churchtown, Southport PR9 7NB. 0704-27547. Open: Tue-Sat 10-6, Sun 2-5 (Oct-Apr open until 5).

Shrimping and lifeboats dominate the local history here, along with natural history, 18th century Liverpool porcelain, Victoriana, a doll collection and archaeology, plus temporary exhibitions.

STALYBRIDGE — Astley Cheetham Art Gallery

Trinity Street, Stalybridge, Manchester SK15 2BN. 061-338 2708. Open: Mon-Wed/Fri 1-7.30, Sat 9-4.

There are permanent collections ranging from 14th century Italian paintings to the Pre-Raphaelites, especially Edward Burne-Jones, and a monthly exhibition programme covering fine art, craft and photography.

STOCKPORT — Lyme Park

Disley, Stockport, Cheshire. 0663-62023. Open: 13 Apr-Sept Tue-Thur/Sat/Sun 2-5. Or by appoint. £ P &

This estate was the home of the Legh family for 600 years, with the house built in about 1550, and the contents reflect the long history of the place.

PASSPORT CONCESSIONS: Holders who use the password - "Are there any vacancies for a housemaid/footman?" - will get a free set afternoon tea in the tea room.

STYAL — Quarry Bank Mill

Styal nr Wilmslow, Ches. 0625-527468. Open: Apr-Sept Daily 11-5, Oct-Mar Tue-Sun 11-4. £ P &

This is a museum of the cotton industry which shows how the millworkers' world was changed in the course of the Industrial Revolution.

PASSPORT CONCESSIONS: Two adults for the price of one.

ULVERSTON — Laurel & Hardy Museum

4C Upper Brook Street, Ulverston, Cumbria. 0229-86164. Open: Daily 10-5. P &

The world's largest collection of material relating to the legendary comic pair, in Stan's home town. There is to be a parade in Ulverston in June to celebrate his 100th birthday.

PASSPORT CONCESSIONS: Free entry to Passport holder; OPPS.

JNR. PASSPORT CONCESSIONS: Free entry to Junior Passport holder; Free Badge.

WARRINGTON — The Museum of the South Lancashire Regiment

Peninsula Barracks, O'Leary Street, Orford, Warrington, Cheshire WA2 7BR. 0925-33563. Open: Mon-Fri 9-2.

The title could be a lot longer, because the museum actually has the regimental collections of the 40th and 82nd Regiments and Volunteer Forces of 1717 to 1881, the South Lancashire Regiment from 1881 to 1958 and the Lancashire Regiment up to the 1970s. It comprises uniforms, badges, medals, regimental records and war diaries.

WIDNES — Catalyst: The Museum of the Chemical Industry

Mersey Road, Widnes, Cheshire WA8 0DF. 051-4201121. Open: Tue-Sun 10-5. £ P &

This is the museum of the chemical industry, and one of the most imaginative of the new generation approaching a subject which may not seem interesting but turns out to be fascinating with the computers, videos, working exhibits and the unique facility of being able to match products with the actual process plants seen from a viewing tower or through special magnifying cameras.

PASSPORT CONCESSIONS: 50% off adult admission charge; OPPS

JNR. PASSPORT CONCESSIONS: Free Badge; 50% off admission charge.

WIGAN — Wigan Pier

Wigan, Lancs. WN3 4EU. 0942-323666. Open: Daily 10-5. £ P &

An award-winning and trend-setting living history museum, where actors recreate scenes from the working life of Wigan. It also claims the world's largest steam mill engine.

WORKINGTON — Helena Thompson Museum

Park End Road, Workington, Cumbria CA14 4DE. 0900-62598. Open: Nov-Mar Mon-Sat 11-3; Apr-Oct Mon-Sat 10.30-4. &

The displays in the mid-Georgian house are of costume, ceramics and other decorative art, and local history with temporary exhibitions in the former stable block.

NORTH EAST

ALNWICK — Dunstanburgh Castle

Craster, Alnwick, Northumberland. 066576-231. Open: Daily 10-6 Summer, 10-4 Winter Tue-Sun. £ (EH)

Perched on a rocky promontory high above the sea, this isolated 14th century fortress has become an important wildlife habitat.

ALNWICK — Royal Northumberland Fusiliers

The Abbot's Tower, Alnwick Castle, Alnwick, Northumberland. 0665-602152. Open: Mon-Fri/Sun 1-4.30. Closed: Oct-Apr. £

Three hundred years of military memories, including the war dog Drummer, 1896-1906, stuffed by a taxidermist and displayed.

PASSPORT CONCESSIONS: Free entry to Passport holder.

JNR. PASSPORT CONCESSIONS: Free entry to Junior Passport holder.

BAKEWELL — Old House Museum

Cunningham Place, off Church Lane, Bakewell. Open: Daily 2-5. £

Originally 16th century, this was the home of the 18th century cotton spinning inventor, Sir Richard Arkwright, and is now a folk museum run by volunteers, with a Victorian kitchen, costumes, tools, lacework and children's toys and games.

PASSPORT CONCESSIONS: 30% off entry fee.

JNR. PASSPORT CONCESSIONS: 30% off entry fee.

BAMBURGH — The Grace Darling Museum

Radcliffe Road, Bamburgh, Northumberland. Open: Apr/May/Sept Daily 11-6, Jun-Aug 11-7. Closed: Oct-Easter.

This museum is dedicated to a single incident which took place over 150 years ago on September 8 1838, which caught the public's imagination then and still does. It was the rescue by 23 year-old Grace Darling and her father, the lighthouse keeper, of nine survivors from the wreck of SS Forfarshire. It even has the original cable used in the rescue.

BARNARD CASTLE — Barnard Castle

Castle House, County Durham. 0833-38212. Open: Daily 10-6 Summer, 10-4 Winter (excl. Mon). £ P ♿ (EH)

The cylindrical tower built by the Balliol family in the 12th century still stands in this extensive castle, staked on the steep banks of the Tees, and there are remains of a 14th century great hall.

BARNARD CASTLE

The Bowes Museum

Barnard Castle, Co Durham DL12 8NP. 0833-690606. Open: Mon-Sat 10-5, Sun 2-5. Nov-Feb closes at 4. £ P &

This is a French chateau in the north of England which has become a museum of European fine and decorative arts with items from the 15th to 19th centuries in period settings plus local antiquities and temporary exhibitions.

PASSPORT CONCESSIONS: Free Poster; Free Guidebook; Free ticket for second visit.

JNR. PASSPORT CONCESSIONS: Free Badge; Free ticket for second visit.

BARNSLEY

Cannon Hall Museum

Cawthorne, Barnsley, South Yorkshire. 0226-790270. Open: Mon-Sat 10.30-12/1-5, Sun 2.30-5. P

John Carr of York remodelled this 17th century building in the 1760s, and it has collections of paintings, furniture, glassware and pottery, plus the regimental museum of the 13th/18th Royal Hussars.

BARNSLEY

Monk Bretton Priory

Barnsley, S. Yorks. 0226-204089. Open: Daily 10-6 Summer, Tue-Sun 10-4 Winter. £ P & (EH)

There are extensive remains of the gatehouse and other buildings from this Cluniac Priory founded in 1158.

THE BOWES MUSEUM

Barnard Castle, Co. Durham DL12 8NP

The Bowes Museum is an enchanted place - a great art Museum in a rural setting, a fascinating personal story, a visual treat and a friendly welcome. You won't really believe it till you've been.

BARTON UPON HUMBER

Baysgarth Museum

Baysgarth Leisure Park, Caistor Road, Barton upon Humber, 0652-32318. Open: Thur/Fri 10-4 Sat/Sun 10-5 & Most BH. P

Porcelain, local history, country crafts, archaeology and geology with new displays on the local industrial heritage due to open half way through 1990 in this 18th century house. Changing exhibitions all year.

PASSPORT CONCESSIONS: 10% off shop purchases; Free car sticker.

BATLEY

Bagshaw Museum

Wilton Park, Batley, West Yorkshire WF17 0AS. 0924-472514. Open: Mon-Sat 10-5, Sun 1-5. P &

Local and natural history displays plus oriental ceramics and ancient Egyptian artefacts in a Victorian gothic mansion, which has a new gallery devoted to mythical and legendary animals.

PASSPORT CONCESSIONS: 10% off shop purchases over £10.

JNR. PASSPORT CONCESSIONS: Free Badge.

BATLEY

Oakwell Hall Country Park

Nutter Lane, Birstall, Batley, West Yorks WF17 9LG. 0924-474926. Open: Mon-Sat 10-5, Sun 1-5. P

This 17th century manor house is set in 87 acres of parkland. It has an exhibition area, period gardens and a nature trail, and there are events as well as exhibitions throughout 1990.

PASSPORT CONCESSIONS: 10% off all shop purchases over £10.

BEAMISH

Beamish, The North of England Open Air Museum

Beamish, Co. Durham. 0207-231811. Open: Apr-Oct Daily 10-6. Nov-Mar Tue-Sun 10-5. £ P

The multi-award winning recreation of Geordie life around the turn of the century, with a town, a railway station, a colliery village and farm. Events in the summer.

BEDALE

Bedale Museum

Bedale, N. Yorks. 0677-24604. Open: Mon-Wed/Fri/Sat 10-4, Sun 11.30-4. Nov-Apr Tue only. P &

At the centre of this little museum is the curious hand-drawn Bedale Fire Engine of 1748. There are also documents, photographs, clothes, toys, craft tools and household utensils.

BEDALE

Crakehall Water Mill

Little Crakehall, Bedale, N. Yorks DL8 1HU. 0677-23240. Open: Easter-Sept Tue-Thur/Sat/Sun 10-5. Closed Oct-Mar. £ P

A corn mill on the site of one mentioned in the Domesday Book, restored ten years ago and currently milling and selling flour using methods and machinery dating from the 18th and 19th centuries.

PASSPORT CONCESSIONS: 50% off adult admission charge.

JNR. PASSPORT CONCESSIONS: Free entry to Junior Passport holder.

BERWICK UPON TWEED

Berwick Barracks

Berwick Upon Tweed, Northumberland. 0289-304493. Open: Daily 10-6 Summer, 10-4 Winter (excl. Mon). £ P   (EH)

The borough museum and the museum of the King's Own Scottish Borderers are housed in one of the earliest purpose-built barracks in Britain to survive relatively unscathed. Built in 1717-21 for officers, men and their families, it now has the award-winning exhibition "By Beat of Drum", which recreates scenes from the lives of English soldiers between 1660 and 1880.

BERWICK UPON TWEED

Berwick Upon Tweed Borough Museum and Art Gallery

The Clock Block, Berwick Barracks, Berwick Upon Tweed, Northumberland. 0289-330933. Open: Apr-Sept Mon-Sat 10-12.30/1.30-6, Sun 11-1/2-6. Oct-Mar Tue-Sat 10-12.30/1.30-4. £ &

Not all of Sir William Burrell's encyclopedic collections went to Glasgow. A great range of fine and decorative art objects came here to become the museum core, but there is also an imaginative 'Window on Berwick' local history display and a new permanent gallery which includes a Cairo bazaar opening in August 1990. Temporary exhibitions too.

BERWICK UPON TWEED

John Sinclair Railway Museum

Ford Forge Heatherslaw, Nr. Etal, Berwick Upon Tweed, Northumberland. 0670-355899. Open: Daily 10-5. Closed: Oct-Apr. P &

Run by volunteers, this museum presents the history of railways in the North East and includes signalling, a booking office, lamps, signs, posters, documents and photographs.

PASSPORT CONCESSIONS: 10% off membership of friend of Museum; Free newsletter.

JNR. PASSPORT CONCESSIONS: Free Pencil.

BERWICK UPON TWEED

The Lindisfarne Wine and Spirit Museum

Palace Green, Berwick Upon Tweed, Northumberland. 0289-305153. Open: Easter-Oct Mon-Sat 10-5, Oct-Easter Mon-Fri 10-5. P

This is a collection of tools of the vintner's trade, including the Customs and Excise instruments, brass measures and early hydrometers.

BERWICK UPON TWEED

Lady Waterford Hall

Ford Village Nr. Berwick Upon Tweed, Northumberland. 0289-082 224. Open: Daily 10.30-5.30 Summer, by appointment only Winter.

This lovely Victorian house in Ford Village near Berwick was built as the village school in 1861 and was decorated with biblical murals by Louisa Marchioness of Waterford, who used local children and their families as models. Temporary exhibitions from Easter to November 1990 on the work of Lady Waterford and the history of Ford.

BEVERLEY

Beverley Art Gallery

Champney Road, Beverley. 0482-882255. Open: Mon-Wed/Fri 10-12.30, Thur 10-12, Sat 10-12/1-4. Oct, Exhibition Sat 10-5, Sun 2-4.

Local artists' work is exhibited in the gallery, which also contains the Beverley Heritage Centre which has an exhibition about the town's history, and the work of the local artist Fred Elwell RA is a major feature.

BEVERLEY — Museum of Army Transport

Flemingate, Beverley, N. Humberside HU17 0NG. 0482-860445. Open: Daily 10-5 (excl. Mon Nov-Feb). £ P &

The largest military museum in the North, under cover on five acres, it tells of Army land, sea and air transport. Special 1990 exhibitions on Dunkirk and after (from June) and the 40th anniversary of the outbreak of the Korean War (autumn).

PASSPORT CONCESSIONS: 20% off all tickets purchased by the Passport holder for his/her family/group.

JNR. PASSPORT CONCESSIONS: 20% off all tickets purchased for family/group.

BISHOP AUCKLAND — Binchester Roman Fort

Bishop Auckland, Co. Durham. 0388-663089. Open: Mon-Wed/Sat/Sun 10.30-6. Closed: Oct-Mar. £ P

This is the excavated section of the Roman fort of Vinovia which includes the most complete remains of a Roman bath house in Britain.

PASSPORT CONCESSIONS: Free Guidebook; Free ticket for second visit.

JNR. PASSPORT CONCESSIONS: Free Pencil; Free ticket for second visit.

BOROUGH BRIDGE — Aldborough Roman Town

Main St, Borough Bridge, N. Yorks. 0423-322768. Open: Daily 10-6 Summer, Oct-Mar Grounds only. £ (EH)

This was the capital of Brigantes, the largest tribe in Roman Britain, and there are remains which include parts of the Roman wall and two mosaic pavements. More remains can be seen in the museum.

BRADFORD — Bradford Industrial Museum

Moorside Mills, Moorside Road, Bradford, West Yorkshire. 0274-631756. Open: Tue-Sun 10-5. P &

Engineering achievements, from early forms of transport to textile machinery, are on display in a former spinning mill. There is also the mill owner's house recalling domestic life at the turn of the century. Check for dates and times of demonstrations.

BRADFORD — Bolling Hall Historic House

Bowling Hall Road, Bradford, West Yorkshire BD4 7LP. 0274- 723057. Open: Tue-Sun 10-5. P

The tower of the original medieval building remains, the hall was extended in the 17th century to create the house with examples of stained glass, and a wing was added in the 18th century. The period rooms are furnished with 17th century oak furniture and other contemporary furnishings.

BRADFORD — Cartwright Hall Art Gallery

Lister Park, Bradford, Yorks. 0274-493313. Open: Tue-Sun 10-5. P &

Purpose-built in 1904 in Lister Park to house Bradford's art collections, it has 20th century paintings, sculpture, local art, crafts, prints and ethnic collections with a busy exhibition programme.

BRADFORD — The Colour Museum

82 Grattan Road, Bradford, BD1 2JB. 0274-390955. Open: Tue-Fri 2-5, Sat 10-4. £ &

This award-winning museum tackles an essential aspect of the complex textiles industry by opening the world of colour, dyeing and textile printing to visitors .

PASSPORT CONCESSIONS: Free entry to Passport holder.

JNR. PASSPORT CONCESSIONS: Free entry to Junior Passport holder.

BRADFORD — National Museum of Photography Film & Television

Prince's View, Bradford, West Yorkshire BD5 0TR. 0274-727488. Open:Tue-Sun/B.H. 11-6. &

The former Museum of the Year explores the art and science of photography, film and television, and features popular interactive displays. It also has Imax, Britain's largest cinema screen.

PASSPORT CONCESSIONS: Free Poster.

JNR. PASSPORT CONCESSIONS: Free Schools information pack.

BRADFORD — West Yorkshire Transport Museum

Ludlam Street Depot, Mill Lane, off Manchester Road, Bradford BD5 0HG. 0274-736006. Open: Sun 11-5. £ P

There are demonstrations and rides on some of the historical vehicles in this collection which includes trams, trolleybuses, buses, and service vehicles, and there are bus simulators, special attractions and vehicles under restoration.

PASSPORT CONCESSIONS: 50% off adult admission charge.

JNR. PASSPORT CONCESSIONS: Free entry to Junior Passport holder.

CLECKHEATON — Red House Museum

Oxford Road, Gomersal, Cleckheaton. 0274-872165. Open: Mon-Sat 10-5, Sun 1-5. P

The house and gardens are dressed in the styles of the 1830s, and there are strong Bronte connections. The barn complex houses changing exhibitions.

PASSPORT CONCESSIONS: 10% off shop purchases over £10.

CORBRIDGE — Aydon Castle

Corbridge, Northumberland. 0434-632450. Open: Daily 10-6 Summer. Closed: Winter. £ P ᕱ (EH)

This was a 13th century knight's residence, with walls and defences added a hundred years later. There are traces of its conversion to a farmhouse in the 17th century, but the original hall, solar and service block remain.

CORBRIDGE — Corbridge Roman Site

Corbridge, Northumberland. 0434-632349. Open: Daily 10-6 Summer, Tue-Sun 10-4 Winter. £ P ᕱ (EH)

This is on the main road between York and Scotland and it was, in succession, a fort, a military depot and then a town. The museum tells its history through finds from the site.

CORNHILL-ON-TWEED — Heatherslaw Corn Mill

Northumberland TD12 4TJ. 089-082 338. Open: Daily 10-6. Closed: Nov-Easter. £

The original 19th century water mill still grinds corn every day, with demonstrations and this year special exhibitions on plight of the salmon and work bondage.

PASSPORT CONCESSIONS: 50% off adult admission charge.

JNR. PASSPORT CONCESSIONS: Free Badge.

COWESHILL

Killhope Wheel Lead Mining Centre

Cowshill, Weardale, Co. Durham. 0388-537505. Open: Daily 10.30-5. Closed: Nov-Mar. £ P

This starkly-named museum is the best preserved lead mining site in England, with displays and working exhibits on the life of the miners with a 34 foot waterwheel dominating the site, and probably the lives of the miners too.

COXWOLD

Byland Abbey

Coxwold, N. Yorks. 03476-614. Open: Daily 10-6 Summer, Tue-Sun 10-4 Winter. £ (EH)

There is an exhibition of carved stones from the site in this beautiful Cistercian abbey, which has a well perserved floor of glazed tiles in the church.

COXWOLD

Shandy Hall

Shandy Hall, Coxwold, York Y06 4AD. 03476-465. Open: Wed: 2-4.30, Sun 2.30-4.30 or by appt. all year. Closed: Oct-May. £ P

A biographical museum dedicated to the Rev. Laurence Sterne, author of the great rococo novel Tristram Shandy, with editions of his work plus prints and pictures in the house where he wrote.

PASSPORT CONCESSIONS: Free Guidebook; Free admission for children accompanied by adult.

JNR. PASSPORT CONCESSIONS: Free entry if accompanied by an adult.

DARLINGTON

Borough of Darlington Museum

Tubwell Row, Darlington, Co. Durham. 0325-463795. Open: Mon/Tue/Wed/Fri 10-1/2-5, Thur 10-1, Sat 10-1/2-5.30.

The social and natural history, and John Dobbin's original painting of the opening of the Stockton to Darlington Railway.

DARLINGTON — Darlington Railway Centre and Museum

North Road Station, Darlington, Co Durham DL1 6ST. 0325-460532. Open: Daily 9.30-5. £ P ♿

At the end of the historic Stockton to Darlington line is a restored Victorian station which houses collections relating to the railways of the North East, including George Stephenson's "Locomotion".

PASSPORT CONCESSIONS: Entry at party rate.

JNR. PASSPORT CONCESSIONS: Entry at child party rate.

DEWSBURY — Dewsbury Museum

The Mansion, Crow Nest Park, Heckmond Wike Road, Dewsbury, West Yorkshire. 0924-468171. Open: Mon-Sat 10-5, Sun 1-5. P

This sits in 42 acres of parkland, and the galleries, recently re-opened, explore the theme of childhood, work and play, featuring a 1940s classroom.

PASSPORT CONCESSIONS: Free Poster; Free Guidebook; Free information pack; holder added to mailing list.

DONCASTER — Conisborough Castle

Conisborough, Doncaster, S. Yorks. 0709-863329. Open: Daily 10-6 Summer, 10-4 Winter (excl. Mon). £ P ♿ (EH)

This features in Sir Walter Scott's "Ivanhoe" and is one of the best 12th century keeps in the country. It has a later curtain wall with solid round towers, and there is a new visitor centre and exhibition.

DONCASTER — Doncaster Museum and Art Gallery

Chequer Road, Doncaster, Yorkshir. 0302-734293. Open: Mon-Sat 10-5, Sun 2-5. P

This is a regional museum of archaeology, local and natural history, geology, painting, sculpture, pottery, glass, jewellery, racing and the King's Own Yorkshire Light Infantry.

DONCASTER — Museum of South Yorkshire Life

Cusworth Hall, Doncaster DN5 7TU. 0302-782342. Open: Mon-Fri 10-5, Sat 11-5, Sun 1-5. P

This is in a Georgian mansion set in parkland. Cusworth Hall has collections illustrating domestic life, childhood, costume, employment and leisure pursuits in South Yorkshire over the past two centuries.

DRIFFIELD — Burton Agnes Hall Preservation Trust

Estate Office, Burton Agnes, Driffield Y025 OND. 0262-89324. Open: Daily 11-5. Closed: Nov-Mar. £ P &

Splendid example of Elizabethan architecture, built 1598-1610, with ceilings and overmantels carved in oak, plaster, stone and alabaster, plus paintings from Gainsborough to Renoir.

DURHAM — D.L.I. Museum and Arts Centre

Aykley Heads, Durham DH1 5TU. 091-3842214. Open: Tue-Sat 10-5, Sun/B.H. 2-5. £ P &

This museum covers the history of the Durham Light Infantry 1758 to 1968, with a new medal room and has an arts centre with a full programme of exhibitions of painting, sculpture and photography in 1990.

PASSPORT CONCESSIONS: Free entry to Passport holder.

JNR. PASSPORT CONCESSIONS: Free entry to Junior Passport holder.

DURHAM — Durham Cathedral Treasury

The College, Durham DH1 3EH. 091-3844854. Open: Mon-Sat 10-4.30, Sun 2.30-4.30. £ &

The great prizes of this collection include the gold and garnetstone cross and portable altar of St. Cuthbert, the 7th century hermit, 10th century ecclesiastical embroidery, Saxon and medieval illuminated manuscripts and silver-gilt altar plate from the 17th and 18th centuries.

DURHAM — Finchale Priory

Brasside, Newton Hall, Co Durham. 091-386 3828. Open: Daily 10-6 Summer, Tue-Sun 10-4 Winter. £ (EH)

This 18th century Benedictine priory was erected on the site of St Godric's hermitage, and there are considerable remains of the church claustral.

DURHAM — Museum of Archaeology

Old Fulling Mill, Archaeology Dept, 46 Saddler St, Durham. 091-3743623. Open: Apr-Oct Daily 11-4, Nov-Mar 12.30- 3. £

This small museum run by the city is in an old fulling mill but its collections are of international stature, illustrating the archeological development of one of our oldest cities.

DURHAM — The Oriental Museum

Elvet Hill, Durham DH1 3TH. 091-3742911. Open: Mon-Sat 9.30-1/2-5. Sun 2-5. Closed: Sat/Sun Nov-Feb. £ P

Durham University's collection which includes Chinese ceramics, jades and Egyptian antiquities, with the star object being the Chinese bed.

PASSPORT CONCESSIONS: 50% off adult admission charge.

JNR. PASSPORT CONCESSIONS: Free Badge.

FILEY — Filey Museum

8-10 Queen St, Filey, N. Yorkshire. 0723-513640. Open: May-Sept Sun-Fri 2-5. Closed: Oct-Apr. £

A volunteer run museum, much visited by holiday makers, it tells of living permanently at the seaside - fishing, the lifeboat service, local history.

PASSPORT CONCESSIONS: Free entry to Passport holder.

GATESHEAD — Bowes Railway Centre

Springwell Village, Gateshead, Tyne & Wear NE9 7QJ. 091-4161847. Open: Sun 12-5, Open as static exhibit each Sat. £

This is the world's only surviving standard gauge rope hauled railway. It was designed as a colliery railway by George Stephenson, opened in 1826, and is not a scheduled ancient monument. Demonstrations and rides some weekends in the spring and summer.

PASSPORT CONCESSIONS: Free Guidebook.

GATESHEAD — Shipley Art Gallery

Prince Consort Road, Gateshead, Tyne & Wea. 091-4771495. Open: Tue-Fri 10.30-5.30, Sat 10.30-4.30, Sun 2-5. &

There are Old Master and Victorian paintings from the Shipley Bequest, a collection of contemporary craft and a programme of changing exhibitions.

GISBOROUGH — Gisborough Priory

Gisborough, Cleveland. 0278-38301. Open: Daily 10-6 Summer, 10-4 Winter (excl. Mon). £ & (EH)

This is an Augustinian priory, founded in the 12th century, with its gatehouse remaining and the east end of the 14th century church.

GOOLE — Goole Museum & Art Gallery

Market Square, Goole, North Humberside DN14 5AA. 0405-762187. Open: Mon-Fri 10-5, Sat 9.30-12.30/2-4.

The museum collections are about the early history of the area and the formation and development of Goole as a port by the Aire and Calder Canal Company, while the art gallery has an extensive collection of marine paintings by the Goole-born artist, Reuben Chappell, the 50th anniversary of whose death it is in 1990.

GREAT GRIMSBY — Welholme Galleries

Welholme Road, Great Grimsby, South Humberside. 0472-242000 Open: Tue-Sat 10-5. P

Model ships, paintings, archaeology, folk life and a Lincolnshire photographic archive from 1850 to the present, with a series of exhibitions throughout the year.

PASSPORT CONCESSIONS: Free Guidebook; 10% off shop purchases; Special Events.

JNR. PASSPORT CONCESSIONS: Free Badge; Free Pencil.

GREAT GRIMSBY — Ironage Settlement

Weelsby Avenue, Great Grimbsy, South Humberside. 0472-242000. Open: Tue-Sat 10-5. During Winter 10-4.

Reconstructed Iron Age roundhouses inside a moated enclosure, all built on the original site.

GRIMSBY — Thornton Abbey

Ulceby, Grimsby, South Humberside. 0469-40357. Open: 10-6 Summer, Sat/Sun 10-4 Winter. £ P &
(EH)

This Augustinian Abbey was founded in 1189, and a magnificent gatehouse of two centuries later remains, with the ruins of the abbey church and other buildings. The exhibition shows finds from and around the gatehouse. Telephone to check that it is open, though.

HALIFAX — Horses At Work - National Museum of the Working Horse

Dobbin's Yard, South Parade, Halifax HX1 2LY. 0422-346835. Open: Mar-Sept Daily 10-5, Oct- 2 Jan 1-4. Closed: Jan/Feb. £ P &

You can take a horse-drawn ride at this unusual museum of horses at work. There is rare horse-powered machinery, authentic vehicles, and shire horses stabled on site.

PASSPORT CONCESSIONS: Free entry to Passport holder.

JNR. PASSPORT CONCESSIONS: Free entry to Junior Passport Holder; Free Schools information pack.

HALIFAX — Museum of the Duke of Wellington's Regiment

Bankfield Museum, Akroyd Park, Halifax.. Open: Mon-Sat 10-5, Sun 2.30-5. P &

Weapons, medals, uniforms, etc. of the regiment, plus some personal possessions of the Iron Duke himself.

HARROGATE — Harrogate Art Gallery

Victoria Avenue, Harrogate. 0423-503340. Open: Daily.

There are permanent collections of English paintings here, alongside temporary exhibitions.

HARROGATE — Nidderdale Museum

King Street, Pateley Bridge, Harrogate. 0423-711225. Open: Late Spring B.H.-Sept Daily 2-5, Oct-Easter Sun only 2-5, Easter-Late Spring B.H. Sat/Sun 2-5. £

Nine large rooms in the Council Offices are devoted to Nidderdale's past, with a cobbler's hop, and a Victorian parlour, kitchen and school room.

PASSPORT CONCESSIONS: 50% off adult admission charge; Free Guidebook.

HARROGATE — Roman Pump Room Museum

Crown Place, Royal Parade, Harrogate. 0423-503340. Open: Mon-Fri 10-5. £ &

This museum traces the history and development of the spa from its beginings in the 17th century to its Edwardian glory, and there are changing exhibitions

HARROGATE — War Room

Broadwater House, 30 Park Parade, Harrogate HG1 5AG. 0423-500704. Open: Wed only 10-5 or by appt. P

Dedicated to all who served in the two world wars, there are exhibitions on the evacuation of Dunkirk (16 May-27 Jun), the Battle of Britain (11 July-19 September) and Fire Over England (26 Sept-10 May). But hurry - there are plans to seal the War Room as a time capsule on the 50th anniversary of the end of the war.

PASSPORT CONCESSIONS: 20% off shop purchases.

HARTLEPOOL — Gray Art Gallery & Museum

Clarence Road, Hartlepool, Cleveland. 0429-268916. Open: Mon-Sat 10-5.30, Sun 2-5. P &

The museum has permanent displays of local and natural history, and oriental collections, and a new Japanese gallery. The art gallery has 19th and 20th century paintings many with local connotations.

HARTLEPOOL — Hartlepool Maritime Museum

Northgate, Hartlepool, Cleaveland. 0429-272814. Open: Mon-Sat 10-5. P

Hartlepool's seafaring heritage, including a ship's bridge, a fisherman's cottage and a notable collection of ship models.

HEBDON BRIDGE — Automobilia British Motoring Museum

Billy Lane, Old Town, Hebden Bridge, W Yorks. 0422-844775. Open: Apr-Sept Tue-Fri 10-5, Sat/Sun 12-5. Oct/Nov/Mar Sun only 12-5. Closed: Dec-Feb. £ P &

A Victorian textile mill has been revived to house this collection of pre-1939 cars, motorcycles and bicycles.

PASSPORT CONCESSIONS: 10% off admission charge.

JNR. PASSPORT CONCESSIONS: Free Badge.

HELMSLEY — Helmsley Castle

Helmsley, N. Yorks. 0439-70442. Open: Daily 10-1/2-6 Summer, Tue-Sun 10-4 Winter. £ P (EH)

In the 16th century a new building was added to incorporate remains of some of the original 12th century interiors of this castle. There is now an exhibition about its history, and another of 19th century watercolours of Yorkshire monuments.

HELMSLEY — Rievaulx Abbey

Helmsley, North Yorks. 04396-228. Open: 10-6 Summer, 10-4 Winter (excl. Mon). £ (EH)

The church in this abbey, which was founded in 1132, has the earliest large Cistercian nave in Europe. There is an impressive 13th century choir and remains of other monastic buildings.

HESSLE — Hessle Whiting Mill

The Foreshore, Hessle. 0482-882255. Open: Daily 10-5. Closed: Nov-Mar. £

Used in the process of making whitewash 100 years ago, and now preserved with most of its internal machinery by Beverley Council.

HEXHAM — Chesters Fort and Museum

Chollerford, Humshaugh, Hexham on Tyne, Northumberland. 0434-681379. Open: Daily 10-6 Summer, 10-4 Winter. £ P ♿ (EH)

This six acre fort housed 500 Roman cavalrymen, and the gatehouse, commandant's house and bath house remain. The museum has a collection of sculpture and Roman inscriptions.

HEXHAM — Housesteads Roman Fort

Haydon Bridge, Hexham, Northumberland. 0434-344363. Open: Daily 10-6 Summer, 10-4 Winter (excl. Mon). £ (EH)

A thousand Roman infantrymen lived on this five acre site, and there was an extensive civilian settlement as well. Walls, gateways, headquarters, granaries and even latrines can be seen with the museum containing altar inscriptions and models.

HEXHAM — Middle March Centre for Border History

Hallgate, Hexham, Northumberland. 0434-604011. Open: Easter-Oct Mon-Fri 10-4.30, Sat 10-4.30, Sun 11-4.30. Nov-Easter by appt. £ P

This examines facets of life among the Borderers during the constant wars and political tension in medieval and Tudor times.

PASSPORT CONCESSIONS: 50% off adult admission; Free Guidebook; 10% off shop purchases.

HOLMFIRTH — Postcard Museum

Huddersfield Road, Holmfirth, W Yorks. 0924-682231. Open: Mon-Sat 10-5, Sun 1-5. ♿

This tells the story of the Bamforths, manufacturers of the original saucy postcard and early film-makers in the town which is the setting for TV's "Last of the Summer Wine".

HOLY ISLAND — Lindisfarne Priory

Holy Island, Berwick on Tweed, Northumberland. 028989-200. Open: Daily 10-6 Summer, 10-4 Winter (excl. Mon). £ P (EH)

There is a new museum here on Holy Island about this important 11th century Benedictine priory built on the site of the monastery St. Aidan founded in 633. It was later the seat of the bishops of the Northumbrian kingdom until the Danes destroyed it in 875.

HORNSEA — Hornsea Museum

Burn's Farm, 11 Newbegin, Hornsea HU18 1AB. 0964-533443. Open: Mon-Sat 10-5, Sun 2-5, Nov-Feb by appt. only.

Runner-up in the Times Shell Community Museum of the Year award in 1989, this is a folk museum set in an ancient farmhouse and outbuildings representing the village life of Hornsea over the last century through room settings and changing displays.

PASSPORT CONCESSIONS: Free entry to Passport holder.

JNR. PASSPORT CONCESSIONS: Free entry to Passport holder.

HUDDERSFIELD — Colne Valley Museum

Cliffe Ash, Golcar, Huddersfield HD7 4PY. 0484-659762. Open: BH/Sat/Sun 2-5. £

These are restored weavers' cottages of 1845 with hand loom weaving, a Spinning Jenny being used, a display of cropping, and clog-making by gaslight.

PASSPORT CONCESSIONS: 50% off adult admission charge; Special visits by arrangement.

JNR. PASSPORT CONCESSIONS: Free Schools information pack; Free Badge.

HUDDERSFIELD — Tolson Memorial Museum

Ravensknowle Park, Wakefield Road, Huddersfield HD5 8DJ. 0484-530591. Open: Mon-Sat 10-5, Sun 1-5. P

A museum of natural history, archaeology and the local past in a Victorian mansion which now includes galleries on textiles, farming, transport and 19th century Huddersfield. Exhibitions and events throughout the year.

PASSPORT CONCESSIONS: 10% off shop

HULL — Fernes Art Gallery

Queen Victoria Sq, Hull. 0482-222748. Open: Mon-Sat 10-5, Sun 1.30-4.30. &

Dutch Old Masters, including Frans Hals; portraits, Elizabethan to modern; the best marine paintings on the east coast and continuous exhibitions and workshops.

PASSPORT CONCESSIONS: 10% off shop purchases; Free Print/Poster for each sale over £2.

HULL — Hull and East Riding Museum

High St, Hull. 0482-222737. Open: Mon-Sat 10-5, Sun 1.30-4.30. P

This has the region's natural history and archaeological collections, including the famous prehistoric Hasholme Boat and Roman mosaics, all being organised now that some of their transport collection has moved to the new Streetlife. A new gallery of the Iron Age is due in 1991.

HULL — Hull University Art Collection

Middleton Hall, Cottingham Road, Hull HU6 7RX. 0482-465035. Open: Mon-Fri 2-4, Wed 12.30-4, during term time. P &

This has British art from 1890 to 1940, including Sickert, Steer, Pissarro, John, Spencer, Gill, Epstein, Moore; and the Thompson Collection of Chinese Ceramics.

PASSPORT CONCESSIONS: Free Poster; Reductions on cards and catalogues; OPPS.

HULL — Old Grammar School

South Church Side, Hull. 0482-222737. Open: Mon-Sat 10-5, Sun 1.30-4.30. &

This is a museum about fun-fairs, circus, seaside, cinema, pop music and theatre, all in what was Hull Grammar School and Hull Merchant's Company. Throughout 1990 the main exhibition is called That's Entertainment.

HULL — Posterngate Gallery

Posterngate, Hull. 0482-222745. Open: Tue-Sat 10-5.30.

There are often exhibits for sale in the temporary exhibitions held here of work by local and national comtemporary artists.

HULL

Spurn Lightship

Hull Marina, Hull.
0482-222737. Open:
Mon-Sat 10-5, Sun
1.30-4.30 Summer,
Wed-Sat 10-5 Winter.

Built in 1927, this was positioned off Spurn Point until 1959. Now visitors can see the master's cabin, the crew quarters, the gallery, the lifeboat and the light mechanism.

HULL

Streetlife: Hull Museum of Transport

High Street, Hull.
0482-222737. Open:
Mon-Sat 10-5, Sun
1.30-4.30.

This is the brand new museum of transport, one of the Hull Museums Service's innovations. It has the old vehicles in period settings, with audio-visual aids to add information and drama.

HULL

Town Docks Museum

Queen Victoria
Square, Hull. 0482-
222737. Open: Mon-
Sat 10-5, Sun 1.30-
4.30.

Hull's maritime museum with collections about whaling, fishing, ship models, figureheads, nautical instruments, paintings, scrimshaw, eskimos and polar bears.

HULL

Wilberforce House

High Street, Hull.
0482-222737. Open:
Mon-Sat 10-5, Sun
1.30-4.30. P

Originally a 17th century merchant's house, it was later the home of William Wilberforce and has collections relating to the great anti-slaver. There are also collections of decorative art, costume, furniture, dolls, silver, guns, period rooms and a river garden.

ILKLEY

Manor House Art Gallery & Museum

Castle Yard, Ilkley
LS29 9DT. 0943-
600066. Open: Daily
10-5. P

This is a Yorkshire manor house of the 16th and 17th centuries set on the site of a Roman fort, and as a museum it covers architecture, history, arts and crafts with a 17th century kitchen on the ground floor and the temporary exhibitions gallery on the first.

IMMINGHAM

Immingham Museum and Gallery

Waterworks St,
Immingham, South
Humberside. 0469-
75777. Open: Tue-
Sun 1-4. P &

Housed in a former Methodist chapel, the collections here are mainly about the Great Central Railway, the development of the docks and local history and archaeology. A local chemist's shop has been reconstructed.

JARROW · Bede Gallery

Springwell Park, Butchersbridge Road, Jarrow, Tyne and Wear. 091-4891807. Open: Tue-Fri 10-5, Sun 2-5. Closed: 2 weeks over Xmas.

The displays in this one-time Civil Defence headquarters are divided between the industrial and social history of Jarrow and temporary exhibitions of work by contemporary artists, often of international standing there is a Patrick Procktor retrospective from April 10 to May 30, 1990 for instance.

KEIGHLEY · Bronte Parsonage Museum

Haworth, Keighley BD22 8DR. 0535-42323. Open: Apr-Sept 11-5.30, Oct-Mar 11-4.30. £ P

The home of the remakable literary family, with rooms set out as in their day and original items of furniture, paintings, drawings, manuscripts and personal treasures. There is a permanent exhibition about the family, and a temporary

one from February 9th on illustrations for the Bronte writings, and on dramatic representations of Emily's Wuthering Heights.

KEIGHLEY · Cliffe Castle Museum & Gallery

Spring Gardens Lane, Keighley BD20 6LH. 0274-758230. Open: Daily Apr-Sept 10-6, Oct-Mar 10-5. P &

The star of this show is Pholiderpeton, resident in the Aire Valley more than two million years ago. There are also gems and minerals, wildlife and local history, and the recreated sumptuous reception rooms, circa 1880, of the original owner of the castle.

KEIGHLEY · East Riddlesden Hall

Bradford Road, Keighley BD20 5EL. 0535-607075. Open: Wed-Fri 2-5.40, Sat/Sun 12-5.30. Closed: Nov-Mar. £ P

Panelled rooms, intricate plasterwork, and mullioned windows with pewter, domestic knick-knacks and oak furniture in a traditional 17th century Yorkshire manor house in the Aire Valley, now owned by the National Trust. Special events spring to autumn.

PASSPORT CONCESSIONS: 50% off adult admission charge.

JNR. PASSPORT CONCESSIONS: Free entry to Junior Passport holder.

KEIGHLEY — Keighley & Worth Valley Railway

Haworth Station,
Haworth, Keighley
BD22 8NJ. 0535-
45214. Open:
July/Aug Mon-Fri 9-5,
Sat & Sun all year 9-5.
P &

Every weekend steam and diesel trains run on
this railway which has been lovingly restored to
its 1950s branch line appearance.

KEIGHLEY — Vintage Railway Carriage Museum

Ingrow Station Yard,
Halifax Road,
Keighley. Open: Mar-
Oct Daily 12-4, Jun-
Aug 11.30-5, Sat/Sun
through year 12-4. £

This is a new, purpose-built, museum on the
Worth Valley Railway which houses the award-
winning collection of coaches belonging to the
Vintage Carriages Trust, illustrating the story of
passenger rail travel from Victorian times.

PASSPORT CONCESSIONS: Free entry to Passport
holder.

JNR PASSPORT CONCESSIONS: Free entry to
Junior Passport holder.

KIRBY WISKE — Sion Hill Hall

Kirby Wiske, nr
Thirsk, North
Yorkshire. 0845-
587206. Open: May-
Sept Sun only 2-4.30.
£ P &

This is at Kirby Wiske and houses the
collections of Georgian, Regency and Victorian
furniture, porcelain, pottery, painting and
clocks of the late H. W. Mawer, who bought the
house specially for them.

KIRKLEATHAM — Kirkleatham Old Hall Museum

Kirkleatham, Redcar,
Cleveland TS10 5NW.
0642-479500. Open:
Mar-Oct Tue-
Sun/B.H. 9-5, Nov-
Feb Tue-Sun 10-4. P
&

Set in an historic building of 1703 with a
modern pavilion attached, this is the local
history museum for the borough of Langbaurgh-
on-Tees with displays on local working and
domestic life and the sea. A new gallery about
nearby seaside resorts opens in April 1990.

PASSPORT CONCESSIONS: Reduction on shop
purchases.

JNR. PASSPORT CONCESSIONS: Free Schools
information pack.

KNARESBOROUGH — Castle & Courthouse Museum

Knaresborough, Yorks. 0423-503340. Open; Easter Weekend/May B.H.-Sept Mon-Sat 10-5, Sun 1.30-4. £

Once a home of English kings, this 14th century castle now houses the museum in a unique Tudor court.

LEEDS — Horsforth Museum

The Green Community Centre, 3-5 The Green, Horsforth, Leeds. Open: Sat 10-4, Sun 2-5.

A reflection of what was once the largest village in England, with a new gallery on Horsforth's evolution opening March 31 along with a temporary exhibition on sports and pastimes.

PASSPORT CONCESSIONS: 10% off shop purchases.

JNR PASSPORT CONCESSIONS: Free Badge; Free Pencil.

LEEDS — Leeds City Art Gallery

The Headrow, Leeds. 0532-462495. Open: Mon/Tue/Thur/Fri 10-6, Wed 10-9, Sat 10-4, Sun 2-5. ♿

There are important holdings of 20th century British art here, including the Henry Moore Centre for sculpture study, and temporary exhibitions all year.

LEEDS — Museum of the History of Education

Parkinson Court, The University LS2 9JT. 0532-334665. Open: Mon-Fri 9.30-3.30. P ♿

This is a diverse collection of educational artefacts, documents, furniture, apparatus, samples of work from trainee teachers and their progress reports.

PASSPORT CONCESSIONS: Free Poster.

LEEDS — Otley Museum

Civic Centre, Cross Green, Otley, Leeds. 0943-461052. Open: Mon/Tue/Fri 10-12.30 or by appointment. Closed: Aug. ♿

A local studies resource centre, managed voluntarily, with a comprehensive collection of Otley material from prehistory.

PASSPORT CONCESSIONS: Free 'Town Trail' guide.

JNR. PASSPORT CONCESSIONS: Free 'Town Trail' guide.

LEYBURN — Middleham Castle

Middleham, Leyburn, N. Yorks. 0969-23899. Open: Daily 10-6 Summer, 10-4 Winter (excl. Mon). £ (EH)

Richard III is still considered something of a hero in these parts particularly here where he spent his boyhood and learned the skills of chivalric knighthood. The 12th century keep still stands within later fortifications and domestic buildings, and there is a replica of the famous Middleham Jewel on display.

MIDDLESBROUGH — Captain Cook Birthplace Museum

Stewart Park, Marton, Middlesbrough. 0642-311211. Open: Tue-Sun 10-6 Summer, 9-4 Winter. £ P &

The life of James Cook, from childhood in Middlesbrough to his voyages of discovery and death on Hawaii.

PASSPORT CONCESSIONS: Special rate family entrance ticket.

MIDDLESBROUGH — Cleveland Gallery

Victoria Road, Middlesbrough, Cleveland TS1 3QS. 0642-225408. Open: Tue-Sat 12-7. P &

This is the contemporary art showcase of the Cleveland County Museum Service, and it has a year-long programme of exhibitions of national importance.

MIDDLESBROUGH — Dorman Museum

Linthorpe Road, Middlesbrough. 0642-813781. Open: Tue-Fri 10-6, Sat 10-5.

This is the local history museum, about the development of Middlesbrough, its natural history and its industry.

MIDDLESBROUGH — Middlesbrough Art Gallery

320 Linthorpe Road, Middlesbrough, Cleveland TS1 4AW. Open: Tue-Sat 10-1/2-6. Closed between exhibitions. &

British 20th century and contemporary art in the permanent collections, with some Old Masters, but with a varied programme of temporary exhibitions mostly with local echoes.

MORPETH — Brinkburn Priory

Long Framlington,
Morpeth,
Northumberland.
066570-628. Open:
Daily 10-6 Summer.
Closed: Winter. £ P
(EH)

This house of Augustinian cannons was founded in about 1135, and the late 12th century church, re-roofed and repaired in 1858, is intact.

MORPETH — Cragside House & Country Park

Rothbury, Morpeth,
Northumberland.
0669-21051. House
Open: Tue-Sun 1-
5.30. £ P &. Park
Open: Daily 10.30-
5.30, House/Park
Sat/Sun all yr.
Closed: Mon-Fri Nov-
Apr. £ P

Administered by the National Trust, the parkland was created by the inventor industrialist Lord Armstrong in the last century and has the hydraulic and hydro-electric plant he installed, plus a new Energy Centre showing the history of power.

PASSPORT CONCESSIONS: Free entry to Passport holder

JNR. PASSPORT CONCESSIONS: Free entry to Junior Passport holder.

MORPETH — Morpeth Chantry Bagpipe Museum

Bridge Street,
Morpeth,
Northumberland
NE61 1PJ. 0670-
519466. Open: Mon-
Sat Jan/Feb 10-4,
Mar-Dec 9.30-5.30. £

One of the most imaginative of local museums, this one has taken the Northumbrian small pipes and set them in the context of bagpipes coming from India to Inverness, with an infra-red sound system bringing them to life. There are concerts and workshops thoughout the year.

PASSPORT CONCESSIONS: 50% off admission; Special family rate; Free Poster; Free admission to special exhibitions.

MORPETH — Wallington Hall

Cambo, Morpeth,
Northumberland
NE61 4AR. 0670-
74283. Open: Apr-
Oct Daily 1-5.30
(excl. Tue). Closed:
Nov-Mar. Gardens
open all year. £ P &

Built in 1688 and altered in 1744, the house now has a Georgian drawing room and a Victorian nursery, a collection of paintings including some by John Ruskin, and a collection of dolls' houses.

MORPETH

Warkworth Castle and Hermitage

Warkworth, Morpeth,
Northumberland.
0665-711423. Open:
Daily 10-6 Summer,
10-4 Winter (excl.
Mon). £ P & (EH)

The ruins date from the 12th century, but the
15th century keep was restored by Anthony
Salvin in the last century. Upstream is a tiny
chapel cut out of the rock.

NEWCASTLE UPON TYNE

Bessie Surtees House

41-44 Sandhill,
Newcastle Upon Tyne.
091-2611585. Open:
Mon-Fri 10-5. (EH)

This is actually two merchants' houses, one
16th and the other 17th century, one half
timbered and the other refronted in brick in the
1720s, standing on the quayside near the Tyne
Bridge. The principal rooms are on display.

NEWCASTLE UPON TYNE

The Hancock Museum

The University,
Newcastle Upon Tyne
NE2 4PT. 091-222
7418. Open: Mon-Sat
10-5, Sun 2-5. £ P

This museum began 200 years ago as a private
collection, and grew, picking up the name of a
pair of Victorian natural historians on the way,
to become so important that it is now part of the
University. But as well as British mammals,
birds, geology, ethnography and the popular
Abel's Ark, there is a corner dedicated to the
naturalist and engraver Thomas Bewick, who
lived and worked all his life not far from here.

PASSPORT CONCESSIONS: 50% off adult
admission charge.

JNR. PASSPORT CONCESSIONS: Free entry to
Junior Passport holder.

NEWCASTLE UPON TYNE

The Hatton Gallery

The University,
Newcastle Upon Tyne.
091-222 6000. Open:
Mon-Fri 10-5.30 &
Sat termtime 10-4.30.
Closed: Sat/Sun
during vacations.

A changing programme of art exhibitions and
permanent displays of the Uhlman Collection
of African sculptures
and Kurt Schwitters'
Elterwater Merzbarn.

*African sculpture from
The Uhlman Collection.*

NEWCASTLE UPON TYNE

John George Joicey Museum

City Road, Newcastle Upon Tyne NE1 2AS. 091-232 4562. Open: Tue-Fri/B.H. Mons 10-5.30, Sat 10-4.30.

This building was an almshouse in the 17th century, and a soup kitchen in the 19th. Now it's one of Tyneside's most joyful museums with displays about Newcastle's history, period rooms and the military history of the 15/19th Hussars.

PASSPORT CONCESSIONS: Free Guidebook.

NEWCASTLE UPON TYNE

Laing Art Gallery

8 Higham Place, Newcastle Upon Tyne. 091-232 7734. Open: Tue-Fri 10-5.30, Sat 10-4.30, Sun 2-5.30. Closed: Mon excl B.H. &

This has fine and applied art, British 19th and 20th centuries in particular, with a special collection of the Northumberland painter John Martin and a large costume collection.

NEWCASTLE UPON TYNE

Museum of Antiquities of the University and Society of Antiquities of Newcastle Upon Tyne.

The University, Newcastle Upon Tyne NE1 7RU. 091-222 7844. Open: Mon-Sat 10-5. &

This is Newcastle University's museum, representing a regional collection of prehistoric to medieval antiquities, and is the main Hadrian's Wall museum with scale models and a reconstruction of the Temple of Mithras, which was recently refurbished.

PASSPORT CONCESSIONS: 5% off shop purchases.

JNR. PASSPORT CONCESSIONS: Free Pencil.

The Hancock Museum

Newcastle Upon Tyne, NE2 4PT
Telephone: 091 222 7418

The Hancock Museum is home to spectacular collections of natural history including British mammals, birds, geology and ethnography. The recently completed display "Abel's Ark" with its animal noises and sound effects, is a fascinating array of animals collected by Abel Chapman, a 19th Century wine buyer, during his extensive travels.

Reader reply service see page 453

NORHAM   Norham Castle

Norham, Berwick Upon Tweed. 028982-329. Open: Daily 10-6 Summer, 10-4 Winter (excl. Mon). £ ♿ (EH)

This was a border castle built about 1160, much altered afterwards but still with its fine Norman keep.

NORTHALLERTON   Mount Grace Priory

Saddle Bridge, Northallerton, N. Yorks. 0609-83494. Open: Daily 10-6 Summer, 10-4 Winter (excl. Mon). £ P ♿ (EH)

This is the finest British example of a Carthusian monastery. It was founded in 1398, and there are remains of a cloistered monastic court and outer court. A monk's cell has been refurbished, and there are exhibitions on Mount Grace and the Carthusians.

PICKERING   Beck Isle Museum of Rural Life

Bridge St. Pickering, N. Yorks. 0751-73653. Open: Apr-Oct Daily 10-12.30/2-5. August 10-6. Closed: Nov-Mar. £

In a listed Regency building a village pub, a Victorian parlour, a nursery and village shops have been recreated, and there is a Victorian fair on July 21.

PASSPORT CONCESSIONS: Free Guidebook

PICKERING   North Yorkshire Moors Railway

Pickering Station, Pickering, N. Yorks. Y018 7AJ. 0751-72508. Open: Daily 10-6. £ P

You can travel back in time by steaming through the moors and the beautiful National Park along 18 miles of track.

PASSPORT CONCESSIONS: Two for the price of one in off peak season.

PICKERING   Pickering Castle

Pickering, N Yorks. 0751-74989. Open: Daily 10-6 Summer, Tue-Sun 10-4 Winter. £ P (EH)

There is an exhibition on the castle opening in 1990. There is a motte and bailey enclosed in a shell keep with later curtain walls, towers, domestic buildings and a chapel.

POCKLINGTON
Penny Arcadia

Market Place,
Pocklington, York.
0759-303420. Open:
May/Sept Daily
12.30-5, Jun-Aug 10-
5. Closed: Oct-Apr.
£

If you thought the Victorians had no fun, this is where you come to be put right: the world's most comprehensive collection of coin-operated amusement machines, with guided tours and demonstrations.

PASSPORT CONCESSIONS: Free Guidebook

PONTELAND
Belsay Hall and Gardens

Belsay, Nr. Ponteland,
Northumberland.
066181-636. Open:
Daily 10-6 Summer,
10-4 Winter (excl.
Mon). £ P &   (EH)

Belsay is one of Britain's most important neo-classical houses, with a 14th century tower house intact and the ruins of a 17th century mansion. There is an exhibition about it and the area, and the High Sheriff's coach is on display.

PRUDHOE
Prudhoe Castle

Prudhoe,
Northumberland.
0661-33459. Open:
Daily 10-6 Summer,
10-4 Winter (excl.
Mon). £ P (EH)

This is a 12th century castle enclosed by earthworks and walls, and part of the inner ward is occupied by an early 19th century Gothick house which has an exhibition about Northumberland castles.

PUDSEY
Fulneck Moravian Museum

55/57 Fulneck,
Pudsey, W. Yorks.
0532- 575474. Open:
Wed-Sat 2-5. Closed:
End Oct-Easter. £

A settlement of followers of the central European Protestant Moravian Church was established here in the mid 18th century and the museum, in two cottages, celebrates it with lace, embroidery, ethnography and a Victorian parlour and kitchen.

REDCAR | RNLI Zetland Lifeboat Museum

5 King St, Redcar, Cleveland TS10 3PF. 0642-499060. Open: Daily 11-4. Closed: Oct-Apr.

Photographs, models and other exhibits about the history of sea rescue in the North East, housed in a former boathouse which also has a reconstruction of a fisherman's cottage.

PASSPORT CONCESSIONS: Storyteller by arrangement.

RICHMOND | Easby Abbey

Richmond, N. Yorks. Open: Daily 10-6 Summer, Tue-Sun 10-4 Winter. £ (EH)

This is a 12th century abbey of White Cannons, with much of the monastic buildings and gatehouse remaining.

RICHMOND | The Green Howards Regimental Museum

Trinity Church Square, Richmond, N. Yorks. 0748-2133. Open: Mon-Sat 9.30-4.30, Sun 2-4.30 (Apr-Oct). Closed: Sat Nov-Feb. £

Over 80 uniforms worn by members of the regiment, and 12 of the 18 Victoria Crosses its heroes have won.

RICHMOND | Richmond Castle

Richmond, N Yorks. 0748-2493. Open: Daily 10-6 Summer, 10-4 Winter. £ P & (EH)

A new visitor centre is due to open in the summer of 1990 in this splendid medieval fortress with a 12th century keep, one of the best of England, and 11th century remains of curtain walls and domestic buildings.

RICHMOND | Richmondshire Museum

Ryders Wynd, Richmond, N. Yorks. 0748-5611. Open: 13 Apr-4 Nov Daily 11-5, 30 Apr-25 May/24 Sept-4 Nov 12-4. £

This is a local history museum, run by volunteers, which includes the Heriot set from television's All Creatures Great and Small, a scale model railway station, farming, lead mining, archaeology, costume, toys and crafts.

RIPON | Ripon Prison and Police Museum

St. Marygate, Ripon, N. Yorks HG4 1LX. 0765-3706. Open: Daily 1-5, Jul/Aug Mon-Sat 11-5, Sun 1-5. Closed: Nov-Mar. £

This is a Victorian prison with the cells converted into a museum. The displays cover the history of crime and punishment, imprisonment and law enforcement.

PASSPORT CONCESSIONS: Free Guidebook.

ROTHERHAM — Brian O'Malley Library & Arts Centre

Walker Place, Rotherham S65 1JH. 0709-382121. Open: Tue-Sat 10-5. P &

There is a continuous programme of temporary exhibitions which include, from time to time, 19th and 20th century paintings from the museum's collections.

PASSPORT CONCESSIONS: 10% off shop purchases.

ROTHERHAM — Roche Abbey

Maltby, Rotherham, S. Yorks. 0709-812739. Open: Daily 10-6 Summer, 10-4 Winter Sat/Sun only. £ P & (EH)

The history of the Cistercian abbey is traced in an exhibition within it. It was founded in 1147, and the walls of the church transepts still stand to their full height.

SCARBOROUGH — Rotunda Museum

Vernon Road, Scarborough, N. Yorks Y011 2PW. 0723-374839. Open: Tue-Sat 10-1/2-5, Sun 2-5 (June-Sept).

A Georgian purpose-built museum in the round, with curved show-cases built against the walls and a moveable stage, to show the permanent displays of archaeology and seaside Scarborough and the temporary exhibitions - toys from June to October 1990.

SCARBOROUGH — Scarborough Art Gallery

The Crescent, Scarborough, N. Yorks. 0723-374753. Open: Tue-Sat 10-1/2-5, Sun 2-5.

The British paintings of the 17th to 20th centuries here include the Laughton Collection, all in an early Victorian Italianate building. Temporary exhibitions or paintings, sculpture, photographs and posters throughout the year.

SCARBOROUGH — Scarborough Castle

Castle Road, Scarborough. 0723-372451. Open: Daily 10-6 Summer, 10-4 Winter (excl. Mon). £ (EH)

There are the remains of a fourth century Roman signal station within the confines of this 12th century castle, where much of the great rectangular keep, on a headland overlooking the town, has survived.

SCARBOROUGH — Wood End Museum of Natural History

The Crescent, Scarborough, North Yorkshire YO11 2PN. 0723-367326. Open: Tue-Sat 10-1/2-5, Sun (Summer only) 2-5.

Built in 1835, this is the former home of the Sitwell family. It has a restored Sitwell wing, a conservatory, an aquarium and displays of local natural history and geology in the main building. In the summer there is an exhibition called Back to Nature celebrating 100 years of the local naturalists' society.

SCUNTHORPE — Normanby Hall and Park

Normanby Country Park, Normanby, South Humberside. 0724-720215. Open: Daily 10-5. Closed: Nov-Mar. P

This is a Regency mansion containing fine furniture, paintings, period room settings and galleries of costume and ceramics. There are also gardens, a deer park and woodland walks.

SCUNTHORPE — Normanby Park Farming Museum

Normanby Hall Country Park, Scunthorpe. 0734-720824. Open: Daily Apr-Oct 1-5. Nov-Mar by appt. only. P

Within the Normanby Country Park, the museum has demonstrations and displays of local rural life, craftsmen's tools, a country kitchen and hand-built carts and waggons.

SCUNTHORPE — Scunthorpe Museum

Oswald Road, Scunthorpe, South Humberside. 0724-843533. Open: Mon-Sat 10-5, Sun 2-5. P

Eighty years of collecting in the region have filled the galleries with archaeology, art, local history, natural science and costume.

SHEFFIELD — Abbeydale Industrial Hamlet

Abbeydale Road South, Sheffield S7 2QW. 0742-367731. Open: Wed-Sat 10-5. Sun 11-5. £

This late 18th century water-powered scythe works has been restored to full working order, with four waterwheels, a crucible steel furnace, a workman's cottage, the manager's house, workshops and warehousing.

PASSPORT CONCESSIONS: One ticket free with one of equivalent or higher value purchased.

JNR. PASSPORT CONCESSIONS: Free entry to Junior Passport holder.

SHEFFIELD — Bishop's House

Norton Lees Lane, Sheffield S8 9BE. 0742-557701. Open: Wed-Sat 10-4.30, Sun 11-4.30. £

This is a Tudor yeoman's house timber-framed with furnished rooms and displays of Sheffield's 17th century past.

SHEFFIELD — Graves Art Gallery

Surrey Street, Sheffield S1 1XZ. 0742-734781. Open: Mon-Sat 10-6.

The permanent collection ranges widely from 16th century British art to oriental painting, with European and non-European art in between; also temporary exhibitions.

SHEFFIELD — Kelham Island Sheffield Industrial Museum

Off Alma Street, Kelham Island, Sheffield S3 8RY. 0742-722106. Open: Wed-Sat 10-5, Sun 11-5. £ P ♿

This is about Sheffield's industry, from the mighty 12,000 horse-power working steam engine to the living skills of the blade-forger and knife-grinder.

SHEFFIELD — Mappin Art Gallery

Weston Park, Sheffield. 0742-726281. Open: Tue-Sat 10-5, Sun 2-5. ♿

The gallery's collection of 18th to 20th century painting and sculpture is balanced with a continuously changing programme of exhibitions of art from the 19th and 20th centuries.

SHEFFIELD — Ruskin Gallery

101 Norfolk Street, Sheffield S1 2JE. 0742-735299. Open: Mon-Fri 10-6, Sat 10-5. ♿

This is an award-winning recently founded gallery which houses the collections of the Guild of St. George which John Ruskin created more than a century ago, and there are continuous temporary exhibitions on Ruskinesque themes. The Ruskin Craft Gallery on the same premises gives exhibitions of contemporary craftwork.

PASSPORT CONCESSIONS: Free Poster.

JNR. PASSPORT CONCESSIONS: Free Badge.

SHEFFIELD — Sheffield City Museum

Weston Park, Sheffield. 0742-768588. Open: Tue-Sat 10-5, Sun 11-5. ♿

It will come as no surprise to know that the biggest and best collection of cutlery in the world is in this museum, and old Sheffield plate as well. There are also archaeological finds from the Peak District, wildfowl and fossils.

SHEFFIELD — Shepherd Wheel

Whiteley Woods, Sheffield. 0742-367731. Open: Wed-Sun 10-1/1.30-5. (closes at 4 in Winter).

Part of the Abbeydale Industrial Hamlet, where waterwheels still drive blade-making machinery.

SHILDON — Timothy Hackworth Railway Museum

Soho Cottages, Shildon, Co. Durham. 0388-772036. Open: Mar-Sept Wed-Sun 10-5, or by appt. £ P

The home and workplace of one of the great railway pioneers, with period settings and a replica of his "Sans Pareil" locomotive which competed in the 1829 Rainhill Trials.

PASSPORT CONCESSIONS: 50% off adult admission charge.

JNR. PASSPORT CONCESSIONS: 50% off admission charge.

SHIPLEY — Brackenhall Countryside Centre

Glen Road, Baildon, Shipley, West York. 0274-584140. Open: Wed-Sun/B.H. 11-5. P ♿

Set in the beautiful Shipley Glen in the Yorkshire Moors, the museum's displays are of local history and the environment.

SHIPLEY — Victorian Reed Organs

Victoria Hall, Victoria Road, Saltaire, Nr. Shipley. 0274-585601. Open: Sun-Thur 11-4. £ P

From the tiny book harmonium to the mighty three manual and pedal organ specially built for Dr. Conway of Ely Cathedral, there are 50 reed organs in the collection of Phil and Pam Fluke.

PASSPORT CONCESSIONS: Free Guidebook.

SKIDBY — Skidby Windmill and Museum

Berverley Road, Skidby. 0482-882255. Open: Tue-Sat 10-4, Sun 1.30-4.30. Closed: Oct-Apr. £ P ♿

Agricultrual tools and craft workshops in a unique specimen of early rural industrial still working.

SKIPTON — The Craven Museum

Town Hall, High Street, Skipton, North Yorkshire. 0756-794079. Open: Apr-Sept Mon-Fri 11-5, Sat 10-12/1-5, Sun 2-5, Oct-Mar Mon-Fri 2-5, Sat 10-12/1.30-4.30, Sun 2-5. Closed: Tue.

This has displays and collections dealing with the geology, archaeology, social history and folk life of the Craven of north west Yorkshire.

SKIPTON — Embsay Steam Railway

Embsay Station, Embsay, Nr. Skipton, North Yorkshire. 0756-794727. Open: Mon-Sat 10-4.15, Sun. 11-4.15. £ P ♿

A steam railway operating along two miles of track to Holywell Halt, with special events all year.

PASSPORT CONCESSIONS: 50% off adult admission charge.

JNR. PASSPORT CONCESSIONS: Free entry to Junior Passport holder.

SOUTH SHIELDS Arbeia Roman Fort & Museum

Baring Street, South Shields, Tyne & Wear. 091-456 1369. Open: Tue-Fri 10-5.30, Sat. 10-4.30, Sun 2-5. Open: B.H. Mons. Closed: Sun Oct-Easter. P

The Roman gateway has been rebuilt on the foundations of the original, and now houses exhibitions about the lot of the Roman squaddie, with excavations still going on and open days with re-enactments.

PASSPORT CONCESSIONS: Free Guide leaflet.

SOUTH SHIELDS South Shields Museum & Art Gallery

Ocean Road, South Shields, Tyne and Wear. 091-456 8740. Open: Tue-Fri 10-5.30, Sat 10-4.30, Sun 2-5. P &

The museum covers the local and industrial history of South Shields with a special gallery devoted to the life and work of one of the town's most famous daughters, who has lent her name to a major tourism drive for the region, the novelist Catherine Cookson.

STOCKSFIELD The Thomas Bewick Birthplace Museum

Mickley, Nr. Stocksfield, Northumberland NE43 7DB. 0661-843276. Open: Tue-Sun 10-5. Closed: Jan/Feb. £ P &

This is Cherryburn, the farm and life-long home of the great naturalist and wood engraver, with an exhibition about his life and work. There are collections of his original blocks, demonstrations from time to time and a farmyard full of 18th and 19th century breeds of animals.

PASSPORT CONCESSIONS: Free Guidebook.

STOCKTON-ON-TEES Preston Hall Museum

Yarm Road, Stockton, Cleveland TS18 3RH. 0642-781184. Open: Mon-Sat 4.30-5.30, Sun 2-5.30. P &

This museum has become famous for its Victorian high street with craftsmen at work in their shops. There are also paintings, including one of Georges de la Tour's gaming series - The Dice Players.

SUNDERLAND Grindon Museum

Grindon Lane, Sunderland. 091-5141235. Open: Mon-Wed/Fri 9.30-12.30/1.30-6, Jun-Sept Sat 9.30-12.15/1.15-4, Sun 2-5. P

Edwardian life in an Edwardian house, where a family seems to have been disturbed in its domestic activities.

SUNDERLAND — Monkwearmouth Station Museum

North Bridge Street, Monkwearmouth, Sunderland. 091-514 1235. Open: Tue-Fri 10-5.30, Sat 10-4.30. Sun 2-5 + B.H.   P ♿

A grand Victorian railway station which reconstructs, in its displays, rail travel in about 1900, and the region's tram.

SUNDERLAND — North East Aircraft Museum

Old Washington Road, Sunderland, Tyne & Wear SR5 3HZ. Open: Daily 11-6. £

A collection of over 25 aircraft, including the most beautiful warplane devised, the Vulcan Bomber, and a unique, to Britain, F-86D Sabre.

PASSPORT CONCESSIONS: 50% off adult admission charge.

JNR. PASSPORT CONCESSIONS: Free entry to Junior Passport holder.

SUNDERLAND — Ryhope Engines Museum

Ryhope, Sunderland, Tyne & Wear SR2 0ND. 091-514 2259. Open: Easter-Xmas Sat/Sun + B.H. £ P

This is an 1868 waterworks with a beam engine under steam on certain days - ring to check which.

PASSPORT CONCESSIONS: Free entry to Passport holders.

SUNDERLAND — Sunderland Museum & Art Gallery

Borough Road, Sunderland, Tyne and Wear. 091-5141235. Open: Tue-Fri 10-5.30, Sat 10-4, Sun 2-5. ♿

Wearside and the surrounding area, with a fascinating North East Before Man permanent exhibition. Special exhibition on bible pictures (until March 18) Wildlife photographs (May 27 to July 1) and the bicentenary of the lifeboat service (Sept 26-Nov 18)

THURGOLAND — Wortley Top Forge Industrial Museum

Cote Lane, Thurgoland, nr Sheffield. 0742-847201. Open: Sun only 11-5. £ P

Once a 17th century water-powered iron forge, the building has been declared a Scheduled Ancient Monument and has become a museum of forging and steam.

PASSPORT CONCESSIONS: Free Poster; Free Guidebook; Free Tour.

TYNEMOUTH — Tynemouth Priory & Castle

Tynemouth, Newcastle. 091-257 1090. Open: Daily 10-6 Summer, 10-4 Winter (excl. Mon). £ & (EH)

There are several layers of history to this site. There was a Saxon monastery on it first, then a Benedictine priory was founded there in 1090, then a castle enclosed it, and in the last war batteries were mounted here to protect the entrance to the Tyne, and there is an exhibition in the gun battery.

TYNEMOUTH — Volunteer Life Brigade Museum

Spanish Battery, Tynemouth, N. Shields. 091-2520933. Open: Tue-Sun 10-3. P &

This museum was the star of the BBC Television series "Watch House"

WAKEFIELD — Yorkshire Mining Museum

Caphouse Colliery, New Road, Overton, Wakefield WF4 4RH. 0924-848806. Open: Daily 10-5. £ P &

Galleries cover the technology of mining and the social history of the Yorkshire coalfield communities with original buildings in the embracing countryside, and there are underground tours guided by ex-miners. There are special events and exhibitions too.

PASSPORT CONCESSIONS: £1 off adult admission charge.

JNR. PASSPORT CONCESSIONS: Free Badge

WAKEFIELD — Stephen G. Beaumont Museum

Stanley Royd Hospital, Aberford Road, Wakefield, W. Yorks. 0924-375217. Open: Wed by appoint. 10-1/1.30-4. P &

In the former West Riding Pauper Lunatic Asylum, the museum plots the development of the care of the mentally ill with original plans, records and documents with a padded cell, equipment, and examples of patients' artistic skill. **JNR. PASSPORT CONCESSIONS:** Free entry to passport holder.

WAKEFIELD — Yorkshire Sculpture Park

West Bretton, Wakefield, West Yorks. 0924-830579. Open: Daily 10-6 Summer, 10-4 Winter. P &

Sculptures on permanent display or temporary loan and placed around this beautiful parkland in an unusual, if not unique, exhibition which was opened in 1977.

WALLSEND — Wallsend Heritage Centre

2 Buddle Street, Wallsend, Newcastle Upon Tyne. 091-2620012. Open: Tue-Fri 10-5.30, Sat 10-4.30, Sun 2-5, BH. P &

The wall, of course, being Hadrian's, this place has a permanent exhibition on the history of Wallsend from Roman times to the present day. **PASSPORT CONCESSIONS:** Free leaflet "5 Minutes From Wallsend Heritage Centre".

WHITBY — Whitby Abbey

Whitby, N Yorks. 0947-603568. Open: Daily 10-6 Summer, Tue-Sun 10-4 Winter. £ (EH)

The monastery which was built on this site in 657 was the home of St. Hilda, and of Caedmon, the first English hymn writer. The Benedictine church which now stands there and dominates the headland was built in the 13th and 14th centuries.

WHITBY — Whitby Museum

Pannett Park, Whitby, N. York. Open: Oct-Apr Mon/Tue 10.30-1, Wed-Sat 10.30-4, Sun 2-4; May-Sept Mon-Sat 9.30-5.30, Sun 2-5. £ &

Run completely voluntarily by the Whitby Literary and Philosophical Society, there is a wide variety of artefacts, including displays on Captain Cook, jet, and the Scoresby whaling captains, plus a large library. **PASSPORT CONCESSIONS:** Reduced entrance fee for groups. **JNR. PASSPORT CONCESSIONS:** Reduced entrance fee for groups.

WHITEWELL-ON-THE-HILL

Kirkham Priory

Whitewell-on-the-Hill, N. Yorks. 065381-768. Open: Daily 10-6 Summer, 10-4 Winter (excl. Mon). £ P ♿ (EH)

There is a remarkable display of late 13th century heraldry in the gatehouse of this early 12th century Augustinian priory.

WOODHORN

Woodhorn Church Museum

Woodhorn Village, Nr Ashington, Northumberland. 0670-817371. Open: Wed-Sun + B.H. Mons 10-12.30/1-4. P ♿

This is a restored Saxon church with a collection of medieval carved stones and changing exhibitions, and with a permanent craft centre.

WOODHORN

Woodhorn Colliery Museum

Woodhorn, Nr Ashington, Northumberland. 0670-856968. Open: Wed-Sun + B.H. 10-4. P

In the midst of the south east Northumberland coalfield, this museum examines the social and industrial history of the mining communities, and there is a working blacksmith and woodworker.

WOOLER

Earle Hill Head Household & Farming Museums

Earle Hill Farm, Wooler, Northumberland. 0668-81243. Open: Fri pm, all Holiday weekends. Closed: Nov-May. £ P

Household and farm antiquities including buttons, lace, needlework, quilts, china, jewellery, toys and the paraphernalia of farm life, and all proceeds to charity.

PASSPORT CONCESSIONS: Free entry to Passport holder

WYLAM

Wylam Railway Museum

Falcon Centre, Falcon Terrace, Wylam, Northumberland NE41 8EE. 0661-852174. Open: Tue/Thur 2-7.30, Sat 9-12. P

Wylam contribution to the development of the railway was principally in giving the world George Stephenson, but there were other pioneer engineers who came from this Northumbrian village and are celebrated in its former school, along with locomotives like Puffing Billy.

PASSPORT CONCESSIONS: Free souvenir postcard with purchases over £1.

JNR. PASSPORT CONCESSIONS: Free souvenir postcard with purchases over £1.

YORK — Archaeological Resource Centre

St. Saviourgate, York Y01 2NN. 0904 643211. Open Mon-Fri 10-5. Sat/Sun call for opening. £ P

In one of the most famously explored cities in Britain, the centre - devised by the people who made most of the discoveries, the York Archeological Trust - gives a chance for visitors to look behind the scenes of archaeology, handle objects from excavations and use the skills of a professional.

PASSPORT CONCESSIONS: Child free if accompanied by one or more adults.

JNR. PASSPORT CONCESSIONS: Free entry if accompanied by paying adult.

YORK — The Bar Convent Museum

17 Blossom Street, York YO2 2AH. 0904-643238. Open Tue-Fri. Closed: Jan. £ ♿

This is a neo-classical convent turned into a museum to tell the story of the Christianity from Roman times. There is an intriguing series of exhibitions throughout 1990.

PASSPORT CONCESSIONS: £1 off adult admission charge.

JNR. PASSPORT CONCESSIONS: Free entry to Junior Passport holder.

YORK — Castle Howard Costume Galleries

Castle Howard, York. 065-384333. Open: Daily 11-4.30. Closed: Nov-Mar. £ P ♿

This is the largest private collection of costumes in Britain, and in 1990 there are to be special exhibitions to celebrate the 25th anniversary of the galleries.

The ARC (Archaeological Resource Centre), St. Saviourgate, York
Telephone 0904 643211. Bookings 0904 613711.

YORK — Fairfax House

Castlegate, York Y01 IRN. 0904-655543. Open: Mon-Thur/Sat 11-5, Sun 1.30-5. Closed: Jan/Feb. £ P

One of England's best Georgian town houses which has the Noel Terry Collection of 18th century furniture and clocks. Exhibition on 18th century posh eating habits from July to October.

PASSPORT CONCESSIONS: 50p off adult admission charge

JNR. PASSPORT CONCESSIONS: 25p off child admission charge.

YORK — Jorvik Viking Centre

Coppergate, York. 0904-643211. Open: Daily Nov-Mar 9-5.30, Spr-Oct 9-7. &

This is a journey back in time to a Viking Street of 1,000 years ago - complete with sound & smell.

YORK — Merchant Adventurers' Guild Hall

Trinity Hall, Fossgate, York Y01 2XD. 0904-654818. Open: 19 Mar-4 Nov Daily 8.30-5, 5 Nov-18 Mar Mon-Sat 8.30-3.30. £ &

The finest surviving medieval guild hall in Europe, with early furniture and portraits, pottery and objects used by the Guild since the 15th century.

PASSPORT CONCESSIONS: Free Guidebook.

JNR. PASSPORT CONCESSIONS: Free entry to Junior Passport holder.

YORK — National Railway Museum

Leeman Road, York YO2 4XJ. 0904-621261. Open: Mon-Sat 10-6, Sun 11-6. £ P &

The best and biggest railway collection in the world, but the central hall closes at the end of February for roof replacement. Instead there is a new exhibition, The Great Railway Show, in the old York Goods Yard beside the museum.

JNR. PASSPORT CONCESSIONS: Free entry to Junior Passport holder; Free Poster.

YORK — Prince of Wales Own Regimental Museum

3 Tower Street, York. 0904-642038. Open: Mon-Fri 9.30-4.30, Sat 11-4.30. £ &

The POW's Own was founded in 1685 and is still going strong. Its museum uses the regimental memorabilia to tell the day-to-day story of the soldier through the last 300 years.

YORK — Ryedale Folk Museum

Hutton-Le-Hole, York Y06 6UA. 07515-367. Open: Daily 10.30-5.30. Closed: Nov-Mar. £ P &

This is an open air museum with rescued buildings transported here to house collections illustrating folk life in Ryedale.

PASSPORT CONCESSIONS: 50% off adult admission charge.

JNR. PASSPORT CONCESSIONS: Free Pencil.

YORK — St. William's College

5 College Street, York YO1 2JF. 0904-637134. Open: Mon-Sat 10-5, Sun 12.30-5. £

This is a 15th century timbered building pierced by a narrow gateway into a quadrangle. The building has displays of architectural artefacts.

PASSPORT CONCESSIONS: Adult Passport holders to enter at the children's rate to the College halls.

YORK — Treasurer's House

4 Minster Yard, York YO1 2JD. 0904-624247. Open: Apr-Oct Daily 10.30-5. Closed: Nov-Mar. £

This was the offficial home of the medieval treasurer's of York Minster, largely rebuilt in the 17th century. It has magnificent rooms with fine furniture, pictures, glass and ceramics and is now owned by the National Trust.

PASSPORT CONCESSIONS: £2 reduction on membership of The National Trust if joining at Treasurer's House, York.

Jorvik Viking Centre, Coppergate, York YO1 1NT
Telephone 0904 643211.   Bookings 0904 613711.

YORK — York Clifford 's Tower

Castle St, York. 0904-646940. Open: Daily 10-6 Summer, 10-4 Winter (excl. Mon). £ P (EH)

This 13th century tower is on one of two mottes which William the Conqueror built in 1068-69 to hold York.

YORK — York Minster

Church House, Ogleforth , York YO1 2JN. 0904-624426. Open: Mon-Sat 10-Dusk, Sun 1.30-Dusk. £ &

The foundations of the cathedral are among the most important archaeological sites in Britain, with Roman, Saxon, Norman and medieval displays. The 13th century Chapter House contains a large collection of carved capitals and pendants, and stained glass from the 13th to 15th centuries.

PASSPORT CONCESSIONS: Adult Passport holder to enter at the children's rate.

YORK — York Racing Museum and Library

The Racecourse, York. 0904-620911. Open: Race days only 11-6 or by appt. P &

This has memorabilia of Fred Archer, perhaps the greatest jockey who ever lived, a touts collections, colours, early race cards and scales.

YORK — Yorkshire Air Museum

Elvington, York Y04 5AV. 0904-85595. Open Tue/Thur 11-4, Sat 2-5, Sun 11-5. Closed: Nov-Mar. £ P &

A restored World War Two airbase with the original control tower, plus a rebuilt Halifax and Mosquito.

YORK — Yorkshire Museum

Museum Gardens, York YO1 2DR. 0904-629745. Open: Mon-Sat 10-5, Sun 1-5. £ &

Digging in the basement here last year they found medieval remains, and have altered their development plans to incorporate them. There are exceptional Roman, Viking, Saxon and medieval objects here.

YORK — Yorkshire Museum of Farming

Murton Park, York YO1 3UF. 0904-489966. Open: May-Oct Daily. 10-5.30. £ P &

Reprieved last year within days of having of to close in a cash crisis, this award-winning museum of farming and the countryside has reconstructed interiors as well, all covering eight acres

NORTHERN
IRELAND

ANTRIM

Shanes Castle Railway

Shanes Castle, Antrim.
08494-28216. Open:
Apr-May/Sept
Sun/B.H. 12-6, Jun
Wed/Sat/Sun 12-6,
Jul/Aug Tue-Thur/
Sat/Sun 12-6. £ P

Visitors can ride the one and a half miles of
track in converted peat wagons, drawn by
narrow-guage steam and diesel engines. These
have been restored and painted in period
liveries.

ARMAGH

Armagh County Museum

The Mall East,
Armagh, Co. Armagh
BT61 9BE.
0861-523070. Open:
Mon-Sat 10-1/2-5. P

This is the regional museum which tells the
county story through its prehistoric weapons
and implements, its relics of city and county
and its 18th and 19th century costume, with an
art gallery showing local portraits,
contemporary work and topographical pictures.
There is a series of temporary exhibitions,
including one marking the tercentenary of the
Battle of the Boyne in 1689 which traces events
from then to the death of William III in 1702,
but that's only on from June 5 to June 29 1990.

ARMAGH

Royal Irish Fusiliers Museum

Sovereign's House,
The Mall, Armagh.
0861-522911. Open:
Mon-Fri 10-12.30/2-4
(excl. B. H.) P

This is about the organisation and business of
the foot regiments and militia which came to
make up the RIF.

BALLYGAWLEY

President Grant's Ancestral Home

Dergenagh,
Ballygawley, Co.
Tyrone. 066252-7133.
Open: Easter-Sept
Daily 10-6. Closed:
Winter. £ P &

Most American presidents seem to be able to
trace their origins back to Ireland, and Ulysees
Simpson Grant's family on the Simpson side
came from here. The museum is a typical 19th
century Irish small-holding with the domestic
implements, furnishing, crops and animals the
Simpsons would have had.

BELFAST

Royal Ulster Rifles Regimental Museum

Regimental
Headquarters. 0232-
232086. Open: Mon-
Fri 10-12.30/2-4, or
by appt. Closed: B.H.

Uniforms, badges and medals, but also archives
including the war diaries and photograph
albums of members of the regiment.

BELFAST — Ulster Museum

Botanic Gardens, Belfast BT9 5AB. 0232-381251. Open: Mon-Fri 10-5, Sat 1-5, Sun 2-5.

This is Northern Ireland's national museum, with displays on art geology, botany, zoology, archaeology and local history. Between April and September 1990 there is a major exhibition called, Kings in Conflict.

PASSPORT CONCESSIONS: Free Guidebook; 10% off purchases over £5.
JNR. PASSPORT CONCESSIONS: Free Pencil.

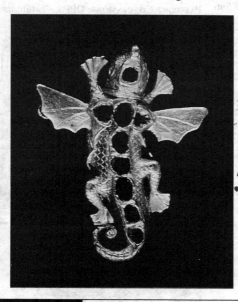

Salamander from Wreck of GIRONA.

COOKSTOWN — Wellbrook Beetling Mill

20 Wellbrook Road, Corkhill, Cookstown, Co. Tyrone BT80 9RY. 06487-51735. Open: Apr-call for details, May/Jun/Sept Sat/Sun/B.H. 2-6, Jul/Aug Daily 2-6 (excl. Tue). £ P

The original machinery, still in working order, was used in the manufacture of linen. The water-powered hammer mill is now administered by the National Trust.

DOWNPATRICK — Down County Museum

The Mall, Downpatrick, Co. Down BT30 6AH. 0396-615218. Open: Tue-Fri 11-5, Sat 2-5, Sun (mid Jun-Sept) 2-5. P

This is a developing regional museum whose displays tell of Down's human and natural history, all set in an 18th century country jail complex which is undergoing a phased restoration.

ENNISKILLEN
Fermanagh County Museum

Castle Barracks, Enniskillen, Co. Fermanagh. 0365-25000. Open: Mon-Fri 10-1/2-5, + Sat (May-Sept) 2-5, + Sun (Jul-Aug) 2-5. P

The history of settlement in the county is related in a medieval castle, with dioramas on prehistory and audio-visuals about Gaelic chieftans, Elizabethan wars and plantation settlers.

PASSPORT CONCESSIONS: OPPS. - exhibition previews.

JNR. PASSPORT CONCESSIONS: Free Badge.

Early Fermanagh Display.

ENNISKILLEN
Royal Inniskilling Fusiliers Regimental Museum

The Castle, Enniskillen, Co. Fermanagh. 0365-23142. Open: Mon-Fri 9.30-12.30/2-4.30. £ P

This is the old castle keep, and traces the regiment's history from 1689 to 1968 through medals, uniforms, flags, documents, weapons and pictures.

HOLYWOOD
Ulster Folk and Transport Museum

Cultra Manor, Holywood, Co. Down BT18 OEU. 0232-428428. Open: May-Sept Mon-Sat 11-6, Sun 2-6, Oct-Apr Mon-Sat 11-5, Sun 2-5. £ P ♿

Original buildings re-located from all over Northern Ireland. Indoor galleries show crafts of the region, and the museum has extensive collections of vintage transport.

Special exhibition from mid-April to October; the costume, jewellery and culture of Bulgaria, on loan from Liverpool.

LISBURN

Lisburn Museum

The Assembly Rooms, Market Sq, Lisburn, Co Antrim BT28 1AG. 0846-672624. Open: Tue-Sat 11-4.45. &

The linen industry is the central theme is the story of the Lagan Valley told here, with the only operational linen hand-loom in Ireland.

MONEYMORE

Springhill

Moneymore, Magherafelt, Co. Londonderry BT45 7NQ. 06487-48210. Open: Apr-call for details, May/Jun/Sept Sat/Sun/B.H. 2-6, Jul/Aug Daily (excl. Thur) 2-6. Closed: Oct-Mar. £ P &

Originally built in the 17th century, this National Trust property remained in the same family for 10 generations. The house contains furniture and paintings, and hand-made wallpaper from the 18th century. There is also an extensive collection of costumes from the 1700s to the present day.

OMAGH

Ulster American Folk Park

Camphill, Omagh, Co. Tyrone. 0662-3292. Open: Summer Mon-Fri 11-6.30, Sat/Sun 11-7. Winter Mon-Fri 10.30-5. £ P &.

The theme of this museum is a curious one: the Ulster folk who went away. With thatched houses, barns, log cabins and craft workshops, it looks at the life of emigrants on both sides of the Atlantic, with a new gallery devoted to a construction of a typical emigrants' ship and the dockside, linking the old and new worlds.

PASSPORT CONCESSIONS: Free entry to Passport holder.

Ship and Dockside Gallery.

JNR. PASSPORT CONCESSIONS: Free entry to Junior Passport holder.

PORTADOWN — Ardress House and Farmhouse

64 Ardress Road, Annaghmore, Portadown, Co. Armagh BT62 1SQ. 0762-851236. Open: Jul/Aug Daily (excl. Tue) 2-6, Apr-Jun & Sept. Sat/Sun 2-6. Closed: Oct-Easter except party bookings. £ P

This is an original 17th century farmhouse with 18th century extensions, and the enclosed cobbled farmyard has an unusual collection of fowl running around in it, as well as (static) old farm machines. Inside there is a permanent display of implements, a dairy and a smithy.

STRABANE — Gray's Printing Press

49 Main Street, Strabane, Co. Tyrone BT82 8AU. 0504-884094. Open: Apr-Sept Mon-Wed/Fri/Sat 2-5.30. £

Dating from the 18th century, this print shop houses vintage printing machines which demonstrate the history of the industry in the Strabane area.

STRANGFORD — Castle Ward

Strangford, Co. Down BT30 7LS. 039686 204. Open: Apr-call for details, Sept/Oct Sat/Sun/B.H. 1-6, May-Aug Daily 1-6 (excl. Thur). Closed: Nov-Mar. £ P &

Built in 1770, Castle Ward was the home of Viscount Bangor. The servants' quarters are linked to the house by an underground passageway. A reconstructed laundry, stables and bakery show the working life of the house. April and May sees organised walks and a craft fair, and performance of a major opera in mid-summer.

SCOTLAND

ABERDEEN — Aberdeen Art Gallery

School Hill, Aberdeen AB9 1FQ. 0224-646333. Open: Mon-Sat 10-5. &

An elegant, neo-classical building of the 1880's with one of the finest provincial collections of paintings in Britain - Raeburn, Ramsay and Reynolds to Paul Nash, Ben Nicholson and Francis Bacon. There are also temporary exhibitions.

ABERDEEN — Aberdeen University Zoology Department Museum

Aberdeen University, Aberdeen AB9 2TN. 0224-272000. Open: Mon-Fri 9-5.30. P

A zoologists' selection from the animal kingdom, particularly important for British birds and insects.

ABERDEEN — James Dun's House

James Dun's House, Schoolhill, Aberdeen. 0224-646333. Open: Mon-Sat 10-5.

Built in the 1760's for Aberdeen Grammar School's rector, James Dun, it was converted for museum use in 1975 and is now the city's special exhibition centre, with changing displays all year.

ABERDEEN — Marischal Museum

Marischal College, University of Aberdeen, Aberdeen AB9 1AS. 0224-273131. Open: Mon-Fri 10-5, Sun 2-5.

This is in Aberdeen University's Marischal College and contains the gifts made to the university over hundreds of years - Egyptian mummies, Greek vases, shrunken heads, eskimo kayaks and gilded buddahs all included. There is also an exhibition with material drawn from all over the world about what it is to be a human being. In 1990 a new gallery opens, called Encyclopedia of the North East.

ABERDEEN — Provost Ross's House

Shiprow, Aberdeen AB1 2BY. 0224-572215. Open: Mon-Sat 10-5. P

This is the third oldest house in Aberdeen, built in 1593, which incorporates the Aberdeen Maritime Museum telling of the Granite City's ties with sea - shipbuilding, fishing, the harbour and North Sea oil.

ABERDEEN — Provost Skene's House

Guestrow, Aberdeen. 0224-641086. Open: Mon-Sat 10-5.

Named after a rich merchant and provost of the city in the late 17th century, room settings are made in different periods from Jacobean to Victorian, and there's tea in the provost's kitchen.

ABERLADY — Myreton Motor Museum

Aberlady, East Lothian Scotland. 087-57288. Open: Easter-Oct Daily 10-6, Nov-Easter 10-5. £ P &

Bicycles from 1890, cars from 1896, motorcycles from 1900, commercial vehicles from 1919, plus Second World War military vehicles, period advertising and related material.

PASSPORT CONCESSIONS: Two adults for the price of one; Free Poster.

JNR. PASSPORT CONCESSIONS: Two for the price of one.

ABRIACHAN — Abriachan Croft Museum

The Old School House, Abriachan, Inverness IV3 6LB. 046-386237. Open: By appoint. only in Summer. P

This is a revivification of a lost crofters' village, begun by the pupils of Inverness High School in 1970 as part of European Conservation Year.

ALFORD — Craigievar Castle

Alford, Aberdeenshire AB3 4RS. 03398-83635. Open: July-2nd Sept Mon-Sun 11-6, 28 Apr-Sept Mon-Sun 2-6. Closed: Oct-27 Apr. £ P

This is a picturesque castle containing a family collection dating from the 17th century and which has magnificent plaster ceilings.

ALFORD — Grampian Transport Museum

Alford, Aberdeenshire AB3 8AD. 09755-62292. Open: Apr-Sept Daily 10.30-5, Oct Sat/Sun 10.30-5. Closed: Nov-Mar. £ P &

This is an extensive local transport history collection housed in a purpose-built building with a railway museum included and summer outdoor events.

PASSPORT CONCESSIONS: 50% off adult admission charge.

JNR. PASSPORT CONCESSIONS: 50% off admission charge for first 2 children.

ALLOWAY — Burns Cottage & Museum

Alloway, Ayr KA7 4PY: 0292-41215. Open: Apr-Jun Daily 10-5, Jul/Aug 9-7, Sept-Oct 10-4, Nov-Mar Mon-Sat 10-4. £ P

Where Scotland's national poet was born in 1759, and many poems, relics and manuscripts (including Auld Lang Syne) and a special exhibition for the 1990 season on Robbie Burns's life and work.

PASSPORT CONCESSIONS: Special family rate ticket.

ANSTRUTHER — Scottish Fisheries Museum

St. Ayles, Habourhead, Anstruther, Fife KY10 3AB. 0333-310628. Open: Apr-Oct Mon-Sat 10-5.30, Sun 11-5, Nov-Mar Mon-Sat 10-4.30, Sun 2-4.30. £ P

This award-winning museum tells of Scotland's fishing industry and the people who made it work, even to actual fishing boats, fishing equipment, an aquarium and a whaling display.

APPIN — Wildlife Museum

Appin Home Farm, Appin, Argyll PA38 4BN. 063171-308. Open: Daily 10-5. P ♿

Taxidermist John Scorgie is the central exhibit of this museum, as he works and talks about the wildlife of the area. His daughter Tina is a goldsmith who also works here and talks about her craft.

PASSPORT CONCESSIONS: OPPS: Personal behind the scenes tour of museum.

ARBROATH — Arbroath Museum, Signal Tower

Ladyloan, Arbroath DD11 1PU. 0241-75598. Open: Apr-Oct Mon-Sat 10.30-1/2-5. + Sun (Jul-Aug) 2-5. Nov-Mar Mon-Fri 2-5, Sat 10.30-1/2-5. P

The sounds, smells and sights of historical Arbroath in the former signal tower, complete with the last manually operated light from the Bell Rock Lighthouse and the secrets of the 'smokie', one of Scotland's many gifts to the gastronomic world.

JNR. PASSPORT CONCESSIONS: Free activity sheets.

ARDERSIER — Queen's Own Highlanders Regimental Museum

Fort George, Ardersier, Inverness. 0463-224380. Open: Apr-Sept Mon-Sat 10-6, Sun 2-6, Oct-Mar Mon-Fri 10-7. P

The 18th century quarters of the Lieutenant Governor and Fort Major of Fort George have been turned into a museum of the regiment created by combining the Seaforth and Cameron Highlanders.

PASSPORT CONCESSIONS: Free entry to Passport holder.

Archaeology, Egyptology, Hieroglyphics…

…all Greek to you?

Read Simon Tait every Saturday.

Not content with editing this excellent Guide, Simon Tait also finds time to produce his own column, every Saturday in *The Times*. His expert guidance and advice will help you get the most out of our museums and galleries.

He'll keep you up to date with exactly what's going on and where. And tell you about any extra concessions or free gifts Museum Passport holders are entitled to.

If you haven't already taken advantage of *The Times* Museums' Passport offer, simply fill in the coupon in *The Times* on Saturdays, for your free Passports to the past.

AUCHTERARDER — Great Scots Visitor Centre

Glenruthen Mill, Abbey Road, Auchterarder, Perthshire 0784-62079. Open: Easter-May 2-5, June-Aug 10-5, Sept-Oct 12-5. £ P &

Scotland's only working textile steam engine is here at Glenruthen Mill, but in the weaving shed the latest technology is brought into play with a computerised lecture on Watt, Baird, Bell, Burns and other great Scots.

PASSPORT CONCESSIONS: 50% off adult admission charge.

AYR — Rozelle Galleries

Rozelle Park Monument Road, Ayr. 0292-45447. Open: Mon-Fri 10-5, Sat 10-5, Sun 2-5 (Apr-Oct). P

More fully, Rozelle House and the Maclaurin Art Gallery, whose wide-ranging list of exhibitions centres on contemporary art either from the permanent collections or from touring shows.

The Fishers - J.Bellany.

BALLATER — Balmoral Castle

Ballater, Aberdeenshire AB3 5TB. 03397-42334. Open: May-July Mon-Sat 10-5. £ P

Queen Victoria's Scottish home and still a palace much in royal use, the grounds are open to the public, and in the ballroom there is an exhibition about the castle's history.

BANCHORY — Banchory Museum

High St, Banchory. 0779-77778. Open: Daily 2-5.20 (excl. Thur). Closed: Oct-May. P

The life and times of the Banchory district, and particularly of the musician J. Scott Skinner.

PASSPORT CONCESSIONS: 10% off shop purchases.

JNR. PASSPORT CONCESSIONS: Free Pencil.

BANFF — Banff Museum

High St, Banff. 0779-77778. Open: Daily 2-5.15 (excl. Thur). Closed: Oct-May. P

The natural history display here won the 1989 Glenfiddich Living Scotland Award. There are also local and social history displays here, and an exhibition devoted to the astronomer James Ferguson, a local boy.

PASSPORT CONCESSIONS: 10% off shop purchases.

JNR. PASSPORT CONCESSIONS: Free Pencil.

BANNOCKBURN — Bannockburn Heritage Centre

Bannockburn, Stirlingshire FK7 0LJ. 0786-812664. Open: Daily 10-6. Closed: 29 Oct-Mar. £ ♿

This museum, which traces the history of Scotland, is established at Borestone from where Robert the Bruce commanded his troops in the battle of 1314 which established the Scots independence from England.

BATHGATE — Bennie Museum

9-11 Mansefield Street, Bathgate, West Lothian. 0506-634944. Open: Mon-Sat 10-4.30. P ♿.

A new museum which only opened in 1988, its curator, Mr Millan, describes it as "a personalised museum" in that the owners of all the artefacts in it are identified, and since the objects are confined to being from Bathgate most of the owners are local too. Part of the building is 200 years old, and the objects in it vary from a weir steam pump to a Roman coin to royal signatures.

PASSPORT CONCESSIONS: OPPS.

BIGGAR — Biggar Gasworks Museum

Biggar, Lanarkshire. 031-2257534. Open: May-Sept Mon-Thur 2-5, Sat/Sun 12-5. Closed: Oct-Apr.

In the only remaining gasworks in Scotland, there is a fascinating look at part of the country's industrial history.

BIGGAR — Gladstone Court (Street Museum)

Biggar ML12 6DL. 0899-21050. Open: Mon-Sat 10-5, Sun: 2-5. Closed: Nov-Mar. £ P.

A reconstructed Victorian shopping centre, with a bank, ironmonger's, photographer's, chemist's dressmaker's, watchmakers, milliner's, printer's, library and schoolroom.

PASSPORT CONCESSIONS: Free entry to Passport holder.

JNR. PASSPORT CONCESSIONS: Free Pencil; Free entry to Junior Passport holder.

BIGGAR — Greenhill Convenanters House

Biggar ML12 6DT. 0899-21050. Open: Daily 2-5. Closed: Mid Oct-Mar. £ P

The farmhouse was transplanted ten miles from Wiston to become the Biggar Museum Trust's museum dedicated to the Covenanters of the 17th century, the free worshippers ruthlessly hunted down.

BIGGAR — John Buchan Centre

John Buchan Centre, Broughton, Biggar ML12 6DT. 0899-21050. Open: Daily 2-5. £ P ♿

Dedicated to the novelist who created Richard Hannay, and who was also Governor General of Canada as Lord Tweedsmuir. His grandfather was the local innkeeper there.

PASSPORT CONCESSIONS: Free entry to Passport holder.

JNR. PASSPORT CONCESSIONS: Free entry to Junior Passport holder.

BIGGAR — Moat Park Heritage Centre

Biggar ML12 6DT. 0899-21050. Open: Mon-Sat 10-5, Sun 2-5. Closed: Nov-Mar. £ P ♿.

The fourth museum of the Biggar Museum Trust's properties, this one is its flagship, opened in 1988 and offering a sweeping view of the history of this part of Scotland from the Neolithic to Victorian.

PASSPORT CONCESSIONS: Free entry to Passport holder.

JNR. PASSPORT CONCESSIONS: Free Pencil; Free entry to Junior Passport holder.

BIRSAY, Orkney — Farm & Folk Museum

Corrigall Farm, Harray and Kirbuster Farm, Birdsay, Orkney. 0856-3191. Open: Apr-Sept Mon-Sat 10.30-1/2-5, Sun 2-7. £ P ♿

Traditional Orcadian crafts such as straw-backed chair making, are displayed and demonstrated in this traditional Orcadian farmhouse.

PASSPORT CONCESSIONS: 50% off adult admission charge.

BLAIR ATHOLL — Atholl Country Collection

The Old School, Blair Atholl, Perthshire. 079-681232. Open: Daily May-Oct 1.30-5.30, Jul-Aug 9.30-12.30/1.30-5.30. Closed: Nov-Apr. £ P ♿

The village school closed in 1972, but the museum in it now still teaches about village life and the glens in the 19th and early 20th centuries, with a reconstructed crofter's living room.

PASSPORT CONCESSIONS: 30p off adult admission charge.

BOAT OF GARTEN

Strathspey Railway Museum

The Station, Boat of Garten, Inverness-shire PH24 3BH. 047983-692. Open: Apr-mid Oct Daily 9-5. P

The collection in this Highland railway station are focussed on railwayana of the Scottish and Highland railways, with the once-redundant line to Aviemore now running steam engines.

BO'NESS

Bo'ness and Kinneil Railway (The Forth Valley Line)

Bo'ness Station, Union Street, Bo'ness, West Lothian EH51 0AD. 0506-822298. Open: Easter-Sept Sat/Sun 10-6, 14 July-19 Aug Daily 10-6, other times call for details. P &

Scottish locomotives, carriages, and wagons are the static part of this collection, but the main item is the seven mile round trip by steam train to Birkhill, where you can see the clay mine. It operates from April to September, but ring for exact dates.

JNR. PASSPORT CONCESSIONS: Free entry to holder for train ride when accompanied by adult.

BO'NESS

Kinneil Museum

Kinneil Estate Bo'ness West Lothian. 0506-824318. Open: Mon-Fri 10-12.30/1.30-5, Sat/Sun 10-5(June-Aug only) Sat only Oct-Mar. P &

Housed in a converted 17th century stable block, the exhibits relate to the surrounding estate including a display on Bo'ness and the natural history of the area.

BRAGAR
Isle of Lewis

Black House

42 Arnol, Bragar, Isle of Lewis PA86 9DB. 031-2443101. Open: Jan-Mar/Oct-Dec Mon-Sat 9.30-4, Apr-Sept Mon-Sat 9.30-7. £

A traditional thatched Lewis farmhouse, it is furnished in equally traditional style and the outbuildings are properly equipped for work. It is in the village of Arnol.

BRODICK, Isle of Arran
Brodick Castle

Brodick, Isle of Arran KA27 8HY. 0770-2202. Open: Daily 1-5, Oct Mon/Wed/Sat. Closed: 20 Oct-12 Apr. £ P

Silver, porcelain and paintings from the collections of the Dukes of Hamilton, William Beckford and the Earls of Rochford are on display in this ancient seat of the Dukes, more recently the home of the late Mary, Duchess of Montrose.

BRODICK, Isle of Arran
Isle of Arran Heritage Museum

"Rosaburn", Brodick, Isle of Arran KA27 8DL. 0770-2636. Open: Mon-Sat 10-1/2-5. Closed: Nov-28 Apr. £ P &.

This is a group of farm buildings which include a smithy and a furnished cottage, and there are displays on shipping, agriculture, archaeology, geology and a school heritage project.

PASSPORT CONCESSIONS: Free Guidebook; 10% off shop purchases.

JNR. PASSPORT CONCESSIONS: Free Badge.

BUCKIE
Buckie Maritime Museum

Cluny Place, Buckie, Moray. 0309-73701. Open: Mon-Fri 10-8, Sat 10-12pm. &

As well as displays about fishing life and other maritime themes, there are the paintings of Peter Anson, who also wrote about the fishermen and their families here.

BURNTISLAND
Edwardian Fair

102 High Street, Burntisland, Fife. 0592-260732. Open: Mon-Sat 10-1/2-5. P

This is a new museum which recreates all the sights and sounds of an Edwardian fair, including sideshows and a lion tamer.

PASSPORT CONCESSIONS: Free Poster.

CAMPBELTOWN
Campbeltown Museum

Public Library, Hall Street, Campbeltown, Argyll PA28 6BJ. 0586-52366. Open: Mon/Tue/Thur/Fri 10-1/2-5/6-8, Wed/Sat 10-1/2-5.

Kintyre's local museum, with natural history and geology, fishing, traditional Scottish weaponry and craftsmen's implements.

CASTLE DOUGLAS
Castle Douglas Art Gallery

Council Offices, Kirkcudbright DG6 4JG. 0557-30291. Open: Call for opening hours. P &.

There is a permanent collection of the paintings of ESG Bristowe here, and temporary exhibitions chiefly of local artists' work.

CERES — Fife Folk Museum

The Weigh House, High St, Ceres, Cupar. 033482-380. Open: Apr-Oct Wed-Mon 2.15-5. Closed: Nov-Mar. £ P &

This has domestic objects, craft tools and agricultural implements from the social and economic history of Fife, seen in a unique set of old buildings.

COATBRIDGE — Summerlee Heritage Trust

West Canal St, Coatbridge ML5 1QD. 0236-31261. Open: Daily 10-5. P &

This is a new museum, with new displays opening all the time, devoted to the last 200 years of Scotland's industrial development, with working machinery, tramway and steam engines.

PASSPORT CONCESSIONS: Free Poster.

COLDSTREAM — Coldstream Museum

Market Square, Coldstream, Berwickshire. 0890-2630. Open: Call for details. Closed: Nov-Mar. £

This uses many items given or loaned by local people to tell the history of this ancient Border town, with a display of material from the Coldstream Guards.

COMRIE — Scottish Tartans Museum

Davidson House, Drummond Street, Comrie, Perthshire PH6 2DW. 0764-70779. Open: Apr-Sept Mon-Sat 10-5, Sun 11-3. Winter call for details. £ &

This museum examines the development of tartans and Highland dress to the degree of having the plants which provided the original dyes growing in the garden, and a weaver's cottage where there are handloom demonstrations.

CRAIL — Crail Museum and Heritage Centre

62/64 Marketgate, Crail, Fife KY10 3TL. 0333-50869. Open: Mon-Sat 10-12.30/2.30-5, Sun 2.30-5. Closed: Oct-Easter. £

This little museum, in an 18th century house, observes the history of Crail, its medieval church, ancient harbour and 200-year-old golf club, with a gallery on 19th century Crail opening at Easter.

PASSPORT CONCESSIONS: 50% off adult admission charge.

CROMARTY — Hugh Miller's Cottage

Church Street, Cromarty, Ross-shire. 03817-245. Open: Mon-Sat 10-12/1-5, Sun 2-5. Closed: Oct-12 Apr. £ P

This thatched cottage is the birthplace of the stonemason who became an eminent geologist, writer and newspaper editor and whose life and work is the subject of the exhibition within.

CULROSS — Culross Palace

Culross, nr Dunfermline, Fife. 0383-880608. Open: Apr-Sept Mon-Sat 9.30-7, Sun 2-7, Oct-Mar Mon-Sat 9.30-12.30/1.30-4, Sun 2-4. £ P

Built by a rich merchant in the days of James VI (and I) and unaltered since, it has wooden walls and ceilings painted with biblical scenes.

CUMBERNAULD — Cumbernauld Central Library and Exhibition Area

Allander Walk, Cumbernauld. 0236-725664. Open: Mon/Tue/Thur/Fri 10-9, Wed 9-5. &

There are art exhibitions here throughout the year.

CUMBERNAULD — Cumbernauld Museum

Ardenlea House, The Wynd, Cumbernauld, Glasgow G67 2ST. 0236-735077. Open: Thur only and by appoint. P

This is in the old village of Cumbernauld, not the new town, and it tells the story of the district from prehistoric times.

PASSPORT CONCESSIONS: 10% off purchases.

CUMBERNAULD — Palacerigg Exhibition Centre

Palacerigg Country Park, Cumbernauld. 0236-720047. Open: Daily 10-4.30. Closed: Mon/Tue in Winter. P &

What was here before? Well, flax farming, Highland cattle, blackface sheep, fireclay mining, peat-cutting, even a colony of Glasgow unemployed at one time, but all comes clear in the exhibition Palacerigg Past and Present. Also an Easter event, a rare breeds workshop in August and WWF sponsored walk in October.

PASSPORT CONCESSIONS: Free Guidebook.

JNR. PASSPORT CONCESSIONS: Free Badge.

CUPAR — Hill of Tarvit Mansionhouse

Cupar KY15 5PD. 0334-53127. Open: Daily 2-6. Closed: Nov-Mar/17 Apr-May. £ P.

This was rebuilt in 1906 by Sir Robert Lorimer for a Dundee magnate, he also designed the gardens. There is a restored Edwardian laundry and potting shed, and collections of tapestries, paintings, furniture, porcelain and objets d'art.

DRUMNADROCHIT — Official Loch Ness Monster Exhibition

Lochness Centre, Drumnadrochit, Inverness-shire. 045-62573. Open: Daily 9-9.30 Summer, 10-5 Winter. £ P &

It must be true if there's a museum about it. Well, if the monster isn't, the interminable search for it is, and this tells the story of it since the first reported "sighting" in 565AD.

DUFFTOWN — Dufftown Museum

The Tower, Dufftown, Moray. 0309-73701. Open: Mon-Sat 10-6. Closed: Oct-early May.

Set in the historic Dufftown Tower, this is a museum of local and social history.

DUMBARTON — Denny Ship Tank

Castle Street, Dumbarton G82 1QS. 0389-63444. Open: Mon-Fri 10-4. £ P

This ship model testing tank was built in 1882 and is fully operational, the workshop showing the construction of models and elsewhere there are displays of some of the notable ships which were tested at the tank.

DUMFRIES — Burns House

Burns Street, Dumfries. 0387-55297. Open: Mon-Sat 10-1/2-5, Sun 2-5. Closed: Sun & Mon Oct-Easter. £

This is where Rabbie lived for the last three years of his life, where he wrote his last poems and songs, and where he died in 1796. His chair is here, so is his gun, recently traced in Canada, early editions of his work and original letters and manuscripts.

DUMFRIES — Camera Obscura

Dumfries Museum, The Observatory, Dumfries. 0387-53374. Open: Mon-Sat 10-1/2-5, Sun 2-5. Closed: Oct-Mar. £

This is on the top floor of Dumfries Museum's windmill tower, installed in 1836 when the building was converted to an observatory. On a clear day you can see the countryside for miles, projected onto a table-top.

DUMFRIES — Dumfries & Galloway Aviation Museum

Control Tower, Heath Hall Trading Estate, Dumfries. 0387-53807. Open: Sat/Sun: 10-5. Nov-Mar by appoint. only. £ P

Outside there are five aircraft with a collection of engines inside, including a Merlin engine from a Spitfire which crashed into Loch Duwon in 1940.

PASSPORT CONCESSIONS: Invitation to view Spitfire which lay in the loch for 40 years - by appoint. only.

JNR. PASSPORT CONCESSIONS: Educational tours given to school groups.

DUMFRIES — Dumfries Museum

Dumfries Museum, The Observatory, Dumfries D62 7SW. 0387 53374. Open: Mon-Sat 10-1/2-5, Sun 2-5. Closed: Oct-Mar Sun/Mon. ♿

One of Scotland's longest established museums and the largest in the south west of the country. It is in the tower of an 18th century windmill and offers fossil footprints left by prehistoric animals, early Christian stone carvings and the everyday things of a Victorian farm, workshop and home among its collections.

DUMFRIES — Old Bridge House

Old Bridge House, Mill Road, Dumfries. 0387-56904. Open: Mon-Sat 10-1/2-5, Sun 2-5. Closed: Oct-Mar.

This is Dumfries' oldest building, made in 1660 from the 15th century sandstone fabric of the Devorgilla Bridge, and is now a museum of the town's social history, with kitchens of 1850 and 1900, an early dentist's surgery and a display devoted to that subject which seems to so fascinate curators at the moment, Victorian childhood.

DUMFRIES — Robert Burns Centre

Robert Burns Centre, Mill Road, Dumfries. 0387-64808. Open: Apr-Sept Mon-Sat 10-8, Sun 2-5, Oct-Mar Tue-Sat 10-1/2-5. P ♿

This is about Robert Burns the exciseman, his job in Dumfries during his last years, as well as Robert Burns the poet, and links him to the town as it was in the 1790s. It's set in an 18th century watermill by the River Nith.

DUMFRIES — Savings Bank Museum

Ruthwell, Dumfries DG1 4NN. 038787-640. Open: Daily 10-1/2-5. Closed: Sun/Mon in Winter. P

The Rev. Henry Duncan, antiquarian, author, artist, geologist and publisher founded the savings banks in 1810: here is the story of him, how he came to do it and what has happened to the banks around the world since.

PASSPORT CONCESSIONS: Multi-language leaflets for reading in the museum.

JNR. PASSPORT CONCESSIONS: Free Schools information pack; Free Pencil.

DUMFRIES — Shambellie House Museum of Costume

New Abbey, Dumfries. 031-225 7534. Open: Mon/Thur-Sat 10-5.30, Sun 12-5.30. Closed: Oct-Apr.

This is mainly women's clothing and fashion accessories from the late 18th to the early 20th centuries, with some children's and men's clothes too. One of the national museums of Scotland.

DUNBEATH — Laidhay Croft Museum

Dunbeath, Caithness. 059-33244. Open: Daily 10-6. Closed: Nov-Easter. £ P &

This has rooms furnished as they would have been in the early years of this century, and there is a cruck-constructed barn and a collection of agricultural implements.

PASSPORT CONCESSIONS: Free entry to Passport holder.

JNR. PASSPORT CONCESSIONS: Free entry to Junior Passport holder.

DUNDEE — Barrack Street Museum

Barrack Street, Dundee DD1 1PG. 0382-23141. Open: Mon-Sat 10-5.

The Tay Whale Skeleton is in the natural history collection, and another gallery explores the influence of nature on the arts. Special exhibitions throughout the year.

DUNDEE — Broughty Castle Museum

Broughty Ferry, Dundee DD5 2BE. 0382-76121. Open Mon-Sat 10-1/2-5, Sun (Jul-Sept) 2-5. P

Local history, arms and armour, seashore life and Dundee's whaling story.

DUNDEE — The Frigate Unicorn

Victoria Dock, Dundee DD1 3JA. 0382-200900. Open: Apr-Oct Mon-Fri/Sun 10-5, Sat 10-4. Nov-Mar Mon-Fri 10-4. Closed: Nov-Mar Sat/Sun. £ P.

The oldest British-built ship still afloat, launched in 1824, and Scotland's only wooden sailing warship now conveys the flavour of life in the Royal Navy during the golden age of sail - not so golden for the tars below deck, though.

PASSPORT CONCESSIONS: 50p off adult admission charge.

JNR. PASSPORT CONCESSIONS: Free Badge.

DUNDEE — McManus Galleries

Albert Square, Dundee DD1 1DA. 0382-23141. Open: Mon-Sat 10-5. &

The full range of a local museum and gallery, with archaeology, local and industrial history, plus a fine art collection of paintings, sculpture, furniture and ceramics and a full temporary exhibition programme.

DUNDEE — Mills Observatory

Balgay Park, Glamis Road, Dundee. 0382-67138. Open: Apr-Sept Mon-Fri 10-5, Oct-Mar Mon-Fri 3-10, all year Sat 2-5. P

The only full time observatory in Britain where, in the winter and under the supervision of the resident astronomer, you can examine the night sky.

DUNDEE — Royal Research Ship Discovery

Maritime House, 26 East Dock Street, Dundee DD1 9HY. 0382-201175. Open: Daily 12-5. Closed: Oct-Mar. £

This is Captain Scott's ship, the one he took to the Antarctic on the trip before his fatal one. It has been restored and refurbishment continues in the town where it was built, but new in 1990 is an exhibition in the ship's galley.

PASSPORT CONCESSIONS: Free "Dundee Heritage" Print.

DUNFERMLINE — Andrew Carnegie Birthplace Museum

Moodie Street, Dunfermline, Fife KY12 7PL. 0383-724302. Open: Apr-Oct Mon-Sat 11-5, Sun 2-5, Nov-Mar Daily 2-4. P &

This is where the lad who went to America to become a great industrialist and philanthropist was born in 1835, and the cottage is furnished as it would have been during his childhood.

DUNFERMLINE — Dunfermline District Museum

Viewfield Terrace, Dunfermline KY12 7HY. 0383-721814. Open: Mon-Sat 11-5. P

Dunfermline is famous for its damask table linen, and this museum concentrates on that, with an 1835 handloom at its centre. There are also more general objects from the district, including clocks, paintings and artefacts found in Bronze Age graves. Throughout 1990 there is an exhibition called Dunfermline's Story.

JNR. PASSPORT CONCESSIONS: Free Badge or Free Pencil.

DUNFERMLINE — Pittencrieff House Museum

Pittencrieff Park, Dunfermline. 0383-721814. Open: Daily (excl. Tue) 11-5. Closed: Nov-Apr. P &

The permanent exhibition gives an introduction to Dunfermline's history with an exhibition about underwear as one of the less-expected local topics, and there are special exhibitions on costume, art, photography and history for the 1990 summer season.

DUNKELD — Dunkeld Cathedral Chapter House

Cathedral Street, Dunkeld, Perthshire PH8 0AW. 03502-249. Open: Mon-Sat 10-7, Sun 2-7. Nov-March 4pm closing. P

The collection or ecclesiastical artefacts goes back to the Picts, and there are books on theology, science and mechanics going back to the 1600's, plus a graphic presentation on the area's social history.

DUNS — Biscuit Tin Museum

Manderston, Duns, Berwickshire TD11 3PP. 0361-83450. Open: Mid May-Sept Thur/Sun 2-5.30, or by appoint. £ P

The home of Adrian Palmer, this late 18th century mansion has a display of over 200 tins made for the Huntley and Palmer biscuit makers.

PASSPORT CONCESSIONS: Free Guidebook.

DUNS — Jim Clark Memorial Trophy Room

44 Newtown Street, Duns, Berwickshire. 0361-82600. Open: Mon-Sat 10-1/2-5, Sun 2-5. Closed: Oct-Mar. £

This is for motor racing enthusiasts; a unique collection of the trophies won by the late Jim Clark, World Motor Racing Champion in 1963 and 1965.

DYSART — McDouall Stuart Museum

Rectory Lane, Dysart, Fife. 0592-260732. Open: Jun-Aug Daily 2-5. P

John McDouall Stuart, who in 1862 became the first man to cross Australia south to north, was born here where the displays tell of him and of the neighbourhood.

ECCLEFECHAN — Carlyle's Birthplace

The Arched House, Ecclefechan, Drumfriesshire. 057-63 666. Open: Daily 12-5. Closed: 26 Oct-Mar. £

This is where the historian Thomas Carlyle was born in 1795, now preserved as a typical artisan's cottage of the period which contains personal relics and manuscript letters.

EDINBURGH — Edinburgh City Art Centre

2 Market Street, Edinburgh EH1 1DE. 031-225 2424. Open: Mon-Sat 10-5, Sun during Festival & Dinosaurs Live Exhibition. P ☾

The city's permanent collections of fine art are on show here as well as temporary exhibitions on four floors of a purpose-built building in the city centre, but it is to close at the end of 1990 to have the top two floors converted into gallery space.

EDINBURGH — Edinburgh University Collection of Historic Musical Instruments

Reid Concert Hall, Bristo Square, Edinburgh EH8 9AG. 031-667 1011. Open: Wed 3-5, Sat 10-1.

Over a thousand stringed, woodwind, brass and percussion instruments - and bagpipes of course - to tell the story of the orchestra, bands and

popular music. Extra opening during the Edinburgh Festival.

PASSPORT CONCESSIONS: Free Guidebook.

Viola da Gamba by Kaiser, Düsseldof, c.1700.

EDINBURGH — The Fruitmarket Gallery

29 Market Street, Edinburgh EH1 1DF. 031-225 2383. Open: Tue-Sat 10-5.30, Sun pm only.

This is a noted international venue for contemporary art, and its exhibition on the painter Calum Colvin re-opens in April 1990.

EDINBURGH — Georgian House

7 Charlotte Square, Edinburgh. 031-225 2160. Open: Mon-Sat 10-5, Sun 2-5. Closed: Nov-Mar. £

A fine example of New Town architecture of the late 18th century, with the north side of the square classed as one of Robert Adam's masterpieces of urban design.

EDINBURGH — Gladstone's Land

477B Lawnmarket, Royal Mile, Edinburgh. 031-226 5856. Open: Mon-Sat 10-5, Sun 2-5. Closed: Nov-Mar. £

A six story tenement on the Royal Mile, originally the home of a burgess called Thomas Gladstone, but now with reconstructed shops displaying 17th century wares, and the main rooms furnished like a typical home of the period.

EDINBURGH — Huntly House Museum

142 Canongate, Edinburgh EH8 8DD. 031-225 2424. Open: Mon-Sat 10-6, Oct-May Mon-Sat 10-5, Sun 2-5 during Festival only.

Edinburgh's local history museum, set in a 16th century house, also has important collections of Edinburgh silver and glass, and Scottish pottery.

PASSPORT CONCESSIONS: 5% off shop purchases over £3.

EDINBURGH — Lady Stair's House

Lady Stairs Close, Lawnmarket, Edinburgh. 031-225 2424. Open: Mon-Sat 10-6, Oct-May Mon-Sat 10-5, Sun 2-5 during Festival only.

This is early 17th century building, once a home of the Earl of Rosebery, is now dedicated to Scotland's three best known writers: Burns, Scott and Stevenson.

PASSPORT CONCESSIONS: 5% off shop purchases over £3.

EDINBURGH — Lauriston Castle

2a Cramond Road South, Davidson Maons, Edinburgh. 031-336 2060. Open: Phone for details. £

Built in the 16th century, the castle was expanded in the 19th century and has been restored with its Edwardian interiors kept as furnished by its last owner, a leading Edinburgh furnisher.

PASSPORT CONCESSIONS: 50% off adult admission charge.

EDINBURGH — Museum of Childhood

42 High Street, Edinburgh. 031-225 2424. Open: Mon-Sat 10-6, Oct-May Mon-Sat 10-5, Sun 2-5 during Festival only.

This was the first museum to be devoted to matters of childhood - toys, dolls, books and hobbies - and is as popular as ever. It is interesting that, with all the magic of electronics and fantasy of science fiction which seem to be entrancing children in the1990s, the most popular items seem to be the nickleodeon and the rocking horse.

PASSPORT CONCESSIONS: 5% off shop purchases over £3.

EDINBURGH — Museum of Communication

James Clerk Maxwell Building, University of Edinburgh, Mayfield Road, Edinburgh EH9 3JL. Open: Mon-Fri 9am-9pm, Sat 9-7, Sun 9-5. Closed: 23 Dec-4 Jan.

Part of Edinburgh University, this museum is all about the electrical transmission of messages.

PASSPORT CONCESSIONS: Opps. The Curator will give a personal tour, opening cupboards, giving explanations, answering questions, book three days ahead.

EDINBURGH — Museum of Fire

Lothian and Borders Fire Brigade, Lauriston Place, Edinburgh EH3 9DE. 031-228 2401. Open: By appt. only.

This museum developed as a back-up for the many educational visits to the fire brigade by the community education department.

EDINBURGH — National Gallery of Scotland

The Mound, Edinburgh EH2 2EL. 031-556 8921. Open: Mon-Sat 10-5, Sun 2-5. &

A world class collection of paintings, drawings and prints from the Renaissance to Post-Impressionism, Velasquez to Van Gogh, alongside the National Collection of Scottish Art. The gallery has been extensively refurbished and restored to give justice to the splendour of William Playfair's building, and make an object of it, too. Cezanne and Poussin are the joint subjects of the year's special exhibition, from August 9 to October 21.

PASSPORT CONCESSIONS: 50% off adult admission charge.

EDINBURGH — National Library of Scotland

George IV Bridge, Edinburgh EH1 1EW. 031-226 4531. Open: Mon-Fri 9.30-5, Sat 9.30-1/2-5. Closed: Mar-Jul (1990 only for modernisation). &

This is the copyright library, entitled to claim works published in the United Kingdom and Ireland, and as a result it has unrivalled collections of books and manuscripts. There are regularly changing exhibitions on all aspects of Scottish culture.

PASSPORT CONCESSIONS: Free Poster; 5% off shop purchases; OPPS.

JNR. PASSPORT CONCESSIONS: Free Badge; Free Pencil.

EDINBURGH — Nelson Monument

Calton Hill, Edinburgh. 031-556 2716. Open: Oct-Mar Mon-Sat 10-3, Apr-Sept Mon 1-6, Tue-Sat 10-6. £ P

This was one of the earliest monuments to Nelson, and after 144 steps up there are splendid views out into the North Sea. Everyday at 1 the time ball drops as a signal to ships lying off shore.

PASSPORT CONCESSIONS: 50% off adult admission charge.

EDINBURGH — People's Story Museum

Canongate Tolbooth, 163 Canongate, Edinburgh EH8 8BN. 031-225 2424. Open: Mon-Sat 10-5, Jun-Sept Mon-Sat 10-6, Sun 2-5 during Festival only. &

This new museum, opened last year and run by the city, is about the lives and leisure of Edinburgh's working people from the 18th century to the present day through reconstructed sets in the old Canongate Tolbooth.

EDINBURGH — Royal Museum of Scotland

Chambers Street, Edinburgh EH1 1JF. 031-225 7534. Open: Mon-Sat 10-5, Sun 2-5. &

Describing this huge museum is like trying to explain the details of a firework display - there are so many gorgeous lights, all part of the same show, so which do you single out? This is Scotland's cultural memory, 9,000 years (and maybe more) of work, arts, personalities, science, technology, geology and incidents. Its presentation is so impressive it was a runner-up in last year's Times Shell Museums Year Award for innovation.

Lennoxlove toilet service.

EDINBURGH — The Royal Scots Regimental Museum

The Castle, Edinburgh EH1 2YT. 031-336 1761. Open: Mon-Sat 9-4, Sun 11-4. Closed: Oct-Apr Sat/Sun. &

The oldest infantry regiment in the British Army, celebrated here in Edinburgh Castle with its colours, uniforms, medals, decorations and pictures.

EDINBURGH — Scottish Agricultural Museum

Inelistgon, Edinburgh. 031-225 7534. Open: Mon-Fri 10-4. Closed: Oct-Mar.

Looking at the old trades and skills of the countryside, this museum reveals the farming methods of our forebears and the changing economic and social conditions they experienced.

EDINBURGH — Scott Monument

East Princes Street Gardens, Edinburgh. 031-225 2424. Undergoing major repairs during 1990 - call for details.

The monument, which dominates Princes Street, was built in 1840 as a tribute to the novelist, and the exhausting climb to the top is rewarded with superb views of the city.

PASSPORT CONCESSIONS: 50% off adult admission charge.

EDINBURGH — Scottish National Gallery of Modern Art

Belford Road, Edinburgh EH4 3DR. 031-556 8921. Open: Mon-Sat 10-5, Sun 2-5. P &

This is the nation's collection of painting, sculpture and graphic art from the 20th century, with major Scottish artists highlighted and leading contemporary artists given a showcase. Oskar Kokoschka is the main exhibition for 1990, from July 14 to September 23.

PASSPORT CONCESSIONS: 50% off adult admission charge.

EDINBURGH — Scottish National Portrait Gallery

1 Queen Street, Edinburgh EH2 1JD. 031-556 8921. Open: Daily 10-5. &

One of the national galleries of Scotland, this one has portraits of the people who have played significant roles in national history from the 16th century to now.

EDINBURGH — Scottish National War Memorial

The Castle, Edinburgh. 031-226 7393. Open: Oct-Mar Mon-Sat 9.30-4.20, Sun 12.30-3.35, Apr-Sept. 9.30-5.05 Sun 11-5.05. £

Designed by Sir Robert Lorimer and built by over 200 Scottish artists and craftsmen to commemorate Scots who died in 20th century conflicts and their regiments.

EDINBURGH — Scottish United Services Museum

The Castle, Edinburgh EH1 2NG. 031-225 7534. Open: Mon-Fri 9.30-5.30, Sun 11-5.30. £ &

This has the national collection of material about the Scottish armed forces which includes weapons, uniforms, equipment, ceremonial objects and regimental regalia, but also fine art photographs and archive material. The exhibition through 1990 tells the story of the Scottish soldier between 1600 and 1914.

EDINBURGH — Trinity Apse, Brass Rubbing Centre

Chalmers Close, High Street, Edinburgh. 031-556 4364. Open: Jun-Sept Mon-Sat 10-6, Oct-May 10-5.

This is the recreated portion of one of Scotland's finest medieval churches, which now houses a brass rubbing centre.

PASSPORT CONCESSIONS: 5% off shop purchases over £3.

ELGIN — Elgin Museum

1 High Street, Elgin, Moray IV30 1EQ. 0343-543675. Open: Call for details. Closed: Oct-Mar.

Re-opening in April 1990 after a major two-year refurbishment, this is one of Scotland's oldest museums with collections including archaeological and social history items, and an internationally important collection of fossil fish and reptiles.

ELLON — Haddo House

Tarves, Ellon, Aberdeenshire. 06515-440. Open: Daily 2-6. Closed: 29 Oct- 12 Apr. £ P ঙ.

Built by William Adam, Haddo House is the family home of the Earls and Marquesses of Aberdeen, containing family relics, particularly of the first Marquess who was Governor General of Canada in the 1890s.

ELLON — Pitmedden Garden & Museum of Farming Life.

Ellon, Aberdeenshire. 06513-2352. Open: May-Sept Daily 10-6. Closed: Oct-Apr. £ P ঙ

Set in the magnificent Great Garden the old farm buildings have been turned into a museum by the Scottish National Trust with a collection of farm tools and domestic implements.

EYEMOUTH — Eyemouth Museum

Auld Kirk, Market Place, Eyemouth, Berwickshire TD14 5JE. 08907-50678. Open: Call for details. Closed: Nov-Easter £

Opened to commemorate the great east coast fishing disaster of 1881 when the community was decimated by the loss of 189 fisherman, the museum got national acclaim for its 15 foot tapestry depicting the melancholy event. There are also happier elements of folk life and fishing recorded here, though.

FALKIRK — Falkirk Museum

15 Orchard Street, Falkirk, Stirlingshire. 0324-24911. Open: Mon-Fri 10-12.30/ 1.30-5, Sat 10-5.

The history of the town, including natural history, with local ironfounding goods and pottery.

FALKLAND — Falkland Palace

Falkland, Fife KY7 7BU, Open: Mon-Sat 10-5, Sun 2-3. Closed: Nov-Mar. £ P

This royal palace, built between 1501 and 1504 on the site of 12th century buildings, was the country residence of the Stuart kings and queens, and it claims the oldest royal - or "real" - tennis court in Britain.

FIFE — Crawford Arts Centre

93 North Street, St. Andrews, Fife. 0334-74610. Open: Mon-Sat 10-5, Sun 2-5. Closed: 2 weeks Xmas.

A changing art exhibition programme complemented by a studio theatre with amateur and professional productions.

FOCHABERS — Fochabers Folk Museum

High Street, Fochabers, Moray IV32 7DU. 0343-820362. Open: Daily 9.30-1/2-5, Apr-Oct 2-6. £ P

This is in a converted church and has a large collection of horse-drawn vehicles, plus over 3,000 exhibits including clocks, model engines, toys and costumes.

PASSPORT CONCESSIONS: Free entry to Passport holder

JNR. PASSPORT CONCESSIONS: Free entry to Junior Passport holder.

FOCHABERS — Tugnet Ice House

Tugnet, Spey Bay, Fochabers, Moray. 0309-73701. Open: Mon-Sat 10-4, Sun 2-5. Closed: Jun-Aug. P

The story of Salmon fishing on the River Spey is told here, in the oldest commercial ice house in Scotland.

FORFAR — Angus Folk Museum

Kirkwynd, Glamis, Forfar, Angus. 030-784 288. Open: Mon-Sun 11-5. Closed: Oct-Easter. £ P &

This is in a row of 19th century estate workers' cottages, restored by the National Trust for Scotland to become, with over 5,000 objects and reconstructed room settings, one of the best folk museums in Scotland.

FORRES — Brodie Castle

Brodie, Forres, Moray. 030-94371. Open: Mon-Sat 11-6, Sun 2-6. Closed: Oct 21-end Mar. £ P

This is the time-honoured home of the Brodie of Brodies, based on a 16th century "Z-plan" with additions made in the 17th and 19th centuries. It contains fine collections of paintings, French furniture and 17th century plasterwork.

FORRES — Falconer Museum

Tolbooth St, Forres, Moray. 0309-73701. Open: Mon-Sat 10-12.30/1.30-4.30, Sun 2-5. Closed: Oct-Apr Sat/Sun. P

This has local history, the story of Forres, natural history and the life of Hugh Falconer, the 19th century botanist, palaeontologist and geologist and vice-president of the Royal Society.

GAIRLOCH — Gairloch Heritage Museum

Auchtercairn, Gairloch, Ross-shire. 0445-832443. Open: Mon- Sat 10-5. Closed: Oct-Mar. £ P

There are displays illustrating all aspects of the history of this West Highland parish in Western Ross.

GALASHIELS — Old Gala House and Boyd Gallery

Scott Crescent, Galashiels. 0750-20096. Open: Apr-Oct Mon-Sat 10-4, Sun 2-4. Nov-Mar (limited opening). P

Just over 400 years old, this is the tradional seat of the lairds of Gala and the oldest building in Galashiels. Its displays are about the house; its successive occupants and the development of the town, while the Boyd Gallery has a programme of temporary exhibitions on mostly contemporary arts.

PASSPORT CONCESSIONS: Free Guidebook; Opps.

GLASGOW — The Burrell Collection

Pollock Country Park, 2060 Pollokshaws Road, Glasgow G43 1AT. 041-649 7151.Open: Mon/Tue/Thur-Sat 10-5, Wed 10-10, Sun 12-6. P &

This award-winning newish museum houses the extraordinarily broad collections of Sir William Burrell, who gave them to the city. The important exhibitions in 1990 are about the Impressionist Camille Pissarro (May 4 to June 17) and the painter Joseph Crawhall (July 9 to August 22).

GLASGOW — Collins Gallery

University of Strathclyde, 22 Richmond Street, Glasgow G1 1XQ. 041-552 4400. Open: Mon-Fri 10-5, Sat 12-4.

This gallery in Strathclyde University has a lively and varied exhibition programme, this year ranging from the inventor of television to Malaysian arts and crafts, plus workshops, demonstrations and talks.

PASSPORT CONCESSIONS: Free Poster; OPPS.

JNR. PASSPORT CONCESSIONS: Free Badge; Free schools information pack; Free Poster/Postcard of your choice.

GLASGOW — Glasgow Art Gallery & Museum

Kelvingrove. 041-357 3929. Open: Mon-Sat 10-5, Sun 2-5. P &

This is the headquarters of the biggest municipal group of museums in Britain, and it is a delightful general museum in a palace of a building created to do the great city - European City of Culture in 1990 - cultural justice.

PASSPORT CONCESSIONS: Please call for details.

GLASGOW — Glasgow Botanic Gardens

730 Great Western Road, Glasgow. 041-334 2422. Open: Gardens 7-Dusk, Glasshouses 1-4.45 (4.15 Winter). &

A sort of plant museum whose main range has a wide variety of specialist collections of orchids, begonias and economic plants, and the unique Kibble Palace with tree ferns and other plants from temperate regions.

GLASGOW — Haggs Castle Museum

100 St Andrews Drive, Glasgow. 041-554 0223. Open: Mon-Sat 10-5, Sun 2-5.

Built in 1585, this was the home of the Maxwell family until they moved to their new mansion, Pollock House, and this one fell into ruin. Now it is a children's history museum, a house-size toy.

PASSPORT CONCESSIONS: Call for details.

GLASGOW — Hunterian Art Gallery

Glasgow University, Glasgow. 041-330 5431. Open: May-Oct Mon-Fri 9.30-5, Sat 9.30-5.30, Sun 2-5; Oct-Apr Mon-Fri 9.30-5, Sat 9.30-1. £ P &

This gallery was purpose-built in 1980 to display the university's Old Masters, modern and contemporary art, and show a complete, reconstructed interior from Charles Rennie Mackintosh's house.

GLASGOW — Hunterian Museum

University of Glasgow, Glasgow G12 8QQ. 041-330 4221. Open: Mon-Fri 9.30-5, Sat 9.30-1. Closed: Certain B.H. &

Scotland's oldest museum, which opened in 1807 and is part of the University of Glasgow, has major displays of Scotland's archaeology and geology, together with treasures of the Hunter Coin Cabinet. There is extended opening in 1990, more time to enjoy the exhibition programme.

PASSPORT CONCESSIONS: Free Guidebook or pack of Postcards.

JNR. PASSPORT CONCESSIONS: Free Guidebook or pack of Postcards.

GLASGOW — Lillie Art Gallery

Station Road, Milngavie, Glasgow. 041-956 2351. Open: Tue-Fri 11-5/7-9, Sat/Sun 2-5. P &

This modern art gallery with a busy exhibition schedule has a permanent collection of 20th century Scottish art with works by Glasgow

School painters and a study collection of drawings by Joan Eardley.

PASSPORT CONCESSIONS: OPPS.

Two Children by Joan Eardley.

GLASGOW — The McLellan Galleries

270 Sauchiehall Street, Glasgow G2. 041-331 1854. Open: Mon-Sat 10-6, Thur 10-10, Sun 12-6. Closed: Between Exhibitions. £ &

Named after Archibald McLellan, the city councillor who died in 1854 and whose art collection became the basis of Glasgow's huge holdings. The galleries which were the 19th century Corporation Galleries of Art have been refurbished and are to open in 1990 - Glasgow's Year of Culture, with Glasgow's Great British Art Exhibition.

GLASGOW — Museum of Transport

Kelvin Hall, 1 Bunhouse Road, Glasgow G3 8DP. 041-3573929. Open: Mon-Fri 10-5, Sat 10-10, Sun 10-6. P &

Scottish Museum of the Year in 1989, it re-opened the year before in Kelvin Hall after moving from the old tramworks in Albert Drive. The vehicles are on show against settings like a reconstructed Glasgow street of 1938 and a car showroom.

GLASGOW — People's Palace

Glasgow Green, Glasgow. 041-554 0223. Open: Mon-Sat 10-5, Sun 2-5. P

This tells the social history of the working people of Glasgow over the last 200 years, straight from their hearths.

PASSPORT CONCESSIONS: Call for details.

GLASGOW — Pollock House

Glasgow Green, Glasgow. 041-632 0274. Open: Mon-Sat 10-5, Sun 2-5. P &

This is the ancestral home of the Maxwells. Built in about 1750, it celebrates the ancient family and also an important collection of Spanish paintings - Murillo, Goya, El Greco included.

PASSPORT CONCESSIONS: Call for details.

GLASGOW — Provands Lordship

Castle St, Glasgow. 041-552 8819. Open: Mon-Sat 10-5, Sun 2-5.

Bishop Andrew Muirhead built this house in 1471 as the manse for St. Nicholas Hospital, and it is now the oldest house in Glasgow containing period displays from 1500 to 1918.

PASSPORT CONCESSIONS: Call for details.

GLASGOW — Royal Highland Fusiliers

518 Sauchiehall Street, Glasgow. 041-332 0961. Open: Mon-Fri 8.30-4.30, Sat/ Sun by appt. only. ♿.

The silver, medals, weapons, pictures, uniforms, library and documents which represent the history of the Royal Scots Fusiliers, the Highland Light Infantry.

GLASGOW — Rutherglen Museum

King St, Rutherglen, Glasgow. 041-647 0837. Open: Mon-Sat 10-5, Sun 2-5. P

The history of the former royal burgh is told here in the old burgh court building.

PASSPORT CONCESSIONS: Call for details.

GLASGOW — Springburn Museum

Ayr St, Glasgow. 041-557 1405. Open: Mon-Fri 10-5, Sat 10-4.30, Sun 2-5. P ♿

A true community museum which not only records the history of what was the greatest steam locomotive building centre in Europe, but present less glorious times just as faithfully.

PASSPORT CONCESSIONS: 10% off shop purchases.

GLASGOW — The Tenement House

145 Buccleuch Street, Garnethill, Glasgow G3 6NQ. 041-333 0183. Open: Daily 2-5. Closed: Nov-Mar. £ P.

The museum is split between a first floor flat restored to the way it originally looked, and a ground floor flat which has other social history displays in a red sandstone block built in 1892 and refurbished in 1983.

GLASGOW — Third Eye Centre

346-345 Sauchiehall Street, Glasgow G2 3JD. 041-332 7521. Open: Tue-Sat 10-5.30, Sun 2-5.30. ♿

This is one of Scotland's main centres for development in the visual and performing arts, with two galleries, foyer exhibition space and two theatres in which to organize its busy

programme of exhibitions and events in 1990.

PASSPORT CONCESSIONS: OPPS; Invitation to Artists talks & tours.

GLASGOW
Thomas Muir Museum

Huntershill Recreation Centre, Crowhill Road, Bishopbriggs, Glasgow. 041-7751 185. Open: Mon/Tue/ Thur/Fri 9.45-8, Sat 9.45-1, Wed 9.45-1/2-5. P

Muir was an 18th century radical and reformer, and the museum is devoted to his life in part of the Muir family home.

GLENCOE VILLAGE
Glencoe and North Lorn Folk Museum

Glencoe Village, Argyll. Open: Mid May-Sept Mon-Sat. Closed Oct-Mid May. £

Set in an old cruck cottage with its roof of heather thatch restored, the museum has toys, dolls, costume, the domestic bits and pieces of local usage place the agricultural, industrial and natural history of this bit of the Highlands.

GOLSPIE
Dunrobin Castle Museum

Golspie, Sutherland. 04083-3177. Open: Mon-Sat 11-4.30, Sun 1-4.30. Closed: Oct-May. £

Pictish stones and big game trophies vie for your attention in this Victorian Museum, along with evidence of local history, ornothology, geology and some ethnography.

GRANGEMOUTH
Grangemouth Museum

Victoria Public Library, Business Road, Grangemouth, Stirlingshire. Open: Mon-Fri 2-5.

The development of the Stirlingshire port and town of Grangemouth, with special displays on the Forth and Clyde Canal.

GRANGEMOUTH
Museum Workshop

7-11 Abbotsinch Road, Grangemouth Stirlingshire. 0324-471853. Open: Jul/Aug Mon-Fri 10-6. P

An industrial museum with a collection of local machines including a refurbished 1929 tram car.

GREENOCK — McLean Museum & Art Gallery

15 Kelly Street,
Greenock, PA16 8JX.
0475-23741. Open:
Mon-Sat 10-12/1-5. P

Late in May 1990 completely refurbished museum displays open to show the collections of big game mounts, including a tiger, ethnographic exhibits, including Japanese swords and samurai armour, and exhibits about Inverclyde's industrial history.

Japanese lacquered cabinet.

GRETNA GREEN — Famous Old Blacksmith's Shop Visitor Centre

Gretna House, Gretna
Green. 0461-38224.
Open: Call for details.
£ P &

Whence heiresses eloped with their Lochinvars to be married by the blacksmith. He'll still perform the ceremony over the famous and doughty anvil, though it has no legal weight any more, and there are collections of horse-drawn vehicles, and a history of Gretna Green.

PASSPORT CONCESSIONS: Free entry to Passport holder.

JNR. PASSPORT CONCESSIONS: Free entry to Junior Passport holder.

HADDINGTON — Jane Welsh Carlyle Museum

Lodge St, Haddington,
E. Lothian EH41 3EE.
062-0823738. Open:
Apr-Sept Wed-Sat 2-5.
Closed: Oct-Mar. £

Thomas Carlyle courted the doctor's daughter in her parents' home here, and it is furnished in the style of the 1830's and decorated with portraits of the Carlyles' powerful circle of friends after their marriage and move to London.

PASSPORT CONCESSIONS: Free entry to Passport holder.

JNR. PASSPORT CONCESSIONS: Free entry to Junior Passport holder.

HADDINGTON — Lennoxlove House

Haddington, East
Lothian. 062082-
3720. Open: Easter
weekend + May-Sept
Wed/Sat/Sun 2-5. £ P

The home of the Dukes of Hamilton, it has 17th century furniture, paintings including two portraits by Raeburn, china and the death mask of Mary Queen of Scots.

HAMILTON — Hamilton District Museum

129 Muir Street, Hamilton, Lanarkshire ML3 6BJ. 0698-283981. Open: Mon-Fri 10-5, Sat 10-12/1-5.

This is a 17th century coaching inn with an 18th century assembly room and a reconstructed 19th century kitchen. The 18th century part has original plasterwork and a musicians' gallery, and there is also a large transport collection.

PASSPORT CONCESSIONS: Free Guidebook.

JNR. PASSPORT CONCESSIONS: Free Pencil.

HAWICK — Hawick Museum and Scott Gallery

Wilton Lodge Park, Hawick, Roxburghshire. 0450-73457. Open: Mon-Sat 10-5, Sun 2-5. Closed: Sat Oct-Mar. £ P

The highlight of this local museum is displays of Hawick renowned knitwear industry, along with local and domestic history and a collection of 19th and 20th century paintings.

PASSPORT CONCESSIONS: Free entry to Passport holder.

JNR. PASSPORT CONCESSIONS: Free entry to Junior Passport holder.

HELENSBURGH — The Hill House

Upper Coloquhoun St, Helensburgh. 0436-3900. Open: Daily 1-5. Closed: Xmas - Jan. £ P

This is Charles Rennie Mackintosh's masterpiece of domestic architecture, built for the publisher Walter Blackie, with an exhibition on Mackintosh and much of his furniture inside.

HELSMDALE — Timespan

Dunrobin Street, Helmsdale, Sutherland KW8 6JS. 043-12327. Open: Mon-Sat 10-5, Sun 2-5. Closed: Mid Oct-Easter. £ P ♿

An award-winning heritage centre based on the "Highland experience", this covers the past and present through life-size displays and special effects.

PASSPORT CONCESSIONS: Special rate family entrance ticket.

HUNTLY — Brander Museum

The Square, Huntly, Aberdeenshire. 0779-77778. Open: Tue-Sat 10-12/2-4. P

Among the local history displays in this museum is a rare and intriguing display of communion tokens.

PASSPORT CONCESSIONS: 10% off shop purchases.

JNR. PASSPORT CONCESSIONS: Free Pencil.

HUNTLY — Leith Hall

Huntly, Aberdeenshire AB5 4NQ. 046-43 216. Open: Daily 2-6. Closed: Oct Mon-Fri, Nov-Easter Sat/Sun. £

This unusual house, built round a courtyard, was the home of the Leith family from 1650 and contains the personal possessions of successive lairds, and Jacobite relics.

HYNISH Isle of Tire — The Skerryvore Lighthouse Museum

The Old Signal Tower, Hynish, Isle of Tire. Open: Daylight hours throughout the year.

Built about 1840 the story of how the lighthouse came to be built is told in the museum which is housed in the tower, and there is a unique and restored harbour with a Fresh water flowing system.

INNERLEITHEN — Robert Smail's Printing Works

High Street, Inner-leithen, Peeblesshire. 0896-830206. Open: Shop May-mid Summer Mon/Wed-Sat 10-1/2-5. Printworks & Shop mid-Summer-Oct/Mon -Sat 10-1/2-5, Sun 2-5. Closed: Shop Jan-Apr/ Nov/Dec. Printworks Jan-mid Jun/Nov/Dec.

This is a "time capsule" of a 19th century printer's shop currently being restored by the National Trust for Scotland, with a Victorian office and working machinery which includes a 100-year-old press originally driven by water.

INVERARAY — Auchindrain Old Highland Township

Inveraray, Argyll. 0499-2314. Open: Mon-Fri 10-5. Closed: Oct-Mar. £

The buildings in this original Highland community have been restored, furnished and equipped in the style of past centuries.

PASSPORT CONCESSIONS: 50% off adult admission charge.

INVERKEITHING — Inverkeithing Museum

The Friary, Queen Street, Inverkeithing. 0383-413344. Open: Wed-Sun 11-5.

The monastic heritage, civic regalia, art works and domestic objects relating to the history of the burgh are the main theme, with the memorabilia associated with Admiral Sir Samuel Greig, who re-organised the Russian navy for Catherine the Great, being of special interest. In the summer of 1990 there is a special exhibition about the construction of the Forth Bridge.

JNR. PASSPORT CONCESSIONS: Free Badge or Free Pencil.

INVERNESS — Culloden Battlefield Visitor Centre

Culloden Moor, Inverness. 0463-790607. Open: Apr-25 May, 10 Sept-21 Oct Daily 9.30-5.30, 26 May-9 Sept Daily 9-6.30. £ P &

This site is almost the antithesis of Bannockburn. In 1746 Bonnie Prince Charlie's Higlanders were defeated here, ending the Jacobite rising. The graves of the clans, the well of the dead, a memorial cairn and Old Leanach Cottage - which survived the battle and is furnished in the period vernacular style - are here.

INVERNESS — Inverness Museum & Art Gallery

Castle Wynd, Inverness IV2 3ED. 0463-237114. Open: Mon-Sat 9-5.

The Scottish Highlands, culture, people, plants and buried past, with a programme of events and exhibitions

INVERURIE — Carnegie Museum

The Square, Inverurie, Aberdeenshire. 0779-77778. Open: Mon-Fri 2-5, Sat 10-1/2-4. Closed: Wed. P

This is a local museum with major archaeological collections and memorabilia of the Great Northern and Scottish Railways.

PASSPORT CONCESSIONS: 10% off shop purchases.

JNR. PASSPORT CONCESSIONS: Free Pencil.

IRVINE — Scottish Maritime Museum

Harbourside, Irvine, Ayrshire. 0294-78283. Open: Easter-Oct Daily 10-5. Closed: Nov-Mar. £

This museum spills over the harbourside, with the undercover displays about Scotland's maritime past, into the harbour itself with vessels afloat and open to the public. There is also a 1910 shipyard worker's house to see. From April to October there is an exhibition about Scottish sea disasters.

PASSPORT CONCESSIONS: 50% off adult admission charge; Special rate family entrance ticket; 5% off shop purchases over £2.

Step into a magical world of cavemen, spacemen, tin soldiers and more, free with The Times.

With over 2000 museums and galleries throughout Great Britain, there's a whole world of excitement and wonder, just waiting to be explored.

With the help of this excellent Guide and free Museums' Passports from *The Times*, children, both young and old, can learn more about our rich cultural heritage. And have great fun at the same time.

Holders enjoy free or reduced entry, plus special offers like free posters, guidebooks to private viewings and discounts in museum shops.

For your free Passports to the past, simply fill in the special coupon, only in *The Times* on Saturdays.

THE  TIMES

JEDBURGH — Jeburgh Castle Jail

Castlegate, Jedburgh, Roxburghshire. 0835-63254. Open: Mon-Sat 10-5, Sun 1-5. Closed: Sept-Mar. £ P

The 19th century prison was built on the original site of Jedburgh castle, and it is the only surviving example of a Howard Reform Prison. The displays show both prison life and something of the history of the town.

PASSPORT CONCESSIONS: Free entry to Passport holder.

JNR. PASSPORT CONCESSIONS: Free entry to Junior Passport holder.

JEDBURGH — Mary, Queen of Scots Visitor Centre

Queen Street, Jedburgh, Roxburghshire. 0835-63331. Open: Daily 10-5. Closed: Nov-Mar. £.

The house was refurbished in 1987 in time for the 400th anniversary of Mary's death. She visited here in 1566, and the exhibition tells her life story.

PASSPORT CONCESSIONS: Free entry to Passport holder.

JNR. PASSPORT CONCESSIONS: Free entry to Junior Passport holder.

KELSO — Floors Castle

Kelso, Roxburghshire. 0573-23333. Open: mid Apr-June/Sept Sun-Thur 10.30-4.45, July/Aug Daily 10-5.30, Oct Wed/Sun only. Closed: Nov-mid Apr. £ P &

Residence of the Dukes of Roxburghe, built by William Adam in 1721, added to by William Playfair in the mid-19th century. It has French furniture, tapestries, porcelain and a unique Victorian collection of birds.

PASSPORT CONCESSIONS: £1 off adult admission charge.

KELSO — Kelso Museum, Turret House

Abbey Court, Kelso, Roxburghshire. 0573-23464. Open: Mon-Sat 10-12/1-6, Sun 2-6. Closed: Oct-Mar. £ P

Displays here include a reconstructed skinner's workshop, a 19th century market place and an interpretation of Kelso Abbey.

PASSPORT CONCESSIONS: Free entry to Passport holder.

JNR. PASSPORT CONCESSIONS: Free entry to Junior Passport holder.

KILBARCHAN — Weaver's Cottage

The Cross, Kilbarchan, Renfrewshire. 05057-5588. Open: 3 Apr-May/Sept-Oct Tue/Thur/ Sat/Sun 2-5, Jun-Aug Daily 2-5 . Closed: Oct-2 Apr. £ P

This is an 18th century craftman's house containing traditional weaving and domestic exhibits. There are weaving demonstrations at certain times.

KILMARNOCK — Dean Castle

Dean Rd. Kilmarnock 0563-22702. Open: Daily 12-5. £ P ♿

This medieval castle, containing arms and armour, tapestries and early musical instruments, is set in a country park which has a nature trail and a children's corner.

PASSPORT CONCESSIONS: Free entry to Passport holder.

JNR. PASSPORT CONCESSIONS: Free entry to Junior Passport holder.

KILMARNOCK — Dick Institute

Elmbank Avenue, Kilmarnock KA1 3BU. 0563-26401. Open: Mon-Sat 10-5. P ♿

This art gallery and museum contains works by Constable, Corot Milais, Alma Tadema and the Glasgow School artists, plus the social, industrial and natural history, geology and archaeology of the area.

PASSPORT CONCESSIONS: OPPS.- Invitation to activity days

KILSYTH — Colzium Museum & Art Gallery

Colzium House, Colzium Lennox Estate, Kilsyth. 0236-735077. Open: Wed only 2-5/5.30-8 or by appoint. Summer, Wed 2-5 Winter. P ♿

The displays here cover three subjects; the history of Kilsyth, Colzium House and its estates, and the Battle of Kilsyth.

KILSYTH — Kilsyth's Heritage

Burngreen, Kilsyth. 0236-823147. Open: Mon/Wed/Fri 9.30-1/2.30-7, Tue 9.30-1/2-5, Thur 9.30-1.30, Sat 9-12.   P

This is a 19th century mansion built next to Colzium Castle and it shows the history of the area, particularly the medieval period.

PASSPORT CONCESSIONS: 10% off shop purchases.

KINGUSSIE — Highland Folk Museum

Duke Street, Kingussie, Inverness-shire. 0540-661307. Open: Apr-Oct Mon-Sat 10-6, Sun 2-6, Nov-Mar Mon-Fri 10-3. Closed: Christmas/New Year period. £ P ♿.

Probably the oldest folk museum in Britain, it deals with clans, costume, handicrafts and social life in the Highlands, and there are summer events and demonstrations.

KIRKCALDY — Kirkcaldy Museum & Art Gallery

War Memorial Gardens, Kirkcaldy, Fife. 0592-260732. Open: Mon-Sat 11-5, Sun 2-5. P

Runner-up in the Scottish Museum of the Year competition in 1989, this collection of local, natural and prehistory with its unique collection of Scottish art, has new permanent exhibitions and displays on Wemyss ware opening in June 1990.

PASSPORT CONCESSIONS: OPPS.

JNR. PASSPORT CONCESSIONS: Free Badge.

KIRKCUDBRIGHT — Hornel Art Gallery and Library

Broughton House, High Street, Kirkcudbright. 0557-30437. Open: Mon/Wed-Sat 11-1/2-5, Sun 2-5. Closed: Mid Oct-Easter. £

When the painter Edward Hornel died in 1933 he left his house, its furnishings (and Japanese garden), library and works of art to the town. The library has important material on Galloway and works by Burns, and there is a permanent exhibition of Hornel's and others' work.

KIRKCUDBRIGHT The Stewartry Museum

St Mary Street,
Kirkcudbright DG6.
0557-31643. Open:
Apr-Oct Mon-Sat 11-4
(Jul/Aug to 5).
Closed: Nov-Mar. £

The scourge of the Royal Navy during the
American War of Independence was Captain
John Paul Jones, but he was not American born;
he started life in Galloway, and the shipping
room of this museum, dedicated mostly to the
history, archaeology and nature of the area, has
a corner devoted to him.

PASSPORT CONCESSIONS: 50% off Adult
admission.

JNR. PASSPORT CONCESSIONS: Free entry to
Junior Passport holder.

KIRKOSWALD Souter Johnnie's Cottage

Kirkoswald, Ayrshire.
06556-274. Open:
Daily 12-5. Closed:
29 Oct-Dec. £ P

Souter Johnnie, the character from Burn's Tam
O'Shanter, was based on John Davidson who
was born in this thatched cottage which now
contains Burns relics and the Souter's
workshop. In the garden is a restored ale house
where the characters from the poem are to be
found in sculpted figures.

KIRKWALL Tankerness House Museum

Broad Street,
Kirkwall, Orkney
KW15 1DH. 0856-
3191. Open: Mon-Sat
10.30-12.30/1.30-5 +
Sun May-Sept 2-5. £

Some of Europe's most important archaeological
finds from the Iron and Bronze ages have been
made on Orkney, and this fine vernacular town
house contains the island's growing collection.

PASSPORT CONCESSIONS: 50% off adult
admission.

KIRRIEMUIR Barrie's Birthplace

9 Brechin Road,
Kirriemuir, Angus
DD8 4BX. 0575-
72646. Open: Mon-
Sat 11-5.30, Sun 2-
5.30. Closed: Oct-
Apr. £ P

This is a two storey house where the creator of
Peter Pan was born, the outside wash-house of
which is said to have been his first theatre, The
house contains mementoes and manuscipts of J
M Barrie and a Peter Pan display.

LANARK — New Lanark Conservation Village

New Lanark Mills, Lanark ML11 9DB. 0555-61345. Open: Daily 11-5. £ P ♿

At the turn of the 19th century Robert Owen turned his theories on the improvement of working conditions into practice by creating a model cotton-spinning village, and now nominated as a World Heritage Site it is being restored as a living village with a population of 150. Its new visitor centre opens at Easter with a presentation on life in 1820 and working exhibits.

PASSPORT CONCESSIONS: Free Guidebook

JNR. PASSPORT CONCESSIONS: Free Badge.

LANGBANK — Finlaystone

Langbank, Renfrewshire PA14 6TJ. 047554-505. Open: Daily 2-5. Closed: Nov-Mar. £

For five centuries this was the home of the Earls of Glencairn, where John Knox and Robert Burns were visitors, and now it is the centre for the Clan MacMillan. There is an international special collection of dolls here, and also landscaped gardens and woodland walks.

PASSPORT CONCESSIONS: 50% off adult admission.

JNR. PASSPORT CONCESSIONS: 50% off admission.

LATHERON — Clan Gunn Heritage Centre & Museum

Old Parish Kirk, Latheron, Caithness. 0955-4771. Open: Mon-Sat 10-5, Sun 11-5. £

This museum examines the history of the far north of Scotland through the Clan Gunn, from the Vikings to the present day.

LAUDER — Thirlestane Castle

Lauder, Berwickshire TD2 6RV. 05782-430. Open: July/Aug Mon-Fri/Sun 2-5. May/June/Sept Wed/Thur/Sun 2-5. £ P ♿

Scottish castle and family home of the more than ordinary sort with collections of toys and the stuff of country life.

PASSPORT CONCESSIONS: 50% off adult admission charge; Special rate family entrance ticket; Car Sticker from Castle Gift Shop.

JNR. PASSPORT CONCESSIONS: Mystery gift from Castle Gift Shop.

LERWICK, Shetland Islands

Shetland Croft House Museum

Voedunrossness, Lerwick, Shetland Islands. 0595-5057. Open: May-Sept Tue-Sun-call for details. £ P

Part of the main Shetland Museum, this is the home of a typical Shetlander in the 1870s, farmer in summer, fisherman in winter, with authentic furnishings and fittings.

PASSPORT CONCESSIONS: Free entry for under-18's.

JNR. PASSPORT CONCESSIONS: Free entry to Junior Passport holder.

LERWICK Shetland Islands

Shetland Museun

Hill Head, Lerwick, Shetland ZE1 0EL. 0595-5057. Open: Mon/Wed/Fri 10-7, Tue/Thur/Sat 10-5. P

This is the regional museum for the islands, covering its archaeology and its farming and seafaring traditions. There are exhibits of textiles and wreck salvage of international importance, and exhibitions throughout 1990.

PASSPORT CONCESSIONS: Free Poster; OPPS.

JNR. PASSPORT CONCESSIONS: Free Badge; Free Pencil; Free Schools Information pack.

LINLITHGOW

The House of the Binns

The Binns, Linlithgow, West Lothian. 0506-834255. Open: Mon-Thur 2-5, Sat/Sun: 2-5. Closed: Oct-Apr. £ P

A 17th century merchants house set in parkland overlooking the timeless Forth where the Dalyell family have lived since 1612.

LIVINGSTON

Mill Farm

Millfield, Livingston Village, West Lothian EH54 7AR. 0506-414957. Open: Easter-Oct Daily 10-5. £ P ♿

The keynote is farmlife for children in this countryside museum, with a restored 18th century watermill, cart and donkey rides and a riverside nature trail.

PASSPORT CONCESSIONS: Free Guidebook; 50% off admission to special exhibitions; Reduced family rate.

MAUCHLINE — Burns House Museum

Castle Street, Mauchline, Ayrshire KA5 5RZ. 0290-50045. Open: Mon-Sat 11.30-5.30, Sun 2-5. Closed: Oct-Easter. £ P ♿

The house Robert Burns and his wife Jean Armour lived in, with Mr & Mrs B seen in their room chatting. There is also an exhibition of Mauchline boxware and a history of curling stones, still made in the village.

PASSPORT CONCESSIONS: 50% off adult admission.

JNR. PASSPORT CONCESSIONS: Free entry to Junior Passport holder accompanied by adult.

MAYBOLE — Culzean Castle

Maybole, Ayrshire KA19 8LE. 06556-274. Open: Daily 10.30-5.30. £ P ♿

One of Robert Adam's finest houses, this one has been restored by the National Trust for Scotland and in the farm buildings there is a display about the area. But in the house is a special room tracing the career of Dwight Eisenhower and his association with Culzean.

MENSTRIE — Nova Scotia Room in Menstrie Castle

Menstrie, Clackmannan. 0738-31296. Open: By appoint. only. £ P

The Scottish National Trust have devised and furnished the room, the birthplace of William Alexander who was James I's representative for the plantation of Nova Scotia.

MILLPORT, Isle of Cumbrae — Robertson Museum & Aquarium

University Marine Biological Station, Millport, Isle of Cumbrae KA28 0EG. 0475-530581. Open: Mon-Sat 9.30-12.30/2-5 (Easter-Sept only). £ P

This is a museum of marine biology in Scotland's oldest marine station, and tells of the hydrography of this part of the Clyde sea area and the fish and invertebrates which live in and by it.

MINTLAW

North East of Scotland Agricultural Heritage Centre

Aden Country Park, Mintlaw, by Petterhead, Aberdeenshire AB4 8LD. 0771-22857. Open: Apr/Oct Sat/Sun 12-5, May-Sept Daily 11-5.   P &

Twentieth century estate life is the theme of this award-winner, house on a farm, with a reconstructed horseman's house and an exhibition on farming life around here over the last 200 years.

MOFFAT

Moffat Museum

The Neuk, Church Gate, Moffat. 0683-20868. Open: Mon-Sat 10.30-1/2.30-5, Sun 2.30-5. Closed: Oct-Mar. £

The theme in this former bakery is Moffat, its occupations, its famous people, its important families and its growth as a spa and tourist centre. The old oven is still on the ground floor, now a museum feature.

MONTROSE

House of Dun

Montrose, Angus. 067-481264. Open: Apr 13-16/21-22/ 28- Oct 21, Daily 11-5.30. £

Designed by William Adam for David Erskine, Lord Dun, in 1730, the exhibition is about the house's own architecture.

MONTROSE

Sunnyside Museum

Sunnyside Royal Hospital, Montrose. 067483-361. Open: Easter-Nov Wed 2.30-3.30 . P &

In the first asylum in Scotland, the museum traces the history of psychiatry including photographs, medical instruments, even a straitjacket.

PASSPORT CONCESSIONS: Free Guidebook.

NAIRN

Cawdor Castle

Nairn IV12 5RD. 06677-615. Open: May-1st Sun in Oct Daily 10-5. Closed: Oct-Apr. £ P &

Is this where Duncan was murdered? Macbeth was Thane of Cawdor, and the king was his guest. The place has been a family home for over 600 years, with the old central tower dating to 1372, fortified in 1454, surrounded by 16th century buildings, and remodelled in the 17th century.

PASSPORT CONCESSIONS: Free Poster.

NEWBURGH — Laing Museum

High Street, Newburgh, Fife. 0334-53722. Open: Apr-Sept Mon-Fri 11-6, Sat/Sun 2-5, Oct-Mar Wed/Thur 12-4, Sun 2-5.

The theme here is Victorian Scotland - emigration, the self-help ethic, new sciences (geology and archaeology), and there is a reconstructed Victorian study and historical reference library, as well as temporary exhibitions.

PASSPORT CONCESSIONS: Free package of museum publications.

NEWTONGRANGE/ PRESTONGRANGE — Scottish Mining Museum

Lady Victoria Colliery, Newtongrange & Prestongrange. 031-663 7519. Open: Tue-Fri 10-4.30, Sat/Sun 12-5. £ P &

The story of Scottish mining is told on two sites near Edinburgh. There is a colliery tour and Scotland's largest steam engine, and at the Victoria Colliery a new exhibition opens in March to celebrate its centenary.

PASSPORT CONCESSIONS: Free entry to Passport holder; Free Poster; Free entry to under-18's; OPPS.

JNR. PASSPORT CONCESSIONS: Free entry to Junior Passsport holder; Free schools information pack; Free Badge; Free Pencil.

NEWTON STEWART — Newton Stewart Museum

York Road, Newton Stewart, Wigtownshire. Open: Easter-Sept 2-5, Jul/Aug 10-12.30/2-5. Closed: Oct-Mar. £ P &

Scottish domestic and agricultural life, costumes, white work, old accounts, photographs in a former Presbyterian church.

NORTH BERWICK — Museum of Flight

East Fortune, North Berwick, East Lothian EH39 5LF. 062088-308. Open: Daily 10.30-4.30. Closed: Nov-Mar. P &

This is the former RAF station from which the R34 left for its double Atlantic crossing in 1919, and is now the home for a collection of aircraft, airship models, engines and rockets.

PASSPORT CONCESSIONS: OPPS.

JNR. PASSPORT CONCESSIONS: Free schools information pack; OPPS.

NORTH BERWICK — North Berwick Museum

School Road, North Berwick. 0620-3470. Open: Apr-Jun Sun/Fri 2-5, Mon-Sat 10-1/2-5. Jun-Sept Mon-Sat 10-1/2-5, Sun 2-5. Closed: Nov-Mar. P

It is always intriguing to see how towns perceive themselves through the museums they create. North Berwick is principally about castles and golf, it seems from this one, but the archaeology, natural and social history are vital supports to these highlights here.

PAISLEY — Coats Observatory

49 Oakshaw Street, Paisley PA1 2DR. 041-889 2013. Open: Mon/Tue/Thur 2-8, Wed/Fri/Sat 10-5.

This is the main seismic station for this quarter of Scotland but it doubles as a museum of traditional astronomical observation and weather recording which has been going on here for over 100 years.

PEEBLES — The Cornice Museum of Ornamental Plasterwork

31 High Street, Peebles. Open: Daily Summer, Sat/Sun Spring & Autumn. Closed: Winter. £

A decorative plasterer's workshop of the turn of the century has been recreated on the premises of present day master plasterers. It illustrates the main methods of ornamental plasterwork, and has the largest surviving collection of plaster masterpieces in Scotland.

PASSPORT CONCESSIONS: Free entry for under-18's.

JNR. PASSPORT CONCESSIONS: Free entry for Junior Passport holder.

PEEBLES — Tweeddale Museum

Chambers Inst, High St. 0721-20123. Open: Mon-Fri 10-5 & Sat/Sun Easter-Oct 2-5. P

This was described as a "centre of learning" when it was opened in 1859, and it still is, teaching about the industry, tradition, wildlife and history of the area, with a picture gallery and changing exhibitions.

PERTH

The Black Watch Regimental Museum

Hay Street, Perth PH1 5HS. 0738-21281. Open: Easter-Sept. Mon-Fri 10-4.30, Sun 2-4.30, Oct-Easter Mon-Fri 10-3.30, Sun 2-4.30. P

The treasures and history of the most famous of the Highland infantry regiment covering 250 years, formally the 42nd/73rd Highlanders.

PASSPORT CONCESSIONS: 5% off shop purchases.

JNR. PASSPORT CONCESSIONS: 5% off shop purchases.

PERTH

Perth Museum & Art Gallery

George Street, Perth PH1 5LB. 0738-324488. Open: Mon-Sat 10-5. P

An adventurous local museum, it has won an award for its local natural history gallery, but also has exhibitions on fine and applied art and human history and a full temporary exhibition programme.

PASSPORT CONCESSIONS: 10% off shop purchases over £1.

JNR. PASSPORT CONCESSIONS: 10% off shop purchases over £1.

PETERHEAD

Arbuthnot Museum

St. Peter Street, Peterhead, Aberdeenshire AB4 6QD. 0779-77778. Open: Mon-Sat 10-12/2-5.

This is a local history museum which also reflects the maritime nature of the town with displays on fishing and whaling and of eskimo artefacts. There is also an exhibition of Scottish and British coins, and temporary exhibitions changing every six weeks.

PASSPORT CONCESSIONS: 10% off shop purchases.

JNR. PASSPORT CONCESSIONS: Free Pencil.

PITTENWEEM

Kellie Castle

Pittenweem, Fife KY10 2RF. 033-38271. Open: Apr Mon-Fri 2-6, May-Oct Daily 2-6. Closed: Nov-Mar. £ P

This is a good example of 16th and 17th century Lowland domestic architecture, with rooms furnished in various styles and an exhibition on Lorimar garden designs.

PORT CHARLOTTE Museum of Islay Life
Isle of Islay

Port Charlotte, Isle of Islay. 049-685358. Open: Mon-Sat 10-5, Sun 2-4. Closed: Dec. £

Run by the Islay Museums Trust, this tells of the island's prehistory, crafts and the tools that were used, its maritime associations and its domestic life. There is an important collection of 16th century stones in the lapidarium below the museum.

PASSPORT CONCESSIONS: Free entry to Passport holders.

JNR. PASSPORT CONCESSIONS: Free entry to Junior Passport holder; Free Badge

ROSEMARKIE Groam House Museum

High Street, Rosemarkie, Ross & Cromarty IV10 8UF. 0381-20961. Open: Mon-Sat 11-5, Sun 2.30-4.30. Closed: Nov-Apr. £

This museum goes back almost to Scotland's prehistory as the Pictish centre for Ross-shire with a collection of sculptures stones, rubbings and reproductions.

PASSPORT CONCESSIONS: 5% off adult admission; Free entry for under-18's.

JNR. PASSPORT CONCESSIONS: Free entry to Junior Passport holder.

ROTHESAY, Bute Museum
Isle of Bute

Stuart Street, Rothesay, Isle of Bute. Open: Apr-Sep Mon-Sat 10.30-12.30/2.30-4.30, Sun 2.30-4.30, Oct-Mar Daily 2.30-4.30. £

Local History, geology, social history and prehistory, with wild flower exhibits in the summer and special events during Highland Week in August.

PASSPORT CONCESSIONS: Free entry to Passport holder.

JNR. PASSPORT CONCESSIONS: Free entry to Junior Passport holder.

ST. ANDREWS Earlshall Castle

Leuchars, by St. Andrews, Fife KY16 0DP. 0334-83205. Open: Call for details. £ P

Built in 1546 by Sir William Bruce, an ancestor of the present owners, the castle was slept in by Mary Queen of Scots and has its own ghost - not hers, Sir Andrew 'Bloody' Bruce's.

ST. MARGARET'S HOPE, Orkney

Orkney Wireless Museum

Church Road, St Margaret's Hope, Orkney. 0856-4272. Open: Daily 10-8. £

Peter MacDonald's unusual collection shows wartime defences and radio at Scapa Flow as well as early domestic radio, and a special feature is the handiwork of Italian prisoners-of-war who were detained on Orkney between 1942 and 1944.

PASSPORT CONCESSIONS: Free entry to under 18's.

JNR. PASSPORT CONCESSIONS: Free entry to Junior Passport holder.

SELKIRK

Bowhill House

Bowhill, Selkirk. 0750-20732. Open: House: Jul Mon-Sat 1-4.30, Sun 2-6; Grounds: 28 Apr-28 Aug Mon-Thur/Sat 12-5, Sun 2-6. £ P &

There are collections of art, tapestry, French furniture, needlework, china and silver in this Georgian/Victorian house, plus historical relics of the Duke of Monmouth, Sir Walter Scott and Queen Victoria.

SELKIRK

Halliwells House Museum and Robson Gallery

Market Place, Selkirk TD7 4BU. 0750-20096. Open: Mon-Sat 10-12.30/1.30-5, Sun 2-4. Closed: Jan-Mar. P

Opened in 1984, this award-winning museum recreates the former use of the building as an ironmonger's shop and his home, with the history of the royal burgh in upstairs galleries and temporary exhibitions in the Robson Gallery.

PASSPORT CONCESSIONS: Free Guidebook.

JNR. PASSPORT CONCESSIONS: Free Badge.

SLEAT
Isle of Skye

The Clan Donald Centre (Museum of the Isles)

Armadale, Sleat, Isle of Skye. 04714-305. Open: Daily 10-5. Closed: Nov-Mar. £ P &

It has an award-winning presentation about the Lord of the Isles in the Hebrides with archives and geneology tracing 1,300 years of their rule.

PASSPORT CONCESSIONS: Special Family rate.

JNR. PASSPORT CONCESSIONS: Free Pencil.

SOUTH QUEENSFERRY
Dalmeny House

South Queensferry, West Lothian. 031-331 1888. Open: Sun-Thur 2-5.30. Closed: Oct-Apr. £ P

Built in the early years of the 19th century for the fourth Earl of Rosebury, the works of art here include the Rothschild collection of 18th century French furniture from Mentmore, the Napoleon Room with family pictures and 18th century British portraits.

SOUTH QUEENSFERRY
Hopetoun House

South Queensferry, Nr Edinburgh, West Lothian. 031-331 2451. Open: Daily 10-5.30. Closed: Oct-Mar. £ P

The Hope family's days of grandeur through their souvenirs contrasted with the artefacts found in their Lanarkshire lead mine are among the displays in their family museum, with the main temporary exhibition of 1990 being on the building of Hopetoun.

SOUTH QUEENSFERRY
Queensferry Museum

District Council Offices, High Street, South Queensferry. 031-225 2424. Open: Mon/Thur-Sat 10-1/2.15-5, Sun 12-5.

This museum tells of the Forth crossing, including the building of the two great bridges, and of the royal burgh of Queensferry, and there is a full-size reconstruction of the strange "Burry Man" who walks through the town every August.

PASSPORT CONCESSIONS: 5% off shop purchases over £3.

STAFFIN, Isle of Skye
Cnoc-An-T-Sithein Museum

6 Ellishadder, Shiffen, Isle of Skye, IU51 9JE. 047-062321. Open: Daily. £ P &

Mr Dugald Ross's museum with fossils, 4,000 year old arrowheads, farming implements and furniture.

STIRLING
Museum of the Argyll and Sutherland and Highlanders

The Castle FK8 1EH. 0786-75165. Open: Easter-Sept Daily 10-5, Oct Mon-Fri 10-5. £ P

The regimental history from 1784 is now on show in the castle and icludes dioramas and a slideshow.

STIRLING — Ruskie Farm & Landscape Museum

Dunverg, Ruskie, Thornhill, Stirling. 0786-85277. Open: By appoint. only. £ P

This is part of the Stewart family's working farm, and it tells the story of the parish of Ruskie and long history of the farm.

PASSPORT CONCESSIONS: Free Guidebook.

STIRLING — Smith Art Gallery & Museum

Dumbarton Road, Stirling. 0786-71917. Open: Tue-Sat 10.30-5, Sun 2-5 Summer, Tue-Fri 12-5, Sat 10.30-5, Sun 2-5 Winter. P &

Stirling's past culture and present appreciation of contemporary art are both celebrated in this highly praised and popular venue.

PASSPORT CONCESSIONS: 10% off shop purchases.

JNR. PASSPORT CONCESSIONS: Free Pencil.

STONEHAVEN — Tolbooth Museum

Old Pier, The Harbour, Stonehaven. 0779-77778. Open: Mon/Thur/Fri 10-12/2-5, Wed/Sun 2-5. Closed: Oct-May. P

A celebration of the town's links with the sea could hardly be more appropriately placed than in its Customs House. There is also an exhibition of cooperage, with barrels, many illegally imported, the exported goods travelled in.

PASSPORT CONCESSIONS: 10% off shop purchases.

JNR. PASSPORT CONCESSIONS: Free Pencil.

STORNOWAY, Isle of Lewis — Museum Nan Eilean (Western Isles Museum)

Town Hall, Stornoway, Isle of Lewis. 0851-3773, Open: Jun-Sept Mon-Sat 10-12/2-5.30, Oct-May 2-5. P

The Gaelic version as its title, Museum Nan Eilean, gives the flavour to its displays and artefacts illustrating the history of the island of Lewis and the town of Stornoway.

STRANRAER — Castle of St. John

Castle Street Stranraer. 0776-5088. Open: Mon-Fri 10-5, Sat 10-1/2-5. Closed: Oct-Mar.

A 16th century tower, later the town jail, now a museum about Stranraer and Wigtown.

STRANRAER — Stranraer Museum

The Old Town Hall, 55 George Street, Stranraer DG9 7JP 0776-5088. Open: Mon-Sat 10-5. &

Polar exploration and the Old Town Hall are among the themes in this local authority museum, which also include archaeology and farming, and a temporary exhibition programme.

STROMNESS, Orkney

Pier Arts Centre

Victoria Street, Stromness, Orkney. 0856-850209. Open: Tue-Sat 10.30-12.30/1.30-5.

Large & small form, Barbara Hepworth, 1934.

Works by Ben Nicholson, Barbara Hepworth, Patrick Heron, Eduardo Paolozzi and Alfred Wallis are included in the permanent collection here, and there is a wide-ranging temporary exhibition programme. The main one in 1990 will be 5,000 Years of Orkney Art, opening in June, and later touring Scotland and England.

TAIN

Tain and District Museum and Clan Ross Centre

Castle Brae, Tain, Ross & Cromarty. 0862-2140. Open: Mon-Sat 10-5. Closed: Oct-Mar. £

Tain is a "royal and ancient burgh" and here is its royal and ancient history, through early artefacts, documents and photographs and the Tain silver collection, plus an audio-visual feature about the Clan Ross.

PASSPORT CONCESSIONS: 50% off adult admission charge.

TARBOLTON

Bachelors' Club

Tarbolton, Ayrshire KA5 5DS. 0292-5419. Open: Daily 12-5. Closed: 29 Oct - Mar. £ P

This 17th century house is named after the club founded there by Robert Burns and his friends in 1780 and it contains period furnishings as well as facsimiles of letters and poems by Burns.

THORNHILL — Drystane Dyking Centre & Farmhouse

Dunaverig, Ruskie, Thornhill, By Sterling. 078-685277. Open: by appoint only. £ P

On a typical small Scottish working farm, called Dunaverig, this museum's features are local history, farm building and implements, and dry stone walls with the craft demonstrated.

PASSPORT CONCESSIONS: Free Guidebook; OPPS.

JNR. PASSPORT CONCESSIONS: Meet the animals; place stones in field wall.

TOMINTOUL — Tomintoul Visitor Centre

The Square, Tomintoul, Moray. 0309-73701. Open: Mon-Sat 9.30-6, Sun 2-5. Closed: Nov-Easter. ♿

This has a reconstructed Scottish Highland kitchen, local smithy and natural history displays along with an exhibition about the development of this Highland area.

TURRIFF — Fyvie Castle

Fyvie, Turriff, Aberdeenshire. 065-16266. Open: 28 May-2 Sept Daily 11-6. Closed: Jan-Apr. £ P

Within this five-towered castle, dating from the 13th century, is a collection of portraits, including works by Batoni, Raeburn, Romney and Gainsborough.

WEEM — Castle Menzies

Weem, By Aberfeldy, Perthshire. 0887-20982. Open: Mon-Sat 10.30-5, Sun 2-5. Closed: Mid Oct-1 Apr. £ P

The largest surviving Z-plan 16th century castle, it contains a collection of Clan Menzies and local memorabilia.

WICK — Wick Heritage Centre

20 Bank Row, Wick, Caithness. Open: Mon-Sat 10-5. Closed: Oct-May. £

You don't have to get a complete working lighthouse into your museum to win awards, but this one has proved that it helps. It also has a cooperage, a fish kiln, a restored fisherman's house and an art gallery.

WIGTOWN — Wigtown Museum

County Hall, Main Street, Wigtown. 0776-5088. Open: Mon-Fri 2-4. Closed: Sept-May. P

Changing local history displays, with special exhibitions this year on the Wigtown Martyrs, Oddfellows, provosts, weights and measures

WALES

ABERDYFI — Outward Bound Sailing Museum

The Wharf, Aberdyfi, Gwynedd. 0654-72464. Open: Easter-Oct Daily 9-5.   P &

This displays the history of sailing and sailing ships in a storage building which dates from Aberdyfi's days as a busy port.

ABERGAVENNY — Abergavenny Museum

The Castle, Castle St, Abergavenny, Gwent NP7 5EE. 0873-4282. Open: Mar-Jun/Oct Mon-Sat 11-1/2-5, Sun 2-5, July-Sept 10.30-1/2-5.30, Sun 2-5.30, Nov-Feb Mon-Sat 11-1/2-4.   £ P

The centrepoint of 1990 for this museum of local history, crafts and archaeology, in a ruined Norman castle, will be Abergavenny's 900th anniversary celebrations. There is a celebratory son et lumiere in August and September, as well as a full programme of events and temporary exhibitions.

PASSPORT CONCESSIONS: 50% off adult admission charge.

JNR. PASSPORT CONCESSIONS: Free entry to Junior Passport holder.

ABERYSTWYTH — Aberystwyth Arts Centre

Elevent Lewis Ceramics Gallery, Penglais Campus, Aberystwyth. 0970-622882. Open: Mon-Sat 10-5. Closed: Mid May-June.   P

This is the ceramics collection of the University College of Wales, with over 1,200 pieces of both historical and contemporary ceramics.

PASSPORT CONCESSIONS: 10% off craftshop purchases.

ABERYSTWYTH — 'Aberystwyth Yesterday'

The Railway Station, Aberystwyth, Dyfed, Wales. 0970-617119. Open: Mon-Sat 10-5.30, Sun 10-5.   P &

Mrs. Margaret Evans's own award-winning collection, made over 50 years, of Aberystwyth's memories manifested in clothes, toys, photographs and much more all in the town's old railway station.

PASSPORT CONCESSIONS: Evening openings for groups with glass of wine on request.

JNR. PASSPORT CONCESSIONS: Special quiz with small prizes for children.

ABERYSTWYTH — Ceredigion Museum

Coliseum, Terrace Rd, Aberystwyth. 0970-617911. Open: Mon-Sat 10-5.   P &

This is an Edwardian theatre which now houses objects relating to the history of the area.

PASSPORT CONCESSIONS: 50% off commemorative mugs; Free Badge to children with Passport holding parents.

BALA — Bala Lake Railway

The Station, Llanuwchllyn, Bala, Gwynedd LL23 7DD. 067-84666. Open: Phone for details.

A narrow gauge railway along the shores of Bala Lake in the Snowdonia National Park, with special events during the summer.

PASSPORT CONCESSIONS: 50% off adult admission charge; 1 free return ticket with one bought for equal value; Special rate family entrance ticket; one child free with each fare-paying adult (return fares only).

JNR. PASSPORT CONCESSIONS: Junior Passport Holder can travel free if accompanied by a fare-paying adult.

BANGOR — Museum of Welsh Antiquities and Oriel

Ffordd Gwynedd, Bangor, Gwynedd LL57 1DT. 0248-353368. Open: Tue-Sat 12-4.30.

This is a study collection of important North Walian artefacts, such as a funeral inscription from of the Dark Ages, a unique Roman sword, furniture from the 17th to the 19th centuries and textiles. It is free, funded by the University College of North Wales, and is in danger of closing because of the shortage of university funds. As the season opens, there are hopes that a consortium of private, local authority and university funding can help keep it open, but it needs public support as well to ensure it does not die.

BANGOR — Penrhyn Castle, Industrial Railway Museum, Doll's Museum

Bangor, Gwynedd LL57 4HN. 0248-353084. Open: Apr-4 Nov Castle: Daily (excl. Tue) 12-5; Grounds: 11-6, July/Aug 11-5. Closed: 4 Nov-May. £ P

This is a "neo-Norman" castle built in the early 19th century, with "Norman" furniture and a fine art collection. There is a railway collection in the stables which includes the famous Fire Queen locomotive. There is also a doll museum here.

PASSPORT CONCESSIONS: Special rate family entrance ticket; OPPS.

JNR. PASSPORT CONCESSIONS: Free Badge; Free Audio Tour.

BEAUMARIS — Beaumaris Castle

Beaumaris, Gwynedd. 0248-810361. Open: Mar-Oct Daily 9.30-6.30, Oct-Mar Daily 9.30-4. £

The last of the bastions against the rebellious Welsh to be built by Edward I, there is an exhibition about how he built them and their subsequent history.

BEAUMARIS — Beaumaris Goal & Courthouse

Beaumaris, Anglesey, Gwynedd. 0248-750262. Gaol Open: Easter/May-Sept Daily 11-6. Courthouse Open: Easter-May Daily 11.30-5.30, except when court is in session. Both Closed: Oct-May. £

The goal is a grim reminder of the harshness of justice in Victorian Britain, and the courthouse is a rare survival from the 19th century. There are documents illustrating prison life then, and the George Scott police memorabilia exhibition.

PASSPORT CONCESSIONS: Free Guidebook.

JNR. PASSPORT CONCESSIONS: Free Badge.

BEAUMARIS — Museum of Childhood

1 Castle Street, Beaumaris, Anglesey, Gwynedd. 0248-712498. Open: Mon-Sat 10-6, Sun 2-5. Closed: Jan-mid-Mar. £ P

This is a collection of childhood memorabilia which stretches from 1800 and includes toys, audio and visual entertainment, china and glass, pictures and samplers.

The Brownie Camera named after the 1st cartoon comic character for children "The Brownies".

BETWS-Y-COED — Conwy Valley Railway Museum

The Old Goods Yard, Betws-y-Coed, Gwynedd. Open: Apr-Oct Daily 10.30-5.30. Closed: Nov-Mar. £

There are two buildings full of railwayana, including locomotives and working layouts, and you can ride on a steam railway.

PASSPORT CONCESSIONS: Free Guidebook; Special family entrance rate.

BLAENAFON — Big Pit Mining Museum

Blaenafon, Gwent NP4 9XP. 0495-790311. Open: 5 Mar-Dec Daily 10-3.30. £ P &

The pit closed in 1980, but it has been preserved as a museum with pithead buildings, like the baths and the winding engine house, remaining. There is a reconstructed miner's cottage interior, and trips into the mine guided by ex-colliers.

BLAENAU FFESTINIOG — Llechwedd Slate Caverns

Blaenau Ffestiniog, Gwynedd. 0766-830306. Open: Daily Mar-Sept 10-5.15, Oct closes at 4.15. Closed: Nov-Feb. £ P &

There are two underground tours here: the Miners' Underground Tramway and the Deep Mine. There are also surface exhibitions.

BRECON — Brecknock Museum

Captain's Walk, Brecon, Powys. 0874-4121. Open Mon-Sat 10-5. P

This is the county museum which covers the wildlife, archaeology, history and culture of Brecknock, and among the reconstructions is a 19th century assize court.

BRECON — South Wales Borderers and Monmouthshire Regiment Museum

The Barracks, Brecon, Powys. 0874-3111. Open: Apr-Sept Mon-Sat 9-1/2-5, Oct-Mar Mon-Fri 9-1/2-5. £ P &

Memorabilia from the 24th Regiment as the Borderers were when they were founded in 1689, its Militia and Volunteer units, from its beginning to its amalgamation with the 41st (The Welch Regiment) in 1969.

BRIDGEND — South Wales Police Museum

Police Headquarters, Cowbridge Road, Bridgend, Mid Glam. 0656-655555. Open: Mon-Thur 10-1/2-4.30, Fri 10-1/2-4. P

Truncheons to typewriters, buttons to a World War Two bike, this is a unique collection of police memorabilia, which centres on the Glamorgan force.

CAERLEON — Roman Legionary Museum

High Street, Caerleon, Gwent. 0633-423134. Open: 15 Mar-15 Oct Mon-Sat 10-6, Sun 2-4, 16 Oct-14 Mar Mon-Sat 10-4.30, Sun 2-4.30. Closed: May Day B.H. £ &

A new museum focussing on the daily life of the Roman garrison which was here, with life-size figures of Roman soldiers and important archaeological finds. One of the National Museum of Wales's branches.

PASSPORT CONCESSIONS: 50% off adult admission charge.

CAERNARVON — Segontium Roman Fort

Caernarvon, Gwynedd. 0286-5625. Open: Mar/Apr/Oct Mon-Sat 9.30-5.30, Sun 2-5.30, May-Sept Mon-Sat 9.30-6, Sun 2-6, Nov/Feb Mon-Sat 9.30-4, Sun 2-4. P

There is a museum of excavated relics here as well as the remains of the fort itself, all guarded by a model of a full equipped Roman infantryman of the second century AD.

CAERNARVON — Seiont II Maritime Museum

Victoria Dock, Caernarvon, Gwynedd. 0286-4693. Open: Daily 1-5. Closed: Nov-Mar. £ P &

You are invited to step back in time by boarding the museum's centrepiece, the steam digger which has been fully restored to working order.

CAERPHILLY — Caerphilly Castle

Caerphilly, Mid Glam. 0222-883143. Open: Mid Mar-mid Oct Daily 9.30-6.30, mid Oct-mid Mar Mon-Sat 9.30-4, Sun 2-4. £ P

This 13th century castle, with the great hall re-roofed, has an exhibition in the gatehouse with models and maps about its long history.

CALDICOT — Caldicot Castle

Caldicot, Gwent. 0291-420241. Open: Mar-Oct Mon-Fri 10.30-1/2-5, Sat 10.30-1/1.30-5, Sun 1.30-5. Closed: Nov-Feb. £ P &

Developed between the 12th and 14th centuries, Caldicot Castle was partially restored by the Victorian antiquarian, J. R. Cobb, as his family home. There are exhibitions in some of the towers.

PASSPORT CONCESSIONS: 50% off adult admission charge.

JNR. PASSPORT CONCESSIONS: Free entry to Junior Passport holder.

CARDIFF — National Museum of Wales

Cathays Park, Cardiff. 0222-397951. Open: Tue-Sat 10-5, Sun 2.30-5. Closed: May Day B.H. £ P &.

Not just internationally important collections belonging to Wales, but essentially collections about Wales, the museum is in the midst of a major expansion programme with new art galleries due to open early in 1990.

PASSPORT CONCESSIONS: 50% off adult admission charge.

CARDIFF — Regimental Museum, 1st Queen's Dragoon Guards

Cardiff Castle, Cardiff, South Glam. 0222-227611. Open: Daily 10-6 Summer, 10-4.30 Winter. £ &.

As well as the usual medals, uniforms and flags, which date from 1685, this museum has weapons from the Swingfire missile of the late 20th century to the flintlock pistol of the early 18th, and uses such techniques as holograms to tell the story.

PASSPORT CONCESSIONS: 20% off all shop purchases; Free Guidebook.

CARDIFF — Welsh Folk Museum

St. Fagans, Cardiff. 0222-555105. Open: Apr (or Easter)- Oct Daily 10-5. Closed: Sun Nov-Mar. P &.

Another out-station of the National Museum of Wales, this was Britain's first open air museum with important working buildings rebuilt here, and skills and crafts demonstrated in them.

PASSPORT CONCESSIONS: 50% off adult admission charge.

CARDIFF — Welsh Industrial & Maritime Museum

Bute Street, Cardiff. 0222-481919. Open: Tue-Sat 10-5, Sun 2.30-5. £ P &.

Divided into three sections this museum, in Cardiff's docklands, sets out the principality's maritime history, its harnessing of different

kinds of power for different industries and its transport, as an off-shoot of the National Museum of Wales.

PASSPORT CONCESSIONS: 50% off adult admission charge.

Optic & machinery from the Bishop Lighthouse, Dyfed.

CARDIFF

The Welch Regiment Museum of the Royal Regiment of Wales

The Black and Barbican Towers, Cardiff Castle, Cardiff CF1 2RB. 0222-229367. Open: Daily 10-6 Summer, 10-4 Winter. £

On three floors of two towers in Cardiff Castle is the history of the regular battalions of the Welch Regiment and its militia, volunteer and territorial battalions between 1719 and 1969 is recalled.

JNR. PASSPORT CONCESSIONS: Free Regimental Brochure.

CARMARTHEN

Carmarthen Museum

Abergwili, Carmarthen, Dyfed SA31 2JG. 0267-231691. Open: Mon-Sat 10-4.30. £ P &

This has the archaeology, natural history, geology and culture of the old county of Carmarthenshire, in the former palace of the bishops of St. Davids, set in seven acres of parkland.

PASSPORT CONCESSIONS: 50% off adult admission charge.

CHEPSTOW

Chepstow Museum

Gwy House, Bridge Street, Chepstow, Gwent NP6 5EZ. 0291-625981. Open: Mar-Oct Mon-Sat 11-1/2-5, Sun 2-5, July-Sept 10.30-5.30. £ P &

Once a market town and port, Chepstow's development is traced here through trades and industries such as shipbuilding and salmon fishing and its social life, and there is a collection of prints and drawings of the Wye Valley.

PASSPORT CONCESSIONS: 50% off adult admission charge.

JNR. PASSPORT CONCESSIONS: Free entry to Junior Passport holder.

The Old Bank.

CLUNDERWEN

Penrhos Cottage

Llanycefn, Clunderwen, Dyfed. Open: Tue-Sat 10-12.30/2.30-6, Sun 2.30-6. Closed: Oct-Apr. £

This is a traditional overnight house or "ty un nos" - built between sunset and sunrise - which squatters would put up in order to claim their land. This one has the original furniture and fittings and the Master Thatcher of Wales has re-thatched it.

CRICCIETH — Lloyd George Memorial Museum & Highgate Victorian Cottage

Llanystumdwy, Criccieth, Gwynedd. 0766-522071. Open: Easter, May-Sept Daily 10-5, or by appoint. £ P

The museum itself is undergoing a change with an extension being built, partly to celebrate the centenary of Lloyd George's entry into Parliament which 1990 is. His boyhood home, Highgate Cottage, is open with displays which include memorabilia and a "talking head".

PASSPORT CONCESSIONS: Free Guidebook.

JNR. PASSPORT CONCESSIONS: Free Biro.

HAVERFORDWEST — Castle Museum and Art Gallery

The Castle, Haverfordwest, Pembrokeshire, Dyfed SA61 2EF. 0437-763708. Open: Apr-Sept Mon-Sat 10-5, Oct-Mar Tue-Sat. £ P

The castle is mostly 13th century, but the museum is in the 19th century jail within the precincts. The displays cover local history, especially the effects of the Norman Conquest, and there is a special exhibition on the influence of the Second World War on the county for 1990 to 1991.

HAVERFORDWEST — Scolton Manor Museum

Scolton, Spittal, Haverfordwest, Dyfed SA62 5QL. 0487-82328. Open: May-Sept Tue-Sun 10-6. Closed: Oct-Apr. £ P ♿

Pembrokeshire's regional museum in an 1841 manor house with period rooms which have displays about the local gentry. Craft displays in the stable block, archaeology, farming and railways in the exhibition hall, and there's a Victorian saddle tank locomotive and signal box.

PASSPORT CONCESSIONS: 50% off adult admission charge.

HOLYHEAD — Holyhead Maritime Museum

Rhos y Gaer Avenue, Holyhead. 0407-2816. Open: Tue-Sun 1-5. Closed: May-mid-Sept. £ P ♿

This covers the maritime history of the western part of the island with emphasis on the ancient port of Holyhead, with marine tools, figure heads and ship models.

HOLYWELL — Greenfield Valley Heritage Park

Abbey Farm, Greenfield, Holywell, Clwyd. 0352-714172. Open: Easter-Oct Daily 10-5. Closed: Nov-Mar.
£ P &

There are reservoirs, Basingwerk Abbey and the Abbey Farm Museum, woodlands, 17th century farm buildings, traditional machinery and farm animals here.

KIDWELLY — Kidwelly Industrial Museum

Kidwelly, Dyfed SA17 4LW. 0554-891078. Open: Easter-Sept Mon-Fri 10-5, Sat/Sun 2-5. Closed: Oct-Easter.
£ P &

Original machinery used to make tinplate by hand until the 1940's is featured here, and a coal complex illustrates the story of the area's mining.

PASSPORT CONCESSIONS: Free entry to Passport holder.

JNR. PASSPORT CONCESSIONS: Free entry to Junior Passport holder.

LAUGHARNE — Little Treasures Doll Museum

Ravenhall, Duncan St, Laugharne, Dyfed. 0994-427554. Open: Easter-Sept Mon-Fri 11-5, Sat/Sun 2-4.
£ P &

This small country museum shows dolls from 1800, dolls' houses, a nursery setting and costume display which change through the season.

PASSPORT CONCESSIONS: Free entry to Passport holder.

LLANBERIS — Museum of the North

Llanberis, Gwynedd. 0286-870636. Open: Daily (1st June-15th Sept) 9.30-6, (16th Sept-31st May) 10-5.
£ P &.

"I know the power of this land, this land of Wales" says Merlin the Magician, and takes you on a guided tour of this history of Wales in a new technological museum, a branch of the National Museum of Wales.

PASSPORT CONCESSIONS: 50% off adult admission charge.

LLANBERIS — Welsh Slate Museum

Llanberis, Gwynedd. 0286-870 630. Open: Easter-Sept Daily 9.30-5.30. Closed: Oct-Easter. P &.

The Dinorwic Quarry was closed in 1969, but most of its machinery and plant have been preserved and the original atmosphere has been recreated in this branch of the National Museum of Wales.

PASSPORT CONCESSIONS: 50% off adult admission charge.

LLANDRINDOD WELLS

Llandrindod Wells Museum

Temple Street, Llandrindod Wells, Powys. 0597-4513. Open: Mon-Sat 10-12.30/2-5, 12.30 closing Sat in Winter.

As its name implies, this is a spa town and its museum reflects that. There are Roman and medieval finds on show and a varied programme of temporary exhibitions.

PASSPORT CONCESSIONS: 10% off shop purchases.

JNR PASSPORT CONCESSIONS: Free Badge.

LLANDUDNO

Llandudno Museum

17-19 Gloddaeth Street, Llandudno, Gwynedd. 0492-76517. Open: - call for details. £ &

This is a new museum not due to open until the summer of 1990, when it will tell the local story over the last 20,000 years or so.

LLANDYSUL

Museum of the Welsh Woollen Industry

Dre-Fach, Felindre, Llandysul, Dyfed. 0559-370929. Open: Apr-Sept Mon-Sat 10-5, Oct-Mar Mon-Fri 10-5. £ P &.

Set in the most important woollen manufacturing area of Wales and next to a working woollen mill, this museum traces the conversion of fleece to fabric. Part of the National Museum of Wales.

PASSPORT CONCESSIONS: 50% off adult admission charge.

LLANFAIR CAEREINION

Welshpool and Llanfair Light Railway

The Station, Llanfair Caereinion, Powys. 0938-810441. Open: Easter-Sept Sat/Sun 10.45-5.15, 18 July-9 Sept Daily. £ P

This an eight-mile-long narrow gauge steam railway which was opened in 1903 and now operates a collection of locos and coaches from all over the world.

LLANGOLLEN — Llangollen Motor Museum

Pentrefelin, Llangollen, Clwyd. 0978-860324. Open: Daily 10-5. Closed: Nov-Easter Sat/Sun. £ P &.

Working British cars and motorcycles in a museum which also specialises in spare parts for older vehicles.

PASSPORT CONCESSIONS: 50% off adult admission charge; Special rate family entrance ticket.

JNR. PASSPORT CONCESSIONS: Free Badge.

LLANGOLLEN — Plas Newydd

Hill St, Llangollen, Clwyd. 08242-2201. Open: Apr-Oct Daily 10-7, or by appt. £ P

Between 1770 and 1831 this was the home of the notorious "Ladies of Llangollen"; it has carved panels, leather-covered walls, household and personal items, pictures, prints and letters.

MACHYNLLETH — Corris Railway Museum

Station Yard, Corris, Machynlleth, Powys SY20 9SH. Open: Mon-Fri 10.30-5 (peak), 12-5. Closed: Oct-May.

A small museum featuring relics, photographs and items of rolling stock from the narrow gauge Corris Railway (1858-1948) and the valley and industries it served.

MACHYNLLETH — Hen Gapel Museum

Hen Gapel, Tre'r Ddol, nr Machynlleth, Powys. 0970-86407. Open: Easter-Oct Mon-Sat 10-5. P &.

Folk objects have been gathered together in this old chapel, which is now jointly run by Ceredigion Museum and the National Museum of Wales.

JNR. PASSPORT CONCESSIONS: Free Badge.

METHYR TYDFIL — Cyfarthfa Castle Museum & Art Gallery

Brecon Road, Merthyr Tydfil, Mid Glam CF47 8RA. 0685-723112. Open: Apr-Oct Mon-Sat 10-6, Sun 2-5; Oct-Apr Mon-Sat 10-1/2-5, Sun 2-4. £ P &.

This is a former ironmaster's mansion housing a collection of pictures, ceramics, silver and furniture, alongside local and industrial history, and there is a major new social history gallery complex opening in April 1990 doubling the display space.

PASSPORT CONCESSIONS: Free entry to Passport holder.

JNR. PASSPORT CONCESSIONS: Free entry to Junior Passport holder; Free Badge or Free Pencil.

METHYR TYDFIL — Ynysfach Engine House Museum

Ynysfach Road,
Merthyr Tydfil, Mid
Glam. 0685-721858.
Open: Mon-Sat 10-5,
Sun/B.H. 2-5. £ P

This new museum is sub-titled "Interpreting the Iron Industry in Merthyr" which it does with artefacts, models and an AV presentation of the world's leading ironworks town in the 18th and 19th centuries.

PASSPORT CONCESSIONS: 50% off admission; Free Guide or Free Coffee.

JNR. PASSPORT CONCESSIONS: 50% off admission or Free Orange Juice.

MONMOUTH — The Nelson Museum and Local History Centre

Priory Street,
Monmouth, Gwent.
0600-3519. Open:
Mon-Sat 10-1/2-5,
Sun 2-5. £

The exhibition of Nelsonia gathered together at the beginning of the century by Lady Llangattock is complemented by local history, including a section on the pioneer motorist and aviator C. S. Rolls, co-founder of Rolls Royce.

PASSPORT CONCESSIONS: 50% off admission charge.

JNR. PASSPORT CONCESSIONS: Free entry to Junior Passport holder.

NEATH — Cefn Coed Colliery Museum

Blaenant Colliery,
Crynant, Neath, W.
Glam SA10 8SN.
0639-750556. Open:
Apr-Sept Daily 10.30-6, Oct-Mar 10.30-4.
£ P

The surface buildings of the old Cefn Coed colliery have been turned into a museum, with a reconstructed mining gallery giving the atmosphere of working life underground.

PASSPORT CONCESSIONS: Free entry to Passport holder.

JNR. PASSPORT CONCESSIONS: Free entry to Junior Passport holder.

NEFYN — Lleyn Historical and Maritime Museum

Old St Mary's Church,
Church Street, Nefyn,
Gwynedd. 0758-720308. Open: Mid
July-mid Sept Mon-Sat 10.30-12.30/2.30-4.30. P

The atmosphere of the area's maritime traditions is recreated here through its visual displays, and the local community from the early 19th century is described.

NEWPORT — Newport Museum and Art Gallery

John Frost Sq, Newport, Gwent. 0633-840064. Open: Mon-Thur 9.30-5, Fri 9.30-4.30, Sat 9.30-4. P &

This has archaeology from the Roman town of Venta Siluram, local history from medieval to modern times, industry from crafts to mining, social history from domestic to Chartism.

NEWPORT — Tredegar House and Park

Newport, Gwent NP1 9YW. 0633-815880. Open: Wed-Sun 12.30-4.30 & Tue in July/Aug. £ P

Tredegar House, the 17th century ancestral home of the Morgan family who were later Lords Tredegar, is one of the most beautiful houses in Britain set in arcadian gardens and country park.

PASSPORT CONCESSIONS: £1 off admission charge.

JNR. PASSPORT CONCESSIONS: Free Badge.

PONTYPOOL — The Valley Inheritance Museum

Park Buildings, Pontypool, Gwent NP4 6JH. 04955-52036. Open: Mon-Sat 10-5, Sun 2-5. Closed: Jan. £ P &

The colourful history of Torfaen, the easternmost of the South Wales valleys, is told here through exhibitions and film.

PASSPORT CONCESSIONS: Free Entry; Free Poster; Free Cup of Tea or Coffee.

JNR. PASSPORT CONCESSIONS: Free Entry; Free Badge; Free Cup of Tea or Coffee or Orange Squash.

PORTHCAWL — Porthcawl Museum

The Old Police Station, John Street, Porthcawl, Mid Glam CF36 3BD. Open: Mon-Fri 2.30-4.30, Sat 10-12/2.30-4.30. Closed: Mon-Wed Xmas-Easter. £

Set in a Victorian police station, the museum was created by the local historical society in the 1970s to explain the area's natural and social history through displays which are regularly changed.

PASSPORT CONCESSIONS: Free entry to Passport holder.

JNR. PASSPORT CONCESSIONS: Free entry to Junior Passport holder.

PORTHMADOG — Porthmadog Maritime Museum

The Harbour, Porthmadog, Gwynedd. 0766-512864. Open: Easter week-end May-Sept Daily 10-6. Closed: Oct-Easter. £ P &

The main exhibition here describes the achievements of the Porthmadog shipbuilders and those who sailed their vessels, and there is a special emphasis on wreck and rescue.

PORT TALBOT — Welsh Miners' Museum

Afan Argoed Country Park, Cynonville, Port Talbot, West Glam. 0639-850564. Open: Daily 10.30-6 Summer, Sat/Sun 10.30-5 Winter. £ P &

This is a community project to record the life of a miner, with a replica coal mine.

PASSPORT CONCESSIONS: 10% off museum goods.

SWANSEA — Glynn Vivian Art Gallery

Alexandra Road, Swansea SA1 5DX. 0792-655006. Open: Daily 10.30-5.30. P &

Finalist in The Times Shell Community Museum of the Year Award, this major regional centre has fine and decorative art collections with three main temporary exhibition areas for its 30 exhibitions, including a sculpture gallery and purpose built sculpture court.

PASSPORT CONCESSIONS: 10% off shop purchases.

SWANSEA — Swansea Maritime and Industrial Museum

Museum Square, Maritime Quarter, Swansea SA1 1SN. 0792-650351. Open: Apr-Sept Daily 10.30-5.30. P &

More than 200,000 visitors last year saw the largest collection of historic vessels in Wales, the fully-operative woollen mill on the first floor, and the other transport, industrial and maritime exhibits set in this last surviving original Swansea Dock warehouse.

PASSPORT CONCESSIONS: 10% off shop purchases.

JNR. PASSPORT CONCESSIONS: Free Pencil; Free Poster.

TENBY

Tenby Museum & Picture Gallery

Castle Hill, Tenby, Pembrokeshire, Dyfed SA70 7BP. 0834- 2809. Open: Easter- Oct Daily 10-6, Nov- Mar Mon-Sat 2-4. £

This museum is dedicated to Pembrokeshire's geology, archaeology, natural history, military and maritime heritage, and among the local artists celebrated are Augustus and Gwen John.

PASSPORT CONCESSIONS: Free Guidebook.

JNR. PASSPORT CONCESSIONS: Free entry to Junior Passport holder.

TYWYN

Narrow Gauge Railway Museum

Wharf Station, Neptune Road, Tywyn Gwynedd LL36 9EY. 0654- 710472. Open: Daily 9.30-5. (until 6 peak season). Closed: Nov-Mar. £ P

A Dublin brewery, a Dundee gas works, a Manchester factory and a Bethesda quarry all depended on their own railways and their steam locomotives are here. Exhibitions and events all summer.

PASSPORT CONCESSIONS: 50% off adult admission charge.

JNR. PASSPORT CONCESSIONS: Free entry to Junior Passport holder.

USK

Gwent Rural Life Museum

The Malt Barn, New Market Street, Usk, Gwent NP5 1AU. 02913-3777. Open: Mon-Fri 10-5, Sat/Sun 2-5. Closed: Nov-Feb. £

A large, award-winning private collection of agricultural and domestic bygones dating from 1800 to 1945 with wagons, vintage machinery, tools, a farmhouse kitchen laundry and dairy, and a display on "The Countryman's Year".

PASSPORT CONCESSIONS: 50% off adult admission charge.

JNR. PASSPORT CONCESSIONS: Free entry to Junior Passport holder.

WELSHPOOL

Powysland Museum and Montgomery Canal Centre

Canal Yard, Welshpool, Powys. 0938-554656. Open: Mon-Fri 11-1/2-5, Sat 2-4.30. Closed: Wed Oct-Mar.

This brand new museum opens at Easter, 1990, and is housed in an old restored canal warehouse, which has an archaeological gallery and displays on the social history of Montgomeryshire.

WREXHAM

Bersham Industrial Heritage Centre

Bersham, Wrexham, Clwyd LL14 4HT. 0978-261529. Open: B.H/Tue-Sat 10-12.30/1.30-4, Sun 2-4 Summer; Sat 12-3.30 Winter. P &

The theme is ironworking which is what the Bersham area of Wrexham is famous for, and the museum occupies the site of the important 18th century Wilkinson Ironworks.

PASSPORT CONCESSIONS: OPPS.

JNR. PASSPORT CONCESSIONS: Free Schools information pack.

Each Saturday throughout 1990, in Simon Tait's museums column, The Times will publish up-to-date information on museums and exhibitions, which may not have been available when this Guide went to press. You can use these pages to make notes on forthcoming events and exhibitions of particular interest to you.

Date	Museum / Exhibition notes

Date	Museum / Exhibition notes

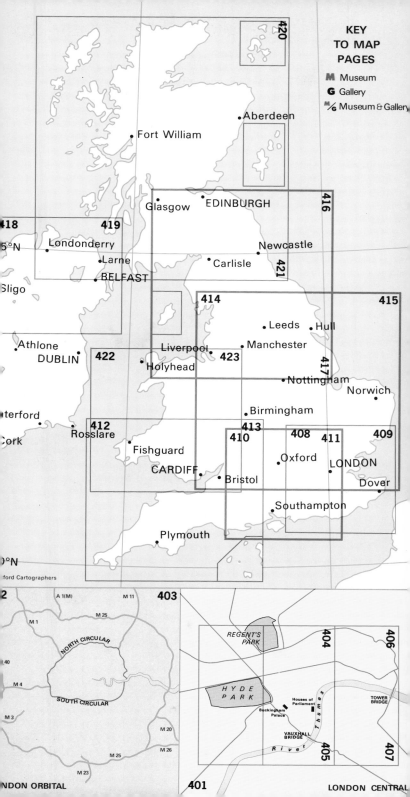

M Museum

G Gallery

M/G Museum & Gallery

420

Aberdeen

Fort William

416

EDINBURGH

Glasgow

418

419

Londonderry

55°N

Larne

Newcastle

421

BELFAST

Carlisle

Sligo

414

415

Leeds

Hull

Liverpool

Manchester

417

Athlone

DUBLIN

422

423

Holyhead

Nottingham

Norwich

Waterford

Birmingham

Cork

Rosslare

412

413

408

411

409

Fishguard

410

Oxford

LONDON

CARDIFF

Bristol

Dover

Southampton

50°N

Plymouth

Oxford Cartographers

2

A 1(M)

M 11

403

M 25

M 1

NORTH CIRCULAR

404

406

REGENT'S
PARK

40

M 4

HYDE
PARK

TOWER
BRIDGE

SOUTH CIRCULAR

M 3

Houses of
Parliament

Buckingham
Palace

M 20

VAUXHALL
BRIDGE

405

407

M 25

M 26

River Thames

M 23

LONDON ORBITAL

401

LONDON CENTRAL

©Oxford Cartographers

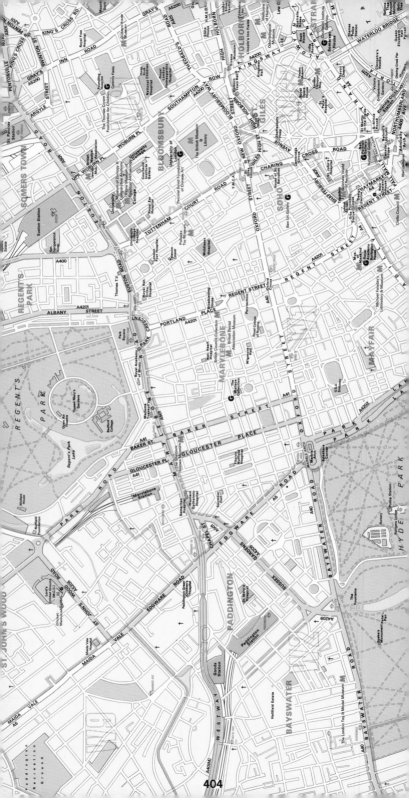

CENTRAL LONDON
Street and Reference Map

	Motorway		Footpath
	Through Route		Important Buildings
	Main Road		Park
	Other Roads		Underground Station
	Railway		Postal district & boundary

This new map has been prepared by Oxford Cartographers from original research and air photography

© Oxford Cartographers

Needham Market
Lavenham
Haverhill
Claydon
Woodbridge
Orford
Ipswich
Wickham Market

52°N

Felixstowe
Halstead
Mistley
Harwich
TED **Braintree** **Colchester**
The Naze
A120
Marks Tey
Wivenhoe
Great Dunmow
Brightlingsea
Witham
E S S E X
Mersea I.
Colne Pt.
Clacton-on-Sea
Maldon
Chelmsford M

entwood
Burnham-on-Crouch
Billericay
Foulness Pt.
Foulness I.
Rayleigh
asildon
Westcliff-on-Sea G
S. Benfleet
Southend-on-Sea M
Canvey
Shoebury Ness
rays
Coryton
Thames Estuary
Tilbury M
Sheerness M
thfleet
Isle of
Herne
Gravesend M
Sheppey
M Bay
North Foreland
Margate M
chester
Gillingham M
Milton
The
Birchington
Broadstair
atham
Regis
Swale
Whitstable
A299
Ramsgate
Meopham Green
Sittingbourne
Faversham
Canterbury
Deal M
M2
Maidstone
Sandwich
K E N T
A28
Ashford
S 187
Dover M
Staplehurst
A20
A2
Goudhurst M
M20
Dover M
Lamberhurst M
Tenterden
Hythe
Folkestone
Rolvenden
Dymchurch
51°N
A21
New Romney
Rye
Lydd
SSEX
Battle M
A259
Dungeness
Winchelsea
Cap Griz Nez
Hastings
Bexhill
ensey M

©Oxford Cartographers

Kineton
Sulgrave
Great Malvern
Pershore
Evesham
Shipston-on-Stour
M Banbury
Adderbury
Brackley
Upton upon Severn
293
A44
Chipping Campden
Moreton-in-Marsh
Deddington
A46
Chipping Norton
Tewkesbury
Stow-on-the-Wold
Winchcombe
A46
Bicester
Woodstock
Huntley
Cheltenham
Charlbury
Bourton-on-the-Water
M Gloucester
GLOUCESTERSHIRE
Painswick
Burford
Kidlington
Oxford
Stonehouse
Stroud
M Minster Lovell
M Witney
Cogges **M**
Cowley
M Com
Cirencester
Fairford
Filkins
N. Hinksey
OXFORDSHIRE
Nailsworth
Lechlade
M Abingdon
Dorchest
Dursley
Highworth
Faringdon
Didcot **M**
Tetbury
Cricklade
Vale of the White Horse
Harwell
Yate
Malmesbury
M/**G** Uffington
M Wantage
Goring
Chipping Sodbury
A429
Wootton Bassett
Swindon **M**/**G**
Lambourn
Pangbourne
Wroughton
277
M4
Chippenham **M**
Avebury
Marlborough
Hungerford
M Read
Bath
Corsham
Calne
A4
Newbury **M**
BEF
Melksham
A361
294
Burbage
A338
Aldermas
Devizes
Vale of Pewsey
A343
M Silchester
Trowbridge
WILTSHIRE
Kingscler
Westbury
A342
Whitchurch
M/**G** Basingsto
Frome
Salisbury
Warminster
STONEHENGE
Plain
Andover **M**/**G**
A359
A303
Amesbury
A34
Mere
OLD SARUM
Stockbridge **M**
HAMPSH
Wilton
Salisbury **M**
New Alres
Shaftesbury
Winchester
A350
Romsey
Eastleigh **M**
M Breamore
Bishop's Waltham
M Fordingbridge
M27
Sturminster Newton
Southampton **M**/**G**
Fareham **M**
Blandford Forum
Lyndhurst
Hythe
Portsmo **M**
A345
Ringwood
NEW
Fawley
Gosport
Wimborne Minster
Brockenhurst
FOREST
Beaulieu
Calshot
M Sou
M/**G** Bournemouth
New Milton
Lymington **M**
Christchurch **M**
Keyhaven
Cowes **M**
R
Wareham
Poole
Newport **M**
Brading
A352
Poole Bay
Yarmouth **M**
Sandown
Isle of Purbeck
The Needles
ISLE OF WIGHT
Sha
Swanage
Durlston Hd.
M Wroxall
Ventno
DORSET

Hartwell · Olney · Bedford · Bromham
Sandy · Potton
swcester · Kempston · Elstow · Biggleswade · Melbourn · Great Shelford
erstone · Newport Pagnell · Shefford · Ashwell · Royston · Saffron Walden
Wolverton · Milton Keynes · Ampthill · BEDS. · Baldock
52°N

Bletchley · Woburn · Letchworth · Hitchin · Stevenage · Buntingford · Stansted
uckingham · Leighton Buzzard · Luton · HERTS. · Welwyn Garden City · Ware · Bishop's Stortford
Vinslow · Linslade · Dunstable · LUTON · Hertford · Harlow · Chipping Ongar
Vhitchurch · Tring · Whipsnade · Harpenden · Hatfield · Hoddesdon · Waltham Abbey · Epping
BUCKS. · Hemel Hempstead · St. Albans · Potters Bar · Cheshunt · Loughton
esbury · Wendover · Berkhamsted · Watford · Borehamwood · Brentwood
Thame · Princes isborough · Chesham · Barnet · Redbridge · Havering
Amersham · Bushey · Haringey · Camden · Barking
High Wycombe · Chalfont St Giles · Harrow · Brent · LONDON · DOCKLANDS
ttington · Beaconsfield · Gerrards Cross · Ealing · Lambeth · Bexley · Dartford
Marlow · Cookham Village · Slough · Eton · Hounslow · Wandsworth · Bromley
Maidenhead · Windsor · Staines · Sunbury · Croydon
Nokingham · Ascot · Egham · Weybridge · Esher · Banstead · Caterham
IRE · Bracknell · Chertsey · Epsom · Leatherhead · Reigate · Crowborough · Tonbridge
andhurst · Camberley · Woking · Farnborough · SURREY · A225 · Edenbridge · Southborough
Aldershot · Fleet · Guildford · Dorking · GATWICK · Horley · East Grinstead
arnham · Alton · Milford · Godalming · 294 · Crawley
Selborne · Liphook · Haslemere · 280 · Billingshurst · Cuckfield · Haywards Heath · Uckfield
Petersfield · Midhurst · Petworth · WEST SUSSEX · Burgess Hill · EAST SUSSEX
Singleton · Pulborough · Bignor · Vale of Sussex · Hurstpierpoint · 248 · Lewes
avant · Arundel · Steyning · DOWNS · Polegate
Chichester · Bognor Regis · Selsey · Littlehampton · Worthing · Lancing · Shoreham-by-Sea · Brighton · Hove · Peacehaven · Newhaven · Seaford
Hayling Island · Selsey Bill · 51°N

411

0° ©Oxford Cartographers

SOUTH WEST/CHANNEL ISLANDS

·361

New Quay
·Trega

·484

52°N

Strumble Hd.

Dinas Hd.

Cardigan
Lampeter

A487
A475
A482

Fishguard
Newcastle Emlyn
415
MYNYDD PENCARREG

PEMBROKESHIRE COAST N.P.

Mynydd Prescelly ·536
·335
MOELFRE

D Y F E D

Llandover
Llanwrda

St. David's Hd.
St. David's
Ramsey I.

A40

Llandeilo

St. Brides Bay
Haverfordwest

St. Clears
Carmarthen
Ammanford

Skomer I.
Milford Haven
Neyland
Kilgetty
Narberth
Kidwelly
Pontardulais
W. GLA

Skokholm I.
St. Ann's Hd.
Pembroke Dock
Llanelli
Burry Port

Pembroke
Tenby
Carmarthen Bay
Swansea
Port Talb

Caldey I.
G o w e r
Mumbles Hd.

St. Govan's Hd.
Worms Hd.
The Mumbles

B r i s t o

Lynton

Bull Pt.
Ilfracombe
Lyn Marti

Lundy I.
Morte Pt.
Combe Marti

Baggy Pt.
A39

Barnstaple or
Braunton
Barnstaple

51°N
Hartland Pt.
Bideford Bay
Westward Ho!
Appledore
Bideford
South Molton

Hartland
Clovelly
A39

Great Torrington
Beaford

Sharpnose Pts.
A388
Chulmleigh
A3

Bude Bay
Stratton
Holsworthy
Hatherleigh
D E

Bude
Dizzard Pt.
Okehampton
A386
619 YES TOR

Boscastle
Dartmoor

Tintagel Pt.
Tintagel
Launceston
A30
DARTMOOR

Camelford
Port Isaac
BROWN WILLY 420
539 GREAT MIS

Pentire Pt.
A39
Bodmin Moor
Tavistock
TOR Ashburt

Trevose Hd.
Padstow
Gunnislake
Buckfastleig

Wadebridge
Callington
Yelverton

St. Columb Major
Bodmin
Fowey
Saltash
Plympton
Ivybrid

Newquay
C O R N W A L L
Liskeard
Torpoint
Plymouth
A38

Kelsey Hd.
Lostwithiel
Rame Hd.
Kingsbridg

St. Agnes Hd.
312
Fowey
Looe
Bigbury Bay
Salcomb

St. Ives
St. Agnes
St. Austell
A390
St. Austell Bay
Bolt H

Zennor
Redruth
Truro
Mevagissey
Eddystone Rocks

St. Just
Camborne
Hayle

Newlyn
Penzance
Marazion
Penryn
St. Mawes

Mousehole
Falmouth
Zone Pt.

and's End
Helston
Falmouth Bay

Mount's Bay
Manacle Pt.

112

Black Hd.
St. Mary's

Lizard
Isles of Scilly

Lizard Pt.

©Oxford Cartographers
5°W
412

Hunmanby
Flamborough Hd.
Bridlington
Great Driffield
Hornsea

HUMBERSIDE
Cottingham
Kingston-upon-Hull
Hedon
Withernsea
Hessle
Barton upon Humber
Immingham
Scunthorpe Grimsby
Cleethorpes
Spurn Hd.
HUMBER-SIDE
Caistor
Kirton in Lindsey

Market Rasen
Louth
Mablethorpe
Wragby Alford
Lincoln Horncastle 302 A158 Spitsby
Woodhall Spa Burgh le Marsh
Tattershall Skegness
LINCOLNSHIRE Wainfleet All Saints
Cranwell
Sleaford Boston

THE WASH

Grantham
Donington
Pinchbeck
Spalding Holbeach Long Sutton
Bourne King's Lynn
The Fens
Market Deeping Crowland
Stamford Wisbech
Peterborough Guyhirn
Old Fletton March
Whittlesey
Oundle Stilton
Ramsey Chatteris
CAMBRIDGESHIRE Ely
Huntingdon St. Ives Soham
Thrapston
Higham Ferrers Godmanchester Cottenham
Rushden Waterbeach Histon
St. Neots Girton Burwell
Colmworth Newmarket
Bedford Cambridge
Potton Great Shelford Duxford
Sandy Haverhill
Biggleswade Melbourn
BEDS. Shefford Royston Saffron Walden
Letchworth Baldock Widdington
Hitchin Buntingford
Luton Stevenage STANSTED Braintree
Welwyn Garden City Stansted
Hemel Hempstead Ware Bishop's Stortford
Berkhamsted Hertford Harlow
St. Albans Hatfield Hoddesdon Chipping Ongar
Watford Potters Bar Epping
Cheshunt
Barnet Brentwood
Harrow Redbridge Havering Basildon
Brent Haringey
Ealing Camden Barking
LONDON Grays
Hounslow Lambeth Bexley Dartford Northfleet
Sunbury Wandsworth Gravesend
Merton Bromley Rochester Gillingham
Esher Chatham
Epsom Croydon
Banstead Sittingbourne

Blakeney Pt.
Sheringham Cromer
Hunstanton Burnham Market Wells-next-the-Sea Glandford
Walsingham Holt North Walsham
Fakenham
Sandringham Blicking Aylsham Winterton on Sea
Reepham Norfolk Broads
Gressenhall NORWICH
East Dereham Acle Great Yarmouth
Swaffham Norwich
Downham Market Wymondham
Watton Attleborough Lowestoft
NORFOLK Mundford
Methwold Bungay Beccles
Littleport Brandon Thetford Harleston
Mildenhall Bressingham Southwold
Ixworth Diss
Bury St. Edmunds Eye Halesworth
Framlingham Saxmundham
SUFFOLK Stowmarket Leiston
Needham Market Wickham Market Aldeburgh
Lavenham Claydon Woodbridge Orford
Sudbury Hadleigh **Ipswich** Orford Ness
Halstead
Colchester Harwich
Marks Tey Wivenhoe The Naze
Great Dunmow Mistley Walton on the Naze
Witham **ESSEX** Brightlingsea
Maldon Mersea I. Clacton-on-Sea
Chelmsford Colne Pt.
Billericay Burnham-on-Crouch
Rayleigh Foulness Pt.
S. Benfleet Southend-on-Sea Foulness I.
Canvey Shoebury Ness
Coryton Thames Estuary
Isle of Sheppey Herne Bay Margate North Foreland
Whitstable Broadstairs
The Swale Faversham Ramsgate

©Oxford Cartographers

54°
53°N
52°N

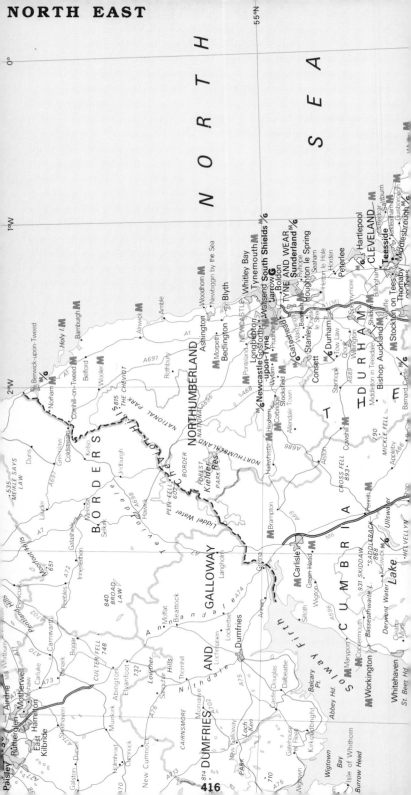

©Oxford Cartographers

Malin Hd.

Glen

Tory I.

Horn Hd.

Sheep Haven

L. Swilly

Tory Sound

Carndo
Inishowen
•615
SLIEVE SNAGH
Peninsula
Buncrana

Bloody Foreland

Milford

752.
ERRIGAL

Derryveagh Mts.

Londonde

A6

Aran I.

Letterkenny

DONEGAL

Dunglow

Gweebarra Bay

Lifford

Stranorlar

Strabane M

Glenties

Ballybofey

Sion Mills

A5

Ardara

Blue Stack Mts.

N15

•312
CROSS HILL

Castlederg

Newtownste
542
MULLAGHO

Glencolumbkille

Killybegs

Donegal

M Oma

L. Derg

DOOLISH MT
.341

TYF

Donegal Bay

Kesh

Dromore

•Finto

Ballyshannon

Lower

Irvinestown

Au

Bundoran

Belleek

Lough

Cloghe

Lough
Melvin

Garrison

Erne

N15

644

FERMANAGH

M Enniskillen

SLI
BEA

Sligo Bay

Manorhamilton

L.
Macnean
Upper

L.
Macnean
Lower

Lisbellaw

Lisnaskea

Sligo

L. Gill

LEI

Upper

542

Swanlinbar

Lough

Erne

C

SLIGO

N4

458

Lough

SLIEVE
RUSHEN
406

SLIEVE
ANIERIN

Ballymote

Allen

587 R

Ballinamore

Belturbet

Tobercurry

N17

L.
Arrow

I
M

Lough

L.Key

Oughter

Cavan

Boyle

Carrick on Shannon

CAVA

L.
Gara

Mohill

Rinn
Lough

Lough
Gowna

Ballyjamesduff

N5

L.Boderg

Bofin L.

Kilglass
Lough

Loug
Shee

ROSCOMMON

Strokestown

Granard

L. Kinale

L. Derrav

Castlerea

Longford

Castlepollard

LONGFORD

N55

N4

Roscommon **418**

L. Derrava

SCOTLAND

420

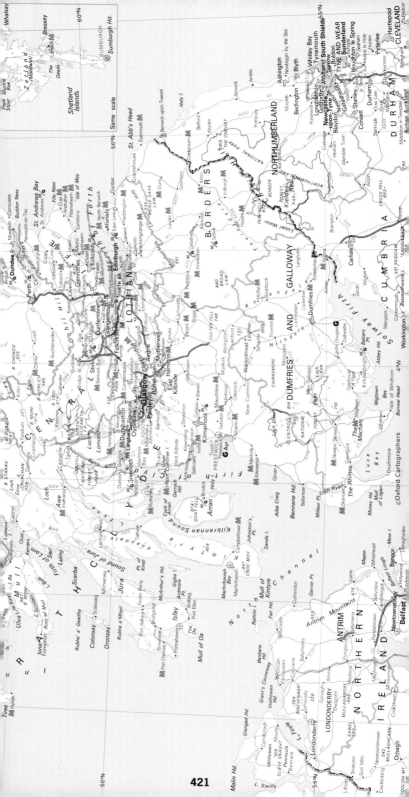

WALES

Carmel Hd.
Amlwch
Holyhead M
Benllech
Great
Valley
Anglesey
Beaumaris
Holy I.
Llanfairfechan
Llangefni
Menai Bridge
Bangor
Menai Straits
Bethesda
Caernarfon M
Llanberis
GLYDER FAWR 99
Caernarfon
Bay
SNOWDON
1085
53°N
G W Y N 734
Blaenau Ff
Nefyn M
YR EIFL
754
Porthmadog Prest
Lleyn
Criccieth
Pwllheli
Harlech
Peninsula
Tremadog
Bay
RH
Aberdaron
Abersoch
FA
Bardsey I.
Barmouth
Barmouth Bay
Tywyn M
Aberdyf M
Cardigan
Borth
mo
Bay
Aberystwyth M
MYNYDD
36
Aberaeron
New Quay
Tr
A487
Lampeter
Cardigan
A475
A48
MY
Dinas
Newcastle Emlyn
Llandysul
PENC
Strumble Hd.
Hd.
415
Fishguard
Dre-Fach
D Y F E D
52°N
PEMBROKESHIRE
Mynydd
335
COAST N.P.
Prescelly • 536.
MOELFRE
St. David's Hd.
A485
A40
Llandeilo
Ramsey I.
St. David's
Clunderwen M
St. Brides Bay
G Haverfordwest
St. Clears
A40
Carmarthen M
Skomer I.
Narberth
Ammanford
Milford
Kilgetty
Laugharne M
Haven
Neyland
Kidwelly M
Skokholm I.
Pembroke Dock
Pontardul
St. Ann's Hd.
Carmarthen
Burry Port
Llanelli
Pembroke
Tenby
Bay
W
Caldey I.
Swansea
St. Govan's Hd.
G o w e r
Worms Hd.
The Mumbles
Mu

B r i s

5°W
422
4°

Enjoy a Museum
tête-a-tête with Simon Tait
-every Saturday.

For the latest update on what's happening in the world of museums and art galleries, read Simon Tait on Saturdays. His excellent weekly column keeps you in touch with what's on and where.

And Museum Passport holders can find out about any extra concessions of free gifts available to them.

If you haven't got your Museums' Passports yet, fill in the coupon in *The Times* on Saturdays, for free Passports to the past.

THE  TIMES

B

C

H

ALPHABETICAL INDEX

ALPHABETICAL INDEX

O

P

S

U

Z

Y

For further information on any of the establishments listed below please tick the relevant boxes and return this coupon to: Spero Communications, Grampian House, Meridian Gate, Marsh Wall, Docklands, London E14 9XT.

☐	The Archaeological Resource Centre	North East	p321
☐	Ayscoughfee Hall Museum	East Midlands	p244
☐	Barbican Art Gallery	London	p42
☐	The Bowes Museum	North East	p283
☐	Cecil Higgins Art Gallery & Museum/ Bedford Museum	South	p108
☐	Chiltern Open Air Museum	South	p113
☐	Courtauld Institute Galleries	London	p46
☐	Dulwich Picture Gallery	London	p48
☐	The English Heritage		p37
☐	Federation of British Artists	London	p57
☐	Glynn Vivian Art Gallery	Wales	p397
☐	The Hancock Museum	North East	p307
☐	Harlow Museum/Mark Hall Cycle Museum	South East	p87
☐	Heritage Brewery Museum	West Midlands	p191
☐	Jane Austen's House	South	p105
☐	Jorvik Viking Centre	North East	p323
☐	Kingston Upon Thames Museum & Heritage Centre	London	p54

✂ --

For further information on any of the establishments listed below please tick the relevant boxes and return this coupon to: Spero Communications, Grampian House, Meridian Gate, Marsh Wall, Docklands, London E14 9XT.

☐	The Archaeological Resource Centre	North East	p321
☐	Ayscoughfee Hall Museum	East Midlands	p244
☐	Barbican Art Gallery	London	p42
☐	The Bowes Museum	North East	p283
☐	Cecil Higgins Art Gallery & Museum/ Bedford Museum	South	p108
☐	Chiltern Open Air Museum	South	p113
☐	Courtauld Institute Galleries	London	p46
☐	Dulwich Picture Gallery	London	p48
☐	The English Heritage		p37
☐	Federation of British Artists	London	p57
☐	Glynn Vivian Art Gallery	Wales	p397
☐	The Hancock Museum	North East	p307
☐	Harlow Museum/Mark Hall Cycle Museum	South East	p87
☐	Heritage Brewery Museum	West Midlands	p191
☐	Jane Austen's House	South	p105
☐	Jorvik Viking Centre	North East	p323
☐	Kingston Upon Thames Museum & Heritage Centre	London	p54

☐ Leicestershire Museums	East Midlands	p229
☐ The London Toy & Model Museum	London	p55
☐ The Lunt Fort	West Midlands	p187
☐ Luton Museum & Art Gallery/ Stockwood Craft Museum & Gardens	South	p123
☐ Margate Museums	South East	p93
☐ Museum & Library of the Order of St. John	London	p59
☐ Museum of Methodism & Wesley's House	London	p60
☐ Museum of The Moving Image	London	p68
☐ National Army Museum	London	p62
☐ Portland Museum	South West	p183
☐ Underground Passages/Museums of Exeter	South West	p157
☐ Russell-Cotes Art Gallery & Museum	South	p109
☐ Tunbridge Wells Museum & Art Gallery	South East	p99
☐ The Wimbledon Lawn Tennis Museum	London	p74

Name

Address

Postcode

☐ Leicestershire Museums	East Midlands	p229
☐ The London Toy & Model Museum	London	p55
☐ The Lunt Fort	West Midlands	p187
☐ Luton Museum & Art Gallery/ Stockwood Craft Museum & Gardens	South	p123
☐ Margate Museums	South East	p93
☐ Museum & Library of the Order of St. John	London	p59
☐ Museum of Methodism & Wesley's House	London	p60
☐ Museum of The Moving Image	London	p68
☐ National Army Museum	London	p62
☐ Portland Museum	South West	p183
☐ Underground Passages/Museums of Exeter	South West	p157
☐ Russell-Cotes Art Gallery & Museum	South	p109
☐ Tunbridge Wells Museum & Art Gallery	South East	p99
☐ The Wimbledon Lawn Tennis Museum	London	p74

Name

Address

Postcode

50% OFF THE 1991 MUSEUMS & GALLERIES PASSPORT GUIDE

As a special introduction, we are offering readers of the 1990 Guide the opportunity to purchase next year's Guide at a 50% saving. Make sure that you don't miss out on the concessions offered at hundreds of Museums and Galleries across the country and be the first to find out about the exhibitions in your neighbourhood.

To ensure that you receive a half-price Guide next year please answer the questions below and return the form to: Museums Guide Offer, Spero Communications, Grampian House, Meridian Gate, Marsh Wall, Docklands, London E14 9XT.

There is no obligation to purchase the Guide but we will send you a pre-publication order form. All answers will be treated in the strictest confidence.

1. Name:

2. Address:

3. Occupation:

4. Are you
   ☐ Male   ☐ Female

5. Your Age:
   ☐ 15-24   ☐ 25-34   ☐ 35-44
   ☐ 45-54   ☐ 55-64   ☐ Over 65

6. Do you, or any member of your household have the
   ☐ ADULT PASSPORT
   ☐ JUNIOR PASSPORT

7. How often do you refer to this Guide?
   ☐ Twice Weekly   ☐ Once a Week
   ☐ Twice a Month   ☐ Once a Month
   ☐ Less than once a Month

8. How many people apart from yourself are likely to consult this Guide (including those in your home and place of work) ?

9. How many times in the past year have you visited a Museum or Gallery?
   ☐ 0-5   ☐ 5-10   ☐ 10-20   ☐ Over 20

10. Do you object to paying to go in to a Museum or Gallery?
    ☐ Yes   ☐ No

11. How many times have you travelled overseas in the past year?

    BUSINESS   PLEASURE

    _____

12. Do you own the house you live in?
    ☐ Yes   ☐ No

13. Do you own more than one property?
    ☐ Yes   ☐ No

14. What is the total annual income of your household?
    ☐ Under £10,000   ☐ £10,000-14,999
    ☐ £15,000-19,999   ☐ £20,000-29,999
    ☐ £30,000-39,999   ☐ £40,000 or over

15. What type and registration car do you drive?

    _____

16. Which newspaper do you read?

    DAILY   _____

    SUNDAY   _____

17. Which of the following credit cards do you use?

    ☐ ACCESS   ☐ VISA
    ☐ DINERS   ☐ AMERICAN EXPRESS

18. Do you have any comments on this year's Guide or suggestions to
    make for improvements in the 1991 Guide?

    _____

    _____

    _____

    _____

    _____

    _____